Time Out

Istanbul

timeout.com/istanbul

Time Out Guides Ltd
Universal House
251 Tottenham Court Road
London W1T 7AB
United Kingdom
Tel: +44 (0)20 7813 3000
Fax: +44 (0)20 7813 6001
Email: guides@timeout.com
www.timeout.com

Published by Time Out Guides Ltd, a wholly owned subsidiary of Time Out Group Ltd.
Time Out and the Time Out logo are trademarks of Time Out Group Ltd.

© Time Out Group Ltd 2010
Previous editions 2001, 2005, 2007

10 9 8 7 6 5 4 3 2 1

This edition first published in Great Britain in 2010 by Ebury Publishing.
A Random House Group Company
20 Vauxhall Bridge Road, London SW1V 2SA

Random House Australia Pty Ltd 20 Alfred Street, Milsons Point, Sydney, New South Wales 2061, Australia

Random House New Zealand Ltd 18 Poland Road, Glenfield, Auckland 10, New Zealand

Random House South Africa (Pty) Ltd Isle of Houghton, Corner Boundary Road & Carse O'Gowrie,
Houghton 2198, South Africa

Random House UK Limited Reg. No. 954009

Distributed in the US and Latin America by Publishers Group West (1-510-809-3700)
Distributed in Canada by Publishers Group Canada (1-800-747-8147)

For further distribution details, see www.timeout.com.

ISBN: 978-1-84670-115-3

A CIP catalogue record for this book is available from the British Library.

Printed and bound by Firmengruppe APPL, aprinta druck, Wemding, Germany.

The Random House Group Limited supports The Forest Stewardship Council (FSC), the leading international
forest certification organisation. All our titles that are printed on Greenpeace approved FSC certified paper
carry the FSC logo. Our paper procurement policy can be found at http://www.rbooks.co.uk/environment.

Time Out carbon-offsets its flights with Trees for Cities (www.treesforcities.org).

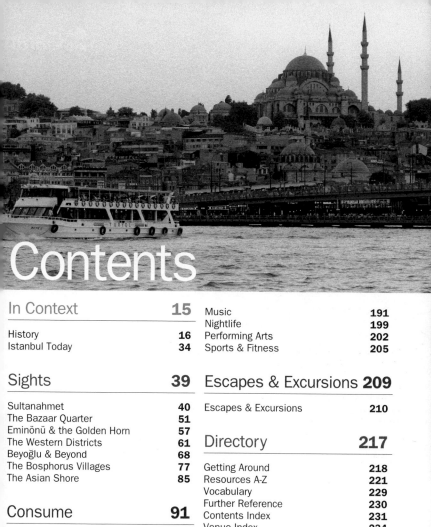

Contents

THE GARANTI BANK ATM.
A MUST SEE
TURKISH LANDMARK.

Open 24/7 for instant cash (TL, $, €, £).
8 languages spoken.

Introduction

Life in Istanbul is conducted on the streets: in the narrow, steep roads of Beyoğlu, in the dark passageways of the Grand Bazaar and on the bridges that link the old city with the new. The city is a constant mill of activity – at once thrilling, bewildering and bewitching, its labyrinthine tapestry of streets home to a trove of unexpected sights. Turn a seemingly inconsequential corner and find impassioned buskers surrounded by passers-by who have stopped to dance; or an unexpected panorama of the impossibly busy Golden Horn; or dozens of men kneeling in prayer outside a mosque too small to accommodate them, or playing backgammon and drinking tea. Add in the call to prayer from the muezzin, horn blasts from tankers gliding up the Bosphorus and the animated chatter of stallholders, and walking the streets is a dizzying experience.

For all Istanbul's captivating sights and medley of sounds, it's the smells that often reside longest in the memory. The frying anchovies in the fish markets along the Golden Horn; the stuffed mussels sold on street corners; grilled corn in summer and roasted chestnuts in winter; the ubiquitous charring kebab. The assault on the senses escalates on streets such as the narrow and restaurant-lined Nevizade Sokak. To squeeze down this path on any evening is to be overwhelmed by the clatter of cutlery, chink of glasses, chatter of Istanbullus and aromas of meat and meze.

There's another Istanbul, too: a city of faith and history, where prayer time is observed, and headscarves and *taqiyah* caps are commonplace. The conservative western neighbourhoods of Fener, Balat and Fatih are typical of this Istanbul, but the city's mixed religious heritage is visible here too: the Church of St Saviour in Chora is home to some of the best Byzantine mosaics and frescos in existence. The historical monuments only get more impressive as you move east, towards the Topkapı Palace, hub of the Ottoman Empire. Among them are Haghia Sophia, dedicated in AD 537, the Suleymaniye Mosque, built in 1557, and the Grand Bazaar, which began trading in 1461.

Over Galata Bridge lies new Istanbul, full of creative and forward-thinking energy. Here bubbles a young population ready to embrace change and foreign influence, armed with guitars, paintbrushes and pens. In today's Istanbul, there's a creative outpouring, only energised by the city's position between East and West, geographically, politically and religiously. Exciting times in an exciting city. **Daniel Neilson, Editor**

BOSS

HUGO BOSS

Istanbul in Brief

IN CONTEXT

The opening section details Istanbul's long and thrilling history:
the power and wealth of the empires that shaped it; the bloody
events and the bizarre personalities. Elsewhere, there's a look at
the 1,500-year story of Istanbul's emotive skyline. Also examined
are the challenges facing Istanbul as it develops and grows as
a modern city, with a unique position between East and West.
► *For more, see pp15-37.*

SIGHTS

Sultanahmet is usually the first port of call for visitors. Sultanahmet
Mosque, Topkapı Palace and Haghia Sophia are all within walking
distance of each other. The world's oldest shopping centre, the
Grand Bazaar, is close by too. Across the Golden Horn is the modern,
secular Istanbul, with hip bars and lively restaurants. There's a slower
pace of life along the Bosphorus, on both European and Asian shores.
► *For more, see pp39-89.*

CONSUME

The quality of food in Istanbul is remarkable. From fish sandwiches
beside the Bosphorus to restaurants with chefs shooting for Turkey's
first Michelin star, Istanbullus eat well. The city is a party town, and
we list plenty of stylish clubs and bars. We also give the lowdown
on shopping opportunities, from carpets to designer clothes.
Completing this section is a rundown of the city's hotels.
► *For more, see pp91-170.*

ARTS & ENTERTAINMENT

Music is an essential part of Istanbul life. Traditional musicians
wander the restaurants of Beyoğlu and gypsy singers frequent
bars for impromptu jams. Meanwhile, in the art world, new galleries
are opening almost monthly, and Istanbul Modern continues to
consolidate its international reputation. We also investigate the
Turkish film industry, examine the city's gay culture, and more.
► *For more, see pp171-208.*

ESCAPES & EXCURSIONS

No trip to Istanbul is complete without a cruise along the Bosphorus.
This guide covers the highlights as far as the Black Sea, hunting out
the best hotels, restaurants and bars. There's also information
about a true retreat from the bustle of the city: the Princes' Islands.
With no cars allowed, only the sound of horses' hooves disturbs
the peace here.
► *For more, see pp209-216.*

Istanbul in 48 Hours

Day 1 The Historic Heart

7AM Get off to an early start. In fact, it can be very early in Istanbul: the daybreak call to prayer is loud among the many mosques of the old city. Breakfast in Turkey is a fortifying affair; it will be needed.

9AM Arrive at the gates of **Tokapı Palace** (*see p45*) as it opens; it gets very busy later on. Be sure to see the Imperial Treasury, to wonder at the opulence of the Ottoman Empire. And don't miss the Harem or Baghdad Kiosk.

12.30AM From Topkapı Palace's Imperial Gate, walk the short distance to Sultanahmet Square and the entrance to the iconic **Haghia Sophia** (*see p40*). Once a glittering cathedral, it became a mosque after the Ottoman conquest and was declared a museum in the early days of the Republic; its cavernous interior is now fairly bare save for some striking Byzantine mosaics. Afterwards, divert briefly to examine the **Sultanahmet Mosque** (*see p42*). For lunch, follow the locals to **Şar** (*see p121*). Its cafeteria-style decor belies its excellent food.

1.30PM It's a short walk to the **Grand Bazaar**. Enjoy getting lost in the vaulted passages and haggling with the shopkeepers. Afterwards, it's time to relax with a çay (tea). Hunt out **Divan** (*see p142*) in the Old Bazaar, or head further up Divan Yolu to try a hookah pipe in a leafy courtyard café.

5PM Take a stroll around Beyazıt Square to the magnificent **Süleymaniye Mosque** (*see p56*).

7PM If you still have energy, head down to the Golden Horn and **Galata Bridge**. As the sun sets, watch the bustle of Istanbul returning home by tram, funicular or ferry.

9.30PM Sultanahment and Eminönü aren't the liveliest areas at night (we've saved the partying for tomorrow), but there are still some good restaurants. **Mozaik** (*see p119*) offers good Anatolian food in an animated atmosphere. If its full try **Rumeli** (*see p121*).

NAVIGATING THE CITY

The best way to explore Istanbul is on foot, perhaps crossing from historic Sultanahmet to Beyoğlu by tram. The street layouts can seem daunting, but in Beyoğlu, Istiklal Caddesi is the street all others lead to. Likewise, Divan Yolu in Sultanahmet is also a useful marker. The main heritage sights are within walking distance of each other in Sultanahmet, and most hotels, restaurants, and noteworthy cultural venues are in one of these two areas. For outlying areas, and the Asian Shore, there's a reasonable public transport network. For details, *see pp218-220*.

THE LOCAL CURRENCY

We have listed prices in **YTL** (New Turkish Lira) throughout this guide, except in the Hotels chapter, where most are in euros. We have quoted prices in US dollars for the few hotels that prefer to quote their prices this way.

Day 2 Culture & Decadence

9AM Start your day with a caffeine jolt at **Şimdi** (*see p145*) or **Kafe Ara** (*see p147*) or and a traditional Turkish breakfast, before climbing up the 14th century **Galata Tower** (*see p71*) for incredible panoramic views of Istanbul.

11AM Once you have your bearings, descend into the streets of **Çukurcuma**, Istanbul's antiques district. Among the meandering streets are shops selling Ottoman furniture and wonderfully kitsch items. Visit **The Works** (*see p169*) for something really quirky or **Eski Fener** (*see p168*) for rural Anatolian treasures.

11AM Climb up to the quiet and increasingly trendy **Cihangir** neighbourhood for some lunch. Two worthwhile options include the open-sided **Meyra** and **Smyrna** (for both, *see p143*). From here, it's a short hop down to **Istanbul Modern** (*see p77*).

3PM Edging round earthy **Karaköy**, sit for a while and watch the ferries and boats weave under **Galata Bridge**. If you fancy an afternoon snack, an anchovy sandwich from the fish market west of the bridge is hard to beat. You'll need some sustenance to climb back up to Galata (or take the Tünel funicular) and **Istiklal Caddesi** – Beyoğlu's principal pedestrian artery.

6PM On any day of the week, Istiklal will by now be packed with parading Istanbullus. Gone are the days when a necktie was de rigueur for a walk along the street, but people will be looking their best. Art lovers will want to check out the galleries. Otherwise, dive into the streets around **Asmalımescit** for a beer. **Badehane** and **KV Café** (for both, *see p144*) are the busiest. For the best views in Istanbul head to **Leb-i Derya Richmond** (*see p147*) for a cocktail as the sun sets.

9PM There's only one place to go for dinner: **Nevizade Sokak**. This boisterous street is rammed with *meyhanes* (taverns) serving mezes and fish dishes. Order a selection of dishes, a bottle of the anise-spirit *rakı* and watch Istanbul at its most exuberant.

PACKAGE DEALS

Given the variety of public transport that you might need to take to make the journey from A to B, you might find it useful to buy a *mavi* (blue) travel pass, valid for a day, a week, 15 days or a month. There's no package pass for the main tourist attractions in Istanbul. To avoid queues at the main sights of Topkapı Palace and Haghia Sophia, buy tickets online and in advance, or through your hotel.

GUIDED TOURS

The whole city is one great outdoor museum, with plenty of free sights in the centre. We've included a handful of mapped walks in the sightseeing chapters. For in-depth guided tours, try **Istanbul Walks** (www.istanbulwalks.net). There's also **City Sightseeing Istanbul** (0212 458 1800, www.city-sightseeing. com), a company that operates bus tours of the city with commentary from a guide.

Istanbul in Profile

SULTANAHMET

The most unmissable sights are in and around Sultanahmet: **Topkapı Palace**, **Sultanahmet Mosque** and **Haghia Sophia**. If this is your first time in Istanbul, this is where you're going to be spending most time. Its spine is Divan Yolu, the main drag and tram route. With stops beside the main mosques and bazaars, the tram is the best way to get around this side of town.
▶ For more, see pp40-50.

THE BAZAAR QUARTER

Seamlessly blending into Sultanahmet is the Bazaar Quarter. At its heart, the **Grand Bazaar** was once the economic centre of the Ottoman Empire, where traders from all corners of the empire would come to do business. The area occupies the highest part of a fat thumb of land enclosed by the Sea of Marmara and the Golden Horn. It is also home to Istanbul University and the majestic Süleymaniye and Beyazıt mosques.
▶ For more, see pp51-56.

EMINÖNÜ & THE GOLDEN HORN

North of Divan Yolu, the streets slope precipitously down to the waterside transport hub of Eminönü. Here, ferries depart for destinations up the Bosphorus and over to the Asian Shore. **Sirkeci Station**, once the terminus of the Orient Express, and the **Egyptian Bazaar** are the only sights around here. But to watch the constant waterborne activity around Galata Bridge is mesmerising.
▶ For more, see pp57-60.

THE WESTERN DISTRICTS

Beyond the Bazaar Quarter are the Western Districts, conservative neighbourhoods such as **Fatih**, **Fener**, **Balat** and, further afield, **Eyüp**. Few visitors make it out here, but there are several interesting churches, mosques and other sights, notably the Byzantine **Church of St Saviour in Chora** and the **city walls**. This quiet, traditional area reveals a very different Istanbul from that of secular districts such as Beyoğlu.
▶ For more, see pp61-67.

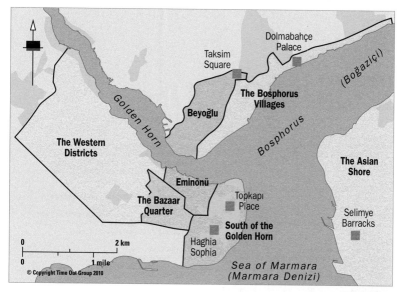

BEYOĞLU & BEYOND
North of the Golden Horn is the 'modern' city, developed largely in the 19th century. Ground zero is Beyoğlu, the place to play after sightseeing. Beyoğlu subdivides into several smaller neighbourhoods, all linked by **Istiklal Caddesi**, a long, pedestrian boulevard whose narrow off-shoots are filled with shops, cafés, bars, clubs and restaurants. North of Taksim are the newer districts of **Harbiye**, **Şişli**, **Nişantaşı** and **Teşvikiye**.
► For more, see pp68-76.

THE BOSPHORUS VILLAGES
Ortaköy, **Arnavutköy** and **Bebek** are picturesque waterside clusters of wooden villas, folksy shops and markets, open-air cafés and restaurants. Linked by bus services, or, better still, the ferry, they make great escapes from the pace of the city. Nearer to the city centre are the more urban **Karaköy** and **Beşiktaş**.
► For more, see pp76-84.

THE ASIAN SHORE
The neighbourhood of **Kadıköy** is home to a lively bar scene, while conservative **Üsküdar** is better known for its historic mosques – as well as the Maiden's Tower, a popular landmark on a small island just off the coast.
► For more, see pp85-89.

Time Out Istanbul

Editor Daniel Neilson
Deputy Editor Ros Sales
Listings Editor Nur Bayol
Proofreader Holly Pick
Indexer William Cook

Managing Director Peter Fiennes
Editorial Director Ruth Jarvis
Business Manager Dan Allen
Editorial Manager Holly Pick
Assistant Management Accountant Ija Krasnikova

Design
Art Director Scott Moore
Art Editor Pinelope Kourmouzoglou
Senior Designer Kei Ishimaru
Advertising Designer Jodi Sher

Picture Desk
Picture Editor Jael Marschner
Deputy Picture Editor Liz Leahy
Picture Desk Assistant/Researcher Ben Rowe

Advertising
New Business & Commercial Director Mark Phillips
International Advertising Manager Kasimir Berger
International Sales Executive Charlie Sokol
Advertising Sales (Istanbul) Time Out Istanbul

Marketing
**Sales & Marketing Director, North America
 & Latin America** Lisa Levinson
Senior Publishing Brand Manager Luthfa Begum
Group Commercial Art Director Anthony Huggins
Marketing Co-ordinator Alana Benton

Production
Group Production Director Mark Lamond
Production Manager Brendan McKeown
Production Assistant Katie Mulhern

Time Out Group
Director & Founder Tony Elliott
Chief Executive Officer David King
Group Financial Director Paul Rakkar
Group General Manager/Director Nichola Coulthard
Time Out Communications Ltd MD David Pepper
Time Out International Ltd MD Cathy Runciman
Time Out Magazine Ltd Publisher/MD Mark Elliott
Group Commerical Director Graeme Tottle
Group IT Director Simon Chappell

Contributors

Introduction Daniel Neilson. **History** Andrew Humphreys, David O'Byrne (*Brotherly Love?* Edoardo Albert; *Ataturk's New Turks* Ros Sales. **Istanbul Today** Daniel Neilson. **Sightseeing** Jon Gorvett (*Hard Times in the Harem* Andrew Humphreys; *Shopping the Bazaar* Ken Dakan; *The Great Icon Controversy* Edoardo Albert; *The City's Narrator* Chris Watt). **Hotels** Andrew Humphreys, Daniel Neilson, Cat Scully (*Hotel Hamams* Emily Troutman). **Restaurants** Rene Ames, Vanessa Able, Daniel Neilson (*Profile Murat Bozok* Daniel Neilson; *School Dinners* Cat Scully). **Bars & Cafés** Vanessa Able, Daniel Neilson (*Hubbly Bubbly* Andrew Humphreys; *Up on the Roofs* Dorian Jones; *Grape Expectations* Cat Scully). **Shops & Services** Daniel Neilson, Jody Sabral, Lucy Wood (*Beyoğlu's Fashion Arcades* Vanessa Able; *The Rug Trade, Market Day* Ken Dakan. **Calendar** John Gorvett. **Children** Yeşim Erdem Holland. **Film** Lucy Wood. **Galleries** November Paynter. **Gay & Lesbian** Ken Dakan. **Hamams** Andrew Humphreys. **Music** Andy Footner (*Doing the Oryantal* Ken Dakan; *Shout Out to Istanbul* **Daniel Neilson**). **Nightlife** Attila Pelit. **Performing Arts** Attila Pelit. **Sport & Fitness** John Gorvett (*Wrestling Moves* Daniel Neilson). **Escapes & Excursions** John Gorvett, Cat Scully. **Directory** Attila Pelit.

Maps john@jsgraphics.co.uk.

Photography Fumie Suzuki, except pages 7 (centre right), 8, 10 (top), 48, 58, 69, 86, 91, 95, 109, 118, 120 (top), 129, 131, 133, 134, 135, 137, 138, 142, 145, 146, 153, 160, 165, 170, 179, 182, 190, 217 Daniel Neilson; pages 25, 29 AKG-images; page 30 AP/Press Association Images; pages 209, 211, 215 Shutterstock.

The following images were provided by the featured establishments/artists:
pages 37, 59, 92, 93, 107, 111, 117, 172, 173, 193, 197, 202, 203

The Editor would like to thank Ceyda Pekenc, Hulya Soylu and Evin Mete at Redmint Communications, Jack and Ena Neilson, Esen Boyacigiller and Deniz Huysal and the staff at *Time Out Istanbul* magazine, and the contributors to previous editions of *Time Out Istanbul*, whose work forms the basis for parts of this book.

The editor flew to Istanbul with Turkish Airlines (www.thy.com, 0844 800 6666).

About the Guide

GETTING AROUND

The back of the book contains street maps of Istanbul, as well as overview maps of the city and its surroundings. The maps start on page 239; on them are marked the locations of hotels (❶), restaurants and cafés (❶), and pubs and bars (❶). The majority of businesses listed in this guide are located in the areas we've mapped; the grid-square references in the listings refer to these maps.

THE ESSENTIALS

For practical information, including visas, disabled access, emergency numbers, lost property, useful websites and local transport, please see the Directory. It begins on page 217.

THE LISTINGS

Addresses, phone numbers, websites, transport information, hours and prices are all included in our listings, as are selected other facilities. All were checked and correct at press time. However, business owners can alter their arrangements at any time, and fluctuating economic conditions can cause prices to change rapidly.

The very best venues in the city, the must-sees and must-dos in every category, have been marked with a red star (★). In the Sights chapters, we've also marked venues with free admission with a FREE symbol.

PHONE NUMBERS

The area code for Istanbul is 0212 (European side) or 0216 (Asian side). Within the city, you don't need to use the code unless you are calling the other side: simply dial the seven-digit number listed in this guide.

From outside Turkey, dial your country's international access code (00 from the UK) or a plus symbol, followed by the Turkey country code (90), 212 or 216 for Istanbul (dropping the initial zero) and the seven-digit number as listed in the guide. So, to reach Istanbul Modern, dial +90 212 334 7300. For more on phones, see p226.

FEEDBACK

We welcome feedback on this guide, both on the venues we've included and on any other locations that you'd like to see featured in future editions. Please email us at guides@timeout.com.

Time Out Guides

Founded in 1968, Time Out has grown from humble beginnings into the leading resource for anyone wanting to know what's happening in the world's greatest cities. Alongside our influential weeklies in London, New York and Chicago, we publish more than 20 magazines in cities as varied as Beijing and Beirut; a range of travel books, with the City Guides now joined by the newer Shortlist series; and an information-packed website. The company remains proudly independent, still owned by Tony Elliott four decades after he launched *Time Out London*.

Written by local experts and illustrated with original photography, our books also retain their independence. No business has been featured because it has advertised, and all restaurants and bars are visited and reviewed anonymously.

ABOUT THE EDITOR

Daniel Neilson has edited several guides for Time Out and written for a number of other Time Out titles. He has also contributed words and pictures to *CNN Traveller*, *Four Four Two*, *The Wire*, *Observer*, BBC's *Who Do You Think You Are?*, *Adventure Travel* and *Total Politics*.

A full list of the book's contributors and photographers can be found on the opposite page.

In Context

Rüstem Paşa Mosque. *See p60.*

History

*Two religious empires,
one secular republic.*

Few cities have occupied the imagination as Istanbul (or Constantinople) has. Fought over throughout its history by armies from Western Europe, the Middle East and Central Asia, capital and centre of two of the world's greatest empires, intriguing, perplexing and often frustrating, it captivates as few other cities can.

Most books will tell you that Istanbul is the only city in the world to straddle two continents, Europe and Asia. In fact it's the other way round: the history of the area defined what we now know as the continents. And the theme of cultural conflict between those continents was already well established by the fifth century BC, when Herodotus devoted much of his *Histories* to the conflict between Greece and Persia, East and West. His writings came to define the 'them and us' attitude that still dominates relations between Europe and Asia, an attitude still present and relevant in current issues such as Turkey's prospective EU membership.

The role of imagined bridge between East and West has been thrust on Istanbul as a legacy of its location, and is more cliché than reality; however, that's not to deny that this eclectic city has both 'Western' and 'Eastern' elements, forged together in unique combination by the force of history to create a city that is hard to define as either.

BLIND BEGINNINGS

Despite its geographical advantages, prehistoric finds around Istanbul have been scarce, probably due to the intensity of occupation that followed. Neolithic sites from about 7000 BC have been found near Kadıköy, and Bronze Age remains dated to 3200 BC unearthed in Sultanahmet.

Around 1600 BC, seafaring Greeks began to found colonies around the Aegean and Mediterranean. By 750 BC, they had passed through the Bosphorus and established settlements on the Black Sea coast of Anatolia and in the Caucasus. The 'clashing rocks' episode from the legend of Jason and the Argonauts was probably inspired by the voyage up the Bosphorus Strait. The first Greek settlement in what is now Istanbul was the colony of Chalcedon, founded around 675 BC in today's Kadıköy, on the Asian shore. According to Herodotus (the best source of classical soundbite), Chalcedon was dubbed 'the city of the blind', its founders having foolishly missed the clear geographical advantages of the opposite European shore.

Within fewer than 20 years, more clear-sighted parties had settled across the water on land now enclosed by the walls of Topkapı Palace. Roughly triangular, bounded on two sides by water, it was a natural fortress, with the Golden Horn to the north, a 6.5-kilometre (four-mile) long, deep-water harbour. The site offered access by sea to Africa, the Mediterranean, and the Black Sea, and lay at the crossroads of routes between Europe and Asia. It was destined to be a city of world importance. Its founding was attributed to a sailor by the name of Byzas, hence the name Byzantium.

Others were quick to recognise the strategic importance of the new city, and it was repeatedly taken by warring powers: the Persians in 550 BC, then the Spartans, then the Athenians. The Byzantines quickly developed a skill for diplomacy and kept their predatory neighbours at bay through a series of alliances. When that failed, the city dug in, successfully weathering a siege from Philip of Macedon in 340 BC.

Good judgement ran out in AD 196 when, after three centuries of independence as part of the Roman province of Asia, the Byzantines backed the wrong side in an imperial power struggle. After a prolonged siege, the stern emperor Septimius Severus had Byzantium's walls torn down, the city put to the torch and a fair chunk of the population put to death. Such a strategic location couldn't lie wasted for long, though, and within a few years the emperor had rebuilt the city on a far grander scale. For all its pomp, like earlier Greek Byzantium, nothing of Severus's city has survived.

NEW ROME

By the end of the third century, the Roman Empire had become too unwieldy to govern effectively from Rome, and was subdivided, with part of the power shifted to Byzantium. The result was to create internal rivalries that ultimately could only be settled on the battlefield. In 324, Constantine, Emperor of the West, defeated Licinius, Emperor of the East, first in a naval battle on the Sea of Marmara, then on the Asian shore at a place called Chrysopolis, today's Üsküdar. With the empire reunited, Constantine set about changing the course of history, first by promoting Christianity as the official religion of the empire, then by shifting the capital from a jaded and cynical Rome to the upstart city on the Bosphorus. On 11 May 330, Constantine inaugurated his new seat of power as 'Nova Roma', a name by which the city has never been known since.

In Nova Roma, more popularly called Constantinople, the new emperor had a city that he could make over as he saw fit. He embarked on a building programme, plundering the empire to bring in the tallest columns, the finest marble and an abundance of Christian relics, including the True Cross itself. To safeguard his new capital, Constantine had walls erected in an arc from near what is now the Atatürk Bridge over the Golden Horn, then looping south to present-day Mustafa Paşa, enlarging the area of the city fourfold. Other than a burnt and badly aged column, little physical evidence of Constantine's work survives, but he laid the foundations for an empire that was to endure for over 1,000 years.

IN CONTEXT

The beginnings were not auspicious, however. On Constantine's death in 337, achievement and stability ended. His three sons quarrelled over the succession and the empire was once again divided between Eastern and Western emperors. Constantinople was largely unaffected by the ensuing two centuries of turbulence, and was even enlarged by the construction of new city walls during the reign of Theodosius II (408-50), completed just in time to halt Attila's advancing hordes. Rome was not so fortunate: it was ripped apart by tribes of Goths and Vandals from the north. With no rival, Constantinople was left to move towards a new era of greatness, reaching its apogee during the era of Justinian (527-65).

CROWD TROUBLE

Justinian's reign was marked by great confidence, which saw the empire extend across most of the Mediterranean coast, including the recapture of the lost dominion of Italy from the 'barbarian hordes'. He was fortunate in having at his service a supremely competent general, Belisarius. Similarly exceptional was Justinian's wife, Theodora, a former street entertainer and prostitute, credited with saving her husband's skin when a revolt broke out among factions at the Hippodrome. Normally rivals, these factions, a cross between political parties and gangs, united to protest at the execution of some of their number. As unrest increased, it was Theodora who dissuaded Justinian from fleeing, and Belisarius who trapped and massacred 30,000 of the rebels in the Hippodrome.

Left presiding over a city of ruins soaked in its citizens' blood, Justinian needed to restore public faith. His answer was to embark on a grand programme of reconstruction, providing for the city spiritually (he endowed over 40 churches) and practically – for example, providing the city with immense water cisterns (among them the **Yerebatan Sarnıcı**, *see p42*). The crowning glory was the new cathedral, Sancta Sophia.

Although the death of Justinian was followed by a prolonged period of decline, largely resulting from internal rivalries, Constantinople remained, as one Byzantine writer put it, 'the city of the world's desire'. There were plenty who acted on those desires. Slavs (581), Avars (617), Persians and Avars (626), Arabs (669-79 and 717-18), Bulgars (813, 913 and 924), Russians (four times between 860 and 1043) and Pechenegs (1087) all marched on the city. Some armies were sufficiently daunted by the walls alone and quit before they'd begun to fight. Others persisted and laid siege. But all failed.

IN CONTEXT

PICTURE PROBLEMS

Trouble was also brewing internally on the theological front when the iconoclast Leo III became emperor in 726. Thus began a 'dark age' of almost 120 years, during which churches were stripped of their decoration and those who stayed faithful to icons (iconodules) were forced to flee to distant monasteries or to worship in secret at risk of denunciation and death. *See p63* **The Great Icon Controversy**.

A restoration in Byzantine fortunes came during the reign of Basil II (976-1025), who succeeded not just in holding the fort but also expanding the empire into Armenia and Georgia. A conscientious ruler, he was also incredibly harsh: in 1014, after taking 15,000 Bulgars prisoner, he had 99 out of every 100 blinded; the remainder were left with one eye to lead their fellow soldiers home. When he saw the ruined army that returned to his capital, Bulgarian Tsar Samuel is said to have collapsed and died two days later.

OUT OF THE DARK

The death of Basil marked a turning point in Byzantine fortunes, and the city entered a period of terminal decline. This was signalled to all when, in 1071, a combination of incompetence and treachery led to the annihilation of a Byzantine army at Manzikert in Anatolia. The victors were a new menace: the Selçuk Turks, who flooded across Asia Minor to the shores of the Sea of Marmara. Meanwhile, to the west, Europe had

emerged from its Dark Ages to become a patchwork of states owing religious allegiance to the Pope in Rome. But theological differences and the Western Church's envy of its older and richer neighbour meant that any common cause was superficial. In 1054, a dispute between papal officials and the Patriarch of Constantinople had resulted in mutual excommunications. The animosity inaugurated the schism between the Roman and Orthodox churches that still exists today.

Threatened by the Selçuk Turks, an increasingly decadent and effete Byzantium was forced to enlist the aid of Latin armies as paid mercenaries. The Latins were crusading to recapture the Holy Lands lost to the Turks and, passing through Constantinople in 1097, they agreed to return to the emperor any formerly imperial territory that they might recapture. This was a promise they failed to keep. Instead, the crusaders set up their own Holy Land states. There followed 50 years of confused bruising between the Byzantine, Latin and Muslim armies, culminating in the Byzantines cutting crusader supply lines and enabling the Selçuks to retake lost territory.

Two or three relatively able emperors, notably John II (1118-43) and Manuel I (1143-80), applied clever diplomacy and judicious use of force to keep the empire intact and even extend its borders; but the good work was undone in 1185 with the accession of the incompetent Isaac II. He was deposed by his brother Alexius III and imprisoned, but Isaac's son escaped and fled west, where he offered enormous sums of money to the armies massing in Venice for the Fourth Crusade, in exchange for helping his father and himself regain the imperial throne. With interest in a long and probably futile struggle in the Middle East never deep, the Latins needed little encouragement to accept.

Threatened with the vastly superior force of the crusaders, the Byzantines agreed to restore Isaac II to the throne. But Alexius III fled with the contents of the treasury and the crown jewels, leaving the reinstated emperor with no money to pay his mercenary allies. On 13 April 1204, the crusaders stormed Constantinople. They sacked the city, stripping it of its treasures and relics and sending them back west; the four gilded bronze horses that now stand over the doorway of St Mark's cathedral in Venice came from Constantinople's Hippodrome. What the crusaders couldn't strip away they destroyed, leaving the city in ruins.

The victorious Latins then appointed one of their own, Baldwin of Flanders, as emperor, and divided up the empire into a patchwork of fiefdoms and city states. Haghia Sophia and many Orthodox churches were converted to the Latin rite. The Latin state lasted until 1261 before the Byzantines mustered enough force to reclaim what remained of Constantinople.

THE OVERWHELMING OTTOMANS

That the Byzantine state was able to survive for another 190 ineffectual years was down to the fact that the rival Selçuk empire had splintered into myriad warring *beyliks*, or fiefdoms. It was only a matter of time, though, before one *beylik* won out. By the first years of the 14th century a new power had emerged: the Osmanlı Turks, named after their first leader Osman, and better known to Westerners as the Ottomans. During the reign of their first sultan, Orhan Gazi (1326-62), the Ottomans conquered most of western Asia Minor and advanced into Europe as far as Bulgaria, establishing a new capital at Adrianople, now Edirne.

Constantinople had become a Byzantine island in an Ottoman sea. Inevitably, the severely weakened, ruined and depopulated city was confronted with a Turkish army at its walls. This first occurred in 1394, and again in 1400, 1422 and 1442; all were repelled, but this only forestalled the inevitable. Soon after becoming Ottoman sultan in 1452, Mehmet II constructed the fortress of Rumeli Hisarı on the European shore of the Bosphorus just north of the city. Fitted with cannons, it gave the Ottomans control of the straits and deprived Constantinople of vital grain supplies.

By April 1453, the Ottoman forces surrounding Constantinople numbered some 80,000; facing them were just 5,000 able-bodied men in a city whose population had

IN CONTEXT

al-Jamal
Badawi

The One and Only Lebanese Restaurant in Istanbu

Sıraevler, Süleyman Seba Cad.
No: 42-46 Akaretler / İSTANBUL
(0212) 236 50 17
www.capamarka.com.tr

from the creators

capa-marka
entertainment group
fun, food & music

' At a time when 'heretics' were being burned alive in western Europe, the Ottoman regime granted all religions freedom of worship.'

fallen to less than 50,000. However, they could not gain access to the Golden Horn because of a great chain that the Byzantines had stretched across its mouth from Galata castle to modern-day Sirkeci. But one night, several weeks into the siege, in an audacious move, the Ottomans circumvented the boom by hauling 70 ships on rollers up over the ridge above Galata and down to the water on the other side, so that by morning they were in the Golden Horn and up against the city walls.

On 29 May, the final assault was launched. The Ottomans forced an opening near the Golden Horn, and poured into the city in their thousands. By dawn it was all over, with an estimated 4,000 defenders lying dead. A contemporary account describes how 'blood flowed through the streets like rainwater after a sudden storm; corpses floated out to sea like melons on a canal'. With the conquest of Constantinople, Mehmet, still only 21 years old, took the name 'Fatih', or Conqueror. He was apparently shocked at the ruined state of the once-great city.

A MULTINATIONAL CAPITAL

Mehmet was intoxicated by the notion of Constantinople and its heritage as capital of Eastern and Western empires. It fitted his own imperial ambitions. Justinian's great cathedral, Haghia Sophia, was reconsecrated as a mosque, and the sultan attended prayer there the first Friday after the conquest. The Ottomans immediately set about repairing the damage sustained during the siege and the decay of preceding centuries. The sultan's *viziers* (ministers) were encouraged to build and endow the new capital with mosques and the beginnings of what would develop into the Grand Bazaar.

Efforts were made to repopulate the half-deserted city. Greeks, who had fled in the preceding years, were offered land and houses and temporary tax exemption. Craftsmen, merchants and those who would enhance the city's wealth were invited regardless of race or religion. At a time when 'heretics' were being burnt alive in western Europe, the Ottoman regime granted all religions freedom of worship and the uncontested right to appoint their own religious leaders. Large numbers of Sephardic Jews expelled from Spain and Portugal took sanctuary in Istanbul, the only multinational, multi-faith capital in Europe.

On the Conqueror's death in 1481, a scuffle for succession was won by his elder son Beyazıt II, succeeded in turn by his son Selim I, known as 'the Grim' for his habit of having his grand viziers executed. Though Selim's reign lasted only eight years, he presided over significant military victories, adding Syria and Egypt to the imperial portfolio. Further south, he saw off a Portuguese threat to Mecca and was rewarded with the keys to the Holy City, the sacred relics of the Prophet, and the title of Caliph, Champion of Islam. This made Istanbul not only the capital of one of the most powerful empires in the world, but, as it was still the home of the Orthodox Patriarchate, also the centre of two major religions.

But it was during the 46-year reign of Süleyman I (1520-66), known as Süleyman the Magnificent, that the city became a true imperial centre. By the time of his death, he ruled an empire that covered North Africa, stretched east to India, and rolled from the Caucasus through Anatolia and the Balkans to Budapest and most of modern-day Hungary. Süleyman's armies reached the walls of Vienna in 1529, where they were turned back after an unsuccessful siege. Key to Süleyman's military successes were the Janissaries, a crack and fiercely loyal fighting force. Originally of entirely Christian origin, selected boys were forcibly converted to Islam and trained as elite soldiers; they were richly rewarded in return. During the 16th century they were the most disciplined, well-armed and effective of all European armies, universally admired and feared.

Under Süleyman, Istanbul became synonymous with grandeur. Its epicentre was the imperial palace, Topkapı, founded by Mehmet the Conqueror, but gilded by the wealth, tributes and taxes from newly conquered territories. Severe and grave, Süleyman surprised all by falling under the spell of a slave girl, Haseki Hürrem, known universally as Roxelana due to her alleged Russian origins. So besotted was Süleyman that in the early 1530s he married Roxelana and dispensed with the company of all other women. In 1538, as a further expression of devotion, he commissioned a promising young

Brotherly Love?

Family life can be a dangerous business.

Wielding absolute power in the most magnificent city on earth, as Emperor of Byzantium or Sultan of the Ottomans, might seem an enviable privilege. Yet despite the unparalleled luxury, there was a dark side to life in the imperial court. Since neither empire had a strict rule of primogeniture, getting to the top – and staying there – presented these rulers with serious challenges.

Between the foundation and fall of Byzantium, there were 107 emperors. Only 34 of them died of natural causes; another eight were killed in battle. Sixty-five were forcibly removed from the throne. Intrigue and assassination were common: emperors had no qualms about killing or mutilating potential claimants or conspirators, since failing to remain in power would generally result in blinding, banishment, or a long and painful death. (Since a deformed man could not be emperor, blinding was considered a more merciful alternative to murder.) When Emperor Andronikos I was overthrown, he was handed over to the mob, who broke his teeth, ripped out his hair, put out an eye, and chopped off a hand; he died three days later.

Things were no better among the Ottomans. The death or decline of the reigning sultan triggered an intense power struggle among his brothers and sons. Given that the sultans had several wives and innumerable concubines, the number of claimants was extensive. Until the 17th century, the sultan's brothers were unlikely to get anywhere near the throne, since fratricide was one of the first acts committed by a new ruler. Garroting was the favourite method of disposing of unwanted siblings, a skill in which the palace mutes excelled.

After the 17th century, the sultan's brothers were confined to the Kafes, or Cage, a secluded building in the Palace where they had no contact with the outside world apart from a few mute servants and a barren women, who formed a harem. Occasionally, one of them might be dragged out and abruptly appointed Sultan. Ibrahim, the last surviving brother of Murat IV, had been a prisoner for 22 of his 24 years when a vizier came to tell him that Murat was dead and he was now Sultan. Ibrahim refused to open the door until Murat's corpse was produced. Ibrahim finally emerged crying: 'The butcher is dead!' He immediately set about making up for lost time. One source notes: 'As Murat was wholly addicted to wine, so was Ibrahim to lust... He frequently assembled all the virgins, made them strip, and himself naked, ran among them neighing like a stallion, and ravish'd one or another.' The party couldn't last. Ibrahim was overthrown by the Janissaries. He was finished off by Kara Ali, the chief executioner, who strangled him with a garter.

Roxelana with Süleyman.

architect, Mimar Sinan, to construct the Haseki Hürrem Mosque complex as a birthday present. This was Sinan's first major commission in Istanbul, launching a glorious career that was to span 50 years, leaving an indelible mark on the city and indeed on most major cities of the Ottoman Empire; see p32 **Story of a Skyline**.

THE RULE OF WOMEN

Süleyman should have been succeeded by his first son, Mustafa, an able soldier and administrator, but Roxelana schemed against it. Mustafa was not her son. She succeeded in convincing the sultan that he was traitorous and Süleyman had him strangled. Selim, Roxelana's son, became heir apparent.

Such bloodletting to secure the imperial throne was not uncommon. Succession was a matter of life or death, for Mehmet the Conqueror had declared, 'For the welfare of the state, the one of my sons to whom Allah grants the sultanate may lawfully put his brothers to death.' They were strangled with a silken bowstring, preferably by deaf mutes who would not hear their cries.

Far from being 'Grim', like the first Selim, Selim II was known as Selim 'the Sot'. His rampant drunkenness rendered him useless as a ruler. The real power behind the throne was Nurbanu ('Princess of Light'), one of Selim's wives, who took control of

'Europe saw the imminent demise of Ottoman rule as a chance to carve up what remained of its empire.'

both the harem and the palace, marking the beginning of an 80-year period referred to as 'the rule of women'. It was an era that saw weak sultans manipulated by their wives and their mothers, the *valide sultanas*, between whom there were often struggles for power (*see p49* **Hard Times in the Harem**).

Selim drowned in his bath and the ruthless Nurbanu had four of his five sons killed, leaving her own child, Murat III, to succeed as sultan. When Murat died in 1595, Mehmet's successor, Ahmet I, stopped the killing, possibly out of fear of dynastic extinction. From Ahmet's time, male relatives of the sultan were instead confined to the Kafes, literally 'cage', a closed apartment hidden deep inside the Topkapı Palace. Here they were kept in complete isolation, apart from a few concubines who had been sterilised by the removal of their ovaries. Guards whose eardrums had been pierced and tongues slit served the prisoners. Although slightly more humane than the earlier fratricidal practices, confinement in the Kafes did little for the captives' mental health. Numerous sultans died prematurely without leaving an heir and their siblings were uniquely unsuited to rule, having spent most of their adult lives incarcerated. In the last years of the empire the problem grew more acute, as successive sultans had little experience of the outside world, or of government. Some simply emerged mad. *See also p24* **Brotherly Love?**

THE TURNING POINT

In 1683 the Ottomans failed in a second attempt to take Vienna. This marked the end of Ottoman military successes and expansions and the beginning of a series of reverses. Within three years the imperial armies had lost Buda to the Austrians, and two years after that, Belgrade. The problem lay not just with addled sultans. In the absence of a strong figurehead, the Janissaries, once the sultan's finest troops, were now completely out of hand, threatening the sultan and killing ministers. Plagues were common. In 1603 a fifth of the population was wiped out, in 1778 a third. Such outbreaks had been eliminated in Europe by the early 1700s by the use of quarantines, but the fatalistic Turks accepted the epidemics as God's will.

Of the advances in science and technology that had begun to revolutionise Western societies and economies in the 18th century, the Ottomans were not only ignorant but arrogantly dismissive. One Turkish dignitary who visited a scientific lab in Vienna in 1748 described it as 'toys' and 'Frankish trickery'.

When Selim III took the throne in 1789, his position was perilous: disobedient guards, recurrent plague, economic decline, military defeats, moribund culture and a restless populace heavily taxed and suffering under poor administration. He looked to the West for inspiration. He established a consultative council and Western architectural influences started to appear at the palaces. More crucially, he attempted to reform the army. For this the sultan earned the enmity of the Janissaries, who felt their privileges were being threatened. They rose up in revolt, deposed Selim and murdered him.

The Janissaries were finally crushed in 1826 by Sultan Mahmut II (1808-39), who had narrowly escaped from the palace with his life the day Selim had been killed. He went on to implement extensive and much-needed reforms, instigating what historian Philip Mansel calls 'revolution from above'. Local government was introduced to Istanbul for the first time, together with the city's first police and fire services.

Mahmut appeared at public functions wearing Western clothes and, most striking of all, banned the wearing of robes and turbans, except by the clergy, introducing the crimson-wool fez from Morocco. This was soon taken to heart by the city, worn by all as a symbol of modernism. More than just a hat, the fez became, in the words of nationalist writer Falih Rifki Atay, 'part of the Turkish soul'.

THE TANZIMAT ERA

Mahmut's successor, Abdül Mecit (1839-61), continued his father's reforming programme, resulting in what was to be a last blossoming of the Ottoman Empire. The sultan further embraced the new era by moving out of Topkapı and into a new Western-style imperial palace at Dolmabahçe. But the real hub of the city was the bridge built across the Golden Horn in 1845. The first bridge to link the two sides of the water, it became the most popular of places; every evening, show-offs from a dozen or more nationalities would dress up like peacocks and promenade up and down the bridge. Between palace and bridge, the largely non-Muslim, European districts of Galata and Pera (modern-day Beyoğlu), originally founded as Italian traders' enclaves in Byzantine times, were rapidly developing into a new commercial and entertainment district centred on the Grande Rue de Pera, location for an increasing number of theatres, cafés, bars and hotels. Istanbul was shifting its locus from south of the Golden Horn to north.

In the middle of the 19th century, the city began to receive its first proper 'tourists', drawn by the oriental mystique of the capital of the Ottoman sultans. Almost immediately, the sightseeing circuit experienced by visitors today was set. In October 1883, the Orient Express rolled into Sirkeci station for the first time.

Political reforms culminated in 1876 in the drafting of a constitution and establishment the following year of the first Turkish parliament – albeit with very limited powers. In any case it was short-lived. In 1877 the Russians seized Ottoman lands in the Balkans and Caucasus. Called to account, Sultan Abdül Hamit responded by dissolving parliament and ruling by decree from his new labyrinthine palace at Yıldız. A paranoid ruler, he hid at Yıldız in constant fear of being bumped off, and had several close members of his family, as well as countless ministers, generals and other court officials, killed. British prime minister William Gladstone called him the 'Great Assassin'. The Turks simply called him 'Abdül the Damned'.

Reform had already progressed too far to allow this reversion to complete imperial rule. Small clandestine groups later known as 'Young Turks' kept up the pressure for change. Most were crushed, but one, the Committee of Union and Progress, succeeded in seizing control of the Ottoman army in Macedonia. By 1908 the CUP was powerful enough to send a telegram to the ageing despotic sultan demanding the restoration of the constitution and parliament. Faced with a rebellious revolutionary army marching on Constantinople, Abdül Hamit acceded to their demands.

Elections to the new parliament saw all but one of the seats won by the CUP, whose elected deputies included Arabs, Greeks, Jews, Armenians and Albanians. It took a pitched battle in Taksim Square to fight off the challenge of Islamic groups, but once that was won reforms were back on the agenda. What should then have been a period of rebirth was instead one of chaos and turmoil, as Europe saw the imminent demise of Ottoman rule as a chance to carve up what remained of its empire.

EMPIRE'S END

In 1912, the Balkan states launched their own offensive, which saw them take all Ottoman possessions in Europe and Bulgarian troops advance to within 40 kilometres (25 miles) of Istanbul. News that Russia, which had long coveted Istanbul and control of the Bosphorus Strait, had joined an alliance with Britain and France left Turkey with little option but to turn to Germany, and the two signed a formal alliance.

Despite a historic victory at Gallipoli, in which they stemmed the Allied invasion and forced a withdrawal, the Ottomans were on the losing side in World War I. In the

IN CONTEXT

aftermath, they could do nothing but watch as the former Ottoman Empire was divided up between European powers. The British and French took over the Arab lands, occupied Istanbul in 1919 and enthroned a puppet sultan there.

Turkish leaders in Istanbul seemed incapable of countering the threat from the Greeks, who ran most of the area west of Istanbul. Groups of disillusioned soldiers began slipping out of the city, under the leadership of Mustafa Kemal, the young Turkish general who had masterminded resistance at Gallipoli. In 1919, Kemal led a revolt from the interior, declaring independence and forming a new government in Ankara. 'Henceforth,' he declared, 'Istanbul does not control Anatolia, but Anatolia Istanbul.' In other words: 'Turkey for the Turks.'

After two years of bitter fighting, the Turks forced the Greeks back to Izmir, which was all but destroyed in the final battle. It was a defining moment for the emergent Turkish state, which was now able to negotiate with the Allies on equal terms. In 1922, the sultanate was abolished and the reigning sultan reduced to little more than a ceremonial figurehead.

LET THE GOOD TIMES ROLL

On 29 October 1923, just a few days after reoccupying Istanbul, Turkey adopted a new secular republican constitution, appointed Mustafa Kemal 'Atatürk' ('father of the Turks') as its president, and chose Ankara as its new capital. The latter was a bold break with almost 1,600 years of tradition, which saw the replacement of one of the world's most fabulous cities by a small, windswept, hillside town that lacked almost every modern amenity, but which was far enough from the new country's borders to make it secure from invasion. Within six months, the 1,300-year-old tradition of the sultanate was completely abolished, and the last members of the Ottoman dynasty were sent into exile, never to return. More sweeping reforms followed, changing the Turkish social, political and cultural world forever (*see right* **Atatürk's New Turks**).

Although supplanted by Ankara as the country's political powerhouse, Istanbul continued to prosper as the undisputed cultural and economic capital of the new republic. The Grand Bazaar remained the centre of commerce, while Pera – now renamed Beyoğlu – entered a wild and heady period buoyed by pro-Western reforms that allowed for previously unthinkable levels of freedom.

As a leader, Atatürk was the personification of good-time Turkey. A man of immense energy, he drank and gambled all night, napped for a couple of hours then got up to conduct the country's affairs. He may have moved the capital to Ankara, but his heart was in Istanbul.

Atatürk died in 1938. His casket was placed in the throne room of Dolmabahçe Palace, where hundreds of thousands came to view the body. Crowds at the palace grew so disorderly that riot police charged and a dozen people were trampled to death. Atatürk's reputation has not been allowed to die: his image is still very visible all over Istanbul.

TURKIFICATION AND TURMOIL

At the renewed outbreak of war in Europe, Turkey, under the leadership of Ismet Inönü, opted to remain neutral. Battle of sorts did go on in Istanbul, however, as the city became the espionage capital of World War II. Packed with refugees from all over Europe, Istanbul was also something of a safe haven for Jews escaping the Nazis.

However, Istanbul's indigenous religious minorities, who at the time still accounted for around one-third of the city's total population, were less fortunate. In 1942, on the pretext of combating war profiteering, the Turkish government introduced an 'asset tax', which was levied primarily on Jews, Armenians and Greeks. Fortunes accumulated over generations were wiped out overnight, as many were forced to sell off their assets to Muslims at a fraction of their worth. Thousands of those who were still unable to meet their payments were deported to labour camps in eastern Turkey.

Atatürk's New Turks

How one man forged a nation.

Every 10 November, at 9.05am, Istanbul comes to a halt for a minute's silence to mark the death of Mustafa Kemal Atatürk, 'father of the Turkish nation': the man who took a nascent Turkish resistance after World War I and galvanised it into an army able to defeat the might of the Allies and regain Turkish lands, taken from a defeated and ailing Ottoman Empire at the end of the war. And the man who unified disparate strands of that defeated empire to work towards his vision for an emerging – and radically new – Turkish nation.

The new Turkish nation was to be totally 'modern'. Some of Atatürk's innovations would be politically inconceivable today – imposing a dress code that made men exchange fezes for hats, for example, or packing provincials off to performances by the newly founded state opera, would be seen as a demeaning imitation of the West. But there was no such discourse around in 1927, when Atatürk explained: 'It was necessary to abolish the fez, which sat on the heads of our nation as an emblem of ignorance, negligence, fanaticism and hatred of progress and civilisation.' Atatürk's theory was simple: the West was advanced; Turkey would copy and reap the benefits. The European calendar was adopted, then the Swiss civil code and the Italian penal code, abolishing the role of religion in law. Women were granted equal rights. But perhaps the most dramatic piece of social engineering was the adoption of the Roman alphabet. Educated people became illiterate overnight and had to learn to read again, while a whole new generation grew up imbibing the new ideology to go with the new script.

Of course, appearing Western was not enough. State intervention in the economy and scientific progress would forge development; social and cultural changes completed the picture. The resulting modernity would become an integral part of a new national identity.

Secularism was another central tenet of the new state, symbolised by the abolition of the caliphate in 1924. Ottomans had not identified themselves as 'Turks'. Their language was Turkish, others called them Turks, but they saw their empire as Islamic, and the caliphate as a divine duty. There was support in some quarters for the idea of a sultan/caliph figure who would act as a sort of Muslim pope. Such an idea was anathema to Atatürk: the Kemalists insisted on the independence of the state from religion. However, this was not quite secularism as understood in the modern West. In Turkey, the state would exercise control over Islam and put it to its service. Here was another crucial marker of the Turkish identity, one that still has repercussions today.

IN CONTEXT

Turkey finally entered the war on the Allied side in February 1945, in order to secure a seat at the United Nations when it was founded later that year. Turkey also sided with the West during the Cold War. Under pressure from its new allies, Turkey introduced parliamentary democracy; in 1950, in the first fully free elections, the Democrat Party (DP) led by Adnan Menderes swept to power with a huge majority.

But the boom proved short-lived. Menderes became increasingly nationalistic and authoritarian. In September 1955, he attempted to exploit tensions over Cyprus by encouraging anti-Greek protests in Istanbul. The protests became a riot and then a pogrom, as mobs attacked the Greek population, killing and looting. The police, apparently under orders not to intervene, stood back and watched. The pogrom sounded the death knell for the Greek community. Today there are only 2,500 Greeks left in Turkey, fewer than the number of expatriate Britons.

In 1960, as Menderes moved to stifle all opposition to his rule, the military staged a coup and, in 1961, hanged Menderes and two of his senior ministers for treason. The 1960s continued to be characterised by political extremism. The streets of Istanbul were the battleground for a low-level civil war between left-wing extremists and far-right groups, who often worked in tandem with elements inside the security forces. In 1971 the military intervened again, toppling the government and appointing an administration of technocrats. Both right and left conducted armed robberies to finance campaigns of assassinations, demonstrations and bombings. On 1 May 1977, unidentified gunmen opened fire on a leftist May Day rally in Taksim Square, killing 39. The violence escalated. By 1980, the daily death toll in Istanbul rarely fell below 20. A succession of weak coalition governments in Ankara seemed unable or unwilling to tackle the problem, with the prime minister Suleyman Demirel dismissing the anarchy as mere hooliganism. On 12 September 1980, to the relief of much of the population, the military seized power again.

For the next three years, Istanbul was under martial law. The ruling military junta banned public meetings, outlawed all existing political parties, closed newspapers and magazines, burned books and arrested tens of thousands of real or suspected political activists, many of whom were subjected to torture. The repression took its toll on public sympathy for the military. When, in 1983, the junta restored civilian rule by allowing free elections, Turks rejected the military's preferred party and voted overwhelmingly for the broad-based Motherland Party and its founder Turgut Özal.

Aftermath of the **Anti-Greek riots**, 1955.

A NEW COSMOPOLITANISM

Faced with an economy that still closely resembled those found throughout Eastern Europe, Ozal implemented a series of market-oriented reforms that helped attract investment, but also brought widespread corruption and sleaze. As the Turkish saying goes, 'He who holds the honeypot is going to lick his fingers.'

Ozal's economic reforms quickened the pace of urbanisation as millions of Anatolian peasants moved to major cities – particularly Istanbul – in search of a better life. These newcomers swelled the population from three million in 1970 to approximately 12 million in 2010, changing the shape of the city. Istanbul has become a collection of villages with names such as 'little Gazientep' and 'little Sivas', named after the Anatolian towns from which most residents originate.

Cheap labour from the *gecekondu* helped fuel the economic boom of the 1980s, although the spread of unplanned suburbs put an unbearable strain on the city's infrastructure, clogging roads and polluting out-of-town reservoirs, leaving some areas without water for weeks at a time. The new arrivals also brought with them the piety of the Anatolian villages, where many paid only lip-service to Atatürk's secularising reforms. In the local elections of March 1994, 40-year-old Tayyip Erdoğan became the city's first Islamist mayor in republican history. Erdoğan used his record as mayor of Istanbul – where even his opponents grudgingly admit he improved services – as a platform to enter national politics. He became prime minister in March 2003 and was re-elected in 2007. He's set to face stiffer opposition in 2011, however, with a resurgent opposition.

THE COST OF EXPANSION

The city continues to grow, not just outwards but upwards, with high-rise office blocks and luxury hotels transforming the skyline. Many belong to large corporations that have grown rich on the back of Ozal's free-market reforms. Others have been constructed by Turkey's drug barons, who launder their profits from the lucrative heroin trade by pumping money into real estate. Over 80 per cent of the heroin entering Europe goes through Istanbul, much of it refined in temporary laboratories set up in the *gecekondu*, then smuggled across the border in trucks. Smugglers also deal in another commodity: people. Nobody knows how many illegal immigrants are smuggled through Istanbul each year on their way to Europe, but estimates range from 150,000 to half a million.

At the same time, the city has regained much of its assertiveness and pride, becoming a regular venue for international conferences, cultural and sports events, including the regular Turkish Grand Prix. Other recent improvements to city life include cleaner streets, pedestrianisation projects, more trees and parks, and a clean-up of the Golden Horn.

There have been setbacks. On 15 November 2003, two truck bombs hit different Istanbul synagogues. Five days later, the British consulate and HSBC bank were hit. More than 60 people were killed. The perpetrators claimed links with Al-Qaeda. Politically, Turkey's EU membership ambitions seem to be no nearer to realisation (*see pp34-37* **Istanbul Today**).

NEW FUTURES

In 2006, the Nobel Prize for Literature was awarded to Istanbul novelist Orhan Pamuk, who has written extensively about his native city. Reviled by nationalists, Pamuk's outspoken criticism of taboo issues, like the treatment of Armenians and Kurds, has got him into trouble with the Turkish state; he has been tried (and acquitted) for 'insulting Turkishness'. But whether or not the Nobel jury's decision was politically motivated, the prize was recognised by Pamuk's friends and foes alike as a coup for contemporary Turkish literature. Brought up in a modern middle-class Istanbul family, Pamuk has, perhaps unwittingly, become a spokesperson for Istanbul's Europe-looking population. He said recently, 'I see Turkey's future as being in Europe, as one of many prosperous, tolerant, democratic countries.'

IN CONTEXT

IN CONTEXT

Story of a Skyline

Istanbul's Byzantine and Ottoman architecture explained.

Haghia Sophia.

When, in AD 330, Constantine began to build his new capital on the Bosphorus, 'Nova Roma' was literally that, a new Rome constructed in the same style as the old one. But the change in location proved significant, as the proximity to Asia Minor and Syria resulted in an infusion of new ideas and methods. Very quickly the traditional Roman column-and-lintel way of building gave way to a more fluid architecture based on arches, vaults and domes. Supplanting stone, the more malleable brick became the building material of choice.

Development continued during the reign of the Emperor Justinian (AD 527-565), possibly the greatest builder in the city's history. He was patron to four great churches: SS Sergius and Bacchus, the smaller **Küçük Haghia Sophia Mosque** (*see p50*); the rebuilt **Haghia Irene** (*see p46*); the Church of the Holy Apostles, which was quarried for the Fatih Mosque; and the great cathedral of **Haghia Sophia** (*see p40*). What distinguished these structures from all that had come before was the dome which had never been built on this scale. With Haghia Sophia, Justinian's goal was to enclose the greatest space possible, creating a physical impression of the kingdom of God, one that was tended by the emperor. To achieve this he is said to have eschewed traditional builders and master craftsmen and instead employed two mathematicians. Such was the impression created that the huge dome was described by Byzantine historian Procopiusas 'appearing to be suspended from heaven by a golden chain'.

Post-Justinian, the Byzantine empire was to continue for another 800 years, during which time architectural styles evolved further. Later structures tended to be more modest in size and more harmoniously proportioned. Decoration came to play a larger part. For all its spatial grandeur, Haghia Sophia is dull, dull, dull on the outside, whereas surviving later churches such as **St Saviour in Chora** (*see p64*) and the 12th-century Church of the Pantocrator (now the **Zeyrek Mosque**; *see p62*) employ multiple domes, narthexes and apses executed in alternating bands of brick and roughly dressed stone. Glazed pottery set into the external walls forms friezes that echo interior mosaics and tiling, which flourished in the later Byzantine period following the miserable repressions of the Iconoclastic era.

The Ottomans, like the Byzantines, especially those of the early era, shared a predilection for centrally planned structures topped by big domes. In that respect, the Haghia Sophia was inspirational, a benchmark.

Once the Ottomans had captured the city in 1453, the task of constructing a dome larger than Justinian's was to occupy imperial architects for more than a century. It was eventually achieved by a master builder named Sinan during the reign of Sultan Süleyman the Magnificent; the dome in question graced Selimiye Mosque in Edirne.

Islam also defined how Ottoman architecture would develop. An egalitarian religion with no hierarchical orders, no saints in need of side chapels, no use for obfuscating trappings like naves and apses, its mosques required nothing more than a single, large, open space. A domed central chamber proved to be the best way of achieving this. It's almost incidental that the external effect is so beautiful – a cascade of gracefully descending curves. Slender, pencil-pointed minarets, originally intended as platforms for the five daily calls to prayer, frame the composition, while surrounding courts keep the secular city at bay.

It was Sinan, trained as a military engineer, who gave Istanbul some of its most memorable architectural triumphs. He constructed an incredible 477 buildings, more than 200 still stand, and more than which 100 were mosques. He exhibited his style exquisitely in **Süleymaniye Mosque** (*see p56*), which still dominates the city's skyline today. Even the much-admired **Sultanahmet Mosque** (*see p42*), built across from the Haghia Sophia in the 17th century, is no more than a reprise of what Sinan had achieved a century earlier.

As the Ottoman empire declined, so European influence made itself felt. This was most definitely not a good thing. From the mid 18th century, the Ottoman simplicity and clarity of function was wedded to the decorative excesses and indulgences of decadent and redundant imported baroque and rococo stylings. Their bastard offspring goes by the name of 'Turkish Baroque'. One of the earliest and most accessible examples is the **Nuruosmaniye Mosque** (*see p53*), completed in 1755. Its large dome rests on four huge semicircular arches filled with long vertical windows that brighten the interior, but the absence of semi-domes makes the profile appear stumpy

By the 19th century, European styles were almost completely dominant, with the 'Turkish' dropping out of 'Turkish Baroque' altogether. Rather than mosques or religious institutions, the defining structures of the time are palaces. **Dolmabahçe** (*see p78*), for example, is a good illustration of the changes taking place, with a showy mix of baroque and neoclassicism, and interiors by Sechan, who worked on Garnier's grand Paris Opera House. Other palaces in a similar ostentatious include **Çırağan** (now a hotel, *see p115*) and **Beylerbeyi** (*see p89*).

Meanwhile, foreign architects had been making their way to Istanbul. A German named Jachmund designed **Sirkeci Station** (*see p57*), terminus of the Orient Express. And an Italian, Raimondo D'Aronco, introduced Istanbul to art nouveau, especially in the suburbs such as Galata and Pera (now Beyoğlu) which were as wealthy, influential and style-conscious as any in Europe. Europe would continue as the prime inspiration for architecture until the founding of the Turkish Republic in 1923.

IN CONTEXT

Istanbul Today

Striving for modernity while looking after the past.

TEXT: DANIEL NEILSON

Magnum photographer Ara Güler, known as the 'Eye of Istanbul', has returned to Galata Bridge repeatedly. Born in 1928, five years after Mustafa Kemal Atatürk founded the Republic of Turkey, Güler has documented the sea change in Istanbul life over the past 60 years. When he started taking pictures in the 1950s, his black and white photos showed a Galata Bridge shrouded in smoke from the coal-fired ferries that plied the waters; the minarets of Haghia Sophia or the Yenı Mosque appear silhouetted against the failing sun. Today, the picture is a lot brighter.

Much has changed in Istanbul in the last few decades, but the Galata Bridge itself remains a centre of activity. It is also an important link – between the old religious city of Constantinople and the modern secular centre of Beyoğlu. This bridge could be said to link the past with the future.

Daniel Neilson is a journalist and the editor of the Time Out Istanbul Guide.

CROSSING THE BRIDGE

Dodging the fishermen casting their lines on the Galata Bridge are sellers of bagel-like *simit*, hawkers of cheap Chinese toys, veiled women pushing prams, backpackers and holidaymakers taking pictures. The city's shiny modern trams glide quietly past. On one side of the bridge, the western shore is dominated by Topkapı Palace, the administrative heart of the Ottoman Empire; it commands a strategic position where the Golden Horn, Bosphorus and Sea of Marmara meet. The skyline is dominated by domes and minarets, symbols of the religious identity of the empire. On the eastern shore, under the 14th-century Galata Tower, is Beyoğlu. To wander its narrow streets – or its main, spine-like thoroughfare, Istiklal Caddesi – on a summer evening is to experience secular Istanbul at its most optimistic and energetic.

BRIDGES WITH EUROPE

Return to Galata Bridge and consider Istanbul's geography. The narrow Bosphorus Strait links the Sea of Marmara and the Black Sea. This provides a vital link for goods to travel to and from the Ukraine, Georgia and Russia. Some 53,000 commercial vessels pass through the Bosphorus every year. Just as the Greeks realised when they founded the settlement of Chalcedon in 675 BC in what is present-day Kadıköy on the Asian shore, the powers of the 21st century recognise the nature of Istanbul's strategic position at the crossroads of Europe and Asia, East and West. The idea may be a cliché but in political terms it remains crucial – and controversial.

The question of European Union membership is emblematic of Turkey's battle for its own identity. Member countries have decided that there is no possibility of Turkey joining the EU until 2013 at the earliest, although, as European Commission President José Manuel Barroso commented in 2006, it's unlikely to happen until 2021. This came as a blow to the Turkish Government in Ankara. However, since Greek debt spiralled out of control at the beginning of 2010, Turkey, with a competitive lira, suddenly became more attractive both as an investment opportunity and as a tourist destination, with British Airways predicting that Istanbul would follow World Cup hosts Cape Town as one of the most popular destinations for visitors in 2010. The city hopes to attract even more than the 26 million visitors (2.43 million from the UK) who came in 2009.

Why has Turkey failed to gain EU membership for so long? Firstly, the Cyprus problem has hindered its chances – the EU has decreed there must be a resolution before membership can be considered. But beyond that, commentators believe that the fact that Turkey is largely a nation of Muslims is part of the problem – elements within the EU believe that Turkish membership would change the organisation in a way they wouldn't like. More specifically, some fear that the government of Prime Minister Recep Tayyip Erdoğan, and his moderately Islamist Justice and Development Party, could align the country too closely with the East, and the danger of Islamist radicalism. They note the proximity of Turkey to the likes of Syria, Iran and Iraq.

Others, including the Obama administration, argue that EU membership would counter whatever risk there is of Turkish political alignment with what the US considers rogue states. In a 2009 visit to Istanbul and Ankara, Obama argued for bringing Turkey into the EU. 'Turkey is bound to Europe by more than the bridges over the Bosphorus,' he said. 'Centuries of shared history, culture and commerce bring you together. Europe gains by the diversity of ethnicity, tradition and faith – it is not diminished by it. And Turkish membership would broaden and strengthen Europe's foundation once more.'

CULTURAL INROADS

While the politicking continues in Ankara, it's Istanbul, as ever, that remains the country's focus. Istanbul plays an enormous role in the Turkish economy, responsible for much of the country's wealth and many of its jobs. It has acted as a magnet for migrants for some 2,700 years now, and there's no sign that this will change. It is also a cultural centre. Becoming one of the European Capitals of Culture in 2010 was considered a boost for EU membership efforts, and a chance for Istanbul to show the rest of Europe just how 'European' it actually is. Modern art, cutting-edge theatre, classical concerts and rock festivals dominated the programme.

BEYOND BEYOGLU

But there's a lot more to Istanbul than a thriving, western-style cultural scene. Stray beyond the triangle of land bordered by the Bosphorus at the bottom and up to the Galata Tower, via Taksim, Cihangir, Teşvikiye, Esentepe and Etiler, and you will find that the rest of this sprawling city can be of quite a different character. You don't need to go too far to find yourself on the 'wrong' side of the tracks – one street should normally do it. Istanbul is a city of highly visible wealth gaps, with the super-clubs along the Bosphorus charging the equivalent of an average worker's weekly wage for a margarita. But despite these economic divides, Istanbul is largely untroubled by the kind of crime that other big cities so often suffer. While street crime has been on the rise in recent years, the city remains generally safe to walk around, even after dark.

There are other divisions too. The large minorities of earlier eras – Jews, Armenians and Greeks – may have gone, but Istanbul today remains a city of different ethnicities and religious groups. There are the Alevis, a religious community that is said to make up around 20 per cent of the city's population, but gets scant official recognition. The Alevis have beliefs that combine elements of Shia Islam with the animist religions of ancient Anatolia. Other minorities include Laz from the Black Sea coast; remnants of the Greek, Armenian and Jewish groups; Kurds (the largest minority), and a few Syriac Christians, a community centred on Mardin and Antioch.

However, the overriding factor in modern Istanbul's demographics is Anatolian immigration: over the past 50 years, mass migration has made parts of the city more like a collection of villages, as pockets of people from the same region set up home in the same area.

DIGGING DEEP

Travel on public transport between Taksim and Atatürk Airport, and you'll use three types of vehicle: a 19th century tram, a 100-year-old funicular and a modern tram. If you're travelling from Beşiktaş, for example, add a bus into the equation. Istanbul's transport network does hang together – if you are patient – but it can be slow and many rely on cars. Here, geography becomes a curse, as some 345,000 cars make their way across the Bosphorus on two bridges every day. At rush hour, a trip from Levent to the Asian shore can take two hours, as opposed to half an hour at other times.

After decades of neglect, however, money is now being invested in upgrading the city's creaking transport infrastructure, and the metro system is now clean, efficient and modern. The city's biggest current undertaking is the Marmaray rail tunnel, which is being dug between Sirkeci Station in Eminönü and Üsküdar on the Asian shore. When completed, it will be the world's deepest rail tunnel, set to alleviate the immense strains on the Bosphorus bridges as part of a new and efficient network. The current completion date is 2013, but the project has been plagued with delays, not least because work has to stop every time workers come across something of archaeological interest, with objects dating back to 6,000 BC having been found. Among the discoveries are items relating to the fourth-century port of Theodosius, and the oldest medieval galley ever found. In fact, so much has been unearthed that the Archaeology Museum (*see p48*) is holding an exhibition especially for artefacts from the dig.

The story of the Marmaray Tunnel can serve as useful shorthand for Istanbul today: the city is meeting the challenges of modernity – with some organisational delay thrown in – while following in the wake of vast historical wealth and heritage. That incredible heritage, and the modern city of today, can perhaps best be understood on a clear day on the Galata Bridge, with Istanbul's bewitching beauty on either side, and the glimmering, busy Bosphorus beneath.

Profile Autoban

The team behind some of Istanbul's most striking interiors.

It helps that the setting is breathtaking: high on a wooded hill overlooking the Bosphorus. It helps, too, that it is on the premises of the Sakıp Sabancı – a quirky museum of calligraphy and paintings. But what really sets **Müzedechanga** (*see p137*) restaurant apart is its design. Split between a large terrace and and multi-levelled interior, the space seamlessly melds. It exudes relaxation and solidity. The mid-century style, combining hardwood, greys and stark white accessories, has made this interior an instant classic. *Wallpaper** thought so, giving Müzedechanga its Best New Restaurant award in 2007.

When restaurateurs Tarik Bayazit and Savas Ertunc were looking to create a new restaurant, they wanted a space that reflected the designed-minded museum it would be part of. There was only one contender to be its designer: Istanbul's Autoban.

Formed by architect Seyhan Özdemir and interior designer Sefer Çağlar in 2003, Autoban has stamped its distinctive mark across the city. The **House Café** (*see p137*) was its first success. All 11 branches were designed by Autoban; each is a beautiful space that plays on the characteristics of its host building and the vibe of the neighbourhood.

'The House Café let us do what we wanted. It's the project we are most proud of,' Seyhan explained.'

Autoban has also been involved in furniture design. 'We decided that we wanted to stamp our own identity on the projects, so we started making our own product,' said Seyhan. For its latest range, Autoban partnered with De La Espada (www.delaespada.com). Its furniture can be seen at the **Witt Istanbul** (*see p105*).

Wandering the streets of Çukurcuma, it is easy to see the source of much of Autoban's inspiration: lots of the shops sell furniture dating from the 1950s to the '70s. Mid-century is now the most widespread style in the bars of Beyoğlu, but House Café began the trend.

'We are, of course, influenced by the Ottoman period, but not directly,' said Seyhan. 'Istanbul is our influence. Some parts are European, some parts are Asian or Arabic and its good to be living in the middle of it.'

Autobam now has more then 20 Istanbul restaurants and bars, and two hotels (the other is the **House Hotel**, *see p107*), in its portfolio. 'We want to be the new face of Istanbul. It's a big challenge but it's a mission,' Seyhan said.

IN CONTEXT

NEED TO KNOW
Autoban's gallery is at Mesrutiyet Caddesi 64/A (0212 243 8641, www. autoban 212.com).

bookinturkey.com

"Turkey Specialist Travel Portal"

- *"B2B & B2C & Domestic & Incoming" Services*
- *All Manner of Services About Travel & Tourism*
- *Affiliate Solutions to Our Partners*
- *Safety Booking with World - Class Technology*
- *High Quality Service with the Reasonable Prices*

Sights

Sultanahmet Mosque. *See p42*

Sultanahmet

Domes and minarets in Istanbul's historic heart.

Sultanahmet is the 'proper' Istanbul: the one with the slim minarets pointing skywards and the domes – the 'Orient' of the Turkish Delight ad. It's a scenic thumbnail of land surrounded by sea on three sides, home to world-famous sites, among them the former church (then a mosque and now a museum) of **Haghia Sophia** and the **Topkapı Palace** complex, epicentre of the Ottoman Empire. These, along with other mosques, museums and assorted historical oddments, are testament to a heritage that encompasses the birth,

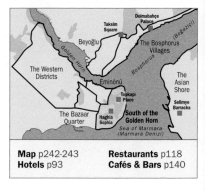

Map p242-243	**Restaurants** p118
Hotels p93	**Cafés & Bars** p140

youthful exuberance, mature middle age and drooling dotage of not one, but two, great empires: Byzantine and Ottoman. And despite the number of tourists who come to explore the area today, its 1,500-year history of power remains as palpable as ever.

SULTANAHMET SQUARE

Focal point for disgorging tour buses and feeding ground for taxis, Sultanahmet Square (Ayasofya Meydanı) is the obvious place to begin. Most of the city's major monuments are just a few minutes' walk from here, including the underground cistern **Yerebatan Sarnıcı**, **Sultanahmet Mosque** (Blue Mosque) and the **Museum of Turkish & Islamic Art**. **Topkapı Palace** is also a short distance from the square.

Most notably, Sultanahmet Square acts as a forecourt to what for close to a thousand years was the greatest church in Eastern Christendom, the **Haghia Sophia** (Ayasofya in Turkish). After the Turkish conquest it served for five centuries as the chief mosque of the Ottoman empire, and is now open to all as a museum.

It's worth remembering that major sights can get very busy, so an early start is a good idea.

★ Haghia Sophia
Ayasofya Camii Müzesi

Sultanahmet Square (0212 522 1750). Tram Sultanahmet. **Open** 9am-5pm Tue-Sun, plus 1st Mon of every month. Galleries close 1hr earlier. **Admission** YTL20. **Credit** AmEx, DC, MC, V. **Map** p243 N10.

The third sacred building on the site to bear the name, the existing Haghia Sophia ('Divine Wisdom') was dedicated on 26 December AD 537 by Emperor Justinian. He had come to power less than a century after the fall of Rome, and was eager to prove his capital a worthy successor to imperial glory. Approached by a grand colonnaded avenue beginning at the city gates, Justinian's cathedral towered over all else and was topped by the largest dome ever constructed – a record it held until the Romans reclaimed their pride just over a thousand years later with Michelangelo's dome for St Peter's (1590). In the meantime, Justinian's dome took on almost fabled status. It was of such thin material, wrote the chroniclers of old, that the hundreds of candles hung high within would cause it to glow at night like a great golden beacon, which was visible to ships far out on the Sea of Marmara.

Adding to the wonder, the church served as a vast reliquary, housing a pilgrim's delight of biblical treasures, including fragments of the True Cross, the Virgin's veils, the lance that pierced Jesus's side, St Thomas's doubting finger, and a large assortment of other saintly limbs, skulls and clippings.

All this was lost in 1204, when adventurers and freebooters on Western Christendom's Fourth Crusade, raised to liberate Jerusalem and the Holy Lands, decided they would be equally content with a treasure-grabbing raid on the luxurious capital of their Eastern brethren. At Haghia Sophia they ripped the place apart, carrying off everything they could, and added insult to thievery by infamously placing a prostitute on the imperial throne.

Further destruction was narrowly avoided in 1453, when the Ottoman Turk armies, led by Mehmet II, breached the walls of the city of Constantinople and put its Byzantine defenders to flight. Those who took refuge in the church were slaughtered, but the conquering sultan allegedly rounded on a looting soldier whom he found hacking at the marble floors, telling him: 'The gold is thine, the building mine.'

Haghia Sophia may have been spared, but it was a loss to Christianity. The Friday after the conquest, the church resounded to the chant, 'There is no god but Allah, and Mohammed is his Prophet'. The church had been converted into a mosque. During its time as a mosque the basilica acquired the addition of four minarets, from which to deliver the Muslim call to prayer. The construction of these minarets was staggered; only two are matching. In 1317, a series of unsightly buttresses was deemed necessary when the church seemed to be in danger of collapse. These aside, what you see today is essentially the church exactly as it was in Justinian's time.

At the death of the Ottoman Empire, with plans afoot to partition Istanbul along national lines, both the Greeks (on behalf of the Eastern Church) and the Italians (on behalf of the Western Church) lobbied for Haghia Sophia to be handed over to them. In Britain, a Saint Sophia Redemption Committee was formed. The Ottoman government posted soldiers with machine guns in the mosque to thwart any attempt at a Christian coup. An expedient solution was effected by the leaders of the new Turkish republic in 1934, who deconsecrated the building and declared it a museum. This action remains controversial, with Islamists periodically calling for it to be restored as a mosque. Comparing the pristine state of the neighbouring mosques with the shabby state of Haghia Sophia, you can't help wondering if they have a point.

At least the cathedral's interior remains impressive, particularly the main chamber with its fabulous dome, 30m (98ft) in diameter. The other

Haghia Sophia.

extraordinary interior features are the mosaics. Plastered over by the conquering Ottomans, they were only rediscovered during renovations in the mid 19th century. Some of the best decorate the outer and inner narthexes, which are the long, vaulted chambers inside the present main entrance. The non-figurative geometrical and floral designs are the earliest and date from the reign of Justinian. Further mosaics adorn the galleries, reached by a stone ramp at the northern end of the inner narthex.

At the eastern end of the south gallery, just to the right of the apse, is a glimmering representation of Christ flanked by the famous 11th-century empress, Zoe, and her third husband, Constantine IX. One of the few women to rule Byzantium, Zoe married late and was a virgin until the age of 50. She must have developed a taste for what she discovered, proceeding to go through a succession of husbands and lovers in the years left to her. On the mosaic in question, the heads and inscriptions show signs of being altered, possibly in an attempt to keep up with her active love life. En route to see Zoe is a slab marking the burial place of Enrico Dandalo, doge of Venice, a leader of the Fourth Crusade, and the man held responsible for persuading the Latins to attack Constantinople. Following the Ottoman conquest of the city, it is said that his tomb was smashed open and his bones thrown to the dogs.

▶ *For a drink after touring Haghia Sophia, Yeşil Ev's beer garden is a pleasant stop; see p141.*

see p141.

INSIDE TRACK
MASKING MOSAICS

The Ottomans plastered over Roman mosaics and some are still being discovered. However, in an attempt to retain a balance between the city's Roman Christian and Ottoman Muslim heritage, many will remain covered. Some of the best mosaics are in the Upper Gallery in **Haghia Sophia** (*see left*).

Sultanahmet Mosque.

FREE Sultanahmet (Blue) Mosque
Sultanahmet Camii
Meydanı Sokak 17 (0212 518 1319). Tram Sultanahmet. **Open** 9am-1hr before dusk (prayer time) daily. **Admission** free. **Map** p243 N11.

Seductively curvaceous and enhanced by a lovingly attended park in front, Sultanahmet Mosque is Islamic architecture at its sexiest. Commissioned by Sultan Ahmet I (1603-17) and built for him by Mehmet Ağa, a student of the great Sinan, this was the last of Istanbul's magnificent imperial mosques, the final flourish before the rot set in. It provoked hostility at the time because of its six minarets – such a display was previously reserved only for the Prophet's mosque at Mecca – but they do make for a beautifully elegant silhouette, particularly gorgeous when floodlit at night.

By contrast, the interior is clumsy, marred by four immense pillars, disproportionately large for the fairly modest dome they support (especially when compared to the vast yet seemingly unsupported dome that caps Haghia Sophia). Most surfaces are covered by a mismatch of Iznik tiles: their colour gives the place its popular name, the Blue Mosque.

In the north-east corner of the surrounding park is the *türbe* or Tomb of Sultan Ahmet I. It also contains the cenotaphs of his wife and three of his sons, two of whom, Osman II and Murat IV, ruled in their turn, Ahmet being the sultan who abandoned the nasty Ottoman practice of strangling other potential heirs on the succession of the favoured son.

The Cisterns

Between the gardens of Sultanahmet Mosque on one side of Sultanahmet Square and Haghi Sophia on the other, **Yerebatan Sarnıcı** (Basilica Cistern), is the grandest of several underground reservoirs that riddle the foundations of this part of the city.

A second cistern, the **Binbirdirek Sarnıcı** (the 'Cistern of 1001 Columns', although there are only 224) is also open to the public.

Yerebatan Sarnıcı
Yerebatan Caddesi 13 (0212 522 1259, www.yerebatan.com). Tram Sultanahmet. **Open** 9am-8pm daily. **Admission** YTL10. **Credit** MC, V. **Map** p243 N10.

Built by the Emperor Justinian at the same time as the Haghia Sophia, it was forgotten for centuries and only rediscovered by a Frenchman, Peter Gyllius, in 1545 when he noticed that people in the neighbourhood got water by lowering buckets through holes in their basements. It's a tremendous engineering feat, with brick vaults supported on 336 columns spaced at four-metre (13-foot) intervals. Prior to restoration in 1987, the cistern could only be explored by boat (James Bond rowed through in *From Russia With Love*). These days there are concrete walkways. The subdued lighting and

SIGHTS

Topkapı Palace

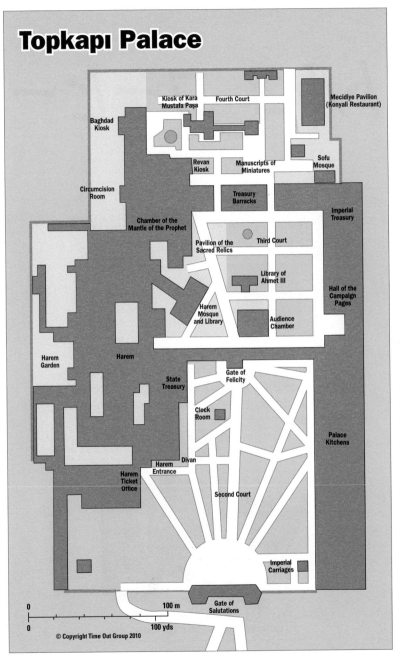

Kiosk of Kara Mustafa Paşa

Fourth Court

Mecidiye Pavilion (Konyalı Restaurant)

Baghdad Kiosk

Revan Kiosk

Manuscripts of Miniatures

Sofu Mosque

Circumcision Room

Treasury Barracks

Imperial Treasury

Chamber of the Mantle of the Prophet

Pavilion of the Sacred Relics

Third Court

Library of Ahmet III

Hall of the Campaign Pages

Harem Mosque and Library

Audience Chamber

Harem Garden

Harem

State Treasury

Gate of Felicity

Clock Room

Palace Kitchens

Divan

Harem Entrance

Harem Ticket Office

Second Court

Imperial Carriages

0   100 m
0   100 yds

Gate of Salutations

© Copyright Time Out Group 2010

SIGHTS

トルコ　コーヒー*

* Turkish Coffee
(in Japan too...)

KURUKAHVECİ MEHMET EFENDİ IS INTRODUCING THE WORLD
TO THE INCOMPARABLE FLAVOR OF TURKISH COFFEE.
TURKISH COFFEE LOVERS ARE ABLE TO ENJOY
THIS EXCEPTIONAL PLEASURE AROUND THE WORLD.

THE WORLD'S NAME FOR TURKISH COFFEE.

www.mehmetefendi.com

INSIDE TRACK LOSING HEADS

Beside the ticket counters at Topkapı
Palace is the Executioner's Fountain. This
is where the chief axeman would wash his
blade after carrying out his grisly work. The
heads of his victims were displayed on top
of the truncated columns on either side of
the fountain.

subterranean cool are especially welcome on hot
days. Look for the two Medusa heads at the far end
from the entrance, both recycled from an even more
ancient building and casually employed as column
bases. There's a café down here and a platform on
which occasional concerts of classical Turkish and
Western music are performed; check with the ticket
office for further details.

Binbirdirek Sarnıcı

*Imran Ökten Sokak 4 (0212 518 1001,
www.binbirdirek.com). Tram Sultanahmet.* **Open**
9am-9pm daily. **Admission** YTL10. **Credit**
AmEx, DC, MC, V. **Map** p243 M10.
Like the more famous Yerebatan cistern, this one is
a Byzantine forest of pillars and brick-vaulted ceilings, but sadly the restorers have put in a false floor
that halves the original height of the chamber (a well
at the centre illustrates the original floor level). No
one has yet figured out what to do with the place and
it currently unsuccessfully accommodates a couple
of cafés, a bar and a restaurant. The admission fee
gets you a free drink.

TOPKAPI PALACE

Directly behind Haghia Sophia are the walls
shielding the Topkapı Palace complex. Part
command centre for a massive military empire,
part archetypal Eastern pleasure dome, the
palace was the hub of Ottoman power for over
three centuries, until it was superceded by
Dolmabahçe Palace in 1853. For lavish decor
and exquisite location, it rivals Granada's
Alhambra. At least half a day is needed to
explore Topkapı; given the high entrance fee
you might want to take a full day to get your
money's worth. If you're pushed for time, the
must-see features are the Harem (although
there's an extra charge), Imperial Treasury
and the views from the innermost courtyard.
Be warned that any part of the Palace may
be closed at any time.

The entrance to the palace is via the
Imperial Gate (Bab-ı Hümayün), erected by
the Sultan Fatih in 1478 and decorated with
niches that during Ottoman times were used
to display the severed heads of rebels and
criminals. The gate leads into the first of a
series of four courts that become more private
the deeper into the complex you penetrate. The
First Court was public and not considered
part of the palace proper. It housed a hospital
and dormitories for the palace guards, hence
the popular name, Court of the Janissaries.
Off to the left is the church of **Haghia Irene**
(Aya Irini Kilisesi), built by Emperor Justinian
and so a contemporary of Haghia Sophia.
It has the distinction of being the only

Topkapı Palace.

SIGHTS

Istanbul on Foot Sultanahmet

Explore Istanbul's historic centre of faith and empire.

Begin at Karaköy Square for a stroll across the Golden Horn into Sultanahmet. It takes imagination to see Galata Bridge as it was in its golden era, a time when Edmondo de Amicis, an Italian writer who visited the city in the 1870s, gave a literary snapshot of the bridge's human comings and goings in his *Constantinople*. At that time the bridge was the centre point of the multicultural Ottoman Empire, and flowing across it were Albanians in petticoats with pistols at the ready, Maltese ladies in black *faldettas* (hooded cloaks), Tartars wearing sheepskin, European ambassadors, necromancers, eunuchs busting skulls making way for the lunchtime social runs of the aristocratic Turkish *hanims* in their charge, and porters limping along under hundreds of pounds of firewood. These days you're much more likely to see amateur fishermen lining the rails, selling their catch to sandwich vendors; there is also a lively line of touristy restaurants and bars on a lower level between the road and the water. It's still a classic Istanbul walk, though, and an exhilarating one.

Straight ahead on the Sultanahmet side of the bridge lies the **Yeni Camii**, or New Mosque, so called because, as a 17th-century construction, it was a relatively late addition to the skyline.

From here, hit the Misr Carsi, the **Egyptian Bazaar**. As well as shops selling Turkish delight, 'Turkish Viagra' (a date stuffed with walnuts), and backgammon boards, the market is home to some quality delis, as well as spice and coffee merchants.

Loop back on to Residaye Caddesi and, with the Golden Horn on your left, head up Muradiye Hudavendigar, which becomes

Alemdar Caddesi. You will pass the flouncy hat entrance of the **Sublime Porte**, once the home of the Ottoman Grand Vizier, but now relegated to the headquarters of the Istanbul governor. Today, the Porte's raw look says little about what used to happen at this juncture of road. Here the Grand Vizier held the dangerous job of wielding true power, while the sultans retreated to the harem, went to seed on wine nominally denied to the Muslim masses, or – in the case of 'Mad Ibrahim' (1640-48) – took to **Alay Koksu**, the polygonal kiosk across from the Porte, where the demented sultan would take potshots at pedestrians with a crossbow. Beyond lies the gate to **Gulhane Park**, where picnickers and sweethearts while away the afternoon. Further up the hill, Istanbul's showcase pieces come tantalisingly into view.

At the top of Alemdar Caddesi, the road leads into Sultanahmet Square. Here, you are at the epicentre of historic Sultanahmet. To the left lies **Haghia Sophia**; **Sultanahmet Mosque** is ahead, visible on the other side of the square past a lovingly attended park with fountains and flowers, a popular place for weekend picnickers. **Topkapı Palace** is around the bend off Soğukçeşme Sokak. There are more sights in this area than can be seen on one visit (it's easy to spend a day at Topkapı Palace). Before deciding what to visit, it might be time for a rest in the mosque's gardens. Alternatively, on the other side of Sultanahmet Square, is a place of greenery and park benches, with a road encircling the park that follows the old chariot tracks. A good place in which to find a shady spot, enjoy an ice-cream, and conclude our walk.

pre-Ottoman-conquest church in the city that was never turned into a mosque. Closed most of the time, the church serves as a concert venue during the **International Istanbul Music Festival** (*see p173*).

Still in the First Court, down the hill to the left, is the superb **Archaeology Museum** (*see p48*), but the palace proper is entered through the Disneyesque gate ahead. Tickets can be bought just before you reach the gate.

A semi-public space, the enormous **Second Court** is where the business of running the empire was carried out. This is where the viziers of the imperial council sat in session in the divan,

overlooking gardens landscaped with cypresses, plane trees and rose bushes. Where once there would have been crowds of petitioners awaiting their turn for an audience, nowadays there are queues lined up waiting to get in to the **Harem**, an introverted complex of around 300 brilliantly tiled chambers on several levels, connected by arcaded courts and fountain gardens. Unfortunately, access is limited: you must wait to join a group that leaves every half-hour and is led through no more than a dozen chambers by an official guide. It's not the ideal way to see the place – locked in a crowd and herded around – but it's the only way. Tickets are sold separately

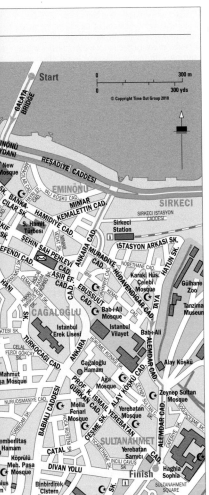

silverware, much of it imported from China and Japan via Central Asia, along the legendary Silk Route. The earliest pieces are Chinese celadon, particularly valued by the sultans because it was supposed to change colour when brought into contact with poison.

All paths in the Second Court converge on the **Gate of Felicity** (Bab-üs Saadet), the backdrop for an annual performance of Mozart's *Abduction from the Seraglio*. The gate also gives access to the **Third Court**.

The Third Court was the sultan's own private domain. Confronting all who enter is the **Audience Chamber** (Arz Odası), which is where foreign ambassadors would present their credentials, until the room's role was supplanted by the Sublime Porte. Although the sultan would be present on such occasions, he would never deign to speak with a non-Turk and all conversation was conducted via the grand vizier.

To the right is the **Hall of the Campaign Pages** (Seferli Koşusu), whose task it was to look after the royal wardrobe. They did an excellent job: there's a perfectly preserved 550-year-old, red-and-gold silk kaftan worn by Mehmet II, conqueror of Constantinople.

Things get even more glittery next door in the **Imperial Treasury** (Hazine). Many of the items here were made specifically for the palace by a team of court artisans, which at its height numbered over 600. A lot of what's displayed here has never left the confines of the inner courts. Not that too many people outside the sultan's circle would have had much use for a diamond-encrusted set of chain mail or a Quran bound in jade. Items like the Topkapı Dagger, its handle set with three eyeball-sized emeralds (one of which conceals a watch face), are breathtaking in their excessiveness.

More remarkable still are the items in the Privy Chamber. It houses the **Chamber of Sacred Relics**. To the sound of the Quran being read live, vistors trail around a series of items including Moses' staff, Muhammad's sword, tooth, beard and cloak.

The final and **Fourth Court** is a garden with terraces stepping down towards Seraglio Point, the protruberance of land that watches over the entrance to the Golden Horn. Buildings are limited to a bunch of reasonably restrained pavilions, while the views over the Bosphorus are wonderful, as are the sea breezes on a sun-beaten summer's day. Most notable is the Baghdad Kiosk, built to celebrate Murad IV's Baghadad Campaign in 1638, its glimmering mother-of-pearl furniture is remarkable. The very last building to be constructed within the palace, the **Mecidiye Pavilion** (Mecidiye Köşkü), built in 1840, now houses a restaurant and café, notable for its covetable terrace seating.

(YTL15), from a window located beside the Harem entrance. (*See also p49* **Hard Times in the Harem**).

Around from the Harem ticket window, a low brick building topped by shallow domes is the former **State Treasury**, present home of an exhibition of arms and armour, which is interesting for the contrast between cumbersome, bludgeonly European swords and the lighter Ottoman model. Across the gardens, a long row of ventilation chimneys punctuates the roof line of the enormous kitchens, which catered for up to 5,000 inhabitants of the palace. They contain a collection of ceramics, glass and

SIGHTS

Archaelogy Museum.

SIGHTS

There are changing exhibitions in various buildings around the year, often celebrating Turkey's diplomatic relationships.

★ Topkapı Palace
Topkapı Sarayı
Bab-ı Hümayün Caddesi, Gülhane (0212 512 0480, www.topkapisarayi.gov.tr). Tram Gülhane or Sultanahmet. **Open** *May-Sept* 9am-7pm Mon, Wed-Sun. *Oct-Apr* 9am-4pm Mon, Wed-Sun. **Admission** YTL20. *Harem* YTL15. **Credit** AmEx, DC, MC, V. **Map** p243 O9.

Archaeology Museum/Museum of the Ancient Orient
Osman Hamdi Bey Yokuşu, Topkapı Sarayı, Gülhane (0212 520 7740). Tram Gülhane. **Open** 9am-5pm Tue-Sun. **Admission** YTL10 (incl Museum of the Ancient Orient & Tiled Pavilion). **Credit** MC, V. **Map** p243 O9.

The collection of classical antiquities displayed here is world class, although many of the galleries are looking a little tired. Within the grounds of Topkapı Palace, the museum was founded in the mid 19th century in an attempt to staunch the flow of antiquities being spirited out of the country by foreigners to fill the museums of Europe. The exhibits were originally housed in the Tiled Pavilion (*see below*) until the commissioning of a new building, since extended on three occasions to keep up with the growing contents. Even so, the bulk of the collection remains in storage due to lack of space and funds.

Greeting visitors is a grinning statue of Bes, a demonic Cypriot demigod of inexhaustible power and strength, qualities required of anyone hoping to get through even a fraction of the 20 galleries within. Starting with the pre-Classical world, they cover 5,000 years of history, with artefacts gathered from all over Turkey and the Near East and grouped thematically. Highlights include a collection of sixth- to fourth-century BC sarcophagi from a royal necropolis at Sidon, in modern Lebanon, of which the finest is known as the Alexander Sarcophagus because of the scenes of the Macedonian general's victory at Issus (333 BC) adorning its side panels.

Up on the first floor, Istanbul Through the Ages is a summary of the city's history presented through a few key pieces, including a serpent's head lopped off the column in the Hippodrome (*see below*) and a section of the iron chain that stretched across the Bosphorus to bar the way of invaders. One great innovation is a small children's area, complete with low cabinets. The museum also occasionally holds special exhibitions – check *Time Out Istanbul* magazine for details.

Across from the museum stands the **Tiled Pavilion** (Çinili Köşk), which dates back to 1472 and the reign of Sultan Mehmet II, Ottoman conqueror of Constantinople. Built in a Persian style, it was an imperial viewing stand that overlooked a large gaming field, now occupied by the main museum building. The pavilion displays some outstanding samples of Turkish tiles and ceramics from the Seljuk and Ottoman periods, dating from between the end of the 12th century and the beginning of the 20th century.

To the south, beside the main entrance, is the **Museum of the Ancient Orient**, containing antiquities from the Mesopotamian, Egyptian and Hittite cultures, including some wonderful monumental glazed-brick friezes from the main Ishtar Gate of sixth-century Babylon. There is also the world's first peace treaty (1283 BC), a clay tablet signed by the Hittite king Hattushilish III and Egyptian pharaoh Rameses II that ended a lengthy conflict between the two ancient rival empires.

THE HIPPODROME & SOUTH

On the north-west side of the Sultanahmet Mosque, a strip of over-touristy tea-houses and souvenir shops fringes the **Hippodrome** (At Meydanı), formerly the focal point of Byzantine Constantinople.

At one time, this ancient arena was used for races, court ceremonies, coronations and parades. Originally laid out by the Roman emperor Septimius Severus during his rebuilding of the city, the arena was enlarged by Constantine to its present dimensions. The modern road exactly follows the tracks of the old racing lanes. Now little more than an elongated park circled by tour buses, the

Hard Times in the Harem

The dark world behind those orientalist fantasies.

From its inception in around 1540 until its dissolution in the early 20th century, the Topkapı harem was home, prison and entire world to almost four centuries of palace women. The word means 'forbidden', a ruling that applied to all men except the sultan, the princes and the eunuch guards. Women had no problem getting in, but once admitted they were in for life. Most entered as slave girls presented to the sultan as gifts: it was forbidden to make slaves of Muslims, so they were all Christians or Jews. Circassian girls who came from what is now Georgia and Armenia were favoured because of their fair skin, although even the fairest was still only valued at a fifth of the price of a good horse. The girls were converted to Islam and 'palace-trained', which means they were taught to sing, dance, play instruments and to give pleasure of a more tactile kind.

But notions of the harem as a sensual hothouse are misplaced. It was a highly competitive and cut-throat environment in which each girl sought to catch the eye of the sultan or a prince and so secure a better station. At any one time, a dozen or so girls would be chosen as imperial handmaids and bedmates. Giving birth to the sultan's child ensured exalted status. If it was a boy, there was even the chance he might one day become sultan and his mother *valide sultana*, 'mother of the sultan' – the most powerful woman in the land. At such high

stakes, with the sex came violence as the women manoeuvred, plotted, poisoned and knifed their way up the harem hierarchy. A mother with the sultan's child was particularly vulnerable – Murat III (1574-95), for example, fathered 103 children, only one of whom was ever going to make the throne.

All the while, harem girls also had to court the favour of the present *valide sultana*, responsible for selecting girls for the sultan, while avoiding the displeasure of the *kızlar ağası*, the chief black eunuch. These latter characters were the go-betweens for the sultan and his mother and so privy to all palace secrets. At the same time, physically and psychologically mutilated as they were, the chief black eunuchs tended to be a dangerous combination of corrupt, scheming and vindictive. Some got their kicks by stuffing girls in sacks and dumping them into the Bosphorus, usually on the instructions of the *valide sultana* (although Sultans Ibrahim and Murat II are both alleged to have ordered their entire harems drowned, one out of boredom, the other through paranoia).

Alev Lytle Croutier sums it up in her fine book *Harem: The World Behind the Veil*, describing it as a world of 'frightened women plotting with men who were not men against absolute rulers who kept their relatives immured for decades'. Far from being a palace of sensual delights, the Topkapı harem must have been more of a nerve-shredding chamber of horrors.

SIGHTS

Hippodrome does retain an odd assortment of monuments, which stand on what was the spina, the raised area around which chariots would have thundered.

Closest to the mosque is an **Egyptian obelisk**, removed from the Temple of Karnak at Thebes (now Luxor). The obelisk was originally carved in around 1500 BC to commemorate the great victories of Pharaoh Thutmosis III. In a self-congratulatory mood, the Byzantine emperor Theodosius had the obelisk moved to Constantinople in AD 390, where it was set upon a marble pedestal and sculpted with scenes of himself and his family enjoying a day at the races.

Next to the obelisk is the bronze **Serpentine Column** (also known as the Spiral Column), carried off from the Temple of Apollo at Delphi, where it had been set to commemorate Greek victory over the Persians in 480 BC. When it

was brought to the Byzantine capital by Constantine, its three entwined serpents had heads but each was decapitated over the years. One detached head survives and is displayed in the Archaeology Museum. A third monument, known as the **Column of Constantine**, is a pockmarked and crumbling affair, once sheathed in gold-plated bronze, but stripped by the looting Fourth Crusaders.

Overlooking the Hippodrome is the grand **Museum of Turkish and Islamic Art**, while down the hill from its south-west corner is the **Sokollu Mehmet Paşa Mosque**, another tour de force by Sinan.

The streets around here twist and turn between creaky wooden buildings – a delight to explore. Head south, downhill toward the sea, for the **Küçük Haghia Sophia Mosque**.

Following Küçük Ayasofya Caddesi back uphill leads past the very worthwhile **Mosaic**

SIGHTS

INSIDE TRACK
MOSQUE ETIQUETTE

At least half of Istanbul's major sights are mosques. Non-Muslims are welcome to visit any of them, but it's best to steer clear of prayer times; noon, especially Friday noon, is the main one (exact times vary throughout the year). Dress modestly: no shorts, short skirts or bare shoulders. Shoes must be removed, although in some places cloth covers are provided to slip over footwear. Headscarves are available for women to borrow, though you might prefer to bring your own. Photography is usually allowed, but it's best avoided during prayers.

Museum and the Ottoman-era shopping centre, the **Arasta Bazaar**, beyond which a sunken terrace café where you can puff an afternoon away with a *narghile*.

FREE Küçük Haghia Sophia Mosque
Küçük Ayasofya Camii
Küçük Ayasofya Caddesi, Sultanahmet. Tram Sultanahmet. **Open** prayer times only, daily.
Admission free. **Map** p243 M12.
Also known as 'Little Haghia Sophia' because of its resemblance to Justinian's great cathedral. Like its larger namesake, it was originally a church, in this case dedicated to Sergius and Bacchus, the patron saints of the Christianised Roman army. Also like its namesake, it's not much to look at from the outside, but possesses a fine interior, including a frieze honouring Justinian and his wife, Theodora. There's also a very pleasant garden, which has an adjoining café.

Mosaic Museum
Büyüksaray Mozaik Müzesi
Arasta Çarşısı, Torun Sokak 103, (0212 518 1205). Tram Sultanahmet. **Open** *Winter* 9am-5pm Tue-Sun. *Summer* 9am-7pm Tue-Sun.
Admission YTL8. **No credit cards.**
Map p243 N11.
Behind Sultanahmet Mosque and slightly down the hill towards the Marmara is a small, 17th-century shopping street, built to provide rental revenue for the upkeep of the mosque. It has been converted into a cluster of tourist shops, known as the Arasta Bazaar. Leading off here is a prefabricated hut that is the unlikely home of a fantastic archaeological find. Uncovered in the mid 1950s, it's an ornamental pavement belonging to the Byzantine Great Palace (Büyüksaray), which stood where the mosque is now, and probably dates from the era of Justinian. The surviving segments depict mythological and hunting scenes, with pastoral idylls disturbingly skewed by bloody depictions of animal combat: elephant versus lion, snake versus gazelle, stags and lizards being eaten by winged unicorns. The museum is also worth a visit for the informative wall panels, particularly the pictorial reconstructions of how the Byzantine palace quarter would have looked.

Museum of Turkish & Islamic Art
Türk ve Islam Eserleri Müzesi
At Meydanı 46, (0212 518 1805). Tram Sultanahmet. **Open** 9am-6.30pm Tue-Sun.
Admission YTL10. **Credit** MC, V.
Map p243 M10.
Overlooking the Hippodrome, the museum occupies the restored 16th-century palace of Ibrahim Paşa. A Greek convert to Islam, Ibrahim was the confidant of Süleyman I and in 1523 he was appointed Grand Vizier. When his palace was completed the following year, it was the grandest private residence in the Ottoman Empire, rivalling any building of the Topkapı Palace. When Süleyman fell under the influence of the scheming Roxelana (*see p25*), he was persuaded that Ibrahim had to go, and the vizier was strangled in his sleep.

The palace was seized by the state and was variously used as a school, a dormitory, a court, a barracks and a prison, before being restored as a museum. The well-planned collections, all housed in cool rooms around a central courtyard, include carpets, manuscripts, miniatures, woodwork, metalwork and glasswork. Items date from the early Islamic period through to modern times, all presented chronologically and geographically, with full explanations provided.

On the ground floor, a gallery showcases modern Turkish and foreign artists. There's an interesting ethnographic section, including a recreation of a *kara çadır* or 'black tent', the residence of choice for many of the nomadic Anatolian tribes who developed the art of the *kilim*. Upstairs, the Great Hall contains what is reckoned to be one of the finest collections of carpets in the world.

▶ *There's an excellent café in a shaded courtyard, with a covered terrace overlooking the Hippodrome next to it.*

FREE Sokollu Mehmet Paşa Mosque
Sokollu Mehmet Paşa Camii
Şehit Mehmet Paşa Sokak 20, Sultanahmet (0212 518 1633). Tram Eminönü or Sultanahmet. **Open** 7am-dusk daily.
Admission free. **Map** p243 M11.
One of Sinan's later buildings (constructed between 1571-72), this mosque has been widely praised by architectural historians for its skilful handling of an uneven, sloping site. If you manage to get inside (hang around long enough, and somebody will usually turn up with a key), notice the lovely tiling and painted calligraphic inscriptions, set among vivid floral motifs. If you don't, the ornate ablution fountain in the courtyard is also beautiful.

The Bazaar Quarter

An ancient – and modern – centre of commerce.

For centuries, this was where the strands of an empire's economy came together, with sellers from Damascus and Yemen bartering hard with buyers from Anatolia, the Balkans and the Aegean. A cacophony of multilingual haggling and braying camels, this was the oriental bazaar *par excellence*. While nowadays the **Grand Bazaar** is given over to a more decorative tourist trade, the experience of shopping here can still be something of a contact sport, as shopkeepers try to sell a multitude of goods, ranging from the beautiful to the tacky, to visitors. Meanwhile, in the surrounding streets, Istanbul's masses still do the real business, descending on the markets to do their weekly shopping – the modern bazaar.

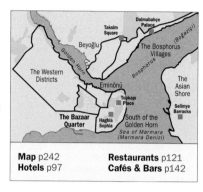

| Map p242 | Restaurants p121 |
| Hotels p97 | Cafés & Bars p142 |

DIVAN YOLU

Narrow, sloping, partially cobbled and given over to purring trams, the street known as Divan Yolu is modestly attractive. There's little indication that this was formerly the ancient Meşe, or Middle Way; the main thoroughfare of Byzantine Constantinople and, later, Ottoman Stamboul. It ran from the imperial centre (today's Sultanahmet) due west over the city's seven hills to the Topkapı Gate in the city wall. From Byzantium, the Meşe continued all the way to Durres (Durazzo) on the Albanian coast. A large marble sliver at the eastern end of Divan Yolu, in the small park behind the Yerebatan Sarnıcı, is all that remains of a Byzantine triumphal arch, known as the **Milion**, which originally marked the point from which all distances were measured.

Modern Divan Yolu is defined by tacky souvenir shops, cheap eateries, money exchange bureaux and bucket-shop travel agencies, with the odd smattering of antiquity. On the corner with Babıali Caddesi is a small, well-tended cemetery with the **Tomb of Mahmut II**. Over the road and down a side street is the **Theodosius Cistern**, sitting under the 'Eminönü Belediye Başkanlığı' building. The **Basın Müzesi** (Press Museum) is rather dull, but has a popular café on the ground floor. Next

door, on the corner with Vezirhanı Caddesi, the big, bulbous, yellow-faced dome belongs to the **Çemberlitaş Hamam** (*see p190*). The buildings fall back here to create a small, pigeon-infested plaza, marked by the equally scruffy **Burnt Column**. Otherwise known as the Hooped Column, this easily overlooked pillar is, in fact, one of the city's oldest monuments. Erected by Constantine to celebrate the city's inauguration as new imperial capital in 330, the column was topped by a statue of the emperor until this was destroyed in an 1106 hurricane. Its present blackened state is the result of one of Istanbul's periodic fires. The iron hoops are structural reinforcements that were added in the fifth century and replaced in the 1970s.

By this point Divan Yolu has turned into **Yeniçeriler Caddesi**, which is lined with a string of small mosques, tombs and *medreses* (theological schools), a couple of which have small courtyards that double up as **narghile** cafés (*see p151* **Hubbly Bubbly**). From here, the Grand Bazaar is immediately to the north.

FREE Theodosius Cistern
Şerefiye Sarnıcı
Piyer Loti Caddesi, Sultanahmet. Tram Sultanahmet. **Open** 9am-5pm Mon-Fri. **Admission** free. **Map** p243 M10.

This unrestored Byzantine reservoir is what the more famous Yerebatan Sarnıçı would have looked like before it was cleaned up for the tourists.

FREE Tomb of Mahmut II

82 Divan Yolu, Sultanahmet. Tram Sultanahmet. **Open** 9.30am-7pm daily. **Admission** free. **Map** p243 M10.

Mahmut II (1808-39) was the sultan who crushed the Janissaries, the Ottomans' elite standing army. He must have been a formidable force in the harem, too, producing 15 sons and 12 daughters, many of whom are now crammed into the domed tomb with him.

GRAND BAZAAR

The Grand Bazaar (in Turkish *Kapalı Çarşı*, or 'Covered Market') is a world apart. A maze of interconnecting vaulted passages, the bazaar has its own banks, baths, mosques, cafés and restaurants, a police station and post office, not to mention thousands of shops, all glittery and fairy-lit in the absence of natural light. Since the rise of the mall it's no longer the biggest shopping centre in the world, but it can still claim to be the oldest.

Part of the building dates back to the ninth century, when it was used as something akin to a Byzantine ministry of finance. Trading proper started in 1461, a mere eight years after the Turkish conquest of Constantinople. The Ottomans ushered in a new economic era, with the city at the centre of an empire that stretched from the Arabian deserts almost to the European Alps. Mehmet the Conqueror ordered the construction of a *bedesten*, a great secure building with thick stone walls, massive iron gates and space for several dozen shops. This survives in modified form as the **Old Bedesten** (*İç Bedesten*), at the very heart of the bazaar. It remains a place where the most precious items are sold, including the finest old silver and antiques. The **Sandal Bedesten** was added later; named after a fine Bursan silk, it was filled with textile traders. It now hosts a carpet auction at 1pm every Wednesday, which is a crowd-pleaser.

A network of covered streets grew up around the two *bedestens*, sealed at night behind 18 great gates. Whenever the economy was booming, the market would physically expand, only to be cut back by frequent fires. As the Ottoman Empire started to decline after 300 years of wealth, so did the legendary splendour of the bazaar. In 1894, a devastating earthquake hit the traders particularly hard. It wasn't until the 1950s that the bazaar began to revive, as the new republic found its economic footing. These days, it's taking tentative steps into the 21st century with chic boutiques, hip cafés, and even a website (www.kapalicarsi.com.tr).

Much of the current prosperity comes from gold – nearly 100 tonnes of it is sold in the bazaar each year. Then there are the 'black bag' shoppers from eastern Europe and former countries of the Soviet Union, so called because of their habit of filling numerous bin bags with cheap clothing.

The bazaar definitely has plenty of inessential knick-knacks, tacky souvenirs, nasty leather jackets, hookah pipes and hippy outfits, but there are some attractive, unusual, and high-quality goods to be had; you just have to know where to look and be prepared to haggle. For guidance on both, *see p54* **Shopping the Bazaar**.

★ Grand Bazaar

Kapalı Çarşı
Beyazıt (0212 522 3173,
www.kapalicarsi.com.tr). Tram Beyazıt or
Çemberlitaş. **Open** 8.30am-7pm Mon-Sat.
Map p288 L9.
▶ *The smaller Egyptian Bazaar in Eminönü has more souvenirs, food and some spices; see p58.*

AROUND THE GRAND BAZAAR

If you can find your way out of the east side of the bazaar, you emerge into daylight beside the **Nuruosmaniye Mosque**.

From here, follow Mahmut Paşa Yokuşu north. This market street is given over to the

SIGHTS

Grand Bazaar.

rag trade: it's lined with wholesalers knocking out fake Lacoste T-shirts and imitation Levi's jeans in insalubrious basement workshops. The street's great stone archways lead into numerous *hans*, medieval merchant hostels with storage rooms and sleeping quarters built around a central courtyard.

To the north, the market extends much further than the limits of the covered area, spilling over into a crazed warren of narrow streets that zigzag all the way to the districts of Tahtakale and **Eminönü** (*see p57*) beside the Golden Horn. If you're lost, just keep heading downhill. On the way, you'll see the contemporary bazaar at its most frenetic.

Exit the Grand Bazaar on the west side for **Çadırcılar Caddesi**. At No.27 is a large derelict courtyard graced with a mosaic of **Yunus Emre**, a 13th-century Sufi poet ('God is our professor and love is our academy', quoth

he). Ascend the staircase to be greeted by wholesaler Ahmet and his stock of Central Asian kaftans, Pakistani fabrics, shamanistic artefacts and jewellery at prices you won't find anywhere else in the bazaar.

West of Çadırcılar, in Sahaflar Çarşısı Sokak, is the **Booksellers' Bazaar**, a lane and courtyard where the written word has been traded since early Ottoman times. Because printed books were considered a corrupting European influence, only hand-lettered manuscripts were sold until 1729, the year the first book in Turkish was published. Today, much of the trade at this historic bazaar is in textbooks (the university is nearby), along with plentiful coffee-table volumes and framed calligraphy for the tourists. Sadly, the booksellers now have to compete with itinerant merchants peddling everything from Byzantine coins to used mobile phones.

FREE Nuruosmaniye Mosque

Nuruosmaniye Camii
Vezirhanı Caddesi, Beyazıt (0212 528 0906).
Tram Beyazıt or Çemberlitaş. **Open** 10am-7pm daily. **Admission** free. **Map** p242 L9.

Constructed on one of the seven hills within the walls of former Constantinople, this was the first mosque in the city built in the style known as Turkish Baroque. Istanbul historian John Freely describes the architecture as possessing a 'certain perverse genius'. Certainly, the courtyard shaded by plane trees is lovely. The extensive manuscript library is also worth a look.

INSIDE TRACK GOLDEN RENT

Many shop owners in the Grand Bazaar still pay their annual rent in gold, particularly jewellery mechants. They can expect to hand over between four and six kilograms of gold a year. On the main avenue, they can expect to pay seven kilograms. However, with rising gold prices, many prefer to pay in the more stable euro or Turkish lire.

Shopping the Bazaar

Insider tips on finding what you want and paying a fair price.

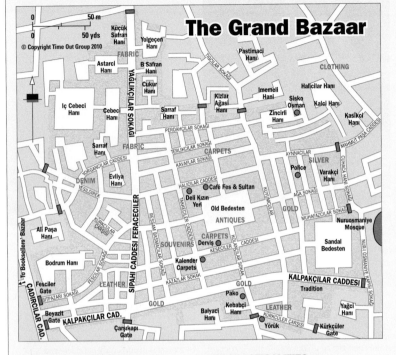

There are 5,500-odd vendors in the Grand Bazaar. Shopkeepers cajole and entreat passers-by in a dozen languages, determined not to permit visitors to indulge in such a non-commercial activity as sightseeing. Remember, you're not dealing with sales clerks but most likely the owners themselves, or at least a trusted brother or nephew. Many still pay their rent in gold – a hefty seven kilos per year for shops on the main avenue (*see p53* **Gold Rent**).

Fortunately, the perception that hardcore hustling is bad for long-term trade has finally started to sink in among the bazaar traders. Visitors will find the Grand Bazaar a kinder, gentler place than it was years ago. But even the sagacious Mehmed the Conqueror, who founded the covered bazaar in the 1460s, would have been surprised by the plasma screens overhead in the bazaar's 65 alleys.

THE PRACTICALITIES

Serious shoppers should come armed with a notepad, a calculator for working out exchange rates and plenty of time – three hours is about the minimum needed for a purchasing expedition here. When you find something you like, jot down the price and the location of the seller. Then find the item elsewhere and get more quotes. Continue for as long as you have the patience.

Don't assume that wildly varying prices for the same item means the higher price you're quoted is a rip-off. Shopkeepers price their goods according to their needs. You may be lucky: someone may require ready cash to pay overheads or buy new stock and will be happy to settle for a quick, cheap sale. Also, it's not true that large, sleek shops in busy central locations always charge more. Even though they pay higher rents, higher turnover often allows them to lower prices.

BARGAINING ETIQUETTE

When bargaining, start somewhere well below your ideal price, because the shop owner will start well above his. Hopefully, you can meet in the middle. Remember that it's considered bad form to enter into an elaborate bargaining process if you're not really interested in buying.

WHERE TO BUY WHAT

There are over a dozen main gates into the Grand Bazaar. At least five of them open on to **Kalpakçılar Caddesi**, an opulent east–west thoroughfare lined with gleaming jewellery shops. On this street, you'll also find **Pako** (at No.87), the place for some of the city's best handbags and purses.

South of Kalpakçılar is the Kürkcüler **Çarşısı**, filled with leather jackets and coats. It's also where you'll find **Yörük** (see p169), a good carpet shop, located at the base of some steps leading up and out of the bazaar.

For more carpets visit the **Rabia Hanı** at the eastern end of Kürkcüler Çarşısı. **Tradition** at No.11 is another well-stocked and hassle-free option.

Running north from Kalpakçılar Caddesi, **Kolonçılar Sokak** is lined with shops that peddle a typical mix of souvenirs, ceramics, tea sets, silks, water pipes, chess sets and carved wood. It crosses **Keseciler Caddesi** (location of the quality rural crafts shop **Derviş**, see p165) before making a beeline for the ancient heart of the bazaar, the **Old Bedesten**. (Check out the Byzantine eagle carved into the stone on the outside face of its eastern entrance.) In here, the atmosphere is hushed, almost scholarly – a suitable setting for dealers in Ottoman-

era prayer beads, icons, chess sets, firearms, pocket watches, painted miniatures, snuff boxes and Soviet memorabilia and art nouveau jewellery.

On the north side of the Bedesten is **Halıcılar Caddesi**, no longer 'the Street of the Carpet Sellers', but instead the front line of gentrification, with quaint **Café Fes** and **Café Sultan** selling Illy coffee and fresh flowers, plus **Abdulla** (see p165), which uses chic packaging to shift traditional products.

West along Halıcılar are some more alternatives to carpets, notably at **Galeri Apollo** (No.22-6), a shop stocked with silky soft goat-hair rugs and calf-skin hides, hand-stitched into patchwork designs.

Halıcılar connects to **Yağlıkçılar Sokağı**, a long, wide, street running north–south and the place for bellydancing costumes, incredible fabrics, lamps, knitwear and more unnecessary souvenirs.

Off Yağlıkçılar is the tranquil **Cebeci Hanı** and, beyond, the **İç Cebeci**, where a large open courtyard is ringed by a second floor, lined with antique and metalwork shops, plus a few places selling fabulous Central Asian fabrics and garments.

To visit the most beautiful *han* in the bazaar, head east from Yağlıkçılar along **Perdahçılar Sokağı**; at the end follow the signs for **Zincirli Hanı**, the lair of the Grand Bazaar's most famous carpet dealer, **Sisko Osman** (see p169).

FOOD & DRINK

Outside the southern entrance to the Old Bedesten are **Julia's Kitchen** (Keseciler Caddesi 92), a great breakfast stop, and **Köşk** (Keseciler Caddesi 98-100), which serves traditional *sulu yemek* ('home-cooked dishes'), served up from bains-marie. **Şark Kahvesi**, at the corner of Yağlıkçılar and Fesciler Caddesi, is an old-style coffee-house decorated with wonderful pictures of old fellows on flying carpets. The courtyard of the **İç Cebeci Hanı** has an excellent kebab shop and a tea house where off-duty merchants spend a serious amount of time over games of cards. **Havuzlu Lokantasi** (Gani Çelebi Sokak 3) is a basic, old fashioned joint that does fine kebabs. Remember that all cafés and restaurants in the bazaar shut by 6.30pm.

BEYAZIT SQUARE

A large, irregularly shaped plaza west of the bazaar, Beyazıt Square was the site of the forum in Roman times. It regained importance when the early Ottomans built a palace here, which served as the pre-Topkapı seat of power until it burned down in 1541. Other significant Ottoman structures still stand, notably the **Beyazıt Mosque**.

Facing the mosque is the monumental gate to Istanbul University. In the 1960s and 1970s, the campus was a favourite battleground for both left and right, and is still a centre for political protest. As a result, the university grounds and **Beyazıt Tower**, built in 1828 as a fire lookout (with so many wooden buildings, fire was a constant hazard) and a prominent city landmark, are currently off limits to all but accredited students.

To the left of the monumental gate is a small *medrese*, which was originally part of the Beyazıt Mosque complex but is now occupied by the **Calligraphy Museum**, which is being restored in 2010.

Follow either of the roads that hug the university walls to reach the architectural perfection of the **Süleymaniye Mosque**. Outside its compound wall, in a walled, triangular garden to the north, is the modest **Tomb of Sinan**, designed by the occupant himself. The mosque's 500-year-old kitchens are now employed by **Darüzziyafe** (*see p121*), where you can have a rather unexceptional lunch in an exceptional setting. Also worth a visit is the neighbouring Lalezar tea-house, which occupies a sunken courtyard with a marble fountain, comfy cushioned seats along the walls, and narghile to puff on.

FREE Beyazıt Mosque

Beyazıt Camii
Beyazıt Square, Yeniçeriler Caddesi. Tram Beyazıt. **Open** 10am-final prayer call daily. **Admission** free. **Map** p242 K9.
Built from 1501 to 1506, this was the second great mosque complex to be founded in the city. The first, the Fatih Mosque, was destroyed, which makes Beyazıt the oldest imperial mosque in town. In effect, it's the architectural link between the Byzantine Haghia Sophia – the obvious inspiration – and the great, later Ottoman mosques such as Süleymaniye. The sultan for whom it was built, Beyazıt II, is buried at the back of the gardens. Still in use, the mosque is full of market traders at prayer times. Outside is the Sahaflar Carsisi (book bazaar), where Sufi booksellers tout travelogues and novels in many diffferent languages.
▶ *For a good, cheap Turkish food after visiting the mosque try Şar (see p121), on the other side of Divan Yolu.*

Calligraphy Museum

Vakıf Hat Sanatları Müzesi
Beyazıt Square, Beyazıt (0212 527 5851, www.vgm.gov.tr). Tram Beyazıt. Museum currently closed for renovations. **Map** p242 K10.
Forbidden to portray living beings by religion (although this was not always strictly adhered to), Islamic artists developed alternative forms of virtuosity. Calligraphy was regarded as a particularly noble art because it was a way of beautifying the text of the Quran. But the sanctity of the text placed restrictions on the flourishes that could be added. Not so with the sultan's *tuğra*, or monogram, which incorporated his name, titles and patronymics into one highly stylised motif – the precursor of the modern logo. The tile art here is excellent and there are a number of brilliantly illuminated Qurans dating from the 13th to 16th centuries. The museum also has a pleasant courtyard that features stone-carved calligraphy. The Dar'ül-Kurra in the courtyard is accessible to visitors during museum opening hours in Ramadan; it contains some holy relics of the Prophet Muhammed. At the time of going to press this museum was closed for much needed restoration and it's unclear when it will open again.
▶ *For more calligraphy displays, visit Sakıp Sabancı Museum (see p84) in Rumeli Hisarı, one of the Bosphorus Villages.*

FREE Süleymaniye Mosque

Süleymaniye Camii
Tiryakiler Çarşısı, off Prof Sıddık Sami Onar Caddesi, Süleymaniye. Tram Beyazıt or Eminönü. **Open** 9am-7pm daily. Closed for refurbishment until 2011. **Admission** free. **Map** p242 K8.
Completed in 1557 under Süleyman the Magnificent, this stunning mosque is arguably the crowning achievement of architect Mimar Sinan. Built on Istanbul's highest hill, it is visible for miles. The approach is along Prof Sıddık Sami Onar Caddesi, once known as 'Addicts Alley' because its cafés sold hashish. This is no longer the case, although the area's tea houses are still very popular student hangouts. The low-rise, multi-domed buildings surrounding the mosque are part of its *külliye* (compound), and include a hospital, asylum, hamam and soup kitchen.

Walk through the gardens and arcaded courtyard, whose columns allegedly came from the Byzantine royal box at the Hippodrome, to enter the mosque – remarkable for its soaring central prayer room, illuminated by some 200 windows. The interior decoration is minimal but effective; it includes stained glass added by Ibrahim the Mad and sparing use of Iznik tiles (which Sinan would later use profusely at the Rüstem Pasha Mosque, just down the hill, *see p60*).

Behind the mosque are several *türbes* (tombs), including Süleyman's own beautifully restored grave. Haseki Hürrem, the sultan's influential wife, a former slave known as Roxelana (*see p25*), is buried beside him. Süleymaniye Mosque is closed until sometime in 2011 for major refurbishment.

SIGHTS

Eminönü & the Golden Horn

Floating fish markets, chugging ferries and vestiges of glamour.

If Sultanahmet is the Istanbul of postcards, Eminönü is the Istanbul of ferry schedules. The commercial hub of the old city and a port since Ancient Greek times, its bustling waterfront leads back to a maze of alleys, mosques and the **Egyptian Bazaar**.

The Orient Express last rolled into Sirkeci Station back in 1961, and the former elegance of the area can still just be discerned under a layer of dust. The most characteristic, and interesting aspect of the area, though, is the hubbub of the waterfront. Watching the ferries, tankers, fishing boats and cruise liners criss-cross the Golden Horn from a vantage point on **Galata Bridge** – a two-tier bridge with cafés and restaurants along its lower deck – is a fascinating way to while away an hour.

Map p242-243   **Restaurants** p121

GULHANE PARK

To get to Eminönü from central Sultanahmet, ride the tram north to the Eminönü stop, or follow the tramlines on foot (a ten-minute walk from Sultanahmet Square). The route curves sharply around the walls enclosing Gülhane Park. Formerly part of the grounds of the Topkapı Palace, the park is now rather dismal, with more concrete than grass. It contains a dire little zoo and, one for connoisseurs of lost causes, the **Tanzimat Museum**, which commemorates the liberalising reforms proclaimed from this spot by Sultan Abdülmecid in 1839 (*see p27*), then roundly ignored by one and all.

Back on the tram tracks, just west of the Gülhane stop, is an ornate gateway with a rococo roof: this is the historic **Sublime Porte** (Bab-ı Ali). At one time, this was the entrance to the palace of the grand vizier, the true administrator of the empire during the dotage of the sultans. Foreign ambassadors were accredited to the 'Sublime Porte', and the term became a synonym for the Ottoman government. The current gate dates from 1843 and is now the entrance to the headquarters of the provincial government.

Opposite, jutting out of a corner of the Gülhane Park wall, is the **Alay Köşkü**, an elaborate platform from which the sultans would observe parades or, in the case of Ibrahim the Mad, take pot-shots with a crossbow at passing pedestrians.

FREE Tanzimat Museum
Tanzimat Müzesi
Gülhane Park (0212 512 6384). Tram Gülhane.
Open 9am-5pm Mon-Fri. **Admission** free.
Map p243 O9.
The exhibits here amount to little more than a wall of portraits, a waxwork bust and some yellowing imperial decrees, all housed in a small wooden hut that's easily mistaken for a public toilet.

EMINÖNÜ

After Gülhane, the tramlines descend to **Sirkeci Station** (Sirkeci Istasyonu). On its completion in 1881, this was the eastern terminus for trains from Europe, including the Orient Express (*see p59* **End of the Line for the Orient Express**). Its street-facing façade has been disfigured by modern additions, but the waterfront profile retains an element of grandeur. Despite the station's relegation to the status of suburban shuttle hub (the only international trains are to Thessaloniki and Bucharest), the original **Orient Express restaurant** (*see p121*), beside platform one, remains largely intact. Sadly, it's too fancy for the commuters and tends to be empty.

Just past takeaway joint Konyalı (*see above* **Inside Track**), the tram tracks swing left, terminating at Eminönü, grandly signposted by the **New Mosque**.

FREE New Mosque
Yeni Camii
Eminönü Meydanı (0212 527 8505). Tram Eminönü. **Open** 7am-dusk daily. **Admission** free. **Map** p243 M8.

Construction on the mosque began in 1598, but suffered a setback when the architect was executed for heresy. It was eventually completed in 1663, after the classical period of Ottoman architecture had passed. It is nonetheless a regal structure, particularly uplifting when seen floodlit. The fact that it is so obviously a working mosque tends to keep visitors at bay, but nobody objects to non-Muslims entering.

THE EGYPTIAN BAZAAR

In front of the New Mosque is a pigeon-plagued plaza busy with itinerant street sellers and dominated on its south side by the high brick arch leading into the **Egyptian Bazaar**, also known as the Spice Bazaar. The market was constructed as part of the mosque complex, and its revenues helped support philanthropic institutions. The name derives from its past association with the arrival of the annual 'Cairo caravan', a flotilla of ships bearing rice, coffee and incense from Egypt.

While the bazaar's L-shaped vaulted hall is undeniably pretty, at first glance its 90 shops seem to be hustling nothing more than an assortment of oily perfumes, cheap gold and sachets of 'Turkish Viagra'. It's a tourist trap, to be sure, but to dismiss it out of hand is to miss one of the world's finest delis: make a beeline for **Erzincanlılar** (shop no.2) for delicious honeycomb and the mature hard Turkish cheese known as *eski kaşar*. Other food shops worth checking out are **Pinar** (no.14) for excellent *lokum* (Turkish delight); **Antep Pazarı** (no.50)

Egyptian Bazaar.

End of the Line for the Orient Express

The rise and fall of the most elegant train journey in the world.

Sirkeci Station. See p57.

A byword for glamour and intrigue, the Orient Express existed in several versions on various routes over the years, the most famous being the Paris-Vienna-Budapest-Istanbul route. Its maiden departure was 4 October 1883 from Gare de l'Est, Paris. Between the Western 'city of light' and the Eastern exoticism of its ultimate destination, the train passed through a patchwork of mercurial Balkan kingdoms, always tinged with the promise of war or revolution. A couple of notorious incidents added to the legend: in 1891, bandits held up the train and took its passengers hostage; in 1929, it was stranded in a snowdrift for six days.

Such episodes could be endured in the comfort of carpeted cabins, decked out with damask drapes and silk sheets for the fold-down beds, or the saloon, which evoked the atmosphere of a London gentlemen's club with its leather armchairs and bookcases. Meals were served in the Wagon Restaurant, beneath gas-lit brass chandeliers at tables set with Baccarat crystal, starched napery and monogrammed porcelain. The kind of passengers who could afford all this tended to be minor royals, wealthy nobility, diplomats and financiers, not to mention spies, nightclub performers and high-class whores – the perfect cast list for thriller-writers such as Agatha Christie and Graham Greene, both of whom famously used the Express as a setting for their novels.

The drawing of the Iron Curtain at the end of World War II signalled the beginning of the end for this train, and its final run was in 1961. Sporadic revivals have proved nothing more than sops to moneyed nostalgia buffs. In the age of EasyJet, spending three days, nine hours and 40 minutes – and the price of a second mortgage on the house – just to get from Paris to Istanbul seems a bit extravagant. But then, it always was.

There's a new museum in Sirkeci Station dedicated to the railways of Turkey. Among the exhibits are tea services from the Orient Express and a medallion commemorating its final journey into Istanbul. There's only one room, but it's obviously been put together by people who care deeply about the railways. Admission is free.

Galata Bridge.

SIGHTS

for pistachios, nuts, honey-covered mulberries and dried figs stuffed with walnuts; and **Güllüoğlu Baklavacısı** (no.88) for pastries. **Özel** (no. 82) has pretty, cheap scarves. Another reason to visit the market is to lunch at **Pandeli's** (*see p123*), a Greek-run restaurant up a flight of steps just inside the main entrance.

Running west from the market, **Hasırcılar Caddesi** is one of the city's most vibrant and aromatic streets thanks to a clutch of delis, including **Namlı Pastırmacı** (*see p164*), spice merchants and coffee sellers, among them **Kurukahveci Mehmet Efendi** (*see p164*), where caffeine addicts queue at the serving hatch to purchase the own-brand bags of beans.

Further along the street, look out for the arched doorways where flights of stairs lead up to the **Rüstem Paşa Mosque**, built in 1561 for a grand vizier of Süleyman the Great.

TAHTAKALE

The view from the Rüstem Paşa's forecourt is dominated by a large dome, which belongs to the nearby **Tahtakale Hamam Çarşısı**, a 500-year-old bathhouse that has been converted into a shopping arcade and a pleasant café occupying the main domed chamber.

This area north of Hasırcılar Caddesi is known as Tahtakale. Its streets heave with locals out to snap up bargain clothing and household accessories. Women shop here to top up their dowries, picking up linens,

bedwear, lingerie and towels. This is also the place to buy the traditional circumcision outfits that consist of a crown, a white satin cape, and a golden staff. Local traders also do a brisk business in wood and wickerware, handmade wooden spoons and coat-hangers, knives and tools. Tahtakale Caddesi is renowned for its 'portable stalls' manned by shifty gents peddling pirated CDs, DVDs, smuggled electronics and cigars. At the first whisper of police, stalls are snapped shut and the owners all leg it.

★ Egyptian Bazaar
Mısır Çarşısı
Yeni Camii Meydanı (0212 513 6597).
Tram Eminönü. **Open** 8am-7pm Mon-Sat.
Map p243 L8.

FREE Rüstem Paşa Mosque
Rüstem Paşa Camii
Hasırcılar Caddesi 90 (0212 526 7350). Tram Eminönü. **Open** 9am-dusk daily. **Admission** free. **Map** p242 L7.
Above the shops, (whose rents pay for its upkeep), the mosque is invisible from the street. It's quite a city secret, although it's one of the most beautiful mosques built by Sinan. Smaller than most of his works, it's also set apart by its liberal and dazzling use of coloured tiles. The first-floor forecourt, with its colonnaded canopy and potted plants high above the crowed alleys, is one of Istanbul's loveliest hideaways.

THE GOLDEN HORN

Eminönü is the departure point for ferries up the Bosphorus, across to Asia and out to the Princes' and Marmara Islands. A few services also head up the Golden Horn, an inlet of the Marmara some 7.5 kilometres (five miles) long. The maritime traffic here is frantic, as hulking vessels skirmish with tiny motorboats for berthing positions. Pedestrian traffic is intense too – watch your wallet.

Mingling with the smell of diesel is the whiff of deep-frying fish. This comes from the small, bouncing boats moored at the dockside, cooking up their day's catch for sale in sandwiches.

The best place to observe the hustle and bustle is from the **Galata Bridge**, the vital link between the two sides of European Istanbul. The current structure, an unsightly concrete ramp with four steel towers at its centre, replaces a much-loved earlier bridge. This one was built in the 1980s to accommodate growing traffic. The lower deck of restaurants, bars and tea houses right on the waterfront provides ring-side seating for cheap beers and boat-watching. It's probably best not to eat along here (or if you do, keep a close eye on the bill); head instead to the fresh fish stalls at the west side of either end of the bridge.

The Western Districts

A different Istanbul.

West of Sultanahmet and the Bazaar Quarter lies the sprawling Western Districts – a collection of old neighbourhoods that make up some of the most religious areas in the city, a dramatic contrast to secular Beyoğlu. In **Fatih**, **Fener** and **Balat**, headscarves, chadors and the baggy *şalvar* trousers worn by devout men are much in evidence. Often neglected by foreign visitors, the area is rich in atmosphere and monuments, peppered with churches, synagogues and Greek Orthodox schools, as well as mosques

| **Map** p244-245 | **Restaurants** p124 |
| **Hotels** p102 | **Cafés & Bars** p142 |

– a reminder that until early last century, around 40 per cent of Istanbul's population were Christians and Jews. Two highlights in this area are the **Church of St Saviour in Chora**, one of the city's foremost Byzantine monuments, and the mosque at **Eyüp**.

SIGHTS

FATIH

Immediately west of the Bazaar Quarter, Fatih is easy to reach by tram from Sultanahmet. Hop off at the Üniversite or Laleli stop and walk north, past rows of leather and suede shops, to the **Şehzade Mosque**, the first royal complex built by Sinan.

Beyond the gardens of the mosque is the mighty **Aqueduct of Valens**. Constructed by the Roman emperor Valens in the fourth century AD, the aqueduct channelled water from the lakes north of the city to Istanbul's cisterns up until the late 19th century. For a city often under siege, a reliable water supply was critical. These days, the aqueduct forms a dramatic entrance to the city as the modern Atatürk Bulvarı thoroughfare passes beneath its two-tiered arches.

Huddled in the shadow of the aqueduct is the attractive little Medrese of Gazanfer Ağa, now the **Cartoon Museum**. A short walk further north is what's now known as the **Zeyrek Mosque**, but was once the Byzantine Church of the Pantocrator. Ten minutes' walk due west is one of the most significant, and under-explored, historical sites in the city: the **Fatih Mosque**. On Wednesdays, streets around the mosque

are taken over by **Fatih Pazarı**, one of the city's largest and best known street markets.

From the Fatih Mosque follow Darüşşafaka Caddesi north; turn right on to Yavuz Selim Caddesi past the fifth-century **Cistern of Aspar** (now a sports complex) to find the lovely **Selim I Mosque** (Yavuz Selim Camii).

★ FREE Cartoon Museum
Karikatür ve Mizah Müzesi
Kavacılar Sokak 12, off Atatürk Bulvarı, Şehzadebaşı (0212 521 1264). Tram Laleli or Üniversite. Open 9am-5pm Tue-Sat. Admission free. Map p242 H8.
Set in a beautiful 17th-century *medrese*, this is one of the city's more unusual museums. Where instructors once lectured students in Islamic philosophy, they now give lessons in illustration, engraving and screen-printing. The permanent collection, with pieces dating back to the 1870s, illustrates the long-standing popularity of caricature and satire in Turkey. One of the most recurring themes is the insidious influence of the West. Temporary exhibitions are devoted to Turkish and foreign cartoonists. The museum also hosts Turkey's only humour library and an archive open to the public on request.
► *For a quirky shop of objects designed by a cartoonist, visit Porof Zihni Sinir (see p156).*

Fatih.

Fatih Mosque
Fatih Camii
Fevzi Paşa Caddesi. Metro Emniyet. **Open** 9am-dusk daily. **Admission** free. **Map** p245 G7.
The grounds of Fatih Mosque are a popular place for pious picnickers. The vast 18th-century baroque structure is built on the site of the Church of the Holy Apostles, burial place of most Byzantine emperors, including Constantine. The church was already in ruins by the time Mehmet II conquered Constantinople. He used it as a quarry for a mosque built in 1470 to celebrate his victory (*fatih* means 'conqueror'). Most of Mehmet's original structure was destroyed by an earthquake in 1766; all that remains is the courtyard and parts of the main entrance. The tomb of the Conqueror stands behind the prayer hall.

Panorama 1453 History Museum
Topkapı Culture Park, Merkez Efendi Mahallesi, Topkapı (212 467 0700, www.panoramikmuze.com). Tram Topkapı.
Open 9am-8pm daily. **Admission** YTL10.
In 1453 Sultan Mehmed II conquered Constantinople, marking the end of the Byzantine Empire in the area. This museum, opened by Prime Minister Recep Tayyip Erdoğan on 31 January 2009, depicts the siege of the city and the principal battle that led to its fall in a 2,350sq m panoramic painting that took three years to complete. To enhance the experience, the multimedia museum uses the sounds of battle and includes objects from the time. In a neat twist, the Panorama 1453 is located by the very walls that were breached by the Janissaries.

FREE Şehzade Mosque
Şehzade Camii
Şehzadebaşı Caddesi, Saraçhane, Şehzadebaşı. Tram Üniversite or Laleli. **Open** 9am-dusk daily. **Admission** free. **Map** p242 H8.
Completed in 1548, Sinan dismissed his first royal mosque complex as 'apprentice work'. It is named after Prince Sehzade Mehmet, son of Suleyman, who died suddenly and prematurely. He is buried in the complex. The square courtyard is as big as the interior of the mosque. The combination of the square plan and the central dome surrounded by four half domes is unprecedented in Islamic architecture.

FREE Selim I Mosque
Yavuz Sultan Selim Camii
Yavuz Selim Caddesi. Bus 90, 99A. **Open** 8am-dusk daily. **Admission** free. **Map** p245 G5.
It may have been built to commemorate Sultan Selim the Grim, nicknamed for his habit of executing senior officials on a whim, but this little-visited mosque is one of the most beautiful in the city, with a lovely courtyard and terrace overlooking the Golden Horn.

FREE Zeyrek Mosque
Zeyrek Camii
Ibadethane Sokak, Küçükpazar. Metro Laleli.
Open 9am-dusk daily. **Admission** free.
Map p242 H7.
Built in the 12th century for the wife of Emperor John II Comnenus (1118-43), the Byzantine Church of the Pantocrator became the imperial residence during the struggles with the Latin crusaders. It was turned into a mosque after the Muslim conquest. Although in a deplorable state of disrepair, it retains some fine internal decoration, including exquisitely carved door frames and marble mosaic floors, which, if you're lucky, one of the caretakers will reveal by drawing back the carpets. Archaeological oddities are displayed on a terrace overlooking the Golden Horn, which belongs to the swish Zeyrekhane restaurant.

FENER & BALAT

Until the early 20th century, Fener was primarily Greek, while Balat was mainly Jewish. Although lacking major monuments, these are fascinating areas in which to wander. The most picturesque approach to the two districts is on foot from the **Selim I Mosque** (*see p61*).

From the mosque, head downhill past the red-brick Fener Greek School for Boys. A little below and to the left is the only Byzantine church still in Greek hands, the **Church of Panaghia Mouchliotissa**. Immediately north of the church is the stretch of Byzantine sea wall breached by the crusaders in 1204. East along Incebal Sokak is the **Greek Orthodox**

The Great Icon Controversy

The theological battle that gripped the Byzantine Empire.

In the eighth and ninth centuries, a Byzantine empire faced with the onslaught of expansionist Islam was also torn apart by an internal controversy: whether or not it was permissible to paint images of Christ and the saints. Should new icons be painted – or should existing ones be destroyed? Strange though it may seem to a modern, secular mindset, this question became the focus of the empire's whole sense of identity.

From the vantage point of the secular 21st century it's easy to say that the Byzantines should have united against the outside threat rather than wasting energy on an internal clash of ideologies. From the vantage point of a Byzantine, it was a matter of crucial importance.

When Emperor Leo III removed an image of Christ from above the doors to the imperial palace in 726, it sparked riots and deaths. However, the emperor was not to be dissuaded. In 730, Leo deposed the patriarch of Constantinople and ordered the removal or destruction of all icons in the city. All resistance was violently suppressed. So what prompted Leo to plunge his empire into a virtual civil war? The answer lies partly in the Byzantine struggle against Islam. The Byzantines saw success or failure as marks of God's favour or disfavour. Encroachment on Christendom by the aggressively iconoclastic Muslims led some to theorise that God had forsaken them because the veneration of icons was a contravention of the second commandment, forbidding the worship of idols.

The icon-lovers developed an underground resistance movement, hiding icons from the imperial troops in monasteries. They found a powerful spokesman in St John of Damascus, a Christian who was chief councillor to the Ummayad rulers of the city. Safely out of the emperor's reach (or so he thought), John wrote in defence of icons. He pointed out that iconographers were only painting what God himself had done: become flesh and blood in the person of Christ. According to the iconoclasts' logic, he argued, the first and greatest idolater was therefore God himself. Infuriated, the emperor allegedly forged a letter in which John offered to betray Damascus to the Byzantines. An unamused Caliph had John's hand cut off.

The icon controversy raged on for over a century, outlasting four religious councils that provided ecclesiastical back-up, several emperors and two empresses. It was these female rulers who eventually decided the case. Empress Irene was the first to reverse the iconoclast policy of her predecessors, and in 843 the Empress Theodora proclaimed the restoration of icons. Since then, the first Sunday of Lent has been celebrated as the triumph of Orthodoxy.

Go into any Orthodox church today and the first things that strike you are the glorious icons, glittering in the candlelight: icons and the faith and art that surround them survived, and it's hard to imagine the Orthodox Church without them. Had the iconoclasts prevailed there would have been none of the later Byzantine religious imagery gloriously preserved in Istanbul – in the Church of St Saviour in Chora.

SIGHTS

Patriarchate, an unprepossessing walled compound that has been the world centre of Greek Orthodoxy for the past 400 years.

Back west along **Yıldırım Street** are some of the city's finest old Greek residences, including the Fener Mansions, which date from the 17th and 18th centuries. Most are in a terrible state of dilapidation. Only one is presently occupied, housing the first dedicated womens' library (**Kadın Kütüphanesi**) in Turkey.

Equally unique is the church of **St Stephen of the Bulgars**, one of Turkey's only examples of neo-Gothic architecture.

Inland from St Stephen, the streets take on a grid pattern in what used to be Istanbul's main Jewish district. This is home to the city's oldest synagogue, the **Ahrida Synagogue**. Around the corner is the fascinating Armenian Orthodox Church of **Surp Hreşdagabet** (Holy Archangels). Heading south-west, towards the city walls, is the **Church of St Saviour in Chora**, now a museum featuring extraordinarily well-preserved Byzantine frescoes and mosaics.

FREE **Ahrida Synagogue**

Ahrida Sinagogu

Kürkçüçeşme Sokak 9, Balat. Bus 35D. **Open** by appointment with the Chief Rabbi (0212 243 5166). **Admission** free. **Map** p245 F3.

Founded by Macedonians from the town of Ohrid (of which 'Ahrida' is a corruption) in the 15th century, the synagogue's congregation later comprised the city's Sephardic Jewish community who had fled Spain during the inquisition. It is still used by the Sephardic community, many of whom speak the medieval Spanish dialect Ladino. The wooden dome, restored in 17th-century baroque style, is exquisite.
▶ *For an insight into Jewish life in Istanbul, visit the Jewish Museum (see p78).*

FREE Church of Panaghia Mouchliotissa
Kanlı Kilise
Tevkii Cafer Mektebi Sokak, Fener (0212 521 7139). Bus 55T. **Open** 9am-5pm daily.
Admission free. **Map** p245 G4.
Otherwise known as St Mary of the Mongols, this 13th-century church was erected in honour of Princess Maria, daughter of Emperor Michael VIII, who was married off to the khan of the Mongols. It was reputedly spared conversion into a mosque thanks to a Greek architect employed by Mehmet II; a decree issued by the Conqueror to this effect has pride of place in the church.

★ Church of St Saviour in Chora
Kariye Müzesi
Kariye Camii Sokak 26, Edirnekapı (0212 631 9241). Metro Ulubatlı or bus 37E, 38E, 91O to Vefa Stadium. **Open** 9am-5pm Mon, Tue, Thur-Sun. **Admission** YTL15. **Map** p244 D4.

Balat.

Often overlooked because it's so far off the beaten track, for Byzantine splendour this church (also known as the Kariye Mosque or Museum) is second only to Haghia Sophia. Built in the late 11th century, its celebrated mosaics and frescoes were added when the church was remodelled in the 14th century. Depicting all manner of Christian themes, from the Day of Judgement through to the Resurrection, the works here are arguably the most important surviving examples of Byzantine art in the world, both in terms of their execution and preservation. Ironically, this Christian art owes its excellent state of preservation to the church's conversion into a mosque in the early 16th century, when the frescoes and mosaics were covered over. They remained concealed until they were rediscovered in 1860. *Photo p67.*
▶ *The Kariye Hotel at the end of the street is worth visiting for its excellent Ottoman restaurant, Asitane (see p124).*

FREE Church of St Stephen of the Bulgars
Mürsel Paşa Caddesi 85-8, Fener (0212 521 1121). Bus 55T. **Admission** free. **Map** p245 G3.
Erected in 1871 for Istanbul's Bulgarian community, this church is still used today by Macedonian Christians. It is constructed entirely from prefabricated iron sections, cast in Vienna and shipped down the Danube to Istanbul.

FREE Church of Surp Hreşdagabet (Holy Angels)
Kamış Sokak, Balat. Bus 35D. **Open** Thur am services only. **Admission** free. **Map** p245 F3.
Tentatively dated to the 13th century, this church was taken over by the Armenians in the early 17th century. Although much of the current structure dates from 1835, the side chapel and *ayazma* (sacred spring) are original Byzantine features. Today, the congregation is composed almost exclusively of headscarved Muslim women – many devout Muslims have a devotion to both Christian and Jewish rituals, taking them very seriously as 'precursors' of Islam.

FREE Greek Orthodox Patriarchate
Fener Rum Patrikhanesi
Sadrazam Ali Paşa Caddesi, Fener (0212 525 2117). Bus 55T. **Open** 8am-5pm daily.
Admission free. **Map** p245 G4.
The central section of the seat of Greek Orthodoxy is permanently closed in memory of Patriarch Gregory V, who was hanged from it in 1821 as punishment for the outbreak of the Greek War of Independence. The main Church of St George is unremarkable save for three unusual free-standing mosaic icons. During celebrations for Orthodox Easter, the church attracts hundreds of pilgrims and provides a focal point for the dwindling Greek community of Istanbul.

Church of Panaghia Mouchliotissa.

CITY WALLS

Constructed during the reign of Theodosius II (408-450), the walls of Constantinople are the largest Byzantine structure that survives in modern Istanbul. These walls withstood invading armies for over 1,000 years, resisting siege on more than 20 occasions until the Ottoman conquest in 1453 (for a vivid representation of this, visit the **Panorama 1453 History Museum**).

The walls encompass the old city in a great arc, stretching some 6.5 kilometres (four miles) from the Golden Horn to the Sea of Marmara. Together with the sea walls that ringed Constantinople, they constituted Europe's most extensive medieval fortifications.

A triumph of engineering, the walls comprise inner and outer ramparts with a terrace in between. The outer wall is two metres (seven feet) thick and around 8.5 metres (30 feet) high, with 96 towers overlooking the 20-metre (70-feet) moat. The five-metre (16-feet) wide inner wall is around 12 metres (40 feet) high and is studded with another 96 towers.

Large sections of the walls have been rebuilt in recent years, drawing criticism from scholars for inappropriate use of modern materials; nevertheless, the restored sections are undeniably impressive.

WALKING THE WALLS

There are several ways to get to the walls, depending on which part you want to visit. It's possible to walk the whole length, along both the inside and outside, although care should

be taken as some sections are deserted apart from vagrants. The best place to begin is on the Marmara coast at **Yedikule**. Take a bus from Eminönü (80) or Taksim (80T) or, for a more scenic ride, a suburban train from Sirkeci to Yedikule. The train passes under the ramparts of Topkapı Palace and winds in and out of what remains of the southern sea walls.

On the Marmara shore, the walls begin with the imposing **Marble Tower** on a promontory by the sea. It has served as both an imperial summer pavilion and as a prison. You can still see the chute through which executed corpses were dumped into the sea.

On the other side of the coastal road is the near-pristine **Gate of Christ**, the first of 11 fortified gates. On the northern side of the railway line is **Yedikule Fortress**, whose entrance is in the north-east wall.

From Yedikule to the **Belgrade Gate** (Belgrad Kapısı) and onwards to the **Silivri Gate** (Silivri Kapısı) it is possible to walk

---

INSIDE TRACK
PILGRIMS PROGRESS

The Church of **Surp Hreişdagbet** (*see left*) is famous for one thing: every 16 September, a miracle cure is reputedly bestowed on one member of the congregation. Muslims with birth defects or incurable illnesses from all over Turkey crowd into the church, hoping to be the lucky one.

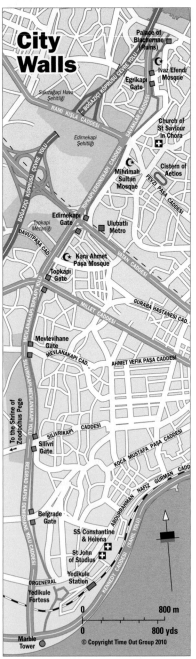

City Walls

along the top of the walls or on the terrace below. Near the Silivri Gate is the **Shrine of Zoodochus Pege** ('life-giving spring'). The **Mevlevihane Gate** bears several inscriptions, including one in Latin boasting how Constantine erected the final phase of the walls in 'less than two months'. Further north beyond Millet Caddesi stands **Topkapı Gate**, or Cannon Gate.

North of Topkapı, the walls descend into the Lycus river valley, now the six-lane Vatan Caddesi. This low-lying stretch was particularly difficult to defend, and it was here that the besieging Ottomans finally broke through in 1453. Over 500 years later, the battlements here remain in the worst state of repair. A little to the north, Mehmet the Conqueror made his triumphal entry into the city through **Edirnekapı** (Edirne Gate). A plaque on the south side of the gate commemorates the event.

Approaching the Golden Horn, the city walls end at the Byzantine **Blachernae Palace**.

Blachernae Palace
Anemas Zindanları
Ivaz Ağa Caddesi, Ayvansaray. Bus 5T, 99A.
Open 9am-7pm daily. **Admission** YTL2.
Map p87.
Constructed around AD 500, the palace was extended in the 11th and 12th centuries, by which time it had become the favoured imperial residence. It's now mostly in ruins. The best-preserved sections are the brick-and-marble three-storey façade, the Palace of the Porphyrogenitus, and five floors of tunnels and galleries below the Ahmet tea garden, which were cleared of rubble in 1999 for a film shoot and are rather awesome in their medieval splendour.

Shrine of Zoodochus Pege
Balıklı Kilise
Seyit Nizam Caddesi 3, Silivrikapı (0212 582 3081). Tram Seyitnizam. **Open** 9am-4pm daily.
Admission free.
Originally an ancient sanctuary of Artemis, the first church on this site was built over the 'life-giving spring' here in the early Byzantine era. Destroyed and rebuilt many times, the present structure dates from 1833. The shrine itself is a pool containing 'sacred' fish, said to have leapt into the spring from a monk's frying pan on hearing him say that a Turkish invasion of Constantinople was as likely as fish coming back to life.

Yedikule Fortress
Yedikule Müzesi
Yedikule Meydanı Sokak, Yedikule (0212 585 8933). Yedikule Station from Sirkeci or bus 80, 80T. **Open** 8am-5pm Mon,Tue, Thur-Sun.
Admission YTL5. **Map** p87.
Impressively restored, this Byzantine 'castle of the seven towers' was remodelled by the Ottomans. Its

Church of St Saviour in Chora. *See p64.*

western face incorporates the Golden Gate (now bricked up), a triumphal arch erected around AD 390. The vertiginous battlements offer wonderful views.

EYUP

Beyond the city walls, a mile west along the shore of the Golden Horn, is the village of Eyüp (pronounced 'eh-oop'). Historian John Freely describes its traditional image as a 'peaceful backwater devoted to religion and death'. These days, the place is on the verge of being absorbed by suburbia, but for the time being it retains both rural and spiritual qualities courtesy of two large, wooded hills above the village whose slopes are free of development by virtue of being devoted to the dead.

The area's popularity as a burial spot derives from the **Eyüp Mosque**, the holiest mosque in Istanbul. Its holy status comes from being the – reputed – burial place of Eyüp Ensari, companion and standard-bearer of the Prophet Muhammad. His tomb is adjacent to the mosque and has a gold-framed footprint of Muhammad and some fancy Iznik tiling. A constant trail of pilgrims queue to supplicate themselves before the cenotaph. A vast *külliye* (complex) surrounds the mosque, with most buildings dating to 1458 and the reign of Mehmet the Conqueror. Non-Muslims are welcome, but visitors should dress modestly. Headscarves are available for women.

Running north from Eyüp's main plaza is an attractive shopping street full of bakeries and interesting food shops. From the top end, flag a taxi and ride all the way up the hill to the

Pierre Loti Café (*see p142*), named after the 19th-century French romantic novelist who lived in Eyüp for several years. You'll be dropped at a modern tourist development with fantastic views from its terrace, but for something with more charm (and equally good views) follow the path down the hill to a modest tea shop with rickety tables beneath the trees.

Also in the area, the Ottoman Empire's first electricity plant, providing electricity for the city from 1911 to 1983, has now been converted into arts and cultural centre **Santralistanbul**.

Santralistanbul

Eski Silahtaraga Elektrik Santrali, Istanbul Bilgi Üniversitesi, Kazım Karabekir Caddesi 1, Silahtar (0212 311 5000, www.santralistanbul.com). Bus 44B. **Open** 10am-8pm daily. **Admission** YTL7. The decommissioned Silahtarağa Power Plant has been converted into one of Istanbul's most exciting multidisiplinary arts centres, opened in 2007. Old equipment has been retained and restored in two of the former engine rooms, which now form the Museum of Energy, and galleries house eclectic exhibitions, covering subjects including architecture and photography as well as painting. Concerts and festivals are also staged here. *See also p181.*

GETTING THERE

Take the 99 bus from Eminönü bus station to Eyüp. It's a 15-minute ride. Alternatively, you can catch a ferry from Eminönü, stopping off at Kasımpaşa, Fener and Balat en route. The first ferry departs Eminönü at 7.20am, with hourly departures until 8pm.

Beyoğlu & Beyond

The city shows its secular side.

Beyoğlu is new Istanbul. Secular
Istanbul. The Istanbul of bars and
restaurants, boutiques and artists'
ateliers. The area's central artery
is the ever-busy **Istiklal Caddesi**,
where the entire city goes to work,
shop and play, making it one of
the liveliest streets on earth. Here,
young Istanbullus go walking and
window shopping, dodging police on
segways and pausing to watch buskers.

Neighbourhoods such as **Çukurcuma**
and **Cihangir**, all accessible from
Istiklal Caddesi, are among the city's
most interesting: the former for antique shops and boutique hotels, the latter
for stylish cafés. And after a day wandering their steep, narrow streets, head
to buzzing **Nevizade Sokak** for dinner.

| Map p246-247 | Restaurants p125 |
| Hotels p103 | Cafés & Bars p142 |

INTRODUCING BEYOĞLU

Beyoğlu is an area with boundaries that are
hard to define, but for our purposes the area
includes everything up the hill from the Golden
Horn, all the way to **Taksim Square**.

Historically, the district went by two
different names: **Galata**, for the hillside just
north of the Golden Horn, and **Pera**, denoting
what's now the lower Istiklal Caddesi area.
Occupied by foreigners since Byzantine times,
these trading colonies across the water from
the walls of Constantinople proper were founded by
merchants from Genoa and Venice. After the
Ottoman conquest in the 15th century, it was to
Galata that the European powers sent their first
ambassadors. By the 17th century, Galata/Pera
was a substantial city in its own right, with a
multiethnic population known collectively as
Levantines. Among them were Italians and many
other communities, defined thus by a Turkish
chronicler of the time: 'The Greeks keep the
taverns; most of the Armenians are merchants or
money-changers; the Jews are the go-betweens in
amorous intrigues and their youths are the worst
of all the devotees of debauchery.'

OLD PERA TO NEW

It was during the 19th century that the area
acquired its present character. The increased
use of iron and brick, instead of the traditional
wood, made it feasible to construct buildings
that could survive the fires that regularly
ravaged the city.

After the foundation of the Republic in
the 1930s, the area officially became known
as Beyoğlu and blossomed with new
restaurants, theatres and concert halls. Older
residents still speak wistfully of never daring
to go to Istiklal Caddesi without a collar
and tie. However, World War II brought
a discriminatory wealth tax that hit the
Christians and Jews hard (Muslims were
exempt). As a result, many left for Greece,
America or Israel. In the 1950s and 1960s,
political tensions caused most of the remaining
Greeks to depart. In their place came a flood
of poor migrants from Anatolia, and Beyoğlu
gradually lost its cachet.

By the late 1980s, Istiklal Caddesi and
the area around it was run-down, sleazy,
even a little dangerous. That began to
change in late 1990 after the simple measure
was taken of turning it into a pedestrian
precinct. The subsequent transformation
has been swift and continues apace.
Passage Markiz on lower Istiklal Caddesi,
a five-storey complex of shops, bars and
restaurants, is a marked contrast to the cut-
rate clothing, music and bookshops often
associated with Beyoğlu.

SIGHTS

Galata Tower. *See p71.*

SIGHTS

The City's Narrator

Orhan Pamuk's books define the city.

Orhan Pamuk has never been shy about giving out his home address, even though the Nobel Prize-winning novelist received death threats and faced imprisonment after speaking out about two Turkish taboos: the Armenian genocide, which the government denies, and the ongoing persecution of the Kurdish minority in the south-east.

Some conservative critics argue that it was really his outspoken dissidence that won Pamuk the world's highest literary accolade. In fact, the prolific Pamuk has long been celebrated for his polished prose and Byzantine plot development, as well as his outspokenness. The Turkish authorities might have secretly been infuriated, but the public – or at least the left-leaning intelligensia – relished this international recognition for one of the nation's best-loved writers.

Pamuk's last name (which means 'cotton' in Turkish) appears above the front door of his childhood home, Pamuk Apartmanı in Nişantaşı, which he called 'the centre of my life' in his 2004 memoir, *Istanbul: Memories and the City*. The family lost the apartment due to dwindling fortunes when Pamuk was a child – a period that inspired his first novel, the three-generation saga *Cevdet Bey and his Sons* – but Pamuk eventually bought it

back. Nişantaşı had changed drastically in the interim, with corner shops giving way to designer boutiques. *The Black Book*, Pamuk's complex 1990 novel about a young lawyer searching for his missing wife, features a Nişantaşı apartment playfully called The-Heart-of-the-City, which is probably modelled on Pamuk's own.

Pamuk now has an office in cosmopolitan Cihangir, the neighbourhood where his family relocated after they lost their Nişantaşı home. Journalists often describe how the bay window in his office perfectly frames two minarets rising from the local mosque; they see a symbolism in the contrast between Pamuk's secular space and a religious world beyond. Pamuk rejects the idea: 'I hate both the concept and the reality of a Muslim world clashing with the West.'

Yet contradictions, if not clashes, are very much a part of Istanbul's identity, and identity is a major theme of Pamuk's writing. 'Istanbul's fate is my fate', he writes in *Memories and the City*. 'I am attached to this city because it has made me who I am.' Pamuk has done for Istanbul what Joyce did for Dublin: the mysteries of human nature lurk around every corner of the city in his brilliant evocations of his birthplace.

This is the place to pick up Cuban cigars, imported wines, Mont Blanc pens and tailored shirts. It's book-ended by an AFM cinema and Sony store just before Taksim Square. Two narrow lanes behind the Galatasaray Lycée also got a makeover a few years ago, when no fewer than 24 derelict buildings were converted into cafés, bars, galleries, restaurants and a boutique hotel, collectively marketed as the **Rue Française**.

The boom in trendy cafés, restaurants and bars has turned Beyoğlu, especially expat-heavy **Çihangir** into the city's hottest destination for many Turks and foreign residents. **Çukurcuma**, the shabby chic antique district nestled between Çihangir and Istiklal Caddesi, is also rapidly heating up. Meanwhile, Galata is already a lost cause for anyone looking for a property bargain. Even **Tarlabaşı**, to the north-west of Taksim Square, one of the city's grimmest, poorest areas, is becoming slowly gentrified.

GETTING AROUND

To get to Beyoğlu from Sultanahmet, simply take the tram across Galata Bridge and down to Kabataş. From there, the new metro will speed you up the hill to Taksim Square. Alternatively, get off the tram at Karaköy and take the one-stop, 19th-century Tünel, an underground funicular that clatters up the steep slope to Tünel Square at the southern end of Istiklal Caddesi. Running all the way between Tünel and Taksim, Istiklal Caddesi is the backbone of the whole area. All Beyoğlu destinations are reachable from here, or from Tünel or Taksim – for this reason we don't list transport for individual destinations in this chapter. An old-fashioned, and always busy, tram runs between Tünel and Taksim.

An alternative route is to walk down the hill and across the Galata Bridge, then take the funicular to Tünel, all of which takes a good 30-40 minutes.

GALATA

Echoing its mercantile origins, Galata remains almost completely commercial. There's even a row of ships' chandlers still trading along Yüzbaşı Sabahattin Evren Caddesi.

Central to the area's history, and easily the most distinctive landmark north of the Golden Horn, the conical-capped **Galata Tower** has spectacular views from its pinnacle.

Just downhill from the Galata Tower on **Camekan Sokak**, Beyoğlu Hospital is a large building with a vaguely gothic tower. It was built in 1904 as the British Seaman's Hospital, designed by Percy Adams, better known as architect of London University's Senate House. The tower afforded clear sightlines to incoming ships, allowing them to signal news of any illness on board, an important consideration in the days before ship-to-shore radio.

Around the corner on **Galata Kulesi Sokak** stands the former British consular prison: the Ottomans allowed favoured nations to imprison their own nationals, and this is where the British convicts were banged up.

On the same street is the former parish church of Galata's Maltese community, the **Dominican Church of St Peter and Paul**. It's a superb neo-classical affair built by the Swiss-born Fossati brothers, dating from 1841 but containing a number of much older relics.

From the 18th century onwards, it was the bankers of Galata who kept a declining Ottoman Empire afloat, albeit at ruinous rates of interest. **Voyvoda Caddesi**, at the bottom of Galata Kulesi Sokak, was the city's banking centre. The financial institutions have since moved out, but the street is still lined with imposing 19th-century mansions. Galata's long Jewish legacy is celebrated at the western end of Voyvoda Caddesi at the **Jewish Museum** (*see p78*), housed in the beautifully restored Zülfaris Synagogue.

South of Voyvoda, **Perşembe Pazarı Caddesi** boasts some fine 18th-century merchants' houses, while 100 metres (320 feet) west on Fütühat Sokak stands the only remaining Genoese church, now the **Arap Mosque**. Just to the north on Yanıkkapı Sokak are more Genoese remains in the shape of the **Burned Gate** (Yanık Kapı), the only remaining gate from the old Galata city walls. It still bears a plaque with St George's cross, symbol of Genoa.

FREE Arap Mosque
Arap Camii
Tersane Caddesi Galata Mahkemesi Sokak. **Open** 9am to dusk daily. **Admission** free. **Map** p246 L6.
Built between 1323 and 1337, and dedicated to St Dominic and St Paul, this was the largest of Constantinople's Latin churches. In the early 16th century, it was converted into a mosque to serve the Moorish exiles from Spain, which is possibly how it got its current name, the 'Arab mosque'. Despite extensive alterations, the design is clearly that of a typical medieval church, with apses and a belfry.

Galata Tower
Galata Kulesi
Galata Square (0212 293 8180, www.galata tower.net). **Open** 9am-8pm daily. **Admission** YTL10. **No credit cards. Map** p246 M5.
Originally named the Tower of Christ, this watch-tower was built in 1348 at the apex of fortified walls. After the Ottoman conquest, it was used to house prisoners of war and later became an observatory; during the 19th century, it was a look-out post to watch for the fires that frequently broke out in the city's largely wooden buildings. In the 1960s, the tower was restored and a horribly cheesy restaurant and nightclub were added. The restaurant, which remains, has improved somewhat. However, it's worth paying the rather hefty entrance fee to ascend to the 360-degree viewing gallery, with commanding views of the entire sprawling metropolis. *Photo p69.*
▶ *For more spectacular views, to be enjoyed with a drink in hand, see p143* **Up on the Roofs**.

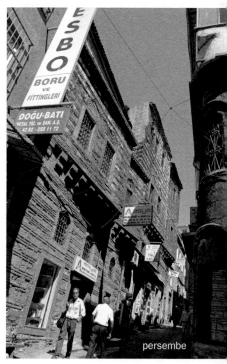

TÜNEL

Opened in 1876, the one-stop funicular that runs from Karaköy up to **Tünel Square** at the southern end of Istiklal Caddesi is, after London and New York's systems, the third-oldest passenger underground in the world.

Tünel, the area around the upper station, is currently in transition from shabby neglect to arty affluence. The proliferation of stylish businesses such as **KV Café** (*see p144*), occupying a 19th-century Italianate passage opposite the funicular, extends as far as Sofyalı Sokak, which is lined with fine bars and restaurants, such as **Sofyalı 9** (*see p134*).

Around the corner from Tünel Square, on Galip Dede Caddesi, is a dervish lodge, the **Galata Mevlevihanesi**, that also goes by the name of the Museum for Classical Literature.

Galata Mevlevihanesi

Galip Dede Caddesi 15 (0212 245 4141). **Open** 9.30am-4.30pm Mon, Wed-Sun. **Admission** YTL2. **Map** p248 M5.

This is the only institution in Istanbul dedicated to the Whirling Dervishes that is open to the public. A peaceful courtyard leads through to the octagonal *tekke* (lodge), a restored version of the 1491 original, which contains various musical instruments and beautifully illuminated Qu'rans. Also within the complex is the tomb of Galip Dede, a 17th-century Sufi poet after whom the street is named.

ISTIKLAL CADDESI

Originally known as Cadde-i Kebir (the high street), and later La Grande Rue de Pera, Istiklal Caddesi gained its present name,'Independence Street', soon after the founding of the Republic. In character, it remains resolutely pre-Republican, thanks to some wonderful early 20th-century architecture. The **Botter House** at nos.475-477 is an art nouveau masterpiece by Raimondo D'Aronco, built for Jean Botter, Sultan Abdül-Hamit's tailor. His daughter offered to leave the building to the city council, but the authorities refused to guarantee its preservation and since her death it has become dilapidated. A few doors up, at no.401, the **Mudo Pera** has an art nouveau interior of highly polished wood.

The street's churches are more restrained, often hidden from the street – the result of a restriction forbidding non-Muslim buildings from appearing on the skyline that held sway until the 19th century. The oldest is **St Mary Draperis** at no.429, a fairly humble building from 1789 that once served as the Austro-Hungarian embassy. This stretch of Istiklal is lined with former embassies, some still serving as consulates, others converted to new uses.

Botter House.

West of the main street is the lively neighbourhood of **Asmalımescit**, home of the city's low-rent art scene. The back streets are full of studios and galleries, as well as countless laid-back cafés, bars, and cheap eateries. Its western boundary is Meşrutiyet Caddesi, address of the swish **Pera Museum**, as well as the famed **Pera Palas Hotel** (*see p103*), with its Orient Express associations and celebrity-filled guest book.

★ Pera Museum
Pera Müzesi

141 Meşrutiyet Caddesi (0212 334 9900, www.peramuzesi.org.tr). **Open** 10am-7pm Tue-Sat; noon-6pm Sun. **Admission** YTL7; YTL5 concessions; free under-12s. **Credit** *café & gift shop only* MC, V. **Map** p248 M3.

In an 1893 building that formerly housed Istanbul's famous Bristol Hotel, this well-run museum combines permanent exhibitions, art galleries, an auditorium, shop and café. Exhibits range from the arcane – a collection of Anatolian weights and measures – to the decorative: Kütahya tiles and ceramics. There is a major collection of 17th- to 19th-century European Orientalist art. Also look out for work by Osman Hamdi, including his most famous painting, *The Tortoise Trainer*. The temporary exhibitions of big name artists, such as Botero, are usually excellent.

▶ *For more on contemporary art in Istanbul, see pp181-83.*

GALATASARY

Hardly big enough to constitute a district, Galatasaray refers to the streets surrounding the **Galatasaray Lycée** (high school), founded in 1868. The current building, which dates from 1907, includes the small **Galatasaray Museum**, dedicated to Istanbul's top football team, which started life at the school.

The slight widening of Istiklal in front of the Lycée is known as **Galatasaray Square**. Recently, it has become the venue for political demonstrations, notably by the 'Saturday Mothers', relatives of the many political activists who have 'disappeared' in the past 20 years. Such demonstrations are illegal, and the 'mothers' are often met by armoured riot police.

Beyoğlu nightlife once revolved around the *meyhanes* (Turkish tavernas) of **Çiçek Pasajı** (Flower Passage), an arcade in what was originally the Cité de Pera building (1876). Its heavily restored façade faces the school gates. These days, it's almost exclusively frequented by tourists, a beautiful setting for an over-priced, mediocre meal (*see p120* **Meyhanes & Meze**). The adjacent Balık Pazarı (**Fish Market**) is lined with shops fronted by wooden trays of piscine still-life on ice. On the east side of the market passage at no.24A, hidden behind big, black doors, is the Armenian Church of the Three Altars – it's rarely open, but take a look inside if you get the chance.

Just beyond the fish market is **Nevizade Sokak**, the liveliest and loudest dining spot in Istanbul, crammed full of pavement restaurants. On the west side are two old arcades, the **Avrupa Pasajı** and **Aslıhan Pasajı**: the former is a mini Grand Bazaar, the latter is full of second-hand book and record shops. The *pasajı* lead through to Hamalbaşı Caddesi and the **British Consulate** (1845), designed by Charles Barry, architect of the British Houses of Parliament, but completed by WS Smith in neo-Renaissance style. The building was bombed in November 2003, in an attack that killed British Consul-General Roger Short and over a dozen others.

The Çiçek Pasajı is the most famous of a host of covered arcades leading off Istiklal Caddesi. A few steps south is **Aznavur Pasajı**, with three floors of teenager's bedroom accessories (incense and candles, comics and clubwear).

Cukurcuma. *See p70.*

SIGHTS

A few steps north is **Atlas Pasajı**, which has more eccentric stock – anything from furry lampshades to tribal masks. (*See also p161* **Beyoğlu's Fashion Arcades**).

The side streets sloping south of Istiklal Caddesi at this point filter down into the appealingly decrepit district of **Çukurcuma**, whose twisting alleys are rife with fascinating antique and junk shops. Among the dealers of carved wedding chests and period furniture are some dim, dusty cubbyholes that offer delightfully off-beat finds such as a temporary London bus stop or cigarette tins painted with scenes of Old Stamboul. Hunt out shops such as **Works** (*see pXX*) and **Popcorn** (*see pXX*).

FREE Galatasaray Museum

Galatasaray Lisesi, Istiklal Caddesi 263 (0212 249 1100). **Open** 1.30-3pm Wed. **Admission** free. **Map** p248 N3.

The official museum of the Galatasaray School sports club, now more famous for its football team. Barely more than a trophy room, the exhibits include photographs, memorabilia and cases crammed with medals and prizes. Microscopic opening hours (which are not always reliable, either), make this one of the world's most difficult museums to visit.

▶ *Why not see a game too? For details, see p206.*

TAKSIM

If Çiçek Pasajı represents old Beyoğlu, the new Beyoğlu is focused on the stretch of Istiklal Caddesi north of Galatasaray, which stretches all the way to Taksim Square. Here, arcades, churches and period architecture give way to malls, mega-stores and multiplexes, as well as endless bars and cafés. Always thronging with shoppers, it feels like Istanbul's Oxford Street.

At its north end, Istiklal Caddesi runs into **Taksim Square**. The name comes from the stone reservoir (*taksim*) on the west side. Built

---

**INSIDE TRACK
MOSQUE CONTROVERSY**

Taksim Square, home to the Independence Monument, is a symbol of secular Turkey. In 1997, a short-lived Islamist government unveiled plans to build a huge mosque on an adjacent lot, but was forced to backtrack in the face of public uproar. Instead, the municipality decided on a YTL730,000 fountain for the site, complete with a blaring sound system and dancing lights.

---

in 1732 on the orders of Mahmut I, the *taksim* was at the end of a series of canals and aqueducts that brought water down from the Belgrad Forest (*see p212*). The centrepiece is the Independence Monument celebrating Kemal Atatürk's new republic.

Despite such picturesque associations, the giant square is one of the world's uglier plazas – little more than a snarled-up transport hub with a small park attached. Even so, the square is generally regarded as the heart of modern Istanbul and symbol of the secular Republic.

BEYOND BEYOĞLU
Harbiye & Şişli

North of Taksim, there is little to capture the visitor's imagination in the residential neighbourhoods of Harbiye and Şişli, save for a couple of museums celebrating Turkey's military conquests and republican ideals. Şişli however, could be the next neighbourhood to become trendy, with shops, restaurants and boutique hotels opening.

★ FREE Atatürk Museum
Atatürk Müzesi

Halaskargazi Caddesi 250, Şişli (0212 240 6319). Bus 46H. Metro Osmanbey. **Open** 9am-4pm Wed, Fri-Sun. **Admission** free.

In northern Şişli, a short bus ride from Taksim Square, is a candy-pink Ottoman house in which Mustafa Kemal once stayed. It now contains three floors of memorabilia of the great Atatürk, from his astrakhan hat to his silk underwear. There's even a wine-stained tablecloth on which he bashed out the new Turkish alphabet over a picnic lunch in 1928. The top floor holds a large collection of propaganda paintings from the War of Independence, depicting scenes of Greek brutality, with the flag of the perfidious British occasionally fluttering in the background.

★ Military Museum
Askeri Müze ve Kültür Sitesi

Vali Konağı Caddesi, Harbiye (0212 233 2720). Bus 46H, 46KY, 69YM/Metro Osmanbey. **Open** 9am-4.30pm Wed-Sun. **Admission** YTL3. **No credit cards**.

The sheer size and wealth of this place says as much about the military's continued clout in Turkey as it does about the country's bloody history. For many years, this was one of the few national museums to enjoy substantial funding, so the collection is nothing if not comprehensive. However, all but the most hardened military enthusiasts will suffer serious battle fatigue long before the interminable procession of rooms and corridors comes to an end. Definitely worth seeing are the gloriously colourful

The Cult of Atatürk

The face of the New Republic's founder is still everywhere in the city.

He's the centre of a personality cult that makes those once surrounding Stalin and Mao Tse Tung look shy. What's more, he's dead and nobody is being forced to put up his posters, erect statues, parrot his slogans, buy the mug, the clock, the teapot, the T-shirt. But masses of people still do. More than 70 years after his death, the image of Mustafa Kemal – better known as Atatürk – remains ubiquitous, from his portrait on Turkish banknotes to his profile carved into hillsides. His name honours airports and stadiums, boulevards and bridges. Back in the 1920s it was seriously proposed that Istanbul be renamed Gazi Mustafa Kemal. In 1999, a coordinated internet voting campaign almost put him on the front cover of *Time* magazine as the readers' choice of 'Man of the Century', until the ploy was scuppered by a Greek and Armenian counter-action.

Many Turks will privately admit that they find the iconography excessive but accept it as a necessary counter to the threat of political Islam. Fervent 'Kemalists' (as the secular nationalist proponents of Atatürk are known) often give the impression that the only thing standing between Turkey and the plunge into Iranian-style Islamic revolution is the image of the 'Father of the Turks' and the slogans surrounding him.

What is beyond debate is Atatürk's status as one of the most influential political figures of the 20th century, not to say a military commander of true genius. His effect on the outcome of the allied landings at Gallipoli in World War I can best be summed up in the official British army history: 'Seldom in history can the exertions of a single divisional commander have exercised so profound an influence not only on the course of a battle but on the destiny of a nation.'

Each year Atatürk is commemorated at 9.05am on 10 November – the anniversary of his death. Sirens blare out across the country signalling a minute's silence. People stand motionless, traffic pulls over and drivers get out to stand. It is a moving, not to say eerie experience, and one that speaks far more eloquently than the kitsch memorabilia.

campaign pavilions of the Ottoman sultans, created from embroidered silk and cotton. Upstairs, in the 20th-century section, there's a decent display dealing with the 1915 Gallipoli campaign, plus some bizarre furniture constructed out of bayonets and gun parts. For sheer morbidity, nothing beats the car in which the Grand Vizier Mahmut Şevket Paşa was assassinated while travelling along Divan Yolu in 1913. The number of bullet holes shows that the gunmen left little to chance.

▶ *For more military history, visit Topkapı Palace; see p45.*

Hasköy

Heading along the banks of the Golden Horn from Beyoğlu, the coastal road is lined with increasingly shabby houses and scruffy little parks where local families hang out. School buses regularly make the journey to Hasköy to visit the **Rahmi M Koç Museum**. This unusual transport museum is worth the ride if you have car-crazy kids with you. If you don't fancy taking a bus, a taxi from Eminönü or Taksim Square takes around 15 minutes. The splendidly eccentric **Miniaturk** (*see p177*) is only a couple of miles further down the coast.

★ Rahmi M Koç Museum

Rahmi M Koç Müzesi
Hasköy Caddesi 27, Hasköy (0212 369 6600, www.rmk-museum.org.tr). Bus 47, 54HM, 54HT. **Open** 10am-5pm Tue-Fri; 10am-7pm Sat, Sun. **Admission** YTL10. *Submarine* YTL4. **No credit cards**.
Founded by the eponymous industrialist, this converted 18th-century foundry on the waterfront is a showcase for the assorted obsessions of one of the wealthiest men in Turkey. The collection includes halls after hall of antique trains, trams, boats and planes. There's even a submarine moored in the Golden Horn. Many exhibits have moving parts that can be manually activated by buttons or levers; there's a walk-on ship's bridge with a wheel, sonar machines and alarm bells. Try to visit on a Saturday or Sunday, when all the working models are in action.

Across the road from the main complex, a domed workshop makes a quaint setting for more industrial curios including the forward section of a US airforce bomber shot down in 1943 and recovered from the seabed off Turkey's coast some 50 years later. Everything is fully labelled in English.

▶ *The museum has two top-class eateries in the pricy Café du Levant, modelled after an old-fashioned Parisian bistro, and Halat (see p136), a fish restaurant with tables on the wharf.*

The Bosphorus Villages

Life on the waterfront.

Running along the banks of one of the world's busiest waterways, a chain of waterfront parks, palaces and *yalıs* stretches from the **Galata Bridge** as far as the fortress of **Rumeli Hisarı**.

Karaköy has been a port since Byzantine times, when the north shore of the Golden Horn was a separate settlement – Galata – distinct from the rest of Constantinople. Much of the maritime traffic has since moved out and the area is being cleaned up, but it still has several monuments reflecting its grittier past. Today, the **Istanbul Modern** gallery, housed in a former warehouse and with collections tracing the development of contemporary Turkish art, is the area's main draw for visitors.

Further up the Bosphorus, the grandiose **Dohlmabahçe Palace** dominates the busy waterfront at **Beşiktaş**, while affluent **Ortaköy** and **Bebek** are known for their waterside restaurants and cafés.

Map p247	**Restaurants** p137
Hotels p115	**Cafés & Bars** p150

GETTING AROUND

Several buses run the route, including 22, 22R and 25E from Eminönü. The metro line (from Taksim) or the new tram (from Eminönü) to Kabataş also place you at a convenient point on the coastal road. A more relaxed way of travelling is to take one of the half-hourly ferry services from Eminönü, stopping at Beşiktaş, Ortaköy and Bebek. Unfortunately, these commuter services only run in the mornings (around 7-10am) and evenings (around 4-8pm).

KARAKÖY

Karaköy has a refreshingly diverse array of religious monuments. One street inland from the harbour, on Kemankeş Caddesi, is the district's oldest building, the Yeraltı Mosque. Not far from here is the **Jewish Museum**, housed in a restored synagogue, and further inland are a couple of curious churches. The **Russian Orthodox Church of St Andrea** on Balyoz Sokak is on the top floor of what

appears to be a 19th-century apartment building, but was actually built as a monastery. The monks have long gone, but the church has experienced a revival thanks to the Russian tourists who have arrived en masse since the collapse of the Soviet Union. Around the corner is the **Church of St Panagia**, belonging to the tiny Turkish Orthodox sect, which broke away from the Greek church in the 1920s. Mass here is said in the Karamanlı Turkish dialect.

North along **Kemeraltı Caddesi**, the road passes in the shadow of the slightly sinister **Tophane**. A former Ottoman cannon foundry built during the reign of Mehmet the Conqueror, the current building, with its distinctive row of ventilation towers, only dates to 1803. Recently renovated, it's now used as an occasional arts and exhibition centre.

Opposite are two impressive mosques. **Kılıç Ali Paşa Mosque** is named after a famed admiral who was born in Calabria, captured by pirates, and then, after gaining his freedom, entered Süleyman's navy and rose to become the commander of the entire Ottoman fleet. The mosque was built in 1580 by the celebrated architect Sinan, who was by this time in his 90s. A little further north is **Nusretiye Mosque**, built in the late 1820s in baroque style by Kikor Balyan, an Armenian architect whose sons would later design the nearby **Dolmabahçe Palace**. Behind the mosque is a row of cafés specialising in narghiles (*see p151* **Hubbly Bubbly**).

The main road continues past the port. Just up the hill is **Inönü Stadium**, home of Beşiktaş football club (*see p205*). Towering over the stadium is the monstrous, high-rise Ritz-Carlton hotel. High-rollers book suites overlooking the stadium when there's a big match on.

★ Istanbul Modern

Meclis-i Mebusan Caddesi, Liman Işletmeleri Sahası, Antrepo No.4 (0212 334 7300, www.istanbulmodern.org). Tram Karaköy. **Open** 10am-6pm Tue, Wed, Fri-Sun; 10am-8pm Thur. **Admission** YTL8; YTL3 reductions. Free for all Thur. **Credit** MC, V.
Created as Turkey's equivalent of London's Tate Modern, Istanbul Modern has grown comfortably into its role since opening in 2004. Housed in a former customs warehouse on the waterfront in Karaköy, the two-storey museum has 8,000 square metres of exhibition space. The permanent collection follows the transformation of Turkish art since the foundation of the Academy of Fine Arts in 1893 and reflects Turkey's shifting economic and political landscape.

On entering the unremarkable building, you'll see a large, site-specific piece from the eighth Biennial – a shattered glass staircase hung from steel chains, created by Monica Bonvicini. Likewise, Richard Wentworth's installation of hundreds of books suspended over the library, for the Centre of Gravity exhibition, proved so popular that it stayed.

The Lower Floor Galleries house temporary exhibitions. These have introduced major international artists, including Anish Kapoor, Juan Munoz and William Kentridge, to a local audience. However, Turkish artists are getting more space than they have in the past with shows from the likes of photographer Pınar Yolaç and painter Burhan Uygur.

One of the museum's galleries is dedicated exclusively to photography; another is devoted to video art. The in-house cinema screens an interesting mix of Turkish and international art-house movies and experimental shorts.

SIGHTS

Jewish Museum. *See p78.*

The museum's restaurant has proved a big hit in its own right. Stunning views across the Bosphorus to the minarets of Sultanahmet and out to the Marmara Sea just about justify bumped-up prices for decent bistro fare.

▶ *For more contemporary art galleries, see pp181-83.*

★ Jewish Museum

Türk Musevileri Müzesi
Karaköy Meydanı, Perçemli Sokak (0212 292 6333, www.muze500.com). Tram Karaköy.
Open 10am-4pm Mon-Thur, 10am-2pm Fri, Sun. **Admission** YTL7. **No credit cards**. **Map** p292 M6.
Housed in the immaculately restored Zülfaris Synagogue (in existence since 1671, but dating in its present form to the early 19th century), a collection of well-presented objects, documents, photographs and storyboards (in English) tells the story of over 500 years of Jewish presence in Turkey. The Jews first arrived in the Ottoman Empire fleeing the pogroms of Christian Europe. They have made significant contributions to Istanbul life, particularly in the financial sector. An ethnography section presents costumes and accessories related to circumcision ceremonies, dowries and weddings. *Photo p77.*

FREE Yeraltı Mosque

Yeraltı Camii
Kemankeş Cadessi. Tram Karaköy. **Open** varies. **Admission** free. **Map** p292 N6.
Often called the Underground Mosque because it's buried beneath a 19th-century wooden mansion, the low, vaulted interior of the Yeraltı Mosque is supported by 54 columns, built on the remains of the Byzantine castle of Galata, which guarded the entrance to the Golden Horn. From here, a great chain was stretched across the waterway, blocking access to enemy ships in times of siege. The upper part of the castle was demolished following the Ottoman conquest, and the remaining lower floor – formerly a prison – was converted to a mosque in 1757.

BEŞİKTAŞ

A celebration of just about everything awful about 19th-century European design, the excessively opulent **Dohlmabaçe Palace** is on most tour group itineraries. Many of its dubious treasures are now housed in the **Depot Museum** next door. Passing the palace, the road is flanked by colonnades of plane trees leading to **Beşiktaş**, an unsightly concrete shopping and transport hub with a statue of Atatürk for a centrepiece. It wasn't always this way: this used to be a quiet suburb of dignified terraced houses and plush mansions. The last remaining terrace is on **Spor Caddesi**, built to house the staff of Dolmabahçe Palace.

Despite having no real harbour, Beşiktaş has strong nautical connections, revealed in the **Naval Museum** beside the ferry terminal. Nearby is the tomb and statue of Hayrettin Paşa, the Ottoman admiral known as Barbarossa. His tomb is only open to visitors on 4 April and 1 July. Nearby **Mimar Sinan University Museum of Fine Arts** houses Turkish 19th- and 20th-century painting.

The Depot Museum

Depo-Müze
Dolmabahçe Caddesi, Dolmabahçe Palace, (0212 236 9000 ext 1339). Bus 25E, 28, 40, 56. **Open** 9am-5pm Tue-Sun. **Admission** YTL2. **No credit cards**. **Map** p293 R2.
Opened in 2004 to commemorate the 150th birthday of Dolmabahçe Palace next door, this rambling collection of pieces salvaged from the palace's storage rooms is housed in what used to be the imperial kitchens. Everything from crystal tumblers to copper cauldrons, samovars to silver candlesticks, French vases to Japanese porcelains are stuffed into this late Ottoman time warp. Many of these antiques have been rescued from the palace cellars, which have regularly flooded over the last few decades.

Dolmabahçe Palace

Dolmabahçe Sarayı
Dolmabahçe Caddesi (0212 236 9000). **Open** *May-Oct* 9am-4pm Tue, Wed, Fri-Sun. *Nov-Apr* 9am-3pm Tue, Wed, Fri-Sun. **Admission** YTL15. *Harem* YTL10. **Credit** MC, V. **Map** p293 R2.
Irrefutable evidence of an empire on its last legs, Dolmabahçe Palace was built for Abdül Mecit by Karabet Balyan and his son Nikoğos. It was completed in 1855, whereupon the sultan and his household moved in, abandoning Topkapı Palace, which had been the imperial residence for four centuries. The outside is overwrought enough – though the façade of white marble is striking when viewed from the water – but it's trumped by the interior, the work of French decorator Sechan, who worked on the Paris Opera. 'Highlights' are the 36m-high throne room with its four-tonne crystal chandelier (a gift from Queen Victoria), the alabaster baths, and a 'crystal staircase' that wouldn't look out of place in Las Vegas. Atatürk died in Dolmabahçe in 1938,

Dolmabahçe Palace.

Istanbul on Foot Karaköy to Dolmabahçe

Churches, mosques and an Ottoman palace.

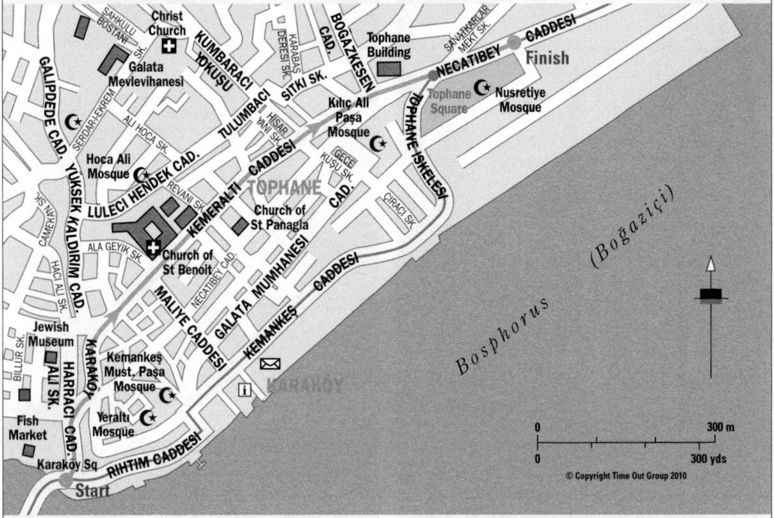

To explore this part of the city, begin at Karaköy Square. Head up busy Haracı Caddesi, then on to Karaköy Caddesi before taking a detour right on to Necatibey Caddesi, and right again to Tulumba Sokak. At the bottom of the street, at the corner of Kemankes Caddesi, one road back from the shore, is the underground **Yeraltı Mosque** (*see p78*). Buried beneath a 19th-century wooden house, the mosque has been described by ohn Freeley, the most eminent Istanbul historian writing in English, as a 'strange and sinister place'.

From the ragged shore lined with fish restaurants, private and municipal ferries run back and forth across the Bosphorus from **Karakoy Iskele**. It was around this spot that Byzantine emperors stretched a chain across the Golden Horn to keep enemy ships from accessing the city's waterways.

Bustling Karaköy Caddesi is a warren of kiosks selling all manner of electronics. These slip away as the street ascends uphill to Galata. The road forks to the right, becoming Kemeraltı Caddesi, home to several churches. **St Benoit** is on the left, and **St Gregory** is further down on the right.

On the left, past Bogazkesen Caddesi, as it intersects with Necatibey Caddesi, lies the last incarnation of a series of Ottoman munitions foundries that occupied the **Tophane** site. This boxy number, built by Selim III in 1803, with eight domes and scrub growing on the roof, now hosts wedding receptions and art exhibitions.

On the right is the baroque **Nusretiye Mosque**. The Balyans, a family of Armenian architects active in Istanbul during the 18th and 19th centuries, built both the mosque and Dolmabahçe Palace up the road. Past the mosque, cafés set back in the park appeal to those in need of a narghile fix. Slump into a bean-bag and have a smoke, or keep walking.

You are now in a convenient spot to take the new tram from Tophane a couple of stops to Kabataş. From here, it's not far along the coastal road to the neo-baroque fantasy that is **Dolmabahçe Palace** (*see p78*), which stretches the length of nearly three football pitches along the water's edge. In 1453, Mehmed the Conqueror, chose this spot – then a small inlet – to haul 70 ships up into Beyoğlu using mules, and down to the Golden Horn, thus avoiding the chain slung across the straits by the Byzantines.

although his apartment is not on the tour itinerary. Visitors are only allowed into the palace, which is still used for state functions, in guided groups.

▶ *If you fancy staying in similar opulence, try the Kempinski Çırağan Palace (p115). The suites are housed in an annexe of Dolmabahçe Palace.*

FREE Mimar Sinan University Museum of Fine Arts

Mimar Sinan Üniversitesi Istanbul Resim ve Heykel Müzesi
Barbaros Hayrettin Paşa Iskelesi Sokak, off Beşiktaş Caddesi (0212 261 4299). Bus 25E, 28, 40, 56. **Open** 10am-4.30pm Mon-Fri. **Admission** free.
The decrepit state of this poorly signposted museum, housed in a waterside mansion, suggests that few visitors find their way here. Shame, because the collection of Turkish art on display in the high-ceilinged halls includes some fine pieces. It all dates from the mid 19th- to mid 20th- century, mostly Orientalist in style. Look out for several notable works by Osman Hamdi Bey, one-time director of the Archaeology Museum. To find the museum, walk down the side-street south of the Naval Museum, pass through the gateway with the armed guard, cross the waterfront plaza and turn right at the end; it's the building on the left.

★ Naval Museum

Deniz Müzesi
Barbaros Hayrettin Paşa Iskelesi Sokak, off Beşiktaş Caddesi (0212 327 4345). Bus 25E, 28, 40, 56. **Open** 9am-5pm Wed-Sun. **Admission** YTL4. **No credit cards.**
Announced by a roadside garden full of cannons, the museum is housed in two separate buildings on the Bosphorus. The larger building holds an extensive collection of model ships, mastheads and oil paintings, along with plenty of booty captured from British and French warships sunk during the abortive Dardanelles campaign of World War I. Upstairs are commemorative plaques to Turkish sailors killed on duty from 1319 to the Cyprus war of 1974, as well as the battle flag of Barbarossa, the notorious 16th-century pirate. Downstairs is just about everything that wasn't nailed down on Atatürk's yacht, the *Savarona*, including a set of silver toothpicks.

The smaller building houses an impressive collection of Ottoman caiques. At one time, these elegant vessels were as symbolic of the city as the gondola is to Venice. Back then, boats rivalled the horse and carriage as the common mode of transport. The sultans' caiques were rowed by Bostancı, an imperial naval unit that doubled as palace gardeners. The largest caique on display, a 1648 model, required some 144 Bostancı to power it along. The oarsmen were apparently required to bark like dogs as they rowed, so that they wouldn't overhear the sultan's conversations. An enterprising Black Sea firm has

Yıldız Chalet Museum. *See p82.*

made modern replicas that convey tourists to the city's smarter hotels, although, regrettably, the banks of oarsmen have now been replaced by an outboard motor.
▶ *For more on military history, visit the Military Museum in Harbiye; see p74.*

YILDIZ

To the north-west of Beşiktaş are the extensive grounds of **Yıldız Palace**, a sprawling complex of buildings of which only a small part is open to the public. On Yıldız Caddesi is one of the most striking monuments in the city, the **Şeyh Zafir Complex**. Comprising a tomb, library and fountain, it commemorates an Islamic sheikh but is designed in art nouveau style by Italian architect Raimondo D'Aronco.

INSIDE TRACK
EYE OF ISTANBUL

Magnum photographer Ara Güler is known as the 'Eye of Istanbul'. He began photographing the city in the 1950s, and many of his moody black and white photos focus on life on and along the Bosphorus. He still lives in Galata, above Kafe Ara (*see p147*), a bar that bears his name. His work can be seen at www.araguler.com.tr.

SIGHTS

A little further along, a side road leads off Yıldız Caddesi into **Yıldız Park**, formerly the grounds of **Yıldız Palace** and now a pleasantly overgrown hillside forest. Sadly, the small tea house built for Abdül Hamit, of which he was the sole patron, is long gone, but there are several former imperial pavilions, including the Şale Pavilion, a D'Aronco-designed building set in private gardens at the top of the park, now open to the public as the **Yıldız Chalet Museum**. While wandering through the park, you might want to stop at the **Imperial Porcelain Factory** and the **Malta Köşkü**, an 1870 pavilion in which Sultan Abül Hamit had his brother Murad imprisoned. It now makes an attractive café-restaurant, with a terrace overlooking the Bosphorus.

Across from the park entrance, between Yıldız Caddesi and the Bosphorus, is what's left of the **Çırağan Palace**. Last of the Ottoman imperial palaces, it was built for Abdül Aziz who died there (probably murdered) in 1876, two years after it was completed. In 1908, it was restored to house the Ottoman parliament; but it burnt down in 1910 and remained a shell until it was rebuilt as a hotel by the Kempinski chain, *see p115*.

Imperial Porcelain Factory

Yıldız Parkı içi (0212 260 2370). Bus 25E, 28, 40, 56. **Open** 9am-noon, 1-6pm Mon-Fri. **Admission** YTL1. **No credit cards**.
Sultan Abdulhamid II established the Yıldız Porcelain Factory in 1890 at the suggestion of the French ambassador Paul Cambon, to provide a ready supply of fancy china for the Ottoman palace. Today, it mass-produces rather cheesy souvenirs in another splendid building designed by the prolific Italian architect Raimondo D'Aronco.

Yıldız Chalet Museum

Yıldız Şale Müzesi
Palanga Caddesi 23, Yıldız Parkı (0212 259 8977). Bus 25E, 28, 40, 56. **Open** 9am-5pm Tue, Wed, Fri-Sun. **Admission** YTL4 Tue, Wed; YTL2 Fri-Sun. **No credit cards**.
The obligatory tour takes you down long, dark, musty corridors leading to 60 rooms furnished with ornate furniture. The Grand Salon, a massive court chamber, now stands empty but for a line of chairs that highlight the sense of lost grandeur. *Photo p81*.

★ Yıldız Palace

Yıldız Sarayı
Yıldız Caddesi (0212 258 3080). Bus 25E, 28, 40, 56. **Open** 9am-4pm Tue-Sun. **Admission** YTL2. **No credit cards**.
Most of the palace dates from the late 19th century, when the paranoid Sultan Abül Hamit II ('Abdül the Damned') abandoned waterfront Dolmabahçe for fear of attack by foreign warships. The sultan was so fearful for his safety that no architect was allowed

to see the complete plans for the new palace, and the labourers who built it were forbiden to communicate. Only the sultan knew the location of all the secret passages. He never slept in the same suite two nights running and placed large objects in the palatial passageways to obstruct any would-be assassins. The rooms open to visitors contain porcelain, furniture and some of Abdül Hamit's possessions, including the carpentry set he used to while away his time after he was deposed in 1908.

ORTAKÖY

Long a thriving social and commercial centre, the coastal area of Ortaköy is a refuge from the crush of the inner city. In the 17th century, Ottoman chronicler Evliya Çelebi noted with a hint of disdain, 'The place is full of infidels and Jews; there are 200 shops, of which a great number are taverns.'

Today, this appealing neighbourhood's narrow, cobbled streets are closed to traffic, its low-rise houses painted in pastel shades. There's a pretty waterfront plaza overlooked by the **Mecidiye Mosque**. Set dramatically on a promontory jutting into the strait, the mosque was built for Sultan Abdül Mecit in 1854 by Nikoğos Balyan, the architect responsible for the Dolmabahçe. Happily, the mosque avoids the vulgarity of the palace; this is one of the most attractive baroque buildings in Istanbul.

Mecidiye Mosque, Ortaköy.

SIGHTS

Beside the ferry landing, waterfront **Ortaköy Square** (Iskele Meydanı) is fringed by open-air cafés and restaurants. The tight nexus of streets inland from the square has been gentrified and filled with gift shops. At weekends, it's the venue for a popular **craft market**.

Nearby are the twin domes of a 16th-century hamam, yet another work by Sinan. Recently restored, it now houses a restaurant.

North of Ortaköy, the road passes under the kilometre-long **Atatürk Bridge**, finished just in time for the Turkish Republic's 50th birthday celebrations in 1973. Beyond the bridge is a string of exclusive nightspots, where Istanbul's socialites and celebrities strut their stuff (*see p201* **Bosphorus Bling**).

ARNAVUTKÖY

Arnavutköy, the 'Albanian Village', is far more low-key than Ortaköy, and has yet to be spoiled by an influx of venture capital. In Ottoman times, the local population was not Albanian, as the name would imply, but predominantly Greek and Armenian. It's overwhelmingly Turkish today, but a small community of Greeks still lives around here, celebrating mass at the Orthodox **Church of Taxiarchs** in the backstreets. Next to the church is a small chapel containing a sacred spring, or *ayazma*, which is down some marble stairs.

Arnavutköy's picturesque wooden *yalıs* overlook the shore, although the traffic sweeping past detracts from the effect. Many local businesses occupy these 19th-century houses with lace-like trim, pulpit balconies and elaborate ornamentation. As more of them are renovated, Arnavutköy is rapidly taking on a fairytale appearance. .

Supposedly enjoying official protection, this architectural heritage has ironically long been under threat from the government itself – plans for a third Bosphorus bridge threatened to rip apart the neighbourhood with great concrete supports. However, opposition from local residents has swayed officials towards a less contentious tunnel project.

BEBEK

Just north of Arnavutköy, a small white light-house marks **Akıntı Burnu**, a promontory jutting out into the straits, named after the strong current that swirls and eddies past the shore. It's a favourite spot for local fishermen who cast out from the shore, but also trawl from rickety wooden boats, battling against a flow so brisk that in days gone by sailing ships often had to be towed around the point by porters.

Bebek.

From Akıntı Burnu it's a ten-minute stroll along a broad, seaside promenade to the next 'village', Bebek. Ranged around a bay backed by wooded hills, this attractive, affluent suburb has the air of a Hampstead-on-Sea, with some pricey cafés and restaurants.

Beside the small waterfront park is a handsome, white art nouveau mansion. Still in service as the (newly refurbished) **Egyptian Consulate**, it was designed by D'Aronco, who would be mightily aggrieved by its cluster of satellite dishes.

At the top end of the park is Bebek's tiny ferry station and an equally diminutive brown stone mosque dating from 1912. Next door, **Bebek Café** is as basic as they come, but it's a pleasant, unaffected place for a coffee. Round the corner, the high street is a bit of a let-down, lined with modern buildings, including a prominent Starbucks, and choked by traffic. Bill Gates was spotted eating breakfast in these parts. Among the shops selling silk ties and antiques is **Meşhur Bebek Badem Ezmesi**, specialising in marzipan, which is beautifully displayed in hardwood cabinets.

Follow any of the streets leading uphill off the high street and almost immediately you're surrounded by greenery and wooden terraces. Head up **Hamam Sokak** opposite the park and after a few minutes' walk you'll find **Café de Pera**, a welcoming place to take a break.

SIGHTS

From Bebek, a wooden promenade winds north towards the fortress of **Rumeli Hisarı**, a ten- to 15-minute walk. Before the castle, a sign points up a steep road beside the **Kayalar Mezarlığı**, one of Istanbul's oldest Muslim cemeteries, to the **Aşıyan Museum**.

FREE Aşıyan Museum

Aşıyan Müzesi
Aşıyan Yolu (0212 263 6986). Bus 25E, 40.
Open 9am-4pm Tue-Sat. **Admission** free.
This attractive wooden mansion was the retreat of celebrated poet Tevfik Fikret (1867-1915), who built it himself. Although the literary exhibits don't amount to much, the views from the upper-storey balconies are wonderful.

RUMELI HISARI

Rounding the headland north of Bebek brings you face to face with the imposing fortress of **Rumeli Hisarı** and below it, the suburb of the same name. The sleepy village is an unlikely setting for the **Fatih Mehmet Bridge**, which at 1,096 metres (3,634 feet) is one of the longest suspension bridges in the world. Completed in 1988, it spans the straits at the same point where King Darius of Persia crossed with his army via a pontoon bridge in 512 BC.

Just before the small central square of the village is another oddity, **Edwards of Hisar**, an upper-crust tailor more suited to Savile Row.

Two bus stops north of Rumeli Hisarı is **Emirgan**, famous for its tulip gardens (best visited in late April or early May), and home to the **Sakıp Sabancı Museum** and the excellent **Müzedechanga** (*see p137*) restaurant and café. The museum is about 100 metres beyond the pencil-sharp minaret of the **Hamidiye Mosque**.

★ Rumeli Hisarı Fortress

Rumeli Hisarı Müzesi
Yahya Kemal Caddesi (0212 263 5305). Bus 25E, 40. **Open** 9am-4.30pm Tue-Mon. **Admission** YTL2. **No credit cards**.
Consisting of three huge towers joined by crenellated defensive walls, the fortress was raised in a hurry as part of Mehmet II's master plan to capture Constantinople. Facing the 14th-century castle of Anadolu Hisarı (already in Ottoman hands) across the Bosphorus' narrowest stretch, Rumeli Hisarı was designed to cut maritime supply lines and isolate Constantinople from its allies. For this, it earned itself the evocative nickname Boğazkesen, the 'Throat-Cutter'. Designed by the sultan himself, work was completed in August 1452, just four months after it commenced. Garrisoned by Janissaries and bristling with cannon, Rumeli Hisarı proved its effectiveness immediately: a Venetian merchant vessel that attempted to run the blockade was promptly sunk.

Having helped secure the Ottoman conquest of Constantinople, the castle lost its military importance and was downgraded to a prison. The castle was restored by the government in 1953. Today, visitors are free to clamber around the walls, enacting childhood fantasies. An open-air theatre in the courtyard hosts popular musical events throughout the summer.

★ Sakıp Sabancı Museum

Istinye Caddesi 22, Emirgan (0212 277 2200, http://muze.sabanciuniv.edu). Bus 22, 22RV, 25E. **Open** 10am-6pm Tue- Sun; 10am-10pm Wed. **Admission** YTL10, YTL3 concessions. **Credit** MC, V.
Owned by one of Turkey's wealthiest businessmen, this museum is housed in a fabulous villa right on the shores of the Bosphorus, built for Egyptian royalty in the 1920s. The steeply sloping lawns are scattered with stone treasures on loan from the Archaeology Museum. Inside are two floors of exceptionally fine ceramics, with informative English texts. It's particularly strong for Ottoman calligraphy and illumination. A modern extension in glass, steel and marble holds a collection of 19th- and 20th-century Turkish art that unfortunately fails to do justice to its coolly elegant surroundings: the paintings play second fiddle to the panoramic views. However, the museum occasionally hosts major touring exhibitions by the likes of Picasso and Rodin, which pull in big crowds.
► *There's an excellent café and restaurant, Müzedechanga (see p137), in the building, with fabulous views over the Bosphorus.*

Rumeli Hisarı.

The Asian Shore

Meet Istanbul's Anatolian side.

It's not like those 'Welcome to Asia' signs beside the Bosphorus Bridge go unnoticed, but some Istanbullus' eyes might glaze over if you mention that over-used tourist board strapline, 'One City – Two Continents'. Historically, 'Stamboul' only comprised the area within the Byzantine Walls on the European side. Only in the last 20 years have the previously unconnected villages of the Asian shore coalesced into the sprawl of suburbs that make up Asian Istanbul.

The two main centres of **Üsküdar** and **Kadıköy** offer shopping and eating, with a regional slant and a sprinkling of historic sights. North of Üsküdar, the settlements still resemble the quiet fishing villages they they so recently were – only with the odd five-star hotel and upmarket restaurant.

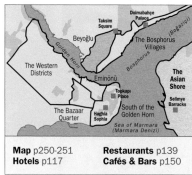

Map p250-251	**Restaurants** p139
Hotels p117	**Cafés & Bars** p150

INTRODUCING THE ASIAN SHORE

While most sights of interest date from the past 100-odd years, there's a long history of human habitation here. The oldest settlement in the Istanbul metropolitan area, Chalcedon, was discovered near Kadıköy and dates from neolithic times, much earlier than anything on the European side. The first Greek city was also founded at Kadıköy in 675 BC – 17 years before the founding of Byzantium.

Separated by water from their more powerful European neighbour, the Asian settlements suffered over subsequent millennia; the ruthless antics of various invading armies explain the lack of substantial early remains. Before the 19th century, only Üsküdar saw any significant development. That changed in 1852 when a steam ferry company, Şirket-i Hayriye (literally 'the good deeds company'), started plying its trade across the straits. Rich Levantines from Beyoğlu began constructing elaborate summer mansions along the shore to the south and east of Kadıköy.

Under the Republic, most of the mansions were demolished and replaced by apartment blocks. These retained their garden settings, which gives the Asian shore, especially between Kadıköy and Bostancı, a greener, more suburban feel than the European side.

For information about settlements further along the Bosphorus, *see pp210-212*.

GETTING THERE

Although two great suspension bridges now span the straits, the best way to get to the Asian Shore is by boat. Between 6am and midnight, ferries depart every 15 minutes from Eminönü (just west of Sirkeci station), Kabataş, Karaköy and Beşiktaş for both Üsküdar and Kadıköy. The pleasant crossing takes around 20 minutes.

KADIKÖY

No trace remains of the Greek or Byzantine settlements of Chalcedon, but modern Kadıköy does retain many hints of its 19th-century incarnation as an area largely settled by Greeks and Armenians. To visitors arriving by ferry, this isn't immediately apparent as the two most visible buildings, Kadıköy Municipality and the local theatre, are in an unlovely modernist style.

Bear right for the main Söğütlüçeşme Caddesi and cut into the alleys beside the Mustafa Iskele Mosque. This is the old bazaar, an area of narrow streets lined with tiny two- and three-storey buildings, many dating from

Time Out Istanbul **85**

Kadıköy.

the 19th century. Some of the best food shopping in Istanbul is on offer here. At the top end of **Yasa Sokak** are delis stocking a huge range of regional Turkish produce. A few steps south on **Mühürdar Caddesi**, opposite a small Armenian church, **Esmer Ekmek** bakes on the premises in a wood-fired oven.

Other than the bakery, Mühürdar Caddesi is almost completely given over to booksellers, most specialising in academic textbooks. Narrow, sloping **Dumlupınar Sokak** has more bookshops, including, at no.17, **Greenhouse Books**, run by Charlotte McPherson, an American who offers tea and coffee as well as a large English-language stock.

Güneşlibahçe Sokak has more great food shops, including one devoted exclusively to honey, another to olive oil, and some fantastic fishmongers. On this street is one of Istanbul's best restaurants, **Çiya** (*see p139*). It's worth the trip over just to experience its regional cuisine. One block east, **Dellalzade Sokak** is lined with antique shops.

The area has a lively café and bar scene centred on **Kadife Sokak** – it's the Asian shore's (slightly downmarket) answer to Beyoğlu, with the feel of a student quarter.

Beyond the cinema, Kadıköy gives way to the posher suburb of **Moda**. A few minutes' walk south is the popular waterfront promenade, with a tiny ferry terminal designed in late-Ottoman revival style by Vedat Tek.

Fenerbahçe

East of Kadıköy is **Rüştü Saraçoğlu Stadium**, home of Fenerbahçe football club (*see p205*). Fener is traditionally one of Turkey's top three teams, with a massive fan base across the city. Such is the fanaticism of local supporters that their neighbourhood is often referred to as the 'Republic of Fenerbahçe'.

Behind the stadium is Bağdat Caddesi, one of the city's best-known streets. For much of its length it's an unremarkable swathe of asphalt, but passing through the plush suburb of **Suadiye** it is lined with upmarket clothing and design stores, beauty clinics, pavement cafés and restaurants. It's the cruising strip of choice for nouveau-riche Istanbul.

HAYDARPAŞA

Across the bay from Kadıköy stands the imposing edifice of **Haydarpaşa Station**, which would look more at home in the Rhineland – not surprising, given that it was a gift from Kaiser Wilhelm of Germany and was designed by German architects. It's the

---

INSIDE TRACK BLIND CITY

Kadıköy was known as Chalcedon when it was founded in 675 BC. It was soon dubbed 'the city of the blind', because its founders had missed the clear geographical advantages of the opposite European shore, which was to become the centre of empires for 2,000 years.

terminus of the Anatolian railway system, the end of the line for trains from as far east as Tehran (serviced by the weekly TransAsya Express). On the waterfront piazza in front of the station is a small but perfectly formed ferry terminal, another Vedat Tek design.

The area north of Haydarpaşa is thinly developed, largely because it belongs to the military and Marmara University, who each own one of the two imposing buildings that dominate the area.

The **Selimiye Barracks** were originally constructed in 1799, during the reign of Selim III, as part of his plan to create a 'new army' to challenge the hegemony of the Janissaries. His plan backfired: he was murdered and his barracks were burnt down. Thirty years later, Mahmut II finally succeeded in defeating the Janissaries and he was responsible for putting up the present building, now part of a restricted military zone. During the Crimean War (1853-6) the barracks served as a hospital run by Florence Nightingale; the north-west corner is preserved as the **Florence Nightingale Museum**.

The other grand building is the former **Haydarpaşa High School**, now Marmara University medical faculty. It's the largest of the many commissions completed by Raimondo D'Aronco. Close by the High School, just off Burhan Felek Caddesi, is the **British Crimean War Cemetery**, containing the graves of Crimean War and World War I dead. As far-flung corners of foreign fields go, it's rather pleasant, with manicured lawns tended by the Commonwealth War Graves Commission. Access is through the gate lodge.

Largest of the area's cemeteries is the **Karaca Ahmet cemetery**, named after a warrior companion of the second Ottoman sultan, Orhan. The cemetery was probably founded back in the mid 14th century; estimates put the number of interments at over a million – by far the biggest boneyard in Turkey.

To get to the barracks and cemeteries, take any Üsküdar-bound dolmuş (YTL1.50) from the ranks south of Haydarpaşa Station.

Florence Nightingale Museum

Birinci Ordu Komutanlığı, Selimiye Kışlası, Harem (0216 343 7310). **Open** by appointment 9am-5pm, preferably weekdays. **Admission** free. A visit to the city's least-known museum requires forward planning: to gain access to the heavily guarded Selimiye army barracks, you must fax your passport details, expected time of arrival and phone number. The army will call back to issue permission. Be sure to take your passport.

Visitors enter through a series of guard posts at which the military rank and level of English improves progressively. During the Crimean War, the vast corridors of the barracks were crowded with

wounded British, French and Turkish soldiers, shipped in from the battlefields of Balaclava and Sebastopol. The overcrowded, unsanitary conditions meant that a hospital stay increased the likelihood of death, rather than recovery, and many of the hospital's former patients are buried in nearby Haydarpaşa Cemetery.

It was here that Florence Nightingale and her team of nurses developed modern hospital and nursing practice. The museum in her honour is housed in a corner tower. The lower floor contains life-sized statues of Turkish soldiers from the Crimean War to the War of Independence, as well as a waxwork of Florence Nightingale with a wounded patient. On the table is her famous lamp. And up a winding, wooden staircase is the room where she stayed.

Florence Nightingale Museum.

Maiden's Tower.

Göztepe

Istanbul Toy Museum

Istanbul Oyuncak Müzesi
*Dr. Zeki Zeren Sokak, off Ömerpaşa Caddesi 17,
(0216 359 4550, www.istanbuloyuncakmuzesi.
com). Bus GZ1, GZ2.* **Open** 9.30am-6pm Tue-Fri.
Admission YTL8; YTL5 concessions. **Credit**
MC, V.
Founded by poet Sunay Akın in 2005 in an old
wooden mansion in Göztepe, the collection at this
museum contains some 4,000 toys from around
the world. Highlights include a French violin made
in 1817, an American doll from 1820, hundred-
year-old porcelain dolls from Germany and a lot of
collectable tin toys.

ÜSKÜDAR

Stepping ashore from the ferry, you are pitched
into the midst of buses, dolmuş and taxis
tearing round the central square. All this
activity is rather misleading because, in
contrast to lively Kadıköy, Üsküdar is a
highly conservative area, populated largely
by migrants from rural Anatolia. During the
Muslim holy month of Ramazan, Üsküdar is the
site of one of the city's largest *iftar* (literally
'break-fast') tents, with masses of food donated
by local businesses for the poor. The main point
of interest for shoppers are the antique shops on
Büyük Hamam Sokak, which is one block
south of the **Mimar Sinan Çarşısı**, a 16th-
century hamam converted into a small market.

Otherwise, the district's attractions are its
mosques. Üsküdar was a favourite place to
build these, because the Asian side lies closer
to Mecca. The Iskele Mosque (1548) opposite
the ferry terminal, and the **Şemsi Ahmet
Paşa Mosque** (1580), down on the shore,
are both the work of Sinan. The Şemsi is
particularly attractive; you can find it by
walking south along the waterfront promenade
past a string of floating fish restaurants. Inland
on Şemsi Paşa Caddesi stands the earliest of
Üsküdar's mosques, the **Rumi Mehmet
Paşa Mosque**, built in 1471 for the grand
vizier. He was of Greek origin, which may
explain the strong Byzantine influence in
the design, which incorporates a cylindrical
drum under the dome.

The **Yeni Valide Mosque** back on Uncular
Caddesi also has a Greek connection. It was
constructed for Sultan Ahmet III, whose Greek
mother was captured at the age of three and
grew up in the harem, where she graduated
from concubine to wife to mother of the sultan
(*valide sultana*). The building is a late example

INSIDE TRACK
THE BOND CONNECTION

The **Maiden's Tower** (*see right*) was used
as a hideout for the villainous Elektra
(Sophie Marceau) in the 1999 James Bond
movie, *The World is Not Enough*.

---

of classical Ottoman style, with an attractive façade but a disappointing interior.

On a small island off the southern shore of Üsküdar is the stubby white **Maiden's Tower**, which for some reason is one of the city's best-loved landmarks.

Maiden's Tower

Kız Kulesi

0216 342 4747. **Open** *Tower* noon-7pm Mon-Sat. *Restaurant* noon-1am Mon-Sat. **Admission** ferry YT4. **Credit** *Restaurant* AmEx, MC, V. **Map** p296 U3.

Although this little island was occupied by a fortress in Byzantine times, the tower dates from the last century. In Turkish it's known as Kız Kulesi, or Maiden's Tower – supposedly after a princess who was confined here after a prophet predicted she would die from a snake bite. The fatal bite was duly delivered by a serpent that arrived in a basket of fruit. In English it's even more randomly known as Leander's Tower, after the Greek hero who swam the Hellespont. The tower has been used as a quarantine centre, lighthouse and customs control point. To get here, walk along the promenade to Salacak (about 15 minutes from central Üsküdar), where boats leave every 15 minutes from noon to 1am. The return trip costs YTL4. These days, the tower is a café-restaurant decked out like an Ottoman banquet hall, which is very popular with wedding parties. It's a scenic spot for an average lunch, but dinner is an expensive, reservations-only affair.

THE ASIAN BOSPHORUS

Just beyond the first Bosphorus Bridge stands **Beylerbeyi Palace**, the last of the great, ugly Ottoman palaces. The eponymous village has a pretty harbour with several tea houses and pleasant restaurants lining the shore. Nearby **Hamidievvel Mosque** is unusual in having a rose garden. At weekends, the area by the ferry jetty is taken over by craft stalls.

Further north, the landscape gets much greener. In the 1990s, property prices here soared as rich commuters from the European shore moved in. The most exclusive properties are the *yalıs*, vast wooden mansions that hug the strip between the road and the sea. As they're mostly invisible from the road, behind high security walls, you'll need to take a Bosphorus cruise (*see p212*) to catch a glimpse of them.

Çengelköy, the next town up, was a humble village until it featured in a long-running TV soap, *Süper Baba*, precipitating an influx of money and car showrooms. The harbour is still pleasant, and there are a couple of waterside fish restaurants with great views. Çengelköy is home to the excellent **Sumahan Hotel** (*see p117*) which overlooks the Bosphorus.

The wide valley to the north of **Kandilli** is split by two narrow rivers, Küçüksu and Göksu Deresi, once together known as the 'Sweet Waters of Asia'. In Ottoman times, the meadows between them were a popular picnic ground for the rich. Even Sultan Abdül Mecit got in on the act, erecting the modest **Küçüksu Palace** on the shore.

Beylerbeyi Palace

Beylerbeyi Sarayı

Abdullah Ağa Caddesi 12 (0216 321 9320). Bus 15 from Üsküdar. **Open** 9.30am-5pm Tue, Wed, Fri-Sun (closes 1hr earlier Nov-Mar). **Admission** YTL10. **No credit cards.**

After being deposed in 1908, Sultan Abdül Hamit II spent the last years of his life here. Facing northwest, the palace gets little direct sunlight – it was intended as a summer annexe to the main palace at Dolmabahçe. Beylerbeyi didn't even have its own kitchen: food was brought over from the European shore by boat. Tours only take 15 to 20 minutes, racing through the sumptuous palace, dripping with crystal chandeliers, and some of its five adjoining pavilions.

Küçüksu Palace

Küçüksu Sarayı

Küçüksu Caddesi, Beykoz (0216 332 3303). Bus 15 from Üsküdar/101 from Beşiktaş. **Open** 9.30am-4pm Tue, Wed, Fri-Sun. **Admission** YTL4. **No credit cards.**

Completed in 1857, this relatively small palace was used by Ottoman sultans for short stays during country excursions and hunting trips. Unlike other imperial buildings, Küçüksu was not surrounded by high walls but by cast iron railings. The ornate façade and twin staircases sweeping around the ornamental pool and fountain create a grand impression, which is echoed inside. The ceilings are richly decorated with plaster motifs and painted designs. And there are so many marble fireplaces that Küçüksu is like a museum dedicated to 19th century fireplace design.

The pavilion was extensively restored in 1994 and the surrounding gardens, fountain and quay are being transformed into a park where the public can enjoy picnics as in centuries past.

SIGHTS

THEMARMARAPERA
Downtown İstanbul

Pera

inviting...

THEMARMARAPERA

*business or leisure... in the heart of nostalgic
Pera district, meeting facilities, rooms and services
just right for the modern day traveller!*

phone 90 - 212 251 46 46 fax 90 - 212 249 80 33
meşrutiyet cad. tepebaşı 34430 istanbul türkiye
www.themarmarahotels.com

TAKSİM PERA ŞİŞLİ ESMASULTAN ÇAMLICA PENDİK SUADİYE ANTALYA BODRUM MANHATTA

Consume

Hotels

Ottoman-era classics or 21st-century hotspots? Beyoğlu or Sultanahmet?

Istanbul's hotels are in the throes of a design revolution. Increasing numbers of immaculately renovated mansions, imaginatively decorated and furnished and kitted out with and the latest technology, are joining the city's roster of hotels. Architects Autoban are behind the effortlessly stylish **Witt** and **House Hotel**, while over on the Asian shore, a remote location adds to the romance of the luxuriously appointed **A'jia** and **Sumerhan**. Some classics have also received a facelift, including Istanbul's most famous hotel, the **Pera Palace**. With a guest book that includes Greta Garbo and Jackie O, discerning travellers can check in to Istanbul's romantic past once again.

WHERE TO STAY

There are basically two choices: south or north of the Golden Horn (the exceptions are the two destination hotels we list on the Asian side, see p117). Most tourists who are visiting for a couple of days will head to one of the many hotels in Sultanahmet to be near the Grand Bazaar and Topkapı Palace. This has traditionally been the centre for the city's budget accommodation. Many hotels in Sultanahmet have rooftop terraces and it's hard to beat morning coffee and croissants nestled between the domes of the Haghia Sophia and Blue Mosque.

To be near the best bars and finest restaurants, find a hotel around Beyoğlu. There are new choices along Meşrutiyet Caddesi such as the newly reopened **Pera Palace** (see p103) and **Mia Pera** (see p105), as well as the likes of **Tomtom Suites** (see p105), **Witt Istanbul** (see p105) and **House Hotel** (see p107) in the trendy district of Cihangir.

Most of the city's high-rise, high-end options for business travellers are clustered around Harbiye, an area of green parkland just north of Taksim Square. There's another cluster of hotels around the business district of 4. Levent, including the **Mövenpick**.

Information & prices

Prices quoted in this chapter refer to the rack rates for standard double rooms. These should at least offer an idea about what you can pay at a given hotel, but note that rates can vary wildly across the city and even in a single property, with some hotels charging more for a view. In all but a few of the high-end hotels, room rates include tax (18 per cent) and breakfast. Prices quoted below are high-season rates, which normally apply from the end of May to the beginning of September, at Christmas and New Year, and during national holidays. Outside these times you can expect a discount of between 10 and 30 per cent. Hotels in the mid-range and budget categories are particularly open to bargaining over rates, especially if you're willing to pay your bill in cash in foreign currency.

Most places quote rates in euros but may accept dollars or sterling. Most take credit cards – Mastercard and Visa being the most widely accepted – but this form of payment can often incur a five to ten per cent surcharge.

Plenty of hotels now take bookings online and there are also a few useful websites for online reservations, notably www.istanbul hotels.com, which brings together about 80 of the city's hotels and offers discounts for online booking. Alternatively, the website www.istanbul.hotelguide.net provides links to local hotel websites. Hotels can also be booked, of course, through www.expedia.com and www.lastminute.com, often at discount rates.

If you arrive without a reservation, there are several booking agents at Atatürk Airport in the international arrivals hall (at the opposite end to the tourist information desk). They have an extensive list of mainly three- and four-star hotels and don't charge any commission.

About the chapter

We have listed prices in this chapter in euros, and occasionally US dollars (in cases where hotels quote their prices in dollars). Hotels in this guide are divided into the following categories: **deluxe** (more than €350 a night for a double); **expensive** (€200-€350); **moderate** (€100-€200); **budget** (€50-€150); and **hostels** (under €50).

At the end of each review, we've listed a selection of hotel services: restaurants and bars, internet access, spas and the like. If you're bringing a car to the city, always check before you arrive. At some hotels parking is limited and my need to be reserved in advance.

South of the Golden Horn

SULTANAHMET

Deluxe

★ Four Seasons
Tevkifhane Sokak 1 (0212 638 8200, www.fourseasons.com/istanbul). Tram Sultanahmet. **Rates** $370-$560 double (excluding tax). **Rooms** 65. **Credit** AmEx, DC, MC, V. **Map** p243 N10 ❶
For 66 years this distinctive building, with its ochre walls and watchtowers, served as the infamous Sultanahmet Prison; inmates included celebrated political prisoners. Sensitively renovated in 1986, the Four Seasons has held on to its position as one of Istanbul's best hotels. With its manicured gardens and elegant gazebo restaurant (Seasons Restaurant, *see p121*), the former prison yard has been transformed into an oasis of calm in the heart of bustling Sultanahmet. Cells have been replaced by 65 plush, high-ceilinged rooms and suites – a modest number that ensures intimacy and superlative service.
Bar. Business services. Concierge. Disabled-adapted rooms. Gym. Internet (wireless). No-smoking rooms. Parking (free). Restaurants (2). Room service. Spa. TV.
▶ *There's another Four Seasons, the Bosphorus, near Beşiktaş; see p115.*

Expensive

Eresin Crown Hotel
Küçük Ayasofya Caddesi 40 (0212 638 4428, www.eresincrown.com.tr). Tram Sultanahmet. **Rates** €350 double. **Rooms** 60. **Credit** AmEx, DC, MC, V. **Map** p243 M11 ❷

The Eresin Crown is unusual as a medium-sized, high-end hotel amid small 'Ottoman' boutique competitors in Sultanahmet: it's on the southern side of the peninsula, a stone's throw from Sultanahmet Mosque. Decor in the public spaces is pretty standard, of the marble and plate glass variety, but the hotel's unique selling point are the 50 or so ancient artefacts discovered when the hotel was being built. Some rooms are on the small side, but all are comfortable and well appointed, with jacuzzis; there are several suites. The Terrace Restaurant has amazing views over the city, the Bosphorus and Sea of Marmara. The Eresin is a choice worth considering if you want to be near the sights, but prefer accommodation with international-style features and facilities.
Bars. Business centre. Internet (wireless). Room service. Restaurants (2). TV.

Yeşil Ev
Kabasakal Caddesi 5 (0212 517 6785, www.istanbulyesilev.com). Tram Sultanahmet. **Rates** €300-€350 double. **Rooms** 19. **Credit** AmEx, MC, V. **Map** p243 N10 ❸
Flagship of the Turkish Touring and Automobile Association's fleet of restored Ottoman properties, the 'Green House' enjoys an unrivalled location on a leafy street midway between the Haghia Sophia and Sultanahmet Mosque. Entering this stately wooden mansion is like stepping on to the set of a 19th-century costume drama. Every room is decked out in reproduction furniture, complete with wood-panelled ceilings, creaky parquet flooring and antique

Four Seasons.

WHERE EAST MEETS WEST,
FIND THE HEART OF ISTANBUL.

Located in the heart of the most dynamic and exotic city of Istanbul, on Taksim Square, Ceylan InterContinental Istanbul awaits you for an unforgettable experience through its rooms with glorious Bosphorus views, a luxurious SPA and Turkish hammam, award winning and fine dining restaurants offering delicious flavors of Ottoman, Turkish and world cuisine and most importantly, its staff ready to assist you anytime with a deep local knowledge.

Do you live an InterContinental life?

CEYLAN
INTERCONTINENTAL.
ISTANBUL

+90 212 368 44 44
istanbul.intercontinental.com.tr
istanbul@interconti.com.tr

Dersaadet.

rugs. The Sultan's Suite has its own hamam. The idyllic garden is one of the highlights, with a pretty pink pond, a fine café and beer garden and the restaurant. With only 19 rooms, booking in advance is essential. Be sure to ask for a room on the first floor, overlooking the cobbled street – with no televisions in the hotel, you'll want the view.
Internet (wireless). Restaurant. Room service.
▶ *The beer garden is a great spot for a drink, especially after a visit to Hagia Sophia (see p40).*

Moderate

Armada
Ahırkapı Sokak 24, Cankurtaran (0212 455 4455, www.armadahotel.com.tr). Cankurtaran rail. **Rates** €75-€165 double. **Rooms** 110. **Credit** AmEx, MC, V. **Map** p243 O11 **④**
Sandwiched between waterside Kennedy Caddesi and the suburban railway line, the Armada scores low on location, although it is only a ten-minute walk up the hill to the sight-studded heart of Sultanahmet. The real advantage is that most rooms have fantastic, uninterrupted Bosphorus views. Modelled on a row of 19th-century houses that once stood here, the building is now a bit stuck in the 1980s. The fancy lobby has a terrapin pond and café, while the 110 rooms, if not exceptional, are comfortable and slightly bigger than the average Sultanahmet room.
Bars (2). Business centre. Concierge. Disabled-adapted rooms. Internet (wireless). No-smoking rooms. Parking (free). Restaurants (4). Room service. TV.

Ayasofya Pansiyonları
Soğukçeşme Sokak (0212 513 3660, www.ayasofyapensions.com). Tram Gülhane. **Rates** €170-€200 double. **Rooms** 64. **Credit** AmEx, MC, V. **Map** p243 N10 **⑤**

In the 1980s, the Turkish Touring and Automobile Association reconstructed this row of nine clapboard houses dating from the 19th century. They were painted in pastel colours and furnished in period style. Rooms are all painted different colours and most have big brass beds. The setting is a dream: a sloping cobbled lane hidden between the high walls of Topkapı Palace and the back of Haghia Sophia. Breakfast is served in the pretty garden or the gazebo of the Konut Evi, a four-storey annexe at the end of the alley. At night, the whole place is lamp-lit. Walt Disney couldn't create more magic.
Bar. Internet (wireless). Parking (free). Restaurants (2). Room service.

Citadel
Kennedy Caddesi Sahilyolu 32, Ahır Kapı Sokak (0212 516 2313, www.citadelhotel.com). Cankurtaran rail. **Rates** €120 double. **Rooms** 31. **Credit** MC, V. **Map** p243 O11 **⑥**
Occupying a striking pink three-storey mansion, this Best Western affiliate has 25 rooms and six suites decked out in Barbie colours. The only thing between you and the Sea of Marmara is – alas – six lanes of speeding traffic. It's not far from the fish restaurants of Kumkapı, though, and the conservatory bar and decent restaurant lessen the feeling of isolation. Free airport pick-ups.
Bar. Concierge. Internet (wireless). Parking (free). Restaurants (3). Room service. TV.

★ Dersaadet
Küçük Ayasofya Caddesi Kapıağası Sokak 5 (0212 458 0760, www.hoteldersaadet.com). Tram Sultanahmet. **Rooms** 17. **Credit** MC, V. **Map** p243 N11 **⑦**
The Dersaadet (one of the many former names for Istanbul) has become one of the most popular boutique hotels south of the Golden Horn for

CONSUME

Have a Great Time in a Timeless City: Istanbul

View from Conrad Istanbul

There is much to discover in Istanbul, whether you are looking for a family holiday, romantic getaway or a single journey. With booming businesses, arts, fashion, shopping, entertainment and a fabulous night life, Istanbul welcomes you to the Hilton Worldwide Istanbul Hotels:

Hilton Istanbul. The longest operating Hilton hotel outside of the Americas and an Istanbul classic, the hotel is located in the city centre of the most exciting part of city, surrounded by gardens, close to business, entertainment and shopping districts.

Conrad Istanbul. Contemporary luxury and timeless elegance opposite an Ottoman Palace with incredible views of the Bosphorus and the city.

Hilton ParkSA. In the heart of Istanbul's stylish Nişantaşı district featuring extensive dining options with breathtaking views of the Bosphorus.

Whichever your choice, Hilton Worldwide Istanbul Hotels will make you feel at home.

Follow us on Twitter to find out more:

twitter.com/HILTONISTANBUL
+90 212 315 60 00

twitter.com/CONRADISTANBUL
+90 212 310 25 25

twitter.com/HILTONPARKSA
+90 212 310 12 00

hilton.com/istanbul

HHONOR
HILTON WORLDWI

WALDORF
ASTORIA

CONRAD
HOTELS & RESORTS

Hilton

DOUBLETREE
by Hilton

EMBASSY
SUITES

Hilton
Garden Inn

Hampton

HOMEWOOD
SUITES
Hilton

HOME2

Hilton
Grand Vaca

independent travellers. The hotel's quaint wooden exterior and 19th-century French-influenced Ottoman decor recreate the charms of the Ottoman golden years. The 17 rooms, across four floors, are all comfortable, and some have good views over the Sea of Marmara. The best room is the Sultan's Suite, which has a low wooden ceiling, big windows and jacuzzi. Sea view rooms have a €15 surcharge. There is a pleasant rooftop breakfast terrace, with both indoor and outdoor tables, overlooking the Bosphorus. It is a superb spot for enjoying an afternoon coffee to the sound of classical music, only interrupted by the call to prayer at Sultanahmet Mosque and the squeak of canaries. This is a no-smoking hotel.

Bars (2). Internet (wireless). Restaurants (2). Room service. TV.

▶ *The Hotel Niles (see below) is run by the same family.*

Empress Zoe

Adliye Sokak 10, off Akbıyık Caddesi (0212 518 2504, www.emzoe.com). Tram Sultanahmet. **Rates** €120-€245 double. 10% discount for cash. **Rooms** 19. **Credit** MC, V. **Map** p243 O11 ❽

Named after a racy Byzantine regent, the Zoe is one of the best and quirkiest of the city's small hotels. Its sunken reception area incorporates parts of a 15th-century hamam; the 'archaeological garden' – ideal for breakfast or a beer. Bear in mind that guests must be agile, as rooms are reached via a wrought-iron spiral staircase. In contrast to the gilt and frills of most other 'period' hotels, the Zoe's 19 rooms are decorated in dark wood and richly coloured textiles. A new wing of suites has recently been added and the garden expanded. Add a fine rooftop bar for a nightcap with a view and this place is sheer class from top to bottom.

Bar. Internet (wireless). Restaurant. Room service. TV.

Ibrahim Paşa Hotel

Terzihane Sokak 5 (0212 518 0394, www.ibrahimpasha.com). Tram Sultanahmet. **Rates** €95-€135 double. **Rooms** 24. **Credit** MC, V. **Map** p243 M11 ❾

Tucked round the corner from the Museum of Turkish and Islamic Art, the Ibrahim Paşa is an eminently likeable small hotel. It doesn't overplay the old Ottoman card and instead is stylishly modern, smart and bright, with just enough judiciously placed artefacts (including some fascinating old photographs in the breakfast area) to remind you that this is Istanbul. Rooms can be small, but judicious use is made of space. The buffet breakfast has a good selection of cheeses, honey, bread, olives and much more. Staff are helpful; the ambience calm and relaxed. There are plenty of minarets and domes on show from the rooftop terrace.

Bar. Internet (wireless). Room service. TV.

Kybele Hotel

Yerebatan Caddesi 33-35 (0212 511 7766, www.kybelehotel.com). Tram Sultanahmet. **Rates** €110-€140 double. 10% discount for cash. **Rooms** 16. **Credit** MC, V. **Map** p243 N10 ❿

The Akbayrak brothers obviously have a thing about vintage glass lamps – the interior of their hotel is hung with 2,000 of them. The eccentricities continue: every room is crammed with kilims, candlestands, empty bottles and quirky knick-knacks. Garish pink and green paint schemes heighten the sense of fun. It all makes sense when you learn that one of the brothers was formerly an antiques dealer, while another spent three years with an Australian circus. The 16 bedrooms are smallish, particularly the singles, but they are comfortable enough and all have fancy marble bathrooms. Breakfast is served in a courtyard as colourful as a gypsy caravan.

Bar. Internet (wireless). Parking (YTL10 day). Restaurant. Room service.

★ Hotel Niles

Ordu Caddesi Dibekli, Cami Sokak 19, Beyazıt (0212 517 3239, www.hotelniles.com). Tram Beyazıt. **Rates** €70-€130 double. **Rooms** 29. **Credit** MC, V. **Map** p242 K10 ⓫

Significantly refurbished in 2010, Hotel Niles is owned by the same family who are responsible for the highly regarded Dersaadet. They have been involved in every detail of the renovations, from the authentic Iznik tiles to the design on the hand-painted ceiling. Each of the ten new suites is based on French-influenced Ottoman guestrooms, done out in light turquoise, equipped with a microwave and hamam-style bathrooms with Marmara marble. Two duplex rooms – with part on the ground floor, part on lower ground – were built using the original bricks with inscriptions in old Turkish script. There's a gym, conference room and leafy roof garden where breakfast is served. Service is flawless.

Bar. Internet (wireless). Room service. TV.

▶ *Dersaadett (see above) is another Sultanahmet hotel run by the same family.*

INSIDE TRACK APARTMENTS

If you're looking for an apartment rather than a hotel, try the following companies. **House Apart** (www.thehouseapart.com), part of the group behind the House Café, has very stylish apartments to rent across the city. **Cihangir Apartments** (www.cihangirapartment.com) has three apartments in one building. **Istanbul Apartments** (www.istapart.com) has two to choose from. Also try **Easy Home Istanbul** (www.easyhomeistanbul.com), which has two blocks of apartments in Tünel and Galatasaray.

CONSUME

PERA PALACE HOTEL
1892

www.perapalace.com

"Pearl of Istanbul" is back...

The fully renovated, legendary Pera Palace Hotel is waiting to welcome its guests to re-live the bygone era of this emperial city within its century old walls while enjoying the Agatha Restaurant, Orient Bar, Patisserie de Pera and SPA facilities.

Meşrutiyet Caddesi No:52 34430 Tepebaşı - Istanbul / Turkey Phone: +90 212 377 40 00 info@perapalace.com

Sarniç

Kuçuk Ayasofya Caddesi 26 (0212 518 2323, www.sarnichotel.com). Tram Sultanahmet. **Rates** €60-€150 double. **Rooms** 21. **Credit** AmEx, MC, V. **Map** p243 N11

Sarniç, the Turkish word for cistern, takes its name from the fifth-century Byzantine cistern beneath the hotel, which guests can explore from 9am to 6pm. After changing ownership, Sarniç underwent major renovations in 2010. Another five rooms were added on the top floor – recommended for the views of the Blue Mosque. All other rooms have been tastefully decorated, and include flatscreen TVs. The small top-floor terrace makes a scenic setting when the sun sets and there's a bar/breakfast room below ground. There are popular half-day cookery courses in the hotel kitchen. The hotel is only a few minutes' walk from the Hippodrome.

Bar. Concierge. Internet (wireless). Massage. Restaurant. Room service. TV.

▶ *For more cookery courses, see p138.*

Hotel Uyan

Utangaç Sokak 25 (0212 516 4892, www.uyan hotel.com). Tram Sultanahmet. **Rates** €70-€130 double 8% discount for cash. **Rooms** 26. **Credit** MC, V. **Map** p243 N11

This attractive corner hotel in a 75-year-old building has 16 spacious standard rooms and ten suites spead over four floors. The standard rooms are simply furnished, with small bathrooms. Deluxe suites have a jacuzzi and sound system in the bathroom. Uyan's main selling point is that it has the highest roof terrace in the neighbourhood, with views over the Sultanahmet Mosque. If you're not an early riser, avoid room 309, which lies directly

underneath the breakfast room. The hotel offers free airport pick-ups. This is a no-smoking hotel.

Bar. Internet (wireless). Restaurant. Room service. TV.

Budget

Hotel Ararat

Torun Sokak 3 (0212 516 0411, www.ararat hotel.com). Tram Sultanahmet. **Rates** €70-€90 double. **Rooms** 12. **Credit** MC, V. **Map** p243 N11

Ararat's best feature is probably its location. Envious of the success of the nearby Empress Zoe (*see p97*), the young Turkish owners of Ararat recruited the same architect, Nicos Papadakis, to revamp their 12-room guesthouse. If the results aren't quite as inspired, the Ararat still breaks the mould, with marbled walls and an orange and ochre colour scheme that works well with the dark, stained-wood floors. Rooms vary widely in terms of size and comfort – some are small with little light, while others have wooden four-posters with wonderful views of Sultanahmet Mosque. Breakfast is served on the roof terrace.

Bar. Internet (wireless). Parking (YTL15 day). Restaurant. Room service.

Hanedan

Adliye Sokak 3, Akbıyk Caddesi (0212 516 4869, www.hanedanhotel.com). Tram Sultanahmet. **Rates** €60 double. 5% discount for cash. **Rooms** 10. **Credit** MC, V. **Map** p243 O11

Hanedan is one of the smartest independent hotels south of the Four Seasons. Clean, bright primrose-yellow rooms, with large beds draped in muslin, all have

CONSUME

Hotel Uyan.

ensuite bathrooms with hairdryers and heated towel rails. The three family rooms have the best Marmara views. There are more unobstructed views from the roof terrace. It can be noisy on summer nights, as neighbouring hotels often host rooftop parties. *Internet (wireless). Room service.*

★ Nomade Hotel

15 Ticarethane Sokak, (0212 513 8172, www.hotelnomade.com). Tram Sultanahmet.
Rates €75 double. **Rooms** 16. **Credit** AmEx, MC, V. **Map** p243 N10 ⓰
The cosy reception area, with comfortable design-minded furnishing, is perfect for watching the bustling pedestrian traffic outside, while the cushion-strewn, flower-filled roof terrace is one of the prettiest in Istanbul, particularly at night. The hotel's new owners refurbished the 16 rooms and reception area in 2010. The rooms are as cosy and uncluttered as before, with pastel walls, ethnic bedspreads, richly hued wall hangings and modern bathrooms. *Internet (wireless). Restaurant. Room service. TV.*

St Sophia

Alemdar Caddesi 2 (0212 528 0973, www.saintsophiahotel.com). Tram Gülhane.
Rates $90 double. **Rooms** 27. **Credit** AmEx, DC, MC, V. **Map** p243 N10 ⓱
In the shadow of the Haghia Sophia, this Best Western affiliate is yet another conversion of a 19th-century house. Extensive renovations have left it a bit over-polished and lacking in atmosphere. The 27 rooms have modern furnishings; those on the top two floors have jacuzzis and balconies that overlook Justinian's great cathedral. *Bar. Café. Internet (wireless). Parking (free). Room service. TV.*

Side Hotel & Pension

Utangaç Sokak 20 (0212 517 2282, www.sidehotel.com). Tram Sultanahmet. **Rates** €30-€60 double. **Rooms** 52. **No credit cards.** **Map** p243 N11 ⓲
Rooms are clean and well looked after here, and have ensuite bathrooms with shower cubicles (the Istanbul norm for this price bracket is a showerhead that falls straight on to the bathroom floor). Rooms vary widely, so ask to look at a few before you make your choice. Pension accommodation is more basic; the cheapest room has a shared but clean bathroom. There are two self-catering apartments for large groups. Breakfast is served on the rooftop terrace. There's free tea available in the rustic, wood-panelled foyer and a small book exchange. *Internet (wireless). TV.*

Turkoman

Asmalıçeşme Sokak 2, off the Hippodrome (0212 516 2956, www.turkomanhotel.com). Tram Sultanahmet. **Rates** €69-€99 double. **Rooms** 20. **Credit** AmEx, MC, V. **Map** p243 M11 ⓳

> **INSIDE TRACK PAY PER VIEW**
>
> With great rooftop views two a penny in Istanbul, hotels often stress the vista from the rooms. What they don't usually mention, though, is that the rooms with the best views may come at a premium. It's a good idea to ask about views when you book.

Located just off the Hippodrome and opposite the Egyptian obelisk, the Turkoman has a roof terrace with amazing views of the Sultanahmet Mosque, although during the summer months the mosque is hidden from the lower floors by foliage. Bright, unfussy and very yellow rooms may verge on the tacky, but they have brass beds, parquet flooring and big windows. Free one-way airport transfer is available as a perk for guests staying more than three nights. *Bar. Café. Concierge. Internet (wireless). Restaurant. Room service. TV.*

Hostels

Orient Hostel

Akbıyık Caddesi 13 (0212 518 0789, www.orienthostel.com). Tram Sultanahmet.
Rates €13-€15 dorm bed; €40 double. **Credit** AmEx, MC, V. **Map** p243 N11 ⓴
For years the Orient has been the mainstay of the Istanbul backpacker scene, base camp for a constant stream of wanderers tramping across Asia or through the Middle East. Besides the full range of budget traveller services, including cheap internet access, money-changing facilities and discounted airline tickets, the Orient has a lively social scene, with barbecues, belly-dancing and film nights. There is also a women-only dormitory. Both the hostels listed here can fill up with local high school students during holiday time, or school groups from further afield. *Bar. Café. Internet. Restaurant.*

Sultan Tourist Hostel

Terbıyık Sokak 3, off Akbıyık Caddesi (0212 516 9260, www.sultanhostel.com). Tram Sultanahmet. **Rates** €16 dorm bed; €48 double. **Credit** MC, V. **Map** p243 N11 ㉑
Another backpacker staple, located virtually next door to the Orient, the Sultan has bright and airy single and double rooms, as well as mixed-sex dormitories, although having only a single shower/toilet on each floor is something of a drawback. There's a restaurant up top, as well as a bar, pub, disco, games room with table tennis and darts, and a computer centre. The Sultan Café on the street is a good place for a beer. *Bar. Internet (wireless). Restaurants (2).*

CONSUME

CONSUME

The Chain Gang

The big names stake their claim in Istanbul.

Many of the big global hotel chains have branches in Istanbul. With a few exceptions, such as the **Four Seasons** (*see p93* and *p115*), **Mövenpick** (*see p113*) and **Kempinski** (*see p115*), don't expect a great deal of character, but rest assured that you'll get the same standard of service and level of comfort you found at the same chain's outlet in Dallas, Kuala Lumpur, or anywhere else in the world.

The **Hilton Istanbul** (Cumhuriyet Caddesi, Harbiye, 0212 315 6000, www.istanbul. hilton.com, map p247 P1) was the first of Istanbul's modern, high-rise hotel blocks. Given the price bracket, it's far from exceptional in terms of rooms, decor and facilities, although the parkland setting is a bonus. It's a ten-minute walk north of Taksim Square. There are also Hiltons in Beşiktaş and Maçka.

The **Grand Hyatt Istanbul** (0212 225 7000, Taşkışla Caddesi, www.istanbul. hyatt. com.tr, map p247 P1) is to be commended for keeping its building low-rise. The Hyatt scores high on business facilities, with an information library and private offices for rent. There's also a luxury 'apart-hotel' with its own separate check-in and elevators. The hotel is a ten-minute walk north-east of

Taksim Square. Sister hotel the **Maçka Palas** (*see p113*), however, breaks the mould completely with its style.

The **Ritz-Carlton** (0212 334 4444, Asker Ocağı Caddesi, www.ritzcarlton.com, map p247 Q1) occupies the blue-glass tower block that dominates the city skyline. The interior is bland, but facilities are good and the Çintemani restaurant is excellent. You'll need a taxi to get anywhere.

The **Swissôtel Istanbul The Bosphorus** (0212 326 1100, Bayıldım Caddesi 2, Maçka, www.swissotel.com, map p247 R1) sits on the hillside above the Dolmabahçe Palace. Rooms are exceptionally comfortable, with gadgets galore. Sports facilities are particularly good, as is the Japanese restaurant, Miyako.

Other chain options in Istanbul include **Radisson Blu** (www.radissonblu.com), which has a property in Ortaköy (0212 310 1500) and one by the airport (0212 411 3838). There are several hotels under the **Best Western** tag, notably the President Hotel in Sultanahmet (0212 516 6980, www.thepresidenthotel.com) and the highly regarded **Regency Suites** (0212 458 5556, www.regencysuitesistanbul.com) also in Sultanahmet.

WESTERN DISTRICTS
Moderate

Kariye Hotel
Kariye Camii Sokak 6, Edirnekapı (0212 534 8414, www.kariyeotel.com). **Rates** €70-€85 double. **Rooms** 26. **Credit** AmEx, MC, V. **Map** p244 D4 ㉒

Another 19th-century Ottoman residence stripped down and dressed up by the Turkish Touring and Automobile Association and pressed into service as a hotel. There are 26 rooms, all done out in early 1900s fashion. There is also a family annex with one master bedroom and a single room. The restaurant, Asitane (*see p124*), is renowned for its authentic Ottoman cuisine. Next door is the Church of St Saviour in Chora (*see p64*), one of Istanbul's essential sights. But the big snag is the location, out by the old city walls and about a half-hour bus ride from Sultanahmet, or around YTL10 in a taxi. But if you had a reason to be in this part of town, this would be the place to stay.
Bar. Concierge. Internet (wireless). Parking (free). Restaurant. Room service. TV.

YEŞILKOY (AIRPORT)
Expensive

Polat Renaissance Istanbul Hotel
Sahil Yolu 2 Caddesi (0212 414 1800, www.polatrenaissance.com). **Rates** €225 double. **Rooms** 414. **Credit** AmEx, DC, MC, V.

Our airport hotel of choice, the Polat Renaissance is a five-minute taxi ride from the terminal in the coastal suburb of Yeşilköy (it's 18 kilometres, or 12 miles, from the city centre). A 27-storey blue glass skyscraper by the sea, the ultra-modern interior features a soaring central atrium. At least half of the 414 rooms have views over the Marmara. All the rooms were renovated in 2010 and are now equipped with LCD TVs, broadband internet access and coffee machines. All the facilities you would expect of a Marriott hotel, including a large heated outdoor pool.
Bars (3). Business services. Concierge. Disabled-adapted rooms. Gym. Internet (wireless). No-smoking rooms. Parking (free). Pool (1 indoor, 1 outdoor). Restaurants (5). Room service. Spa. TV.

North of the Golden Horn
BEYOĞLU
Deluxe

Pera Palas.

Pera Palas

Meşrutiyet Caddesi 98, Pera (0212 251 4560, www.perapalas.com). **Rates** call for details. **Rooms** 388. **Credit** AmEx, DC, MC, V. **Map** p248 M4 ㉓

Built in 1892 as the last stop on the Orient Express, the Pera Palas is the most aristocratic of hotels. The same company that ran the famed Paris-to-Istanbul trains built it and in the early days its pampered guests were carried on cushioned sedans from Sirkeci station to waiting hotel transport. After a two-year closure for a €23 million refurbishment, it will open its doors again in September 2010 – as a 'museum hotel'. Care has been taken to restore the hotel meticulously, to an authentic version of its former glory, while incorporating the technology needed for modern comforts. Many of the 145 rooms have brass plaques with the names of famous past guests: Sarah Bernhardt, Greta Garbo, Jackie Onassis, Atatürk (whose room remains as it was when he stayed) and Agatha Christie, who wrote part of *Murder on the Orient Express* during a stay here.

Bar. Business centre. Café. Concierge. Gym. Internet (wireless). No-smoking rooms. Parking. Restaurant. Room service. TV.

Expensive

Ceylan Inter-Continental

Asker Ocağı Caddesi 1, Taksim (0212 368 4444, www.istanbulintercontinental.com.tr). **Rates** €275 double. **Rooms** 388. **Credit** AmEx, DC, MC, V. **Map** p247 P1 ㉔

The Inter-Continental is an 18-floor Goliath. Renovated in 2008, the style remains brash, the tone set by a golden staircase spiralling up from the lobby and a glitzy, palm-filled atrium. Decor aside, the hotel is well appointed, although most of the 388 rooms are a bit smaller than others in this price category. Those on the Club Floor (actually the top four floors) are preferable, but pricey. Mick Jagger and Liz Taylor are some of the celebrities who have stayed in the four lavish Presidential Suites. The Safran restaurant was recommended by Académie Internationale de la Gastronomie and top-floor City Lights bar offers spectacular views but steep prices. The hotel is a ten-minute walk from central Taksim Square.

Bar. Business services. Concierge. Disabled-adapted rooms. Gym. Internet (wireless). No-smoking rooms. Parking (free). Pool (outdoor). Restaurants (3). Room service. Spa. TV.

ERESIN **CROWN** HOTEL
ISTANBUL

ERESIN **TAXIM** PREMIER
ISTANBUL

BEST WESTERN
ERESIN **TAXIM** HOTEL
ISTANBUL

ERESIN HOTELS PRESENTS...
THE THREE FLAVORS OF ISTANBUL.

Eresin Hotels really offers something for everyone, because each of our three boutique hotels has something special to offer, whether that's Turkey's only "hotel-museum", comfortably efficient accommodations for business travelers, or a home-away-from-home. But the one thing all our hotels share is friendly, welcoming professional staff dedicated to providing your travelers with superior service during their stay in Istanbul. Tailormade service and boutique hotels sure to suit your travelers' tastes... Eresin Hotels.

ERESIN HOTELS
I S T A N B U L
www.eresinhotels.com.tr

Küçük Ayasofya Cad. No: 40 Sultanahmet
34122 Istanbul-Turkey
• Tel: +90 212 638 4428
• Fax: +90 212 638 0933
• E-mail: eresin@eresincrown.com.tr

www.eresincrown.com.tr

Topçu Caddesi No: 16 Taksim
34437 Istanbul-Turkey
• Tel: +90 212 256 0803
• Fax: +90 212 253 2247
• E-mail: eresin@eresinpremier.com.tr

www.eresinpremier.com.tr

Topçu Caddesi No: 16 Taksim
34437 Istanbul-Turkey
• Tel: +90 212 256 0803
• Fax: +90 212 253 2247
• E-mail: eresin@eresintaxim.com.tr

www.eresintaxim.com.tr

Marmara Taksim

*Taksim Square, Taksim (0212 251 4696,
www.themarmarahotels.com).* **Rates** €283-€303
double. **Rooms** 376. **Credit** AmEx, DC, MC, V.
Map p249 P2 ㉕

One of four Marmara hotels in Istanbul (with sister
establishments in Manhattan and across Turkey),
this location is a Taksim Square landmark. It is the
the place to stay if you want to be at the heart of the
action, though bear in mind that Taksim Square is
far from picturesque. It isn't quite as polished as its
international rivals, although it remains popular
with businessmen. The rooms have the facilities and
feel of a big chain hotel. Most have decent views, but
the best lookout spot is from the top-floor Tepe
Lounge or the Panorama restaurant.
*Bars (3). Business centre. Café. Concierge. Gym.
Internet (wireless). No-smoking rooms. Parking
(free). Pool (outdoor). Restaurants (2). Room
service. Spa. TV.*
Other locations Mesrutiyet Caddesi, Tepebasi
(01212 251 4646); Muallim Naci Caddesi,
Yalıçıkmazı Sokak 20, Ortaköy (01212 244 0509);
Ortaklar Caddesi 30, Mecidiyeköy (0212 370 9400).
▶ *The street-level Kitchenette (see p127) is a
stylish location for a long brunch.*

Mia Pera

*Meşrutiyet Caddesi 53, Pera (0212 245 0245,
www.miaperahotel.com).* **Rates** €229-€249
double. Rooms 61. **Credit** AmEx, MC, V.
Map p248 M4 ㉖

One of the latest additions to Beyoğlu's burgeoning
hotel scene is also one of the most stylish. Only the
façade of this 19th-century French style Ottoman residence remains intact. Once through the glass doors,
Mia Pera is a thoroughly modern experience. Copies
of *Wallpaper** magazines are stacked next to coloured
glass vases on the shelves in the lobby. Down three
steps are the bar, restaurant and breakfast room (the
breakfast buffet is excellent). The single rooms are on
the small side, but thoughtfully designed. Deluxe
rooms are significantly larger and there are also four
duplex suites. The highlight, however, is the basement spa and heated oval pool – a relaxing and warm-
ing hamam style affair. Massages are available.
*Bar. Business centre. Café. Concierge. Gym.
Internet (wireless). No-smoking rooms. Parking
(free). Pool (indoor). Restaurant. Room service.
Spa. TV.*

Richmond Hotel

*Istiklal Caddesi 227 (0212 252 5460,
www.richmondhotels.com.tr).* **Rates** €180-€230
double. **Rooms** 111. **Credit** AmEx, MC, V.
Map p248 M4 ㉗

The Richmond is the best hotel on Istiklal Caddesi,
Beyoğlu's main thoroughfare. This always busy
pedestrianised street, lined with shops, cafés, bars
and plenty of grand old apartment blocks ripe for
conversion, has been oddly overlooked by hotel
developers. The Richmond has retained the building's
historic façade, but the interior has been ripped out,
and rooms are undergoing a second renovation in
2010. What the interior lacks in style, the hotel makes
up for with a relaxed atmosphere and friendly staff.
Standard rooms are simple and streamlined, while the
executive suites cater mainly to business travellers.
*Bars (2). Business services. Café. Concierge.
Disabled-adapted rooms. Gym. Internet (wireless).
No-smoking rooms. Restaurants (2). Room
service. TV.*
▶ *The sleek Leb-i Derya bar-restaurant (see
p127) at the Richmond probably has the best
view of any of Istanbul's rooftop bars. The
central oval bar is popular for cocktails.*

★ Tomtom Suites

*Boğazkesen Caddesi, Tomtom Kaptan Sokak 18
(0212 292 4949, www.tomtomsuites.com).* **Rates**
€190-€280 double. **Rooms** 20. **Credit** AmEx,
MC, V. **Map** p248 N4 ㉘

It's the size of Tomtom Suites that's immediately
striking. The standard rooms are 35-45sq m (376-
484sq ft), and the senior suites 55-65sq m (582-700sq
ft). The high ceilings of this converted Franciscan
nunnery only add to the impressive proportions. The
beds are enormous, and each room has a jacuzzi.
Named for its road and nearby mosque, Tomtom
Suites was restored and repurposed in 2008 with a
modern classic design that has maintained original
features such as the staircase. Modern artwork and
a glass loft, which can be seen rising to the fourth
floor, greet the visitor. The terrace restaurant and
patio has panoramic views over the Golden Horn.
The restaurant serves an Ottoman-inspired menu.
*Bar. Business services. Café. Concierge. Disabled-
adapted room. Internet (wireless). No-smoking
rooms. Restaurant. Room service. TV.*

★ Witt Istanbul

*Defterdar Yokusu, 26, Cihangir (0212 293
1500, www.wittistanbul.com).* **Rates** €169-
€499 double. **Rooms** 17. **Credit** AmEx, MC,
V. **Map** p249 O4 ㉙

Designed by Autoban (*see p36*) in a modern-meets-
retro style, the Witt Istanbul is a deeply impressive
suite hotel. Attention to detail is apparent everywhere: every element has been painstakingly considered, from the open-plan arrangement of the suites
to the staff uniforms. The lobby, bar and
dining/breakfast areas are low lit, with only black
tiles reflecting the light. Suites are spacious, and
include a kitchenette with sink, kettle, microwave,
Nespresso machine and hobs. There is also a seating
area, large beds and a desk with an iPod dock. the
Ross Lovegrove-designed marble bathrooms have
showers with five showerheads and bespoke towels.
Walls are soundproofed. Not all suites have a great
view, so ask for one that does. The location is convenient for both the hip cafés along Akarsu Sokak and
the antique shops of Çukurcuma. *Photo p107.*

CONSUME

Witt Istanbul. See p105.

Bar. Business services. Café. Concierge. Internet (wireless). No-smoking rooms. Restaurant. Room service. TV.

Moderate

★ 5 oda

Şahkulu Bostan Sokak 164, Galata (0212 252 7501, www.5oda.com). **Rates** €140 double. **Rooms** 5. **Credit** AmEx (4% commission), MC, V. **Map** p248 M5 **30**

This new guesthouse, on a quiet street just off Istiklal Caddesi, is perfectly located for the bars and shopping of Beyoğlu. The five rooms are accessed through a reception/kitchen area; a small glass-sided elevator takes you to the upper floors. They are long and airy, with large windows at either side. The architect has used the space well, with an open-plan design that includes a kitchen area with sink, hob, fridge and coffee-making facilities, a couple of chairs and a glass table. With modern design, using wood and white-painted bare brickwork, they are relaxing spaces. Bathrooms are small, with only room for a shower, basin and toilet. Breakfasts, which can be served in guestrooms, are excellent.

★ Eklektik Guest House

Kadribey Cikmazi 4, Galata (0212 243 7446, www.eklektikgalata.com). **Rates** €85-€125 double. **Rooms** 8. **No credit cards**. **Map** p248 M5 **31**

This thoroughly charming guesthouse, on a quiet cul-de-sac, is popular with gay visitors, but the friendly and knowledgeable staff make everyone feel very welcome. Each of the eight smallish rooms is decorated to a theme: from clean lines, white walls and wood in the Zen Room to drapes and ornate lamps in the Colonial Room, and black linens – and a mirror ball in the bathroom – in the Black Room. Downstairs is the new Hamam Room, with heated floors and a Marmara marble bathing area. The shower in the corner of most rooms is an unconventional touch, but it doesn't seem to bother the patrons, neither does the lack of a lift. There is a small terrace with views over the Bosphorus. Staff will arrange tours, transport or restaurant bookings. The breakfast, served around one large table, is superb. *Photo p109.*
Concierge. Internet (wireless). Parking (YTL20). Room service. TV.
▶ *Eklektik is close to several gay venues, such as the Sugar Café (see p187).*

★ House Hotel

Firuzağa Mahallesi, Bostanbaşı Caddesi 19, Çukucuma (0212 252 0422, www.thehouse-hotels.com). **Rates** €120-€190 suites. **Rooms** 20. **Credit** AmEx, MC, V. **Map** p248 N4 **32**

This stunning new hotel is partly owned by the House Café (*see p137*) group, and the same sensitive design aesthetic shines through here. It's located in a converted mansion built in 1850, on a quiet street in the Çukucuma antique district. Going through the elegant but unassuming entrance, you'll find the original tiled floors and Italian marble staircase. Upstairs, each of the 20 well-equipped suites has been designed with the neighbourhood in mind – the tiles in the bathrooms list traditional family names of

Çukurcuma. Decor is a subtly modern take on the traditional, with mixed shades of wood adding pattern to parquet flooring, panelled walls painted white and sleek, updated chandeliers. Furnishings in dove grey add a slightly ethereal touch to the white. All the furniture was designed for the hotel by Autoban (also behind the Witt, *see p105*, and House Café). The bar, on the top floor (bear in mind there are no lifts), has Chesterfield sofas from which to admire views over the Galata Tower.
Bar. Café. Concierge. Internet (wireless). Restaurant. Room service. TV.
▶ *Two larger House Hotels will open in Ortaköy and Nişantaşı at the end of 2010 and another four are planned for 2011. See the website for details.*

★ I'zaz Lofts
Balik Sokak 12 (0212 252 1382, www.izaz.com). **Rates** $110-$150. **Rooms** 4. **Credit** AmEx, MC, V. **Map** 248 N3 ㉝
There are only four ('lofts') at I'zaz, each replete with considered design touches. They're well appointed, with large beds, a desk, flatscreen TV, iPod dock and coffee-making facilities. Visitors should bear in mind that the upper rooms can only be accessed by a staircase. The location is excellent for the bars and restaurants of Nevizade, although the hotel entrance is on a nondescript street, just out of earshot of the action. There's a lovely seating area with vast views over the minarets of Kasımpaşa and the western side of the city. I'zaz's hands-off philosophy means it can feel more like an apartment outfit than a hotel: if they want to, guests can cook for themselves in the communal kitchen (where there's always a pot of coffee on the go) or do their own laundry. But staff are also on hand and can cater to most whims. *Photo p111.*
Internet (wireless). TV.

Madison Hotel
Recep Paşa Caddesi 15, Taksim (0212 238 5460, www.themadisonhotel.com.tr). **Rates** €100-€120 double. **Rooms** 108. **Credit** AmEx, MC, V. **Map** p247 P1 ㉞
North-west of Taksim Square, between Tarlabaşı Bulvarı and Cumhuriyet Caddesi, are a number of quiet streets that are home to a handful of good mid-range hotels, including this one. The Madison

---

INSIDE TRACK BREAKFAST

Breakfast is big news in Istanbul hotels. They are usually extensive and delicious, with cheeses, olives, fresh breads, honeycomb, preserves and cold meats. Some of the best breakfasts can be found at **5 Oda** (*see p107*), **Eklektik** (*see p107*), **Mia Pera** (*see p105*) and **Sumahan** (*see p117*).

Eklektik Guest House. *See p107.*

is a modern four-star place with decent-sized rooms. Insipid colour scheme aside, there's little cause for complaint. Bathrooms are small but clean and practical, decked out in marble, and some thoughtful person has even thought to put an extra telephone next to the toilet. All the rooms were renovated in 2010. The indoor pool-side bar is a relaxed place to hang out.
Bar. Concierge. Gym. Internet (wireless lobby access). No-smoking rooms. Parking (free). Pool (indoor). Restaurant. Room service. Spa. TV.

Taksim Square Hotel
Sıraselviler Caddesi 15, Taksim Square (0212 292 6440, www.taksimsquarehotel.com.tr). **Rates** €100 double. **Rooms** 87. **Credit** AmEx, DC, MC, V. **Map** p249 P2 ㉟
Right in the centre of town, this modern, high-rise hotel is modestly priced but lacks charm. Just 32 of the 87 rooms have a view across the rooftops to the Bosphorus; in the rest, guests have to be content with looking down on the street life on busy Sıraselviler and the diners on the rooftop terrace of Burger King opposite.
Bars (2). Business services. Café. Concierge. Disabled-adapted room. Internet (wireless). Restaurants (2). Room service. TV.

Taksim Suites
Cumhuriyet Caddesi 49, Taksim (0212 254 7777, www.taksimsuites.com). **Rates** €169 double suite. **Rooms** 21. **Credit** AmEx, MC, V. **Map** p247 P1 ㊱

CONSUME

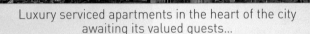

These self-catering suites make an ideal base for business people. The Miyako suites take their inspiration from the east, while the Park and Avenue suites look towards Scandinavia. Fully equipped with everything from microwaves to fax machines, the five options range from a 45sq m (480sq ft) studio to a 109sq m (1,150 sq ft) penthouse with remote-controlled skylights and Bosphorus views. Additional treats include breakfast in bed (or the Taksim Lounge), jacuzzis, a fitness room and accommodating staff who will buy your groceries if you leave a shopping list at reception. Another plus is the excellent location just minutes from Taksim Square.
Business services. Concierge. Gym. Internet (high-speed). Room service. Spa. TV.

Budget

★ Büyük Londra Hotel
Meşrutiyet Caddesi 53, Tepebaşı (0212 245 0670, www.londrahotel.net). **Rates** €80 double. **Rooms** 54. **Credit** MC, V. **Map** p248 M3 ⑰
The Londra was built in 1892, so it's roughly the same age as the nearby Pera Palas (*see p103*). But while the Pera Palas is grand, the Londra is homely and eccentric. Caged parrots peer dolefully from their cages on the windowsills in the lounge-bar (*see p145*). Portable coal burners, wind-up gramophones, valve radios and plenty of other ancient junk clutter the corridors. Hemingway stayed here in 1922, sent by the *Toronto Daily Star* to cover the Turkish war of independence, and the place is still favoured by artists, writers and film crews. Some of the 54 rooms are a little down-at-heel, but they are clean. The upper floors have 'super' rooms with double glazing, plush carpets and jacuzzis.
Bar. Internet (wireless). Room service. TV.

Galata Residence
Felek Sokak 27, off Bankalar Caddesi, Karaköy (0212 292 4841, www.galataresidence.com). **Rates** €75-€120 apartment. **Rooms** 15. **Credit** MC, V. **Map** p246 M6 ㉚
An apartment hotel with history. The house formerly belonged to the Kamondos, an important Levantine banking family, who gave their name to the sculpted steps that lead up to the residence from Voyvoda Caddesi. The solid brick building later served as a Jewish school. It is now split into 15 comfortably furnished apartments, which each sleep four. Smaller two-bedroom apartments are available in the next building. The decor is homely in an old-fashioned way, with four-poster beds, vintage armchairs and sofas. Each apartment has a fully equipped kitchen, but there's also a restaurant on the roof and a bare-brick café in the vaulted cellar. It is close enough to walk across the bridge to Eminönü and the bazaar, but just downhill from the Galata Tower and Beyoğlu.
Café. Internet (high-speed). Restaurant. Room service. TV.

Residence
Sadri Alışık Sokak 19, off Istiklal Caddesi (0212 252 7685, www.hotelresidence.com.tr). **Rates** €52 double. **Rooms** 46. **Credit** AmEx, DC, MC, V. **Map** p247 O3 ㊴
The Residence is a bit difficult to find as it's tucked away on a narrow side street, but it's worth the effort. The rooms, though small and basic, are bright and well equipped and recently refurbished. The location is great too, right among the bars of Beyoğlu.
Bar. Restaurant. Room service. TV.

Vardar Palace Hotel
Sıraselviler Caddesi 16, Taksim (0212 252 2888, www.vardarhotel.com). **Rates** €60-€75 double. **Rooms** 40. **Credit** AmEx, MC, V. **Map** p249 O3 ㊵
Two minutes from Taksim Square, the 40-room Vardar occupies a drab-looking 19th-century building on a narrow strip, where Sıraselviler narrows to almost canyon-like proportions. Inside, however, the hotel is bright, pleasant and deserving of its three-star status, although the airiness of the high-ceilinged rooms is sabotaged by a dark colour scheme. Front-facing rooms can get noisy.
Concierge. Internet (wireless). Room service. TV.

Villa Zurich
Akarsu Yokuşu Caddesi 36/36A, Cihangir (0212 293 0604, www.hotelvillazurich.com). **Rates** €100 double; €120-€150 sea view. **Rooms** 45. **Credit** AmEx, MC, V. **Map** p249 O4 ㊶

I'zaz Lofts. *See p109.*

CONSUME

Ten minutes' walk down Sıraselviler Caddesi from Taksim Square, in Cihangir, the Villa Zurich is conveniently close to the centre but pleasantly removed from all the hustle. The area itself is worth exploring – a lively mix of local shops and teahouses mixed with hip cafés and gourmet delis. The hotel is vaguely European in character, with 43 comfortable, if unremarkable, guest rooms and two suites. There is a popular seafood restaurant, Doğa Balik, on the rooftop, with fabulous views.
Bar. Concierge. Internet (wireless). No-smoking rooms. Parking (free). Restaurant. Room service. TV.

NIŞANTAŞI, ŞIŞLI & LEVENT
Deluxe

Bentley Hotel
Halaskargazi Caddesi 23, Harbiye (0212 291 7730, www.bentley-hotel.com). Metro Şişli. **Rates** €240-€280 double. **Rooms** 48. **Credit** AmEx, MC, V.
Istanbul's first (self-proclaimed) 'hip' hotel, the Bentley's minimalist chocolate-and-cream lobby looks like the reception area of an upmarket ad agency. Rooms are similarly smart and understated. Best options are the corner rooms with curving glass walls (a pity there's not much of a view). The two penthouse suites have wine minibars, plasma TVs and espresso machines. One comes with an adjacent single room. These are stylish amenities, as you would expect from a member of the Design Hotels group, but there's nothing groundbreaking.
Bar. Business services. Concierge. Gym. Internet (high-speed). No-smoking rooms. Parking (free). Restaurant. Room service. Spa. TV.

★ Park Hyatt Maçka Palas
Tesvikiye, Bronz Sokak 4 isli Şişli, Şişli (0212 315 1234, www.istanbul.park.hyatt.com). Metro Şişli. **Rates** €187-€260 double. **Rooms** 90. **Credit** AmEx, DC, MC, V.
Leave your preconceptions of international chain hotels in the atrium lobby. This Park Hyatt in Şişli is one of a new generation of large, corporate-looking hotels that are responding to the boutique phenomenon. Converted from what used to be the Italian Embassy in Ottoman days, the building is impressive. Each of the 90 rooms has plenty of space, with modern gadgets for the business traveller. Bathrooms have a steam room, which in cheaper rooms is shared with the shower. Some also have a hamam-style area with heated marble floors. Other nice touches include a filtered water sink, alongside a regular one, iPod docks and deep stand alone baths. Photos from Ara Güler, known as the 'Eye of Istanbul', are hung around the hotel. In the lobby is a wine lounge, but more impressive is the Terrace, with a small pool. The Prime restaurant serves flawless steaks and seafood, grilled in the open kitchen, alongside an impressive, but not cheap, wine list.

THE BEST ROOFTOP VIEWS

Of the Western Districts
Büyük Londra (*see p111*).

Of the whole city
Richmond Hotel (*see p105*).

Of the Bosphorus
TomTom Suites (*see p105*).

Bars (2). Business services. Café. Concierge. Disabled-adapted rooms. Gym. Internet (wireless). No-smoking rooms. Parking. Restaurant. Room service. Spa. TV.

The Sofa Hotel
Teşvikiye Caddesi 123, Nişantaşı (0212 368 1818, www.thesofahotel.com). Metro Nişantaşı. **Rates** €350-€530 double. **Rooms** 82. **Credit** AmEx, DC, MC, V.
The Sofa Hotel offers minimalist chic in the heart of Nişantaşı's upmarket shopping and dining area, and is also within walking distance of the Istanbul Convention and Exhibition Center. The design-led bedrooms are comfortable, and the well-equipped bathrooms feature rainshowers, natural soaps and fluffy bathrobes. There's a decent spa and fitness room, and the in-house restaurant, Longtable, serves modern New York cuisine in handsome surroundings. Try the signature saffron martini.
Bar. Business services. Café. Concierge. Disabled-adapted rooms. Gym. Internet (wireless). No-smoking rooms. Parking (YTL15 day). Restaurant. Room service. Spa. TV.

Expensive

★ Mövenpick
Buyukdere Caddesi, 4. Levent (0212 319 2929, www.movenpick-hotels.com). Metro 4.Levent. **Rates** €120-€400 double (excluding 8% tax & breakfast). **Rooms** 249. **Credit** AmEx, DC, MC, V.
The pick of the hotels in corporate 4. Levent, the Swiss-owned Mövenpick is a good business option, but its location very near 4. Levent metro stop means it is handy for central Taksim Square too. The 249 rooms are well designed, with plain wood and natural colours, as you would expect from Mövenpick, and rooms on the higher floors have good views. For guests paying the executive rate, there's an airport-style lounge on the 20th floor. Others have to make do with the chic Baradox lobby bar and lounge. The dimly lit and cavernous wellness centre has a new gym, sauna, jacuzzi and a refreshing swimming pool.
Bars (2). Business services. Concierge. Gym. Internet (high-speed, €18 a day). No-smoking rooms. Parking (free). Restaurant. Room service. Spa. TV.

YAŞMA
HOTEL

In the middle of old town Istanb
for different needs

BOSPHORUS VILLAGES
Deluxe

★ Çırağan Palace Hotel Kempinski
Çırağan Caddesi 32, Beşiktaş (0212 258 3377, www.kempinski.com). Bus DT1, D2. **Rates** €500-€1,350 double. **Rooms** 313. **Credit** AmEx, DC, MC, V.
The hotel is partly set in a magnificent 19th-century palace on the Bosphorus, built for Sultan Abdülaziz, an ill-fated ruler who killed himself wi th a pair of scissors. In 1908, the palace became the seat of parliament, but burned down two years later. In 1986, following an ambitious restoration, parts of the original complex were incorporated into this luxurious, 313-room extravaganza belonging to the Kempinski chain. Only 11 suites are in the palace itself – including the €30,000-a-night Sultan's suite (breakfast included) – along with the Tuğra restaurant, which showcases Ottoman cuisine, and other public rooms. All other bedrooms are in the annex. Non-residents can enjoy the hotel's art and culture programme, which includes art exhibitions. There are free classical concerts held on the first and last Saturday of every month (call to reserve). In summer, take advantage of the stunning outdoor infinity pool, which appears to flow into the Bosphorus. *Photo p117.*
Bars (2). Business centre. Concierge. Disabled-adapted room. Gym. Internet (wireless). No-smoking rooms. Parking (free). Pools (1 indoor, 1 outdoor). Restaurants (2). Room service. Spa. TV.

★ Four Seasons Bosphorus
Çırağan Caddesi 28, Beşiktaş (0212 381 4000, www.fourseasons.com/bosphorus). Bus DT1, D2. **Rates** €430-€490 double. **Rooms** 170. **Credit** AmEx, DC, MC, V.
The second Four Seasons property in Istanbul is a very different proposition from the Sultanahmet hotel. This one, near Kempinski's Çırağan Palace, is a 19th-century palace on the Bosphorus. Its classic design will reassure those used to the Four Seasons brand, although there are Ottoman touches throughout. Rooms and suites all have a TV, DVD and CD player, and a deep marble bath. The grounds are delightful for taking a stroll before dinner to watch the ships roll past. If it's warm outside, the pool bar and terrace is the spot to take dinner.
Bars (2). Business centre. Concierge. Disabled-adapted room. Gym. Internet (wireless). No-smoking rooms. Parking (free). Pools (1 indoor, 1 outdoor). Restaurants (2). Room service. Spa. TV.

Hotel les Ottomans
Muallim Naci Caddesi 168, Kuruçeşme (0212 287 1024, www.lesottomans.com). **Rates** €1,200-€5,400 suite. **Rooms** 12. **Credit** AmEx, DC, MC, V.
Opened in spring 2006, this all-suite hotel is designed to lure celebrities, heads of state and millionaires bored of the Çırağan Palace. In an impeccably restored white wooden *yalı* (mansion), with spectacular views of the Boğazici Strait, the style is Oriental opulence – to excess, some might say. Think brocade drapes, Arabic-script inscriptions and giant chandeliers. With just 12 suites, the emphasis is on exclusivity. Butler, yacht and limousine service are all part of the package. The Passionate Suite is, of course, billed as the perfect honeymoon destination – with feng shui to 'add a completely new freshness and purity to your life as a couple'. There's an intimate Ottoman restaurant with an impressive cellar and a fabulous Caudalie spa (*see p116* **Hotel hamams**).
Bar. Business services. Concierge. Gym. Internet (wireless). No-smoking rooms. Parking (free). Pool (indoor). Restaurant. Room service. Spa. TV.

Expensive

Bebek Hotel
Cevdet Paşa Caddesi 34, Bebek (0212 358 2000, www.bebekhotel.com.tr). **Rates** €240 street view; €330 sea view. **Rooms** 21. **Credit** AmEx, MC.
Far from the centre and the sights, this is primarily a business hotel. From the outside, the four-storey building is nothing special, but inside the 21 suites are all gleaming dark wood, brown leather, pink marble and rattan furniture. The real wow factor here is the view, and nine of the rooms have balconies over the Bosphorus. Is it worth the extra €90? We'd have to say yes. However, if you get stuck with a room overlooking the street, you can enjoy the same view from the waterfront bar downstairs. Beware of Bebek in the summer, when the traffic into town can be agonisingly slow.
Bars (2). Café. Concierge. Internet (wireless). Parking (free). Restaurant. Room service. TV.

Princess Hotel Ortaköy
Dereboyu Caddesi 10, Ortaköy (0212 227 6010, www.ortakoyprincess.com). **Rates** €160 double. **Rooms** 90. **Credit** AmEx, DC, MC, V.
Few people other than those doing business up in nearby Levent and Maslak choose to stay in Ortaköy, but if scurrying around the mosques isn't on your agenda, this rather bland option is worth considering. A modern hotel with 90 generously sized rooms, its most appealing feature is probably

---

THE BEST HISTORICAL CONVERSIONS

A whitewashed waterside mansion
A'jia (*see p117*).

Luxury in a former *rakı* distillery
Sumahan (*see p117*).

Luxury in a palace, a very big palace
Çırağan Palace (*see above*).

CONSUME

Hotel Hamams

Get clean, feel beautiful.

Turkey is famous for its hamams, but for those who prefer their treatments more spa-like and less spartan, many Istanbul hotels now have their own, western-style spas – and most include Turkish baths. Spa facilities aren't restricted to hotel guests, and a few hours' pampering can be a perfect pick-you-up. All the spas recommended below include an indoor pool, sauna, Turkish bath and steam room.

If you can't afford a room at the exclusive **Les Ottomans Hotel** (*see p115*), check into the basement Caudalie Vinothérapie spa instead. Facilities include a tiled hot tub and indoor pool with natural light filtered through the glass bottom of the above-ground pool. For around YTL140 a day, visitors can use the pools, exercise equipment, sauna (with flat-screen TV), steam room, Turkish bath and 'salt inhalation therapy' room. There's even a meditation room, complete with a cascade of lavender-infused water. Best of all, indulge in one of the treatments using grape-based Caudalie products.

Another luxury hotel that's big on spa treatments is the **Çırağan Palace Kempinski** (*see p115*). In summer, you can take full advantage of your environment by booking a poolside massage in a private cabana with views of the Bosphorus. Otherwise, the treatments are given in the palace section that dates back to 187. A vast range of treatments using Decléor products is available. The Traditional Çırağan Body Scrub (€120) is pure bliss.

An Asian-inspired ambience, expert staff and Molton Brown products are the hallmarks of the Laveda Spa at the **Ritz-Carlton** (*see p102*). One of the city's most exclusive spas, its menu features a 'Traditional Turkish Hamam' treatment, including massage (€100).

The treatments at the **Ceylan Intercontinental** (*see p103*) begin with a warm steam bath, followed by a full body scrub and a foam massage (YTL 130).

The **Four Seasons Bosphorus** (*see p115*) has given new direction to the hamam experience with treatments you can enjoy with your partner. Body masks and deep body massages are available (YTL180).

For a more traditional experience, the **Grand Hyatt** (0212 225 7000, Taşkışla Caddesi, www.istanbul.hyatt.com.tr, map p247 P1) has a Turkish bath in which to enjoy a body scrub.

CONSUME

its proximity to the waterfront bars, cafés and fish restaurants. You can avoid the traffic that clogs Istanbul's roads by catching a ferry down the Bosphorus to the sights in Sultanahmet.
Bar. Business services. Café. Concierge. Gym. Internet (wireless). No-smoking rooms. Parking (free). Pool (outdoor). Restaurant. Room service. Spa. TV.

W Istanbul
Suleyman Seba Caddesi 22, Akaretler, Beşiktaş (0212 381 2121, www.wistanbul.com.tr). **Rates** €160-€360 double (excluding tax). **Rooms** 136. **Credit** AmEx, DC, MC, V.
The ultra-styled design of W hotels around the world continues with this Beşiktaş property. The hotel is in a newly redeveloped area whose terraced buildings were once housing for officers from the nearby Dolmabahçe Palace. The Akaretler (www.akaretler.com.tr) houses have now become clothing stores – lots of them are home to designer brands – and this W. The lively interior – perhaps best summed up as mid-20th century and modern meets Ottoman – has oriental touches among the dark corridors, with flashes of neon. Satiny reds add a gypsyesque touch to the bedrooms, but they are less overtly styled, comfortable and modern, with BOSE stereos and iPod docks. There is a champagne bar by the lobby, but most of the action happens in the bar upstairs or the restaurant another flight up. With a monthly rotation of international DJs, it is a lively bar that adheres to the W lifestyle ethos of music and fashion. There is also a day spa and café.
Bars (2). Business centre. Concierge. Gym. Internet (wireless). No-smoking rooms. Parking (YTL30). Restaurants (2). Room service. Spa. TV.

CAMPING

Ataköy Tatil Köyü
Rauf Orbay Caddesi, off Ataköy Tatil Köyü, Bakırköy (0212 559 6014). **Rates** $10 per tent (two-man); $6 per caravan; $2.50 extra for car. **Credit** DC, MC, V.
On the Marmara coast about 15 kilometres (10 miles) from the city centre, this campsite is conveniently situated near Ataköy train station, from where there are regular trains into Sirkeci. The site is clean and has good facilities, including a tennis court, pool (summer only) and bar. Make sure you don't get a pitch too close to the noisy road.

THE ASIAN SHORE

Deluxe

★ A'jia

Ahmet Rasim Paşa Yalısı, Çubuklu Caddesi 27, Kanlıca (0216 413 9300, www.ajiahotel.com). **Rates** €260-€460 double. **Rooms** 16. **Credit** AmEx, DC, MC, V.

The first boutique hotel on the Asian Shore, A'jia opened in 2004 to great acclaim. The white washed *yalı* (mansion) was built in 1876 and has at various times been an army barracks, housed Atatürk's advisor Ahmet Rasim Pasha and, later, a primary school. It's now a stunning residence, lapped by the Bosphorus. The 16 sleek rooms contrast successfully with the traditional exterior. Each of the rooms facing the water has a balcony, and breakfast,and dinner can be taken on a large deck overlooking the Bosphorus. It's little wonder that the A'jia is a favourite venue for weddings and honeymoons. A'jia has its own boat, which can be used at any time to cross to Emigan opposite, or the fort at Rumeli Hisarı. *Bar. Concierge. Disabled-adapted rooms. Internet (high speed). No-smoking rooms. Parking (free). Restaurant. Room service. TV.*

► *The hotel is well-placed for the Müzedechanga restaurant (see p137) in the Sakip Sabanci museum directly opposite on the European shore. The free boat will drop guests off and pick them up again.*

★ Sumahan

Kuleli Caddesi 51, Çengelköy (0216 422 8000, www.sumahan.com). **Rates** €195-€380 double. **Credit** AmEx, DC, MC, V.

This converted distillery, dating from 1875, enjoys a fabulous waterfont setting in Çengelköy, a sleepy fishing village way off the tourist radar. The architect owners have created polished contemporary interiors featuring grey marble, exposed stonework, and picture windows with extraordinary views of mosques and minarets shimmering beyond the Bosphorus bridge. Many rooms come with mini-hamams, and beds face the waterfront. Kordonbalik restaurant serves superlative seafood – at a price. There are scheduled boat trips across the Bosphorus. *Bar. Business services. Café. Concierge. Disabled-adapted rooms. Gym. Internet (high speed). No-smoking rooms. Parking (free). Restaurant. Room service. Spa. TV.*

Hostel

★ Hush

Caferağa Mahallesi Miralay Nazım Sokak 20, Kadıköy (0216 330 9188, www.hushhostel istanbul.com). **Rates** €10 dorm; €30 double. **Credit** MC, V. **Map** p251 W8 ㊷

Hush is the first hostel on the Asian shore, and perfectly located for a night out along the lively Kadife Sokak, an area lined with bars and restaurants. As its name suggests, the hostel is on a quiet side street, in a four-storey wooden building dating from the 1920s. Accommodation is in four double rooms, two mixed dorms and one female-only dorm. There's also a cosy lounge and a leafy garden and bar with reasonable prices. It's also reasonably handy for the Sabiha Gökçen Airport. The amiable owners will advise you where to go, and may even join you.

Çiragan Palace Hotel Kempinski. *See p115.*

CONSUME

Restaurants

Turkish chefs are reinventing the national cuisine.

Istanbul's culinary scene is on the move. Meze, often accompanied by the anise-flavoured spirit *rakı*, remains perennially popular, but young Istanbullus are also discovering a fusion cuisine that mixes fresh ingredients from the Bosphorus, spices from the bazaars and techniques learned in the restaurants of France, the US and UK. Fine-dining establishments such as **Mikla** (*see p127*) and **Mimolett** (*see p131*) could even be in line for Turkey's first Michelin star.

Beyond the world of white tablecloths and sommeliers, there's Istanbul's street food, traditional, delicious, economical dishes such as grilled intestine, *kokoreç*, or fried anchovies, fished from the Bosphorus just minutes before cooking.

THE LOCAL SCENE

The quintessential Istanbul eating experience remains the *meyhane* (taverna). These places are cheap and frequently boisterous. The meze (shared small dishes) is washed down with plenty of *rakı* (anise-flavoured spirit).

Filling the table with myriad meze to share keeps everyone happy, even vegetarians. *Meyhanes* are found around the city, but there's a heavy concentration around **Nevizade Sokak** (*see p131*) in Beyoğlu. Often the dishes are available to see first, useful when the translated menu includes dishes such as 'sensitive meatballs'. A budget option for Turkish food is canteen-style *lokantas*, where workers eat *hazır yemek* (ready-made dishes) served from bains-marie.

Fish is another local speciality. Most visitors are directed to **Kumkapı** (*see p123*), which has the greatest concentration of seafood restaurants and is close to the hotel district of Sultanahmet. But there are plenty of other enticing options away from the hordes. A city staple is **Doğa Balık** (*see p131*) in Cihangir, or **Balıkçı Sabahattin** (*see p119*) in Sultanahmet.

Taste a real kebab at a *kebapçı* or *ocakbaşı*. There are more varieties than you can shake a skewer at. *See p129* **Kebab Cuisine**.

Practicalities

Few restaurants have a dress code, but invariably the Istanbullus look fabulous when they go out, especially at high-end places.

Tipping is expected; ten per cent is sufficient. Service charges are rarely included except at high-end places, where tips are expected anyway. Reservations are a must on Friday and Saturday, and advisable during the week at the most popular restaurants.

Alcohol is expensive in Turkey. *Rakı* is usually served with fish dishes in *meyhanes*, although the ever improving Turkish wine (*see p146* **Grape Expectations**) is increasingly popular, and can cost between YTL25-YTL150 in restaurants.

ABOUT THE LISTINGS

Throughout the chapter, we've listed the price range of starters – these are the meze dishes which can be either an appetiser or a selection can serve as the meal itself. The price range of main courses is also provided to offer a rough indication of meal cost. Restaurants often close when the last patron leaves. If paying by credit card, check the machine is working before ordering.

If a restaurant is on a side street (*sokak*), we have also used the name of an adjoining main street where possible.

SULTANAHMET

Big on sights it may be, but Sultanahmet is woefully underserved by decent restaurants. It would be unfair say that all the eateries are tourist traps, but it wouldn't be far off the mark. Below are a few exceptions.

Amedros

Hoca Rüstem Sokak 7, off Divan Yolu (0212 522 8356). Tram Sultanahmet. **Open** 11am-1am daily. **Starters** YTL8-YTL14. **Main courses** YTL16-YTL30. **Credit** DC, MC, V. **Map** p243 M10 **❶** **Turkish**

Though it's a European-style bistro, Amedros also does good Ottoman dishes. The house special is *testi kebabı*, lamb roasted with vegetables in a sealed clay pot that is cracked open at the table. In summer, candlelit tables are lined up in the cobbled alley; in winter, diners are warmed by a crackling fire.

Balıkçı Sabahattin

Seyit Hasan Kuyu Sokak 1, off Cankurtaran Caddesi (0212 458 1824, www.balikci sabahattin.com). Tram Sultanahmet. **Open** 11am-12.30am daily. **Starters** from YTL7. **Main courses** YTL15-YTL45. **Credit** AmEx, MC, V. **Map** p243 N11 **❷** **Seafood**

Most visitors staying around Sultanahmet head to Kumkapı for fish, unaware that there's a far better option on their doorstep. It benefits from a gorgeous setting: a street of picturesque old wooden houses, periodically rattled to their foundations by the commuter trains passing in and out of Sirkeci. There's no menu: instead, bow-tied waiters present you with a tray of various meze and, later, a huge iced platter of seasonal fish and seafood from which to choose. Entertainment comes in the form of skittering cats skilled at doleful looks and pleading meows. Reservations essential.

Djazzu

Alemdar Mahallesi, Incili Çavuş Çıkmazı 5-7 (0212 512 2242). Tram Sultanahmet. **Open** 11am-1.30am daily. **Starters** YTL8-YTL24. **Main courses** YTL18-YTL24. **Credit** AmEx, MC, V. **Map** p243 N10 **❸** **Modern European**

In a small alleyway by Şah Bar (*see p141*), just off Incili Çavuş Sokak, Djazzu's attractive pavement seating area and inside tables beat its considerable competition in the design stakes. The menu is also a gear above the usual Turkish cuisine of the area, with a fusion, Mediterranean-influenced menu cooked by a Japanese chef. The marinated *maguro* (tuna) is excellent. There's a good selection of Turkish wines too, but we felt service could do with smartening up on a recent visit.

Dubb Indian Restaurant

Alemdar Mahallesi, Incili Çavuş Sokak 10 (0212 513 7308, www.dubbindian.com). Tram Sultanahmet. **Open** noon-11pm daily. **Starters** YTL7-YTL15. **Main courses** YTL13-YTL35. **Credit** AmEx, DC, MC, V. **Map** p243 N10 **❹** **Indian**

Istanbul is not exactly brimming with Indian restaurants, and this little gem in the heart of Sultanahmet might be the closest that you'll get to eating authentic dishes from the subcontinent. There's a wide variety of curries, thalis and dishes from the tandoor, plus Indian bevvies like salty or sweet lassi. All the bread is baked in house daily. There's a set menu at YTL36. The roof terrace – up seemingly endless flights of stairs – is worth the climb.

★ Mozaik

Divanyolu Caddesi, Incili Çavuş Sokak 1 (0212 512 4177). Tram Sultanahmet. **Open** 9am-midnight daily (bar 2am). **Starters** YTL7-YTL18. **Main courses** YTL12-YTL29. **Credit** AmEx, DC, MC, V. **Map** p243 N10 **❺** **Turkish**

A cut above many of Sultanahmet's more slapdash establishments. When it is too chilly to sit on the pavement, the interior, with wooden floors carpeted with old kilims, copper platters and creaking stairs between the restaurant's three floors, offer romantic potential for dinner à deux. The international menu covers a lot of ground – everything from chicken mandarin to T-bone steak – but the special is *abant kebap*, a spectacular West Anatolian dish. After dinner, head for the basement bar.

Pudding Shop

Divanyolu Caddesi 6 (0212 522 2970, www.puddingshop.com). Tram Sultanahmet. **Open** 7am-11pm daily. **Starters** YTL8. **Main courses** YTL8-YTL17. **Credit** AmEx, MC, V. **Map** p243 N10 **❻** **Turkish**

A landmark in hippie history. In the pre-*Lonely Planet* days of the late 1960s and early 1970s, the Pudding Shop (founded 1957) was a bottleneck for all the overland traffic passing through on its tie-dyed, spliff-addled way east to Kathmandu. In addition to the food, the place served up travel information, courtesy of the two brothers who owned it, a busy bulletin board, and the like-minded company. It even crops up in the movie *Midnight*

INSIDE TRACK
EAT LIKE A SULTAN

For the kind of food that pleasured the palates of sultans, such as *imambayıldı* ('the imam fainted'; slow-roast aubergines with onions and tomatoes), *dilberdudağı* ('lady's lips'; pastry soaked in syrup), *karnıyarık* ('slit stomach'; aubergine stuffed with minced meat) and *kadınbudu köfte* ('ladies' thighs'; battered, fried meatballs), visit a restaurant serving traditional Ottoman cuisine, using recipes directly from the kitchens of Topkapı. Expect elaborate dishes mixing rice, fruit and vegetables with meat and fish. Try **Asitane** (*see p124*) for the real Ottoman deal, or **Rumeli** (*see p121*) for updated twists on the same theme.

CONSUME

Meyhanes & Meze

For an evening of authentic meze head for Çiçek Pasajı and Nevizade Sokak.

Everyone needs a place to let loose. The British down pints in pubs, the French guzzle wine in brasseries, and the Greeks smash plates in tavernas. The Turks? They make merry in the *meyhane*, the age-old Istanbul version of a tapas bar. This is where locals meet, eat meze, drink *rakı* and are cajoled by house musicians into belting out folk songs.

The city's most famous *meyhane* district is the **Çiçek Pasajı**, an elegant 19th-century arcade off Istiklal Caddesi. With its neo-classical façade, barrelled glass roof, old-fashioned street lamps and cascading plastic flora, the atmosphere is not what it once was. Many joints use waiters' recommendations rather than menus, so try to confirm prices in advance to avoid confrontations with unscrupulous staff.

Locals prefer neighbouring **Nevizade Sokak**, an alley lined with restaurants leading off **Balık Pazarı** (Fish Market). Though home to some of the city's best *meyhanes*, the area also has more than its fair share of cheap beer joints. Rows of tables are set outside as if for one giant street party, which is what the place looks like most evenings: every seat is filled by garrulous diners, attended by dashing waiters, wandering minstrels and hopeful street vendors. If you have just one night in Istanbul, spend it on Nevizade Sokak.

Krependeki Imroz.

Most *meyhanes* also have two or three floors of indoor dining, sometimes with a roof terrace. They don't differ much in terms of food and prices, but everyone has their favourites. We like **Boncuk** (*see p133*), which specialises in Armenian dishes and features live *fasıl* music. **Krependeki Imroz** (*see p133*), founded in 1941 and one of the oldest *meyhanes*, deserves a mention for its excellent staff, solid food and reasonable prices. Imroz is the Greek name for Gökçeada, one of the Aegean islands, and home to the Greek owners. **Cumhuriyet Meyhanesi** (*see p133*), once frequented by Atatürk, is notable for its *fasıl* musicians. For quality fish (rather than a thrilling atmosphere), **Mer Balık** (*see p133*) is better than most establishments in the area. The lantern fish kebab is outstanding.

When ordering from the heaped tray of meze, the more dishes the merrier, since sharing is what it's all about. Cold dishes cost about YTL5, hot ones YTL6-YTL10, and seafood appetisers YTL10-YTL20. For two people, six dishes are usually enough; you can order main courses later if you have room. Most dishes can be chosen from the fridges, or will be paraded before you on a tray. Or go for a set menu of meze, fish, meat and dessert, with unlimited *rakı*, beer or wine, which costs about YTL40-YTL80 a head.

Nevizade Sokak.

Express. Smartened up for the 21st-century tourist – plate-glass windows, gleaming display cabinets and slick staff – the restaurant still doles out basic canteen-style fare, no better or worse than half a dozen similar restaurants along this strip.

Rumeli

Ticarethane Sokak 8, off Divanyolu Caddesi (0212 512 0008). Tram Sultanahmet. **Open** 9am-midnight daily. **Starters** YTL6-YTL17. **Main courses** YTL15-YTL29. **Credit** AmEx, DC, MC, V. **Map** p243 M10 **❼** **Modern Turkish**
Rumeli's food is far superior to the tourist fodder served at the cluster of establishments at the bottom of Divan Yolu. A former printworks, with a cavernous interior of exposed brick, stone and stained floorboards, the restaurant spans several floors from the cobbled side-street up to the roof terrace. Traditional Ottoman dishes are given a Mediterranean twist, along with excellent salads, pasta, and a very decent wine list. There are dishes from the Kurdish and Armenian regions too. Staff are charming.

Seasons Restaurant

Four Seasons Hotel, Tevfikhane Sokak 1 (0212 638 8200, www.fourseasons.com). Tram Sultahahmet. **Open** noon-3pm, 7-11pm. **Starters** YTL18-YTL26. **Main courses** YTL29-YTL50. **Credit** AmEx, DC, MC, V. **Map** p243 N10 **❽** **Modern European**
Still a high-end Sultanahmet establishment with an international menu, the Seasons Restaurant can't compare with the flair of newer restaurants like Ulus 29, Topaz and Mimolett. In a glass enclosure in the gardens of the Four Seasons Hotel, the restaurant aims at elegance – but the look is still very hotel-like, and diners are mainly tourists or hotel guests.
▶ *The Four Seasons on the Bosphorus (see p115) has a good Mediterranean restaurant, Aqua, in a lovely dining room.*

THE BAZAAR QUARTER

Darüzziyafe

Şifahane Sokak 6, Süleymaniye (0212 511 8414, www.daruzziyafe.com.tr). Tram Beyazıt, Eminönü or Laleli. **Open** noon-11pm daily. **Starters** YTL7-YTL19. **Main courses** YTL27. **Credit** AmEx, MC, V. **Map** p242 J8 **❾** **Turkish**
The former soup kitchens of the Süleymaniye Mosque complex now turns out more varied fare. Although the menu runs to several pages, the food is still canteen cooking – great for lunch (and a favourite with tour buses) but too prosaic for dinner. The setting, a large courtyard filled with rose bushes and trees, is potentially lovely but rendered institutional by cheap furniture and neglect. The restaurant is located to the north of the mosque, separate from the row of small eateries which line its west side.

★ Şar

Yeniceriler Caddesi 47, Beyazıt (0212 458 9219). Tram Beyazıt. **Open** 6am-11.30pm daily. **Starters** YTL3-YTL5. **Main courses** YTL6-YTL15. **Credit** MC, V. **Map** p242 K10 **❿** **Turkish**
Among tourist restaurants south of the Golden Horn, this canteen stands as an island of Turkish food for Turkish people. The pick-and-point system also serves as a good introduction to the dishes. Pick your starter, main, salad, drink and dessert, pay and head upstairs. Şar has been here since 1957 and is known for its hearty food, such as the moussaka-like *gizli kebap* or the *pide çeşitleri*, a Turkish pizza. It's one of the cheaper options in the area. No alcohol.
▶ *There is another, more upmarket, branch around the corner on Tiyatro Caddesi.*

EMİNÖNÜ & THE GOLDEN HORN

Two blocks south of Sirkeci Station, narrow **Ibni Kemal Caddesi** is a street full of cheap eateries serving the local working population. The presence of neighbouring Hoca Paşa Mosque means no alcohol is served, but a meal costs less than YTL15 per person. The underslung section of the **Galata Bridge** is also crammed with budget fish restaurants, with menus in English and beer by the flagon. Much better, however, are the floating fish stalls on the west side of the bridge. Order an anchovy sandwich and watch the fishermen.

Hamdi Et Lokantası

Kalçın Sokak 17, Tahmis Caddesi (0212 528 0390). Tram Eminönü. **Open** 11am-midnight daily. **Starters** YTL7-YTL10. **Main courses** YTL12-YTL23. **Credit** AmEx, DC, MC, V. **Map** p243 L7 **⓫** **Turkish**
Right on Eminönü square, Hamdi is a favourite among Istanbul natives, particularly business lunchers and carnivorous fans of south-eastern Turkish food. Hamdi serves meat *alaturca* at its very best, grilled to succulent perfection on the *mangal*. The restaurant occupies four floors, but the top one is the most memorable. In an enclosed glass terrace, it offers sweeping views of the Golden Horn and Beyoğlu. It's particularly lovely in the summer, when the windows are opened. Otherwise, opt for the curious Oriental Saloon on the first floor, kitted out with cuckoo clocks and startled nymphs.

Orient Express Restaurant

Sirkeci Station, Istasyon Caddesi (0212 522 2280, www.orientexpressrestaurant.net). Tram Sirkeci. **Open** 11.30am-midnight daily. **Starters** YTL6-YTL12. **Main courses** YTL15-YTL25. **Credit** MC, V. **Map** p243 N8 **⓬** **Turkish**
An essential stop for fans of the Orient Express and Agatha Christie, this time-warp is bang in the

CONSUME

centre of Sirkeci station, the final stop of the world's most famous train. In warmer weather, tables are set outside on the station platform. The only obvious change in the dining room since the restaurant's launch in 1890 is the incongruous concrete fishpond in the centre, which jars with the Oriental backdrop. The walls are adorned with black and white stills from the 1974 movie *Murder on the Orient Express*. Food is standard Turkish fare, reasonably priced. It's a shame the restaurant is usually empty.

▶ *For more on the Orient Express, see p59.*

Pandeli

Mısır Çarşısı 1, Eminönü Square (0212 527 3909, www.pandeli.com.tr). Tram Eminönü. **Open** 11.30am-7.30pm daily. **Starters** YTL6-YTL12. **Main courses** YTL15-YTL25. **Credit** AmEx, DC, MC, V. **Map** p243 L8 ⑬

Turkish

Not a bad place for lunch if you're shopping in the Egyptian Bazaar. Occupying a wonderful set of domed rooms above the bazaar entrance, Pandeli is very much the essence of genteel old Stamboul. Decorated throughout in blue and white Iznik tiling, it's worth a visit for the lovely interior alone. The food, by contrast, is run of the mill Turkish and pricey – and waiters have a tendency towards brusqueness too. Ask for a table in the front room with views of the Golden Horn. Note the early closing time.

KUMKAPI

Situated inside the city walls on the Sea of Marmara coast, this former fishing port is now an inner-city neighbourhood of cobbled lanes lined with seafood restaurants, where persistent hawkers attempt to waylay passers-by. A shortish taxi ride from Sultanahmet, Kumkapı is not a bad choice for fresh fish, although the popularity restaurants along **Çapari Sokak** have long been eclipsed by the *meyhanes* at Nevizade and fancy fish places up the Bosphorus.

In total, there are around 50 restaurants in Kumkapı. There are a few that locals rate highly, including **Akvaryum Fish Restaurant**, which has live *fasıl* music, as does **Çapari**, one of the district's oldest establishments. **Kartallar Balıkçı** is famous for its *balık çorbası* (fish chowder) and *buğulama* (steamed fish casserole) – and has a large celebrity quotient among its clientele. In business since 1938, **Kör Agop** is known for its top quality fish and *fasıl*.

As at the Grand Bazaar, prices are conspicuously absent from menus, so make sure to agree on the bill in advance. Most places offer fixed meal deals, kicking off with meze followed by fish of the day

INSIDE TRACK FINE FISH

For the day's catch in refined surroundings, head up the Bosphorus to the village of **Arnavutköy**, which is packed with fish restaurants and has a scenic walkway by the water. A little further along the Bosphorus is upmarket **Poseidon** (*see p137*) in **Bebek**, and **Rumeli Iskele** (*see p138*) up at **Rumeli Hisarı**.

and dessert. Expect to pay around YTL50 per person with alcohol (*rakı*, local wine or beer).

Fasıl musicians roam between the restaurants serenading outdoor diners, while an odd assortment of street vendors flog anything from fresh almonds to Cuban cigars.

Akvaryum Fish Restaurant

Çapari Sokak 39 (0212 517 2273). Kumkapı station. **Open** 10.30am-1am daily. **Credit** MC, V. **Map** p242 K11 ⑭ **Seafood**

Çapari

Çapari Sokak 22 (0212 517 7530, www. capari.net). Kumkapı station. **Open** 10am-2am daily. **Credit** MC, V. **Map** p242 K11 ⑮ **Seafood**

Pandeli.

CONSUME

Menu & Glossary

USEFUL PHRASES

Can I see a menu? **Menüye bakabilir miyim?**
Do you have a table for (number) people? **(Number) kişilik masanız var mı?**
I want to book a table for (time) o'clock. **Saat (time) için bir masa ayırmak istiyorum.**
I'll have (name of food). **Ben (name of food) istiyorum.**
I'm a vegetarian. **Et yemiyorum.**
Can I have the bill please? **Hesap, lütfen.**

BASICS

breakfast **kahvaltı**
lunch **öğle yemeği**
dinner **akşam yemeği**
dessert **tatlı**
menu **menü**
service charge **servis**
cup **fincan**
glass **bardak**
fork **çatal**
knife **bıçak**
spoon **kaşık**
napkin **peçete**
plate **tabak**
baked **fırında pişmiş**
boiled **kaynamiş**
fried **kizarmiş**
grilled **ızgara**
roast **kavrulmuş**
bread **ekmek**
thin flat bread **pide** or **lavaş**
brown bread **kepekli ekmek**
pasta **makarna**
rice **pilav**

soup **çorba**
cheese **peynir**
hardboiled/softboiled egg **katı yumurta/rafadan yumurta**
yoghurt **yoğurt**
garlic **sarımsak**
salt **tuz**
red/black/hot pepper **pul/kara/acı biber**

MEAT

beef **dana**
chicken **tavuk**
lamb **kuzu**

FISH

fish **balık**
anchovy **hamsi**
bluefish **lüfer**
bonito **palamut**
crab **yengeç**
lobster **istakoz**
mackerel **uskumra**
monkfish **fener**
sardines **sardalya**
sea bass **levrek**
sea bream **sarıgöz/sinarit**
shrimp **karides**
sole **dil**
swordfish **kılıç**
tuna **torik**

VEGETABLES

aubergine **patlıcan**
carrots **havuç**
cucumber **salatalık**
lentils **mercimek**
lettuce **marul**

Kartallar Balıkçı

Capriz Sokak 32 (0212 517 2254, www.valentinokartallar.com). Kumkapı station. **Open** 10am-midnight daily. **Credit** MC, V. **Map** p242 K11 ⓰ Seafood

Kör Agop

Ördekli Bakkal Sokak 7 (0212 517 2334). Kumkapı station. **Open** noon-2am daily. **Credit** AmEx, MC, V. **Map** p242 K11 ⓱ Seafood

THE WESTERN DISTRICTS

These relatively poor, religiously conservative parts of town draw few visitors, and hence have few restaurants. Asitane is close to the Byzantine church of **St Saviour in Chora** (*see p64*).

★ Asitane

Kariye Hotel, Kariye Camii Sokak 18, Edirnekapı (0212 534 8414, www.asitanerestaurant.com). Bus 28, 77MT, 87. **Open** 11.30am-11pm daily. **Starters** YTL8-YTL15. **Main courses** YTL20-YTL30. **Credit** AmEx, DC, MC, V. **Map** p244 D4 ⓲ Turkish

It may be a trek to Edirnekapı, but it's worth it for this one-of-a-kind restaurant, which specialises in authentic Ottoman food. Authentic means just that: the same dishes that were served at the circumcision feasts of Sultan Süleyman's sons, Beyazıd and Cihangir, in 1539. Expect lots of sweet and sour fruit and meat combos: *kavun dolması* is melon stuffed with mincemeat, rice, almonds, currants and pistachios; *nirbaç* is a stew made with diced lamb, meatballs and carrots, spiced with coriander, ginger, cinnamon, pomegranate and crushed walnuts. The leafy garden is lovely in summer.

CONSUME

okra **bamya**
onions **soğan**
peas **bezelye**
peppers **biber**
potatoes **patates**
spinach **ıspanak**
tomatoes **domates**
courgette **kabak**

FRUIT & NUTS
fruit **meyve**
apples **elma**
banana **muz**
cherries **kiraz**
grapes **üzüm**
hazelnuts **fındık**
honeydew melon **kavun**
lemon **limon**
peanuts **fıstık**
pistachio nuts **şam fıstığı**
oranges **portakal**
walnuts **ceviz**
watermelon **karpuz**

MEZE
börek flaky savoury pastry with parsley and/or white cheese, minced meat, spinach or other vegetables.
çerkez tavuğu shredded chicken served cold in a walnut cream sauce.
çoban salata 'shepherd's salad', composed of tomatoes, cucumbers, hot peppers and onions with lemon and olive oil.
dolma cabbage, grape leaves, pepper or squash, served cold and stuffed with rice, pine nuts, currants and spices.

When served hot, dolma are usually also stuffed with minced meat.
imambayıldı aubergines cooked with onion, tomato and olive oil, served cold.
karnıyarık baked aubergines stuffed with minced meat, onion, tomato, and spices
kısır Turkish-style tabouleh salad with parsley, bulgar, lemon, tomato, onion, olive oil, pomegranate, and mint
lahmacun spiced minced meat on a thin crust pizza-like bread called pide
mücver deep-fried patties made with grated courgette in a batter of egg and flour
zeytinyağli cold dishes with olive oil

MAINS
güveç casserole cooked in a clay pot
karides güveç shrimps cooked with onions in a peppery tomato sauce
köfte meatballs
pirzola lamb chops

DRINKS
apple juice **elma suyu**
beer **bira**
cherry juice **vişne suyu**
coffee **kahve**
Turkish coffee **Türk kahvesi**; without sugar **sade**; a little sugar **az şekerli**; medium sweet **orta şekerli**; sweet **şekerli**
milk **süt**
orange juice **taze portakal suyu**
peach juice **şeftali suyu**
red wine **kırmızı şarap**
tea **çay**
water **su**
white wine **beyaz şarap**

CONSUME

BEYOĞLU

Beyoğlu has the biggest and best selection of restaurants. Its narrow backstreets are loaded with traditional restaurants and *meyhanes*, with the heaviest concentration around **Çiçek Pasajı** and **Nevizade Sokak** (*see p131*). The main drag, Istiklal Caddesi, is lined with *lokantas*, serving wholesome fast food, Turkish style. In Beyoğlu, too, you'll find Istanbul's most cutting-edge restaurants, often with superb rooftop views.

360
Mısır Apartmani 32/309, Istiklal Caddesi (0212 251 1042, www.360istanbul.com). **Open** noon-4pm Mon-Thur; 6pm-2.30am Fri; 6pm-4am Sat; 6pm-2.30am Sun. **Starters** YTL12-YTL25. **Main courses** YTL18-YTL39. **Credit** DC, MC, V. Map p248 N3 ⓳ **International**

On the roof of the historic Mısır apartment block, 360 has magnificent 360-degree views of the city. The spacious dining area is a high-tech fusion of steel and glass, with brick walls. The international menu includes dishes as diverse as Thai green curry and slow roast cherry duck, but the pizzas are a good bet. Reservations are essential on Fridays and Saturdays, with two sittings per night. It turns into a fairly boisterous club and cocktail after midnight, when the venue, and the view, are at their best.
▶ *For more bars and restaurants with a view, see p143* Up on the Roofs.

★ Canim Ciğerim
Asmalımescit Sokak 1, Asmalımescit (0212 252 6060, www.asmalicanimcigerim.com). **Open** noon-midnight daily. **Main courses** YTL18. **No credit cards. Map** p248 M4 ⓴ **Turkish**

11 leblon
restaurant-bar-lounge

The only place that meets gourmet food,
colorful cocktails and cheering music
in one of the most historical building in Istanbul

General Yazgan Sokak Tünel Geçidi İş Hanı B Block No: 2/A Tünel Beyoğlu İstanbul

There are only three choices at this perennially popular neighbourhood restaurant: beef, chicken or lamb. Once the meat of choice is ordered, a plate of mint, a plate of parsley, some spicy tomato sauce, a pile of flat bread and grilled veg will be plonked down, followed by around nine skewers of meat. It isn't licensed. Eat inside or on the terrace.

Gani Gani
Kuyu Sokak 13, Taksim (0212 244 8401, www.naumpasakonagi.com). **Open** 10am-midnight Mon-Thur, Sun; 10am-1am Fri, Sat. **Starters** YTL3-YTL6. **Main courses** YTL10-YTL25. **Credit** AmEx, MC, V. **Map** p249 O3 **㉑** Turkish

Popular with locals, this unusual eaterie buried in the backstreets near Taksim Square offers Anatolian eating at its best. Set on six floors, the place feels like a showcase for rural artefacts. Most of the seating – either in private dining rooms or cosy communal spaces – is traditional Anatolian style, with low tables surrounded by kilims and cushions on the floor. Authentic eastern Turkish specialities include *çiğköfte* (*a la turca* steak tartare made with cracked wheat and chili), *mantı* (ravioli with yoghurt sauce), *pide* or *lahmacun* (Turkish-style pizzas), plus a range of kebabs. Narghiles (waterpipes) are available. No alcohol.

Hacı Abdullah
Atfı Yılmaz Caddesi 9/A, off Istiklal Caddesi (0212 293 8561, www.haciabdullah.com.tr). **Open** 11am-10.30pm daily. **Starters** YTL6. **Main courses** YTL13-YTL20; set menu YTL40. **Credit** AmEx, V, MC. **Map** p248 N3 **㉒** Turkish

One of the oldest restaurants in Istanbul, Hacı Abdullah is deservedly famous for traditional Ottoman fare. Three old-school dining rooms are brightened by a few contemporary flourishes. Opt for the pale pink room at the rear, complete with skylight and chandelier. The restaurant is renowned for its pickles, stored in colourful jars, and bizarrely described in the English menu as 'the symbols of pooped politicians'. An array of pre-cooked dishes is on display in the front room. No alcohol is served.

Kitchenette
Taksim Square, in Marmara Hotel, Taksim (0212 292 6862, www.kitchenette.com.tr). **Open** 10am-10pm. **Starters** YTL8-YTL25. **Main courses** YTL15-YTL33. **Credit** AmEx, DC, MC, V. **Map** p249 P2 **㉓** French/Modern European

From the can-do-no-wrong Istanbul Doors Group, which also owns Angelique (*see p150*) and Vogue (*see p139*), this recent venture is brasserie, bakery, bar and breakfast joint. The space is stunning, with chrome booths and long wooden tables making for a large, but atmospheric, interior. The in-house bakery provides the bread for the large breakfasts.

There is also a wide selection of pastas, meat dishes and salads. It's not cheap, but for a long brunch in stylish surroundings it's worth it. There are Turkish wines by the glass (YTL13).
▶ *There's another branch in Kanyon shopping mall; see p153.*

★ Leb-i Derya Richmond
Sixth Floor, Richmond Hotel, Istiklal Caddesi 445 (0212 243 4375). **Open** 11am-2am Mon-Thur, Sun; 11am-4am Fri, Sat. **Starters** YTL14-YTL28. **Main courses** YTL28-YTL40. **Credit** AmEx, DC, MC, V. **Map** p248 M4 **㉔** Modern European

Located on the sixth floor of the Richmond Hotel on Istiklal Caddesi, Leb-i Derya has probably the best views of any restaurant in the city, even by Istanbul standards. The tables are placed by vast windows: very romantic, especially if the meal is timed with the setting sun. Using the best ingredients, the dishes are simple but perfectly rendered. Highlights include parmesan crusted sea bass, beef cheek ragu and scallop ravioli. And while the menu changes with the seasons, one constant is the extraordinary Forty-Spice Steak. The restaurant stops serving lunch in July and August due to the greenhouse effect of its glass panelling. Reservation recommended.
▶ *For the Richmond Hotel, see p105.*

Lokanta
Meşrutiyet Caddesi 145-147 (0212 245 5810). **Open** noon-3pm, 6.30pm-2am Mon-Thur; noon-3pm, 6.30pm-5am Fri, Sat. **Closed** July-Oct. **Main courses** YTL15-YTL33. **Credit** DC, MC, V. **Map** p248 M4 **㉕** Turkish

Lokanta roughly translates into English as 'canteen', appropriate given the plain decorative style. No matter, it's all about the food, notable for top-quality ingredients and an unfussy approach. The atmosphere is low-key and casual, and the place is usually busy, with a constant hum of conversation – just like a *lokanta*. This is a very enjoyable place to spend time during winter weekends; in summer the same menu and staff move upstairs to their fashionable terrace venue, which has a panoramic view.

★ Mikla
The Marmara Pera, Meşrutiyet Caddesi 167-185, (0212 293 5656, www.mikla restaurant.com). **Open** 6.30pm-11.30am Mon-Sat. **Starters** YTL24-YTL36. **Main courses** YTL44-YTL71. **Credit** AmEx, DC, MC, V. **Map** p248 M4 **㉖** Modern European

On the roof garden of the 18-storey Marmara Pera Hotel, Mikla is one Istanbul's most exclusive eateries. The project of Turco-Finnish chef Mehmet Gürs, the menu reflects both sides of his heritage and is brief but inventive. Starters are big enough to share (just as well, as prices are steep). Mains might include grilled grouper with tomatoes, aubergines, anchovies,

CONSUME

capers, olive oil and poached artichoke, or pistachio-crusted lamb chops with potato, pistachio purée and pomegranate molasses. The place doesn't fill up until 10.30pm; you'll miss the buzz if you book too early.
▶ *Other fine-dining restaurants include Topaz (see p134) and Mimolett (see p131).*

Nature & Peace
Büyükparmakkapı Sokak 21-23 (0212 252 8609, www.natureandpeace.com). **Open** 11am-11.30pm Mon-Thur, Sun; 1-11.30pm Fri, Sat. **Set lunch** YTL11-YTL22. **Main courses** YTL15-YTL26. **Credit** AmEx, DC, MC, V. **Map** p249 O3 ㉗ **Vegetarian**
Vegetarian restaurants are rare in Istanbul, and even this pretender to the title serves several chicken dishes. The set lunch is great value and the dinner menu includes a soup and salad with any main course; pasta and falafel are reliable choices. One of the most popular dishes is a lentil 'meatball', with cabbage and nettle soup. The small, unpretentious space is cosy, if slightly musty.
▶ *Zencefil (see right) is another good vegetarian restaurant.*

Rejans
Emir Nevrus Sokak 7A, Galatasaray (0212 243 3882, www.rejansrestaurant.com). **Open** noon-3pm, 7pm-midnight Mon-Sat. **Starters** YTL5-YTL20. **Main courses** YTL16-YTL52. **Credit** MC, V. **Map** p248 N3 ㉘ **Russian**
Founded by White Russians who relocated to Istanbul in the wake of the Russian Revolution, Rejans was reputedly one of Atatürk's favourite restaurants. Left-wing Turkish intellectuals would come here to gripe over borscht and vodka. Since the red star was spurned in favour of the gold card, Rejans is now frequented by visiting Russians with deep pockets, who knock back flavoured vodkas as they gorge on 'tsar's zakuski'. If the Slavic food is so-so, Rejans still oozes charm, with its polished wood, high ceilings, musicians' gallery and a drunken door-man to hang customers' coats on hooks personalised with the names of long-dead regulars.

Tokyo Restaurant
İpek Sokak 1, off İstiklal Caddesi (0212 293 5858, www.tokyo-restaurant.com). **Open** 11am-11pm daily. **Starters** YTL10-YTL20. **Main courses** YTL19-YTL30. **Credit** AmEx, DC, MC, V. **Map** p249 O2 ㉙ **Japanese**
With its modern-traditional scarlet decor and tatami rooms, Tokyo is a hit with the local Japanese. The menu includes dozens of noodle, rice and teriyaki dishes, plus good sushi and sashimi. The sushi chefs show off their skills behind an open counter.

Zarifi
Çukurlu Çeşme Sokak 13 (0212 293 5480, www.zarifi.com.tr). **Summer venue** *Muallim Naci Caddesi 44, Kuruçeşme (0212 293 54 80).*

Open 8pm-4am daily. **Starters** YTL5-YTL10. **Main courses** YTL22-YTL35. **Credit** AmEx, MC, V. **Map** (winter venue) p249 O3 ㉚ **Turkish**
An update on the *meyhane* that's very popular with fashionable young Turks. Zarifi's extensive menu covers all the classic *meze* and grilled meats, as well as Ottoman dishes and recipes inherited from the former Greek residents of the Pera neighbourhood, like shrimp *saganaki* and octopus stew. The sound-track is equally eclectic – a mix of Turkish folk, chill-out tunes and mainstream pop. Once the *rakı* is flowing freely, the spirit of the *meyhane* usually takes over and spontaneous table-top dancing breaks out. This winning formula is duplicated every summer at Zarifi's supper club at the New Yorker in Kuruçeşme.

Zencefil
Kurabiye Sokak 8 (0212 244 4082). **Open** 11am-midnight Mon-Sat. **Starters** YTL4-YTL8. **Main courses** YTL6-YTL20. **Credit** MC, V. **Map** p249 O2 ㉛ **Vegetarian**
Probably the best vegetarian restaurant in Istanbul (though purists may be infuriated by the fact that chicken makes an occasional appearance on the menu). The setting is urban café meets country kitchen, with shelves lined with jars of produce and giant blackboards listing the daily specials, from soups to spicy stews and freshly baked breads. The home-style food is unfalteringly delicious, likewise the homemade lemonade.

Cihangir

Rehabilitated from its dirty days as a shady part of town, Cihangir is now one of Istanbul's most coveted neighbourhoods. This transformation has been accompanied by the long overdue arrival of a decent selection of restaurants, cafés and bars catering to the area's predominantly arty and foreign residents. In warm weather, restaurants and cafés spread their tables out on to **Akarsu Caddesi** and stay open well into the small hours.

★ Beşinci Kat (5.Kat)
5th floor, Soğancı Sokak 3, off Sıraselviler Caddesi (0212 293 3774, www.5kat.com). **Open** 10am-2am Mon-Thur, Sun; 10am-3am Fri, Sat. **Starters** YTL8-YTL22. **Main courses** YTL16-YTL46. **Credit** AmEx, DC, MC, V. **Map** p249 O3 ㉜ **International**
With its bright colours, velvet furnishings and an eye-catching floor piece of a nude young Norma Jean Baker, 5.Kat has one of the city's most striking inte-riors. As its name implies (*kat* means floor), it occu-pies the fifth floor of a backstreet building. A giant neon angel shines at street level. A rooftop terrace, lit with red lanterns, opens during the summer and has fabulous views over the Asian Shore. The menu

CONSUME

Kebab Cuisine

No longer just filling fodder for boozers, kebabs are going gourmet.

Not too long ago, sophisticated Istanbullus would turn their noses up at the kebab (the word *kebap* means simply 'roast meat'), dismissing it as uncouth provincial grub. Kebabs are synonymous with south-eastern Turkey. The stereotypical kebab restaurateur is a mustachioed sort from rural Droolsville. But over the years the foodie snobs have gradually come around. So much so that these days it's a case of *kebap c'est chic*.

For all its south-eastern associations, the initial spotting of the gourmet potential of grilled meat took place in western Turkey. Back in 1867, a chef in the city of Bursa, 250 kilometres (155 miles) south of Istanbul, by the name of Iskender Usta hit upon the idea of layering slabs of boneless lamb on to a spit, then revolving the resulting meaty mass in front of glowing coals. He then shaved off thin layers with a long knife, and there you have the birth of the döner kebab and Turkey's contribution to worldwide post-booze bingeing. Not content to stop there, Iskender Usta went on to jazz up the döner with *pide* bread, tomato and yoghurt to create his namesake, the Iskender kebab.

His contribution to kebab cuisine was enshrined in law in 2002, when Usta's descendents were awarded a patent to protect their family delicacy from imitators. Thousands of restaurants throughout Turkey were obliged to relabel their 'Iskender kebabs' as 'Bursa kebabs' in order to forestall potential lawsuits.

His name may be protected but Iskender's crown has been lost for good. The current king of kebabs is Beyti Guler. His family opened Beyti's (Orman Sokak 8 Florya, 0212 663 2990, www.beyti.com) restaurant, in the outskirts of Istanbul, back in 1945. By the 1960s, Turcophile diplomat and author Lord Kinross was declaring that it served 'the best meat in Europe'. The plaudits continued and the celebrity guests kept coming – Richard Nixon, Jimmy Carter and Arthur Miller have all eaten here. And, of course, there's a trademark 'Beyti kebab'.

With these varieties and many more, the kebab has come a long way since Mr Usta sliced his first döner. Here's our quick guide to help you choose:

Adana kebap minced lamb seasoned with red peppers and grilled on a spit.
begendi kebap chunks of beef cooked with onions and tomatoes and served on a bed of puréed aubergine.
beyti kebap chopped lamb flavoured with a hint of garlic and red pepper. Served either wrapped in filo pastry or on cubes of toasted pide bread.
Çöp şiş tiny bits of slightly fatty lamb grilled on a skewer, then rolled up in paper-thin *pide* with onions and parsley.
döner kebab compressed meat sliced in strips off a vertically rotating spit. Beef or chicken.
fistikli kebab minced low-fat suckling lamb studded with pistachios.
Iskender kebab slices of döner drizzled with tomato sauce and melted butter served with a side of yogurt on cubes of toasted *pide* bread.
ppatlican kebab minced lamb grilled with chunks of aubergine.
şiş kebap chunks of marinated lamb, chicken or fish grilled on skewers.
testi kebab diced meat, tomatoes, shallots, garlic and green peppers simmered in a clay pot for several hours.

CONSUME

RESTAURANT & CAFE

Göksu Marine Restaurant & Cafe welcome the word to a delightful journey at an Anatolian fortress near the Göksu river....

One of the most sought after places in Istanbul, Göksu Marine Restaurant & Cafe serves unique dishes from Turk and from around the world with its famous Turkish hospit and welcoming service. The saloon is decorated in the sty of a luxury boat, while the garden showcases colourful flowers, a 200 year pergola, willow trees and Black Sea vines. Göksu Marine will entertain you with classical Turk live music sung atop the rowing boat on the river.

Göksu Marine Restaurant & Cafe, has a wonderful view across the Göksu River. It can host 110 people in the salo 180 seated in the garden, and up to 500 for a cocktail reception.

Göksu Marine is open every day from 9 am to 11 pm. On the weekends it is open from 10 am until midnight, with Breakfast Buffet running until 2 pm.

Guests are served breakfast, lunch and dinners, and special celebrations, such as weddings, engagements, birthdays, meetings or any other special day.

Göksu Marine has its own dock, where guests can moor their boats or we can even come and pick you up with our own transfer boat. We have a parking area for up to 150 cars and a valet service for the guests.

We take pride in welcoming you with our renowned hospitality and the quality of service, which has received accolades from the Ministry of Tourism and Culture.

Göksu Marine Restaurant&Cafe

Anadolu hisarı, Körfez cad. Kızılserçe sk. No:18/20 Beyko
Tel : (0216) 332 03 94 • Fax : (0216) 332 43 43
www.goksu-marine.com • info@goksu-marine.com

is a culinary mish-mash (Turkish, French, Italian, oriental) but everything is good. There are two fixed price menus, including two 'local' drinks, for YTL65 and YTL75. 5.Kat's actress proprietor, Yasemin Alkaya, keeps a close eye on proceedings, even after hours, when dance music takes over from chilled jazz, and the atmosphere gets clubby.

▶ *For more bars and restaurants with a view, see p143* **Up on the Roofs**.

Doğa Balık
Akarsu Yokuşu Caddesi 46 (0212 243 3656).
Open noon-midnight daily. **Starters** YTL5-YTL15. **Main courses** YTL15-YTL50. **Credit** AmEx, MC, V. **Map** p249 O4 ❸❸ **Turkish**
Don't let the entrance, via the lobby of the Villa Zurich Hotel, put you off: Doğa Balık is a splendid neighbourhood fish restaurant. The dining room is on the seventh floor and is best known for its roof terrace, which has stunning views across to Sultanahmet and Beyoğlu. The cooking is equally impressive. The kitchen specialises in lightly cooked greens (up to 18 varieties) and perfectly grilled seasonal fish drizzled with garlicky olive oil. This is the quintessential Aegean comfort food – and it's good for you, too. On Wednesday, Friday and Saturday evenings, there's live traditional music.

▶ *For the Villa Zurich Hotel, see p111.*

★ Mimolett
Sıraselviler Caddesi 55/A (0212 245 9858, www.mimolett.com.tr). **Open** noon-3pm, 7pm-midnight Mon-Sat; *bar* noon-2am Mon-Sat. **Starters** YTL18-YTL29. **Main courses** YTL49-YTL72. **Degustation menu** YTL125-YTL145. **Credit** AmEx, DC, MC, V. **Map** p249 O3 ❸❹ **Modern European**
Head chef Murat Bozok worked at Michelin-starred restaurants in France and the UK (including a stint as head chef at Gordon Ramsay's Devonshire), before returning to his native city to open Mimolett, one of Istanbul's new breed of fine-dining restaurants. The menu is a Michelin-friendly selection of modern European dishes; Turkish twists, seen in dishes such as a lamb chop and sweetbread *dolma*, bring originality and a sense of place. Quality is incredibly high, and the service flawless. The opulent, yet modern, interior befits a restaurant of this stature, but the terrace is the best place to take dinner, just as the sun sets and the moon rises over the Bosphorus. Mimolett also has a bar and wine shop.

▶ *For a profile of Murat Bozok, see p135.*

★ Miss Pizza
Hayvar Sokak 5, off Akarsu Caddesi (0212 251 3279). **Open** noon-midnight daily (last orders 10.30pm). **Pizzas** YTL12-YTL33; **Side orders** YTL15-YTL20. **Credit** AmEx, MC, V. **Map** p249 O4 ❸❺ **Pizza**
Arguably the best pizzeria in town, this stylish but cosy eaterie in the heart of Cihangir is a big hit

with resident foreigners. Selen and Elif, who both have backgrounds in textiles, were inspired to create Miss Pizza by their trips to Italy. An Italian chef created the menu and taught them to make pizza dough. Pizza *funghi*, made with gorgonzola and porcini mushrooms marinated in truffle oil, is our recommendation here. Besides pizza, there are good cheese and charcuterie platters and salads. There are only a few tables, but you can also order home delivery. Reservations are essential on Fridays and Saturdays.

Other location Meşrutiyet Caddesi 86 (0212 251 3234).

Tünel/Galata/Nevizade Sokak

Filled with an interesting mix of restaurants, cafés and bars frequented by locals, the narrow, atmospheric streets stretching from **Tünel**

Beşinci Kat (5.Kat). *See p128.*

Square down to the **Galata Tower** are a trendy but low-key area. **Nevizade Sokak**, **Çiçek Pasajı** and a few neighbouring streets form the city's most famous *meyhane* district.

Boncuk
Nevizade Sokak 7A (0212 243 1219). **Open** 11.30am-2am daily. **Credit** MC, V. **Map** p248 N3 ** Turkish**
For review, *see p120* **Meyhanes & Meze**.

Cumhuriyet Meyhanesi
Sahne Sokak 47, Balık Pazarı (0212 293 1977). **Open** 9.30am-2am daily. **Credit** MC, V. **Map** p248 N3 ** Turkish**
For review, *see p120* **Meyhanes & Meze**.

★ Iskele Balik
Near Karaköy Square (no phone). **Open** 7am-midnight daily. **Main courses** YTL5-YTL15. **No credit cards. Map** p246 M6 ** Seafood**
There are dozens of restaurants around the fish market by Galata Bridge and on the bridge itself. This one, on the west side of the bridge, is consistently the most popular with locals. Take a seat on the patio out back, under a makeshift roof, and order the anchovies. A large plate of fried fish, two big hunks of soft bread and a small salad will arrive, priced YTL6.

★ Krependeki Imroz
Nevizade Sokak 16 (0212 249 9073). **Open** 11.30am-2am daily. **Credit** MC, V. **Map** p248 N3 ** Turkish**
For review, *see p120* **Meyhanes & Mezes**.

Lokal
Müeyyet Sokak 5/A, off Istiklal Caddesi (0212 245 5744). **Open** 10am-midnight daily.

Starters YTL7-YTL15. **Main courses** YTL15-YTL25. **Credit** AmEx, MC, V. **Map** p248 M4 ** Modern European/International**
Once one of the hippest eateries in town, Lokal has graduated to classic status. On a tiny side street off Asmalımescit, Lokal is easy to locate thanks to the films projected on the wall opposite, ranging from footage of skateboarders to spaghetti westerns. Menus bound by kitsch LP covers read like an encyclopedia of global fusion: pesto linguine, chicken tikka, pad Thai, salmon teriyaki and chicken wings. All are surpisingly good. There are two recent Lokal additions in the side streets around the original. One focuses on Italian food, while the one opposite Tünel offers coffee, smoothies and snacks.

★ Mer Balik Restaurant
Hüseyin Ağa Mahallesi 23, off Istiklal Caddesi, (0212 292 8358, www.beyoglumer.com). **Open** 11.30am-2am daily. **Credit** MC, V. **Map** p248 N3 ** Turkish**
For review, *see p120* **Meyhanes & Meze**.

★ Refik
Sofyalı Sokak 10-12 (0212 243 2834). **Open** noon-3pm, 7-11.30pm Mon-Fri; 7pm-midnight Sat. **Main courses** YTL20-YTL25. **Set menu** YTL75. **Credit** AmEx, MC, V. **Map** p248 M4 ** Turkish**
Established in 1954, this upmarket *meyhane* is a great starting point to immerse yourself in meze culture and acquire a taste for *rakı*. Gravel voiced Refik Arslan still meets patrons at the door, including a devoted clientele of leftie hacks and intellectuals. Most regulars smoke and drink more than they eat, but the place is renowned for seafood dishes from the Black Sea. There's no music, as it would interfere with the animated conversation.

CONSUME

Iskele Balik.

Topaz.

signature main course is *kuzu kafes* for two (YTL95) which is lamb with fig-flavoured potatoes, grilled baby squash and two sauces. Live music often accompanies dinner.

★ Topaz
Ömer Avni Mahallesi, Inönü Caddesi 50, Gümüşsuyu (0212 249 1001, www.topaz istanbul.com). **Open** noon-midnight daily. **Starters** YTL20-YTL36. **Main courses** YTL24-YTL6. **Degustation menu** YTL98-YTL110. **Credit** AmEx, MC, V. **Map** p247 Q2 **45** **Modern European**

Views from Topaz are superlative: picture windows run the length of the restaurant, which looks over the first Bosphorus bridge. The interior is comfortably modern, sleek and luxurious, and the food and service matches the look. Alongside the carte, there are two six-course *degustation* menus: the first is a modern interpretation of traditional Ottoman cuisine, with dishes such as artichoke with wild rice and grilled lamb loin with smoked aubergine purée. The second is a more modish Mediterranean selection, albeit with Turkish touches: cherry soup with shrimps and foam of rak and liquorish jelly, and oven braised beef cheek with goose liver crème brûlée, perhaps. All ingredients are rigorously sourced. The service is flawless, and the French sommelier can recommend Turkish or international wines. Cocktails are great too. Book ahead for a table by the window.

NIŞANTAŞI

Few visitors make it up the hill to this upmarket neighbourhood, with its impressive selection of designer boutiques and equally swanky eateries.

Hünkar
Mim Kemal Öke Caddesi 21 (0212 225 4665). Metro Osmanbey. **Open** noon-midnight daily. **Starters** YTL7-YTL15. **Main courses** YTL12-YTL20. **Credit** AmEx, MC, V. **Turkish**

The original Hünkar opened in 1950 in the far-flung, working-class Fatih neighbourhood. This offshoot in Nişantaşı has taken the old-school Ottoman brand upmarket. Diners include Chanel-suited ladies who lunch and deal-clinching businessmen who schmooze over homely dishes like sheep's trotter soup, stuffed cabbage, anchovy pilaf, or the signature dish *hünkar beğendi* – 'sultan's delight' – a rich lamb stew with aubergine purée. Decorative touches (jars of preserves, copper artefacts) maintain one foot in the past; street side seating allows clients to keep an eye on the present.

Longtable
Sofa Hotel, Teşvikiye Caddesi 123 (0212 224 8181, www.thesofahotel.com). Metro Osmanbey. **Open** 7pm-2am Mon-Sat. **Starters** YTL17-YTL32. **Main courses** YTL26-YTL35. **Credit** AmEx, DC, MC, V. **Modern Turkish**

Sofyalı 9
Sofyalı Sokak 9, Tünel (0212 245 0362, www.sofyali.com.tr/eng). **Open** noon-1am Mon-Sat. **Starters** YTL4-YTL10. **Main courses** YTL13-YTL25. **Credit** AmEx, MC, V. **Map** p248 M4 **43** **Turkish**

A *meyhane* maybe, but *très* genteel. This cosy local haunt feels like someone's front room – someone with money, taste and a fine old house. The ground floor space is small, with mustard walls, exposed brickwork, wooden floors and hanging lanterns. But tables spill into the alley and there are two floors upstairs. Even so, reservations are a must, as the city's literati and gay crowd love this place. The food is a cut above – superior meze, followed by meat and fish dishes prepared with the freshest ingredients and a lightness of touch.

Şişli

Naz Turkish Cuisine
Swissôtel The Bosphorus, Bayıldım Caddesi 2, Maçka (0212 326 1175, www.nazturk.com). **Open** 11.30am-midnight daily. **Starters** YTL5-YTL21. **Main courses** YTL 25-YTL45. **Credit** AmEx, MC, V. **Map** p247 R1 **44** **Turkish**

Housed in a model of an 18th-century *yalı* (mansion) next to the Swissôtel in Maçka, Naz serves traditional Ottoman cuisine. Avoiding any ostentatious faux-Ottoman decor, the interior is austere. Aimed at tourists and business people, the food offers an introductory selection of superior mezes. The

Profile Murat Bozok

After years abroad, Istanbul's best chef has returned to his homeland.

Persistence pays. Murat Bozok wrote to three Michelin-starred chef, Pierre Gagnaire, seven times before receiving a reply. After the eighth letter, Gagnaire relented and invited Murat to work in London's Sketch. It was his first job in a Michelin-starred restaurant, and a move that would propel the Turkish chef up the culinary ladder. But his latest journey will be the most challenging yet: Murat hopes to bring Michelin stars to Istanbul for the first time with his restaurant Mimolett.

Murat Bozok was born in Istanbul in 1975. As a child he was exposed to his mother's and grandmother's traditional Turkish cooking. And it's the touches of Turkish culinary heritage at his new restaurant, **Mimolett**, which is earning accolades from around the world. Dishes such as wild sea bass with ravioli, scallops and red pepper purée, or lamb chop and sweetbread dolma, use ingredients recognisable from other Istanbul restaurants, but Bozok employs French cooking styles and avant-garde techniques such as foams, to turn his food into a fine and delicate experience.

After a false start in the family textile business, Murat decided to go to the USA and follow his dream of being a chef – telling his family he was studying management. After work experience at the Ritz Carlton New York and Chicago, and prolific letter writing, he finally started work for Pierre Gagnaire. From Sketch, he worked at Gordon Ramsay's eponymous restaurant at Royal Hospital Road, the Connaught, L'atelier de Robuchon in Paris, and Petrus, where he became sous-chef. His final assignment was head chef at Gordon Ramsay's Devonshire gastropub.

In December 2009, Mimolett (named after Murat's favourite cheese) was opened in a lusciously converted 100-year-old house near Taksim Square. There's a bar and a 'wine boutique' with more than 400 wines, 50 by the glass.

Adapting to the Turkish palette may be a challenge for Bozok at Mimolett, but together with chef Mehmet Gurs and his Scandinavian/Turkish fusion menu at **Mikla** (*see p127*), and the more traditional Mediterranean and Ottoman food being cooked at **Topaz** (*see p134*), Bozok is helping to create a new Turkish cuisine.

'I've always questioned why there isn't a star in Turkey,' Murat said. 'I'm determined to be the one. There's a buzz, but we are at the beginning of the journey.'

NEED TO KNOW
For a review of a **Mimolett**, see p131.

CONSUME

Müzedechanga.

Longtable replaces Tuus, the previous restaurant at the Sofa Hotel (*see p113*). The interior design is eclectic and light-hearted, bordering on the kitsch. There is a catwalk-like walkway down the centre of the restaurant, running parallel to the bar – the longtable of the name. The menu majors on dry-aged meat: veal medallions, New York steak and 23 types of seasoned ribeye steaks. There are also chicken and fish selections, salads, pizzas and pastas. There's live soul music Tue-Sat between 9-11pm.

Salomanje
Belkıs Apartmanı 4/1-2, Atiye Sokak (0212 327 3577). Metro Osmanbey. **Open** 11.30am-2am Mon-Sat. **Starters** YTL9-YTL14. **Main courses** YTL22-YTL30. **Credit** MC, V.
Modern European
This place is a hit with Nişantaşı's most stylish residents, although entering the undersized venue you might wonder why. With a bar, a handful of tables and a small terrace out the back, the decor is unremarkable but cosy. The menu combines Turkish and international standards. In summer, Salomanje moves to Sortie nightclub in Kuruçeşme, *see p201*.

LEVENT & ETILER

A couple of Istanbul's wealthier business districts – comprising glass skyscrapers, monolithic malls, and bumper-to-bumper SUVs – Levent and Etiler are home to a handful of fine restaurants.

Sunset Grill & Bar
Yol Sokak 2, off Adnan Saygun Caddesi, Ulus Parkı, Ulus (0212 287 0357, www.sunsetgrillbar. com). Metro Levent. **Open** noon-3pm, 7pm-2am daily. **Starters** YTL15-YTL40. **Main courses** YTL35-YTL80. **Credit** AmEx, DC, MC, V.
International

A gorgeous setting for a romantic tryst – a tree-lined terrace set on a hilltop high above the Bosphorus. The menu is an unlikely but well-executed mix of Californian fusion, meat-heavy modern Turkish dishes and superior sushi. The restaurant is a five- or ten-minute walk from Levent metro station. Predictably, it's hugely popular at sunset, when you are advised to book ahead.

Ulus 29
Kireçhane Sokak 1, Adnan Saygun Caddesi, Ulus Parkı, Ulus (0212 265 6181, www.group-29.com). Metro Levent. **Open** noon-3pm, 7pm-midnight daily. **Starters** YTL18-YTL30. **Main courses** YTL30-YTL60. **Credit** AmEx, DC, MC, V. **Mediterranean**
Someone to impress? Something to celebrate? Ulus 29 fits the bill. Thanks to yet another spectacular hillside setting (just above the Sunset Grill & Bar, *see above*), the views from the semi- circular verandah are unbeatable. Models make eyes at moguls against an opulent oriental backdrop, decked with muslin drapes and lit by oil lamps. The restaurant is immaculately designed by local nightlife impressario Metin Fadıllıoğlu and his interior designer wife, Zeynep, who make gracious hosts. Food is impressive, focusing on the eastern Mediterranean.

HASKÖY

Halat
Kumbarhane Caddesi 2, Hasköy (0212 297 6644). Bus 47E, 54HT. **Open** 10am-midnight Tue-Sun. **Starters** YTL7-YTL15. **Main courses** $10-$14. **Credit** AmEx, DC, MC, V.
French
In addition to being a world-class museum, the Rahmi Koç has a couple of excellent restaurants in the Café du Levant, a fancy French bistro, and Halat,

CONSUME

with quayside dining under canvas awnings. The menu ranges from a 'tea-time' selection of sandwiches and tarts to breaded crab claws and heavenly desserts. Black-waistcoated staff and classical music suggest formality, but the vibe is laid-back. The views – across the Golden Horn to the tumbling orange roofs of Balat – are stunning.

▶ For the Rahmi Koç museum, see p76.

THE BOSPHORUS VILLAGES

This string of waterfront settlements starts at **Beşiktaş** and runs north through **Ortaköy**, **Arnavutköy** and **Bebek**, as far as **Rumeli Hisarı**. Restaurants in this district tend to be pricey, cashing in on their seaside setting, but remain popular.

Banyan Ortaköy
Muallim Naci Caddesi Salhane Sokak 3, Ortaköy (0212 259 9060, www.banyanrestaurant.com). Bus 40, 40T, 42T. **Open** noon-2am daily. **Starters** YTL12-YTL20. **Main courses** YTL25-YTL40. **Credit** AmEx, DC, MC, V. **Asian**
With spectacular views of the original Bosphorus bridge and floodlit Ortaköy mosque, Banyan comes into its own on summer nights. Bonsai trees scattered around the tables lend an exotic twist to the refined interior. Living up to the slogan 'Food for the Soul', all ingredients are organic and ethically sourced. The menu is a melange of Asian influences. Chinese, Japanese, Vietnamese and Indian delicacies are all beautifully presented and prepared. This is fusion food at its best – good for the soul, but hard on the wallet.

★ The House Café
Salhane Sokak 1, off Muallim Naci Caddesi, Ortaköy (0212 227 2699, www.thehouse cafe.com.tr). Bus 40, 40T, 42T. **Open** 9am-2am Mon-Thur, Sun; 8am-2am Fri, Sat. **Starters** YTL8-YTL22. **Main courses** YTL15-YTL35. **Credit** AmEx, DC, MC, V. **Modern European**
The expansion of the House Café group is something of a phenomenon. Since opening the original branch in Teşvikiye (the Ortaköy branch was the second), another nine venues have been added to the list. With industrial-chic interior, from Istanbul super-designers Autoban, all the locations offer lovely surroundings in which to enjoy a mishmash of global comfort food made with gourmet ingredients. This Ortaköy café has a blissful terrace right on the Bosphorus. Weekend brunch is a fixture for the young and well-heeled. Try the superlative House burger, thin-crust pizzas, imaginative bruschetta and salads. Pint-sized fresh fruit cocktails are a joy to behold and delicious to boot. A hotel is to be built above the restaurant, due to open at the end of 2010.
Other locations Throughout the city.

Mangerie
Cevdetpaşa Caddesi 69, Bebek (0212 263 5199, www.mangeriebebek.com). Bus 40, 40T, 42T. **Open** 8am-midnight daily. **Starters** YTL7-YTL12. **Main courses** YTL20-YTL34. **Credit** MC, V. **Modern Turkish**
Tucked away behind the fancy waterside eateries in Bebek, this delightful restaurant is worth seeking out. (Head for the Küçük Bebek end of the high street and follow the steps leading up past a hairdresser.) The airy interior is all white wood, with a balcony that looks over the rooftops to the Bosphorus. The relaxed atmosphere makes this an ideal lunch spot, with simple salads and sandwiches served on a great breads, baked on the premises. *Zeytinyağlı*, seasonal vegetables and fruits stewed in olive oil, is recommended.

★ Müzedechanga
Sakıp Sabancı Caddesi 22, Emirgan (0212 323 0901, www.changa-istanbul.com). Metro Levent, then Bus EL1, EL2. **Starters** YTL23-YTL39. **Open** 10.30am-1am Tue-Sun. **Credit** MC, V. **Turkish-Mediterranean**
In the Sakıp Sabancı Museum, Müzedechanga is much more than a museum café. A spin-off from the acclaimed Changa restaurant in Taksim, it's housed in a space remodelled with a modern mixture of glass, wood and steel, with custom-made furniture by renowned local designers, Autoban. The terrace has amazing views across the manicured museum gardens to the Bosphorus. The Turkish-Med menu, supervised by consutant chef Peter Gordon of Sugar Club fame, is faultless and well-priced for this quality. Highly recommended.
▶ *The original Changa is at Sıraselviler Caddesi 47, Taksim (0212 249 1348).*

Poseidon
Küçük Bebek, Cevdet Paşa Caddesi 58, Bebek (0212 263 3823, www.poseidonfish.com). Bus 40, 40T, 42T. **Open** noon-midnight daily. **Starters** YTL7-YTL25. **Main courses** YTL20-YTL40. **Credit** AmEx, MC, V. **Seafood**

THE BEST
MODERN RESTAURANTS

For inventive Turkish/
Scandinavian fusion
Mikla (*see p127*).

Turkey's best chance for
a Michelin star
Mimolett (*see p131*).

Where Mediterranean and Ottoman
cuisines meet
Topaz (*see p134*).

CONSUME

A supremely stylish affair, Poseidon, with a beautiful location on the Bosphorus in Bebek, serves superior seafood at vertiginous prices. Sampling the meze menu will hike up the bill, but specialities like stuffed calamari, marinated sea bass and fish croquettes are worth it for the high quality. The catch of the day is priced by the kilo. Your dining companions will be well-bred and well-manicured big spenders. The large deck is virtually suspended above the Bosphorus and has gorgeous views of Bebek bay, but the view from inside is almost as magical.

Rumeli Iskele

Yahya Kemal Caddesi 1, Rumeli Hisarı (0212 263 2997). Bus 40, 40T, 42T. **Open** noon-2am daily. **Starters** YTL3-YTL10. **Main courses** YTL7-YTL44. **Credit** AmEx, MC, V. **Seafood**
Despite competition from newer, shinier seafood restaurants, this place is always packed. The best tables are on the waterfront deck, with a view of the hilltop castle of Anadolu Hisarı across the strait. The menu holds few surprises – meze and Mediterranean fish – but the food is good. Service is unobtrusive and efficient.

School Dinners

Learn to cook Turkish.

Centuries of complicated history have produced a varied and sophisticated Turkish cuisine, a combination of Middle Eastern, Mediterranean and Balkan influences. Staple ingredients found in a Turkish kitchen are cheeses (salty and white), herbs (dill, parsley, mint), spices (pepper, garlic, cumin, red pepper flakes), yogurt, aubergines, tomatoes, minced meat and fish. Bread is hardly stuff for peasants, but a food to respect. Baked daily and in many different ways, you will never find a table without tempting, fabulous fresh bread.

Saying goodbye to Turkish food, from simple *simit* (ubiquitous bagel-like bread) and *börek* (cheese or meat filled pastry) to more sophisticated dishes, can be hard for food-loving visitors. Several astute cooks have discerned a market here, and their kitchens now host Turkish cooking classes designed specifically for tourists.

Cooking Alaturka (Akbiyik Caddesi 72A, Sultanahmet, 0212 458 59 19, www.cookingalaturka.com) is one such kitchen. Dutch expatriate and professional chef, Eveline Zoutendijk, offers two slots for classes a day. Taught in English (French, Dutch and Turkish also available), students prepare a typical 'home-style' menu with a hand from Eveline and her sous-chef, Feyzi Yildirim. After the class, the group sits down to eat their dishes in Eveline's charming restaurant. It is a friendly and informative approach to learning about Turkish ingredients and methods of cooking. Half a day's course is YTL130 per person, which includes the meal at the end, accompanied by wine.

Turkish Flavours (Vali Konağı Caddesi Uğur, Apt 14/3, Nişantaşı, 532 218 06 53, www.turkishflavours.com) is run by Selin Rozanes, who, in addition to organising culinary itineraries, invites visiting foodies to learn how to cook Turkish dishes in her home. Recipes are seasonal and easy to follow, and classes have a casual 'hands on' approach. She charges $100 per person.

The **Istanbul Culinary Institute** (Meşrutiye Caddesi, 59 Tepebasi, 0212 251 22 14, www.istanbulculinary.com) has courses in English, but check its website to see the schedule as each class is devoted to a particular dish. Classes range from YTL100-YTL190.

Finally, for visitors with children, **In the Kitchen with the Kids** (Çocuşumla Mutfatktayız Tepecik Yolu 28/2, Etiler, 0212 358 1825, www.mutfaktayiz.com) designs cooking courses for parents and their kids. Classes takes place one weekend per month; phone to book a place. Courses cost YTL89 (plus tax) for parent and child.

Vogue

Spor Caddesi 92, BJK Plaza A Blok 13, Akaretler, Beşiktaş (0212 227 2545, www.istanbuldoors.com).
Open noon-2am daily; 10.30am-4pm Sun. **Starters** YTL20-YTL35. **Main courses** YTL30-YTL55. **Credit** AmEx, DC, MC, V **Modern European**
Despite being eclipsed by newer, trendier joints, Vogue has managed to retain its stylish clientele and high standards. Curiously situated on the top floor of an office block, the restaurant serves sophisticated Californian-fusion dishes and freshly prepared sushi. Reservations are still essential at weekends.
▶ *Vogue is owned by the Doors group. It's other restaurants include Kitchenette (see p127) and Angelique (see p150).*

THE ASIAN SHORE

Çiya and **Kanaat** offer a fantastic array of classic, and more unusual, Turkish dishes at bargain prices, while exclusive **A'jia** and **Körfez** are worth crossing a continent to visit.

★ A'jia

A'jia Hotel, Ahmet Rasim Paşa Yalısı, Çubuklu Caddesi 27, Kanlıca (0216 336 3013, www.ajiahotel.com). Ferry from Beşiktaş or Eminönü to Üsküdar then taxi. **Open** 7am-midnight daily. **Main courses** YTL20-YTL50. **Credit** AmEx, MC, V. **Modern European**
A'jia's remote location – a boutique hotel in a converted *yalı* on the shores of the Bosphorus – makes for a peaceful setting. Far from the hustle of the city centre, the waterfront terrace has sweeping views of European Istanbul, while the sleek interior marries Ottoman elegance with contemporary designer pieces. Highlights of the international menu include fresh pasta and octopus carpaccio.
▶ *For the hotel, see p117.*

★ Çiya

Güneşlibahçe Sokak 43-44, Kadıköy (0216 418 5115, www.ciya.com.tr). Ferry from Eminönü or Karaköy to Kadıköy. **Open** 11am-10pm daily. **Starters** YTL4-YTL8. **Main courses** YTL7-YTL12. **Credit** AmEx, MC, V. **Map** p251 W7 ❹⓺ **Turkish**
Most of the little local eateries on Güneşlibahçe are indistinguishable, but Çiya is so good – and so successful – that it is taking over most of them. Çiya Sofrası specialises in traditional dishes from around Turkey. Opposite is Çiya Kebapçı, heaven for kebab aficionados, where chefs in white hats conjure up a mind-boggling selection of skewered meats and freshly made flat breads in the open kitchen. The interesting starters are on a buffet. Choose what you like and then your plate will be weighed. Dishes can also be seen before you buy: stuffed artichoke, meatballs, a fabulous stuffed intestine stew or a bit of everything. Or just let the affable waiters choose for

Poseidon. *See p137.*

you. The venues are smart and clean, with tiled white floors, pine furniture, and sepia photos of pastoral scenes. Friendly staff are the picture of brisk efficiency. Do not miss a meal here. No alcohol.

Kanaat

Selmanipak Caddesi 25, Üsküdar (0216 341 5444). Ferry from Eminönü or Beşiktaş to Üsküdar. **Open** 6am-11pm daily. **Starters** YTL4-YTL8. **Main courses** YTL6-YTL12. **No credit cards. Map** p250 W2 ❹⓻ **Turkish**
Kanaat is a perfect example of a historical *lokanta* that appears to have changed little since it was founded in 1933. The vast menu of traditional but increasingly hard-to-find Turkish dishes is excellent value. Choose from dozens of stuffed, stewed and spiced vegetables and a mouthwatering array of grilled, baked and roast-meat dishes, from rich lamb stew to spicy meatballs. There's a separate section dedicated to desserts. Baked quince with clotted cream and delicate milk puddings with various combinations of dried fruit and nuts are especially memorable.

Körfez

Körfez Caddesi 78, Kanlıca (0216 413 4314, www.korfez.com). Bus 40, 40T, 42T to Rumeli Hisarı, where a special shuttle departs from opposite Edwards of Hisar; or ferry from Eminönü or Beşiktaş to Üsküdar, then 15min taxi ride. **Open** noon-4pm, 7pm-midnight daily. **Starters** YTL8-YTL13. **Main courses** YTL30-YTL79. **Credit** AmEx, MC, V. **Seafood**
Gourmands from all over Istanbul regularly make the pilgrimage to Kanlıca, midway up the Bosphorus, for what many locals swear is the finest fish in Istanbul. As with most seafood restaurants, the emphasis is on whatever is freshest, but try not to miss the signature dish, *tuzda balık* or 'fish in salt' – a whole fish baked in a crust of sea salt, a method which preserves all the flavour and succulence. Booking is essential.

Bars & Cafés

Cocktails with stunning views or a glass of tea in a corner café.

Bar culture, as understood in the West, came late to Turkey. Atatürk was partial to *rakı*, and the drink has a long history here, but for most common folk coffee was as strong as it got. All that has changed – dramatically. Once confined to seedy taverns frequented by older men, alcohol consumption has come out of the closet, with bars filling up around Beyoğlu at 5pm, and staying busy all night – even on school nights. Initially, the favoured style was Parisian Left Bank meets student squat – bare brick, wooden floors and flea-market furnishings – but interiors have increasingly got the *Wallpaper** factor. Cocktail bars are often enhanced by killer locations, either set beside the Bosphorus or up on the rooftops.

WHERE TO DRINK

There is now a new take on the traditional men-only coffee- or teahouse, the *kıraathane*, thanks to the current popularity of the *narghile* (hookah pipe) with young people of both sexes: *see p151* **Hubbly Bubbly**. These joints don't serve alcohol. Otherwise, most places blur the boundaries between bar and café, serving coffee and food throughout the day, and becoming increasingly smoky and boozy after night falls.

Heaven for bar-hoppers, Beyoğlu has a density of drinking venues that would do any German city proud. There's not much worthwhile on the main drag, Istiklal Caddesi, but the surrounding side streets are packed with watering holes, ranging from the good, the bad to the ugly. An evening in Ortaköy or Arnavutköy is pleasant, but quality options are limited. The same is true in swanky Nişantaşı and Teşvikye. A night on Kadife Sokak in Kadıköy, on the Asian Shore, has the potential to turn into something enjoyable regrettable, but getting home could prove to be a problem.

Café culture, as it's known in Western Europe and the US, has come to Istanbul with zeal. It was kick started by the wonderful House Café chain, which was the first to encourage a lazy coffee with free Wi-Fi access, good food and award-winning design from Autoban (*see p37* **Profile**). Starbucks has a firm foothold in the city, with apparently more than 80 outlets. Gloria Jean's is a homegrown competitor with branches across the city. A new addition, along the same lines as House Café, is Big Chefs (Meşrutiyet Caddesi 176, www.bigchefs.com.tr).

WHAT TO DRINK

There are now countless places where you can order a cocktail with confidence (try **Leb-i Derya** for a well-mixed cocktail with a view). Local vintners are also producing and marketing a greater variety of wine (*şarap*) of steadily improving quality (*see p146* **Grape Expectations**), although ordering an unspecified glass of house red or white will still generally result in remorse. There are some reliable labels, though: you won't go wrong with Kavaklıdere's Angora (red and white), Çankaya (white) and Yakut (red), or Doluca's Villa Doluca (red and white). Wine isn't particularly cheap, and there's a very high tax on imported booze. Turks consume twice as much *rakı* – the anise-flavoured spirit similar to the Greek ouzo or French *pastis* – as all other alcohol combined; it's generally drunk with *meze*; it's especially good with fish.

SULTANAHMET

With the exception of **Mozaik** restaurant's basement bar (*see p119*) and the **Şah Bar** (*see right*), there's a shortage of decent bars in Sultanahmet. Options are limited to a row of nondescript tourist cafés east of the

Hippodrome, the odd rowdy backpacker joint on **Akbıyık Caddesi** and one or two somnolent hotel bars. Or forgo the booze and give your lungs a workout at one of the local *narghile* cafés.

Enjoyer Café
Incili Çavuş Sokak 25 (0212 512 8759).
Tram Sultanahmet. **Open** 9am-2am daily.
Not licensed. Credit MC, V.
Map p243 N10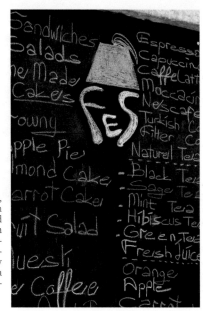
For review, *see p151* **Hubbly Bubbly**.

Fes Café
Ali Baba Türbe Sokak 25-27 (0212 526 3071).
Tram Çemberlitaş. **Not licensed. Open** 9am-9pm daily. **Credit** MC, V. **Map** p243 M9
On a quiet back street near Nuruosmaniye Mosque, just off Nuruosmaniye Caddesi, this café's modern design blends surprisingly well with its antiquated surroundings. With a sister establishment smack in the centre of the Grand Bazaar, Fes Café is something of a local institution. The fresh-pressed lemonade and mint tea are refreshing after a heavy shopping session. Be sure to check out Abdullah, a little shop in the café that sells gorgeous natural textiles, plus an assortment of olive oil-based soaps.

★ Meşale
Arasta Bazaar 45 (0212 518 9562). **Open** 24 hours daily. *Tram Sultanahmet.* **Not licensed.**
Credit MC, V. **Map** p243 N11
For review, *see p151* **Hubbly Bubbly**.

The North Shield
Ebusuud Caddesi 2 (0212 527 0931,
www.thenorthshield.com). Tram Gülhane. **Open** noon-1am Mon-Thur, Sun; noon-4am Fri, Sat.
Licensed. Credit MC, V. **Map** p243 N9
The North Shield transports its regulars to suburban middle England. Think tartan carpets, Famous

Grouse mirrors, etched glass screens, wooden benches and a dark, polished bar. There's even Abba, Elton John and Santana on the sound system. Homesick Brits get together here and at five other North Shields around town. It's big on sports, especially football and rugby.
Other locations Throughout the city.

Şah Bar
Alemdar Mahallesi, Incili Çavuş Çıkmazı, (0212 519 5807). Tram Sultanahmet.
Open noon-2am daily. **Licensed. Credit** MC, V. **Map** p243 N10
This is a true drinking bar, with loud Western music, Efes flowing and a rowdy backpacker crowd enjoying the vibe. It's something rare in Sultanahmet, and welcome for that. There are some snacks, but it's best to visit after dinner elsewhere for drinking into the night and singing along to soul classics.

Yeşil Ev Beer Garden
Kabasakal Caddesi 5 (0212 517 6785). Tram Sultanahmet. **Open** 7am-11pm daily. **Licensed. Credit** AmEx, MC, V. **Map** p243 N11
This idyllic garden of towering laurel, linden and horse chestnut trees belongs to the quaint Yeşil Ev guesthouse. It's the finest place for an aperitif this side of the Golden Horn. In winter, guests are sheltered in a large conservatory amid hanging plants. Pricey, but worth it.
▶ *For the Yeşil Ev hotel, see p93.*

INSIDE TRACK ON THE RAKI

When it comes to alcohol, Turkey is best known for *rakı* – the anise spirit that turns milky when mixed with water, hence its nickname 'lion's milk' (*aslan sütü*). Careful drinkers fill a third of their glass with *rakı* and top up with water and ice. Unlike beer, *rakı* contains no malt, which allegedly saves drinkers from killer hangovers. Even so, you can have a very bad *rakı* experience unless you wash it down with plenty of water and soak it up wth copious meze. *Rakı* should never be drunk without an edible accompaniment. White Turkish cheese and melon is a classic combination.

CONSUME

Cuppa.

THE BAZAAR QUARTER

Divan
Kapalıçarşı Cevahir Bedesten 143-151 (0212 520 2250). Tram Beyazıt Kapalıçarşı. **Not licensed. Open** 9am-7pm Mon-Sat. **Credit** MC, V. **Map** p242 L9 ❼
This place in the Old Bazaar, or Cevahir Bedesten, stands out. It's a simulated slice of the suave old days of the Republic, with burgundy walls, red leather couches, a huge Turkish flag draped from the ceiling, and a crystal chandelier beside a giant portrait of Atatürk. The extensive coffee menu features the likes of frappuccinos, plus decent sandwiches and sweets.

Beyazıt

Erenler Çay Bahçesi
Çorlulu Ali Paşa Medresesi, Yeniçeriler Caddesi 36/28 (0212 528 3785). Tram Beyazıt. **Open** *Summer* 7am-3am daily. *Winter* 7am-midnight daily. **Not licensed. No credit cards.** **Map** p242 L10 ❽
For review, *see p151* **Hubbly Bubbly**.

INSIDE TRACK COFFEE TIME

Turkish coffee is still a familiar ritual: boiled in a miniature copper or brass beaker known as a *cezve*, it is served in miniature porcelain cups (*fincans*). Types include *çifte kavrulmuş* (double-roasted), *dibği* (ground with a mortar), *mirra* (bitter with cardamon), *közde* (coal-cooked) and *melengiçi* (with nettle tree). After draining your cup, turn the remaining sludge upside down to have your fortune read from the dregs. As the Turkish saying goes: *Bir fincan kahvenin kırk yıllık hatrı vardır* (one cup of coffee brings 40 years of gratitude).

WESTERN DISTRICTS

Eyüp

Pierre Loti
Balmumcu Sokak 5, off Gümüşsuyu Caddesi (0212 581 2696). Bus 55ET. **Open** 8am-midnight daily. **Not licensed. No credit cards.**
On a hilltop with a stunning vantage point over the Golden Horn, this café is dedicated to French naval officer Pierre Loti, who was so obsessed with Istanbul that he took to masquerading as a Turk and remodelled his house as a 'Sultan's palace'. Legend has it Loti would sit at this spot for hours, gazing over the city and gathering inspiration for his literary masterpiece, *Aziyade*. To get to this modest tea-house, climb up through the scenic cemetery near Eyüp Mosque or take a cable car, which is signposted from the mosque.

BEYOĞLU

Cihangir

This bohemian enclave boasts countless style-conscious cafés and bars. Most are concentrated along and around Akarsu Sokak. Things really liven up after dark and at weekends, when a leisurely brunch can easily last all day.

★ Cuppa
Yeni Yuva Sokak 22A (0212 249 5723, www.cuppa juice.com). **Open** 9am-10pm daily. **Credit** AmEx, MC, V. **Not licensed. Map** p249 O4 ❾
On one of the smaller streets behind Cihangir's main drag, this juice bar is the perfect antidote to Beyoğlu's boozy bars. Choose from around 40 fruit and veggie cocktails, plus nutritious extras like wheatgrass, guarana or Echinacea. The healthy menu extends to salads, wraps and sandwiches. The decor, like many

places in the area is retro, with classic furniture, shelving holding up *National Geographic* magazines and *Peanuts* cartoon books, and a record player providing the tunes. WiFi is available.

▶ *You'll find lots of fruit juice stalls along Galipdede Caddesi, off Tünel Square.*

Meyra

Akarsu Caddesi 46 (0212 244 5350). **Open** 9am-4am daily. **Licensed**. **Credit** MC, V. **Map** p249 O4 ⑩

Meyra (formerly Leyla) is a popular café that is unpretentiously cool. The retro designer furniture, chalkboard specials and airy interior with large windows opening on to street tables make it the perfect location for whiling away an afternoon. Menu highlights include all-day themed breakfasts, with geographical themes running from Istanbul to Oslo, Madrid and London. The English breakfast is a generous plate of bacon and eggs, with orange juice, tea and a selection of rolls. Salads, burgers and meat dishes are also available. There's wine by the glass and Efes beer is on tap. The bar is open late.

★ Smyrna

Akarsu Caddesi 29 (0212 244 2466). **Open** 9am-4am daily. **Licensed**. **Credit** AmEx, MC, V. **Map** p249 O4 ⑪

Up on the Roofs

Head up high for stunning views.

Yesterday I watched you from a noble hill,
Noble Istanbul
I know every street, every alleyway,
I love you Istanbul
Yahya Kemal Batah (1884-1958)

Now, as then, the best way to see Istanbul is from above, as Istanbul's nightlife impresarios have discovered – a revelation that has revolutionised dining and drinking in recent years. Rooftop bars and restaurants have sprung up everywhere, desperately trying to outdo each other with the most sweeping skyline and exotic cocktail list.

The frontrunner of this trend is **5.Kat** (*see p128*), owned by actress Yasemin Alkaya: it's a heady mix of art deco and kitsch, starlit romance and late-night shenanigans. Another pioneer of the roof terrace scene is **Leb-i Derya Richmond** (*see p147*). Four years ago, owner Cem Sancer was bowled over by the view from what was then a dilapidated building down a narrow side street off Istiklal Caddesi. Sancer transformed the sea of rubble into a vertiginous oasis for Istanbul's international elite. A recent addition to Leb-i Derya's portfolio is another bar with equally breathtaking views over the Bosphorus (Kumbaracı Iş Hanı 57/7, Kumbaracı Yokuşu, Tünel (0212 293 4989).

Nu Teras (*see p147*) is another stunner: up on the seventh floor, and with amazing views over the Golden Horn, this is a place to be seen – it's summer central for hip Istanbullus.

In recent years, scores more bars, restaurants, cafés and cake shops have launched open-air outposts offering

nu Teras. *See p147*.

fabulous cityscapes. **360** (*see p125*) is a restaurant, bar and club rolled into one, this glass-walled pleasure palace sits atop one of Beyoğlu's most famous apartment blocks, smack in the middle of Istiklal Caddesi. As its name suggests, it boasts 360-degree views, with sky-high prices to match.

Rooftop revelry is not confined to the rich. Many of Beyoğlu's meyhanes and humble coffee shops have also opened up their top floors to the elements – though they can't all boast the same views.

Badehane.

CONSUME

Traditionally, Cihangir's favourite hangout has been the cluster of teahouses by the mosque, where local loafers can spend a whole day or evening ensconced beneath the plane trees, nursing a dirt-cheap glass of tea. Nearby Smyrna is where the teahouse regulars come when they're feeling flush, to rub shoulders with the actors and artists who live in the area. The fabulous decor has been put together using items from junk shops in the area and is a mix of the antique, modern and downright whimsical. The old typewriters reflect the bohemian vibe. Food includes a variety of salads, pastas and meat dishes. Laid-back enough for daytime lounging and lunching, Smyrna shifts up a few gears after dark.

Susam Café
Susam Sokak 11 (0212 251 5995). **Open** 9am-2am daily. **Licensed**. **Credit** AmEx, MC, V. **Map** p249 O4 ⑫
Quaint little Susam has a menu with hot and cold coffees, teas, freshly squeezed juices, lemonade, cookies, cakes and other sweets. There are waffles and pancakes too. Mains include toasted sandwiches, salads, sandwiches, meat and chicken as well. There's food to go tool.

Galata & Tünel

The cobbled streets found around **Galata**, **Asmalımescit** and **Tünel** are home to some of the city's most exciting and distinctive venues. Residents come from all over the city to catch live Turkish music at **Badehane** or jazz and pop bands at **Babylon** (*see p191*).

★ Badehane
General Yazgan Sokak 5, Tünel (0212 249 0550). **Open** 9am-3am daily. **Licensed**. **Credit** AmEx, MC, V. **Map** p248 M4 ⑬
A modest, single-room venue just off Tünel Square, Badehane began as an eaterie, but quickly evolved into one of the most popular bars in town. On Wednesdays, live gypsy music (including local legend Selim Sesler) gets the crowd dancing around the tiny, packed tables. There is also live music on Tuesdays and at weekends – see in-house posters for details. In summer, the café spills out on to the street, where backgammon tournaments take place, and friends meet for large beers and a smoke.
▶ *For more live music venues, see pp191-98.*

★ Enginar
Şah Kapısı Sokak 4A, Kuledibi, Galata (0212 251 7321). **Open** noon-2am daily. **Licensed**. **Credit** AmEx, MC, V. **Map** p246 M5 ⑭
The neighbourhood around the Galata Tower has had a major facelift in the last few years: streets have been repaved and cafés have spread their tables across the spruced-up square surrounding the tower. Enginar, one of the area's most popular bars, has a claim to fame as a set for a local soap opera, and with its stained-glass windows and rustic interior, it's a perfect pit-stop after a tour of the tower or midway on the steep climb from Karaköy to Tünel. There's occasional music during the winter months.

KV Café
Tünel Geçidi 10, Tünel (0212 251 4338, www.kv.com.tr). **Open** 8am-2am daily. **Licensed**. **Credit** MC, V. **Map** p248 M4 ⑮

Opposite Tünel station, an elaborate iron gate leads to an enchanting 19th-century arcade overgrown with potted plants. Of the handful of cafés lucky enough to share this secret passageway, KV is the largest and most atmospheric. Couples cosy up on wrought-iron furniture, snacking on cakes or lingering over cheese and wine. Inside, the café occupies three beautiful bare-brick rooms with tiled floors, arched windows, and unusual antiques. At dusk, the setting is even more romantic, lit by candles and Victorian lamps, with live piano music wafting through the arcade. The music programme is usually from September to March.

Otto Sofyalı

Sofyalı Sokak 22/A, Tünel (0212 252 6588, www.ottoistanbul.com). **Open** 11am-2am Mon-Sat. **Licensed. Credit** AmEx, MC, V. **Map** p248 M4 ⑯
With their authentic pizzas, light bites and good cocktails, Otto has been an important part of Istanbul food and drink, as well as nightlife, since the first branch opened back in 2005 (at the Santralistanbul arts centre; *see p67*). This branch has a similar industrial chic look as the others. Its most noticeable detail is the bar, which spans from the entrance all the way down to the back of the narrow venue.
Other locations Santralistanbul, Silahtar Mahallesi (0212 427 1889); Asmalımescit Mahallesi, Şehbender Sokak 5/1 (0212 292 7015).

Şimdi

Asmalımescit Sokak 5, Tünel (0212 252 5443). **Open** 8am-2am daily. **Licensed. Credit** AmEx, MC, V. **Map** p248 M4 ⑰

This relaxed refuge off Istiklal is one of the most stylish all-day café-bars anywhere in Istanbul. Hipsters hang out in the retro front room, where low seating and low lighting encourage lounging. And with free wireless internet, you can bring your own laptop or use the Mac provided. There's an above-average selection of wine by the glass, accompanied by addictive balls of spiced cheese. Simple but delicious Mediterranean dishes are served in the dining area at the rear.

Galatasaray

Discerning drinkers head to the stylish cafés and bars around the **Galatasaray Lycée**, where Istanbul's intellectuals, designers and media types congregate. Photographers favour **Kafe Ara**, named after Magnum snapper Ara Güler, who lives upstairs.

Büyük Londra

Meşrutiyet Caddesi 53 (0212 293 1619). **Open** 4pm-2am daily. **Licensed. Credit** MC, V. **Map** p248 M3 ⑱
Fans of colonial watering holes tend to head for the bar at the Pera Palas Hotel; that's because they don't know about the Büyük Londra. Another late 19th-century time warp, it may be a little less grand than the Pera Palas, but it's way more eccentric. The two gilded salons are plushly carpeted and decked with giant chandeliers. The immaculate barman occasionally sallies forth from the tiny bar at the back to change the 78 on the wind-up gramophone. Otherwise, the soundtrack is provided by caged songbirds on the windowsills. Open late and rarely crowded, Büyük Londra is an open secret

Enginar.

Grape Expectations

Turkey has 3,000 years of wine-making heritage. It's taken that long to succeed.

Wine may not the first thing that comes to mind when discussing Turkish products. Turkish delight, *kater* cheese, evil eye ornaments... But wine? That may be about to change. Wine writers Oz Clarke and Charles Metcalfe, and Masters of Wine Susan Hulme and Tim Atkin, toured Turkey's wine-producing areas in 2010 and returned pleasantly surprised. An impressed Tim Atkin reported, 'This historic but little-known wine-producing country has an exciting range of indigenous varieties that deserve to reach a wider audience. I am very impressed by the quality.' Judges at the 2010 London International Wine Fair agreed. Turkish wines scooped numerous medals and awards, and at the 2010 Decanter World Wine Awards, out of 11,000 entries, a Turkish producer, Kavaklidere, was awarded a silver medal.

It's been a challenge to get Turkish wine up to competitive standards when the favoured local booze, anise-based *rakı*, fills bar glasses and accompanies meals as a matter of course. In addition to convincing local taste, the fact that the country's three principal producers – Doluca, Kavaklidere and Kayra – have dominated winemaking has pushed small-scale vineyards to the sidelines up until now. However, with international acknowledgement and increased exposure, there are signs that Turkey is on its way to becoming a significant exporter. 'There's a long wine history in Turkey, but at the moment there's not much competition,' explained Murat Bozok, head chef of Mimolett (*see p131*), one of Istanbul's leading restaurants. 'When there is, the quality of wine will go up. We have a lot of boutique vineyards and the baby boom generation are beginning to learn about wines.'

Educating the average consumer about Turkish wines is half the battle. Not only have they probably never considered them, but it's also tough trying to pronounce the names of the grapes. Below is a short rundown.

RED

Öküzgözü (*okoo-zgoo-zu*). Translates as 'bull's eye', referring to its large, dark grape. Medium body, not too fruity. It doesn't taste as heavy as it looks. Öküzgözü is to Turkey what malbec is to Argentina.

Boğazkere (*bo-aahz-kere*). Dark and rich but typically used to make light-bodied blends. However, the single variety, premium quality, makes for a full-bodied, tannic, fully loaded glass.

Kalecik Karası (*kal-ee-jik kar-a-si*). Not so deep in colour, but lively on the palate. Soft tannins, with aromas of dried fruits, cocoa and spices. It is a classy number. If you like pinot noir, you'll like this.

WHITE

Emir. Refreshing and dry with lingering floral and faintly fruity notes. Low acidity. It's also used to make excellent bubbly. The type of wine you can drink on its own and not feel like a hobo.

Narince. An aromatic white with a smooth texture. The flavour of this grape varies greatly because it can be aged for quite a while, though younger bottles have a nice, fresh flavour.

Sultaniye (*sul-ta-na*). The Ottoman sultans drank this by the gallons. Light and citrous with a low level of acidity. The perfect wine to sip sitting by the Bosphorus with a freshly cooked fish sandwich.

If you'd like to learn more and sample some of Turkey's top tipples, visit **La Cave** (Sıraselviler Caddesi 109A, Cihangir, Beyoğlu, 0212 243 2405, www.lacave sarap.com) or **Sensus** (Bereketzade Mahallesi, Büyükhendek Caddesi 5, Galata, Beyoğlu, 0212 245 5657, www.sensus wine.com). Both offer 'flights' by wine regions for around YTL20 for five samples.

CONSUME

that's good to know. Hemingway stayed here in 1922, sent by the *Toronto Daily Star* to cover the Turkish war of independence, and the bar is still favoured by artists, writers and film crews.

▶ *The Büyük Londra is also a good, moderately priced hotel (see p111).*

Cezayir

Hayriye Caddesi 12 (0212 245 9981, www. cezayir-istanbul.com). **Open** 9am-2am Mon-Thur, Sun; 9am-4am Fri, Sat. **Licensed. Credit** MC, V. **Map** p248 N3 ⑲
Behind the Galatasaray Lycée, this fabulous 19th-century building was originally a school for the Italian Workers' Association. Now beautifully converted into a glamorous bar and restaurant, Cezayir throngs with the city's literati and glitterati late into the night (note the opening hours). The baroque silver and white dining room is stunning. The back room, with original floor tiles, soaring ceilings and a long wooden bar, is a stylish place for sharing some of the most inventive meze in Istanbul. There's a louche lounge with large mirrors and sofas, and a garden at the back that opens on to the twee restaurants of French Street.

Kafe Ara

Istiklal Caddesi, Tosbağa Sokak 2, off Yeniçarşı Caddesi (0212 245 4105). **Open** 8am-midnight Mon-Thur, Sun; 10am-midnight Fri, Sat. **Not licensed. Credit** MC,V. **Map** p248 N3 ⑳
A continental-style café owned by local Magnum photographer Ara Güler, whose evocative black and white shots of Istanbul adorn the walls and place mats. In fine weather, tables in the little alley opposite the Galatasaray Lycée fill up fast. In winter, the smart, split-level interior buzzes with cultured patrons armed with portfolios, notebooks, or laptops. No alcohol is served, but the fresh-pressed lemonade and milkshakes are great. Snack on sandwiches, pasta and desserts. *Photo p148.*
▶ *To view photos by Ara Güler, see www.araguler.com.tr.*

★ Leb-i Derya Richmond

Richmond Hotel, Istiklal Caddesi 445 (0212 243 4375, www.lebiderya.com). **Open** 11am-2am Mon-Thur, Sun; 11am-4am Fri, Sat. **Licensed. Credit** AmEx, MC, V. **Map** p248 M4 ㉑
On the top floor of the Richmond Hotel, right on Istiklal Caddesi, this bright and airy bar and restaurant has one very attractive proposition: the best views in Istanbul. The food is excellent, but avoid lunch in summer as the glassed-in terrace creates a greenhouse effect. Instead, go in time for sundowners, with breathtaking views of the Bosphorus and the Sea of Marmara.
▶ *Don't miss its other, equally spectacular, venue nearby at Kumbaracı Iş Hanı 57/7, Kumbaracı Yokuşu, Tünel (0212 293 4989).*

INSIDE TRACK TEA TIME

Turkish tea, made from black tea leaves grown in the Black Sea region, brewed in a teapot and sipped from elegant little tulip-shaped glasses, is as ubiquitous as it ever was.

Limonlu Bahçe

Yeniçarşı Caddesi 98 (0212 252 1094). **Open** *Nov-Mar* noon-11pm daily. *Apr-Oct* 9.30am-2am daily. **Licensed. Credit** MC, V. **Map** 248 N3 ㉒
Part-way down the precipitous slope of Yeniçarşı, Limonlu Bahçe is set in a big, bucolic garden. This pretty setting draws a self-conscious young crowd who loll on cushions, flop in hammocks or gather around chunky wooden tables. There are plenty of tight T-shirts and cute tattoos on display. And if there aren't enough staff, nobody seems to mind.

Nu Teras

Meşrutiyet Caddesi 67 (0212 245 6070, www.nupera.com.tr). **Open** *June-Oct* 6.30pm-2am Mon-Thur, Sun; 6.30pm-5am Fri, Sat. **Licensed. Credit** AmEx, DC, MC, V. **Map** p248 M4 ㉓
On the rooftop of the Nu Pera building, Nu Teras is the epitome of hip Istanbul – with the backdrop of a stunning view of the Golden Horn. The area behind the bar is given over to long tables for diners, who

Cezayir.

CONSUME

tuck into the same nouvelle Turkish cuisine as at Lokanta (*see p127*), the winter venue on the ground floor. Dancing is tolerated, but swaying is considered cooler. Unlike other new venues that were crowded out then swiftly abandoned, Nu Teras is a survivor that can be considered a classic.

▶ *For more bars with views, see p143* **Up on the Roofs**.

Pano

Hamalbaşı Caddesi 12B (0212 292 6664). **Open** 11am-2am daily. **Licensed**. **Credit** AmEx, MC, V. **Map** p248 N3 ㉔

Over a century old, Pano is an Istanbul institution. This atmospheric wine bar is like an updated take on a typical Greek taverna, with wood-panelled interior and rows of giant barrels above the bar. The later it gets, the more people pile in, and there's often standing room only. Then customers squeeze around the narrow counters, sampling Turkish and imported wines by the glass or bottle. Beer is also plentiful and cheap. Tasty finger food includes a generous cheese platter. Only the lucky few will find a table for a proper meze dinner.

▶ *For more on Turkish wines, see p146* **Grape Expectations**.

Public

Meşrutiyet Caddesi 84 (0212 251 5131). **Open** noon-midnight Mon-Thur; noon-4am. **Licensed**. **Credit** MC, V. **Map** p248 N3 ㉕

Public is a new Beyoğlu venture among the hotels and design bars of Meşrutiyet. By day, it serves an impressive range of snacks and light lunches.

The evening menu is more substantial, with Mediterranean dishes and a few Turkish standards. The music gets going at night too; some of Istanbul's more cutting-edge DJs and a few international names have put in an appearance. After dark, Public is all about the partying.

Zoe

Tomtom Mahallesi, Yeniçarşı Caddesi 58/5 (0212 251 7491). **Open** noon-2am daily. **Licensed**. **Credit** MC, V. **Map** p248 N3 ㉖

Despite the gruff bouncers manning the red velvet entrance, Zoe is actually a relatively laid-back bar/restaurant that puts equal emphasis on food and drink. It's one of many venues that makes the most of its rooftop; in the summer, lively groups of customers party under the stars.

Nevizade

Nevizade Sokak is a safe bet for a lively night out. Young Turks down *rakı* in packed *meyhanes* or huddle around tankards of beer in the nearby pubs.

Gizli Bahçe

Nevizade Sokak 27 (0212 249 2192). **Open** noon-3am daily. **Licensed**. **Credit** MC, V. **Map** p248 N3 ㉗

The only way to tell this place apart from the dozens of other establishments on Nevizade Sokak is by the '27' crudely painted on the wall. There's a mellow bar on the ground floor and a livelier space up two flights of stairs, littered with low tables and arm-

Kafe Ara. *See p147.*

chairs. The name means 'Secret Garden' – and that's upstairs, too. The music is an odd medley of modern electro and obscure 1980s tracks. The door policy can be uncharacteristically picky for the area.

James Joyce

Balo Sokak 26, off Istiklal Caddesi (0212 244 7970, www.theirishcentre.com). **Open** noon-2am Mon-Thur, Sun; noon-4am Fri, Sat. **Licensed.** **Credit** AmEx, MC, V. **Map** p248 N3 ㉘

The first and only Irish pub in Istanbul. The decor is predictably clichéd, although recently renovated, but the punters are a mixed bag of worldly Turks, expats and tourists who come for the decent range of fairly pricey beers (Guinness included). Irish breakfast is served all day and there's often live music. The place gets packed for international football matches, when the atmosphere can be electric. There's also regular live music on the new stage.

Şahika

Nevizade Sokak 17 (0212 249 6196). **Open** noon-4am daily. **Licensed.** **Credit** MC, V. **Map** p248 N3 ㉙

Another lively but laidback venue with dozens of stools and tiny tables packed into the small space outside, from where a predominantly younger crowd watches the world go by. Inside, wooden stairs lead to five levels of dining rooms and a summer roof terrace where the good times roll to a mix of 1980s, electronica and alternative rock. The simple menu is good value for money.

Taksim

Almost every side-street off mile-and-a-half long Istiklal Caddesi is riddled with bars and cafés. The greatest concentration are near **Taksim Square**, with venues for every tribe: Africans, Anatolians, goths, bikers, students, intellectuals, gays and transvestites. Those in search of a cheap beer or a puff on a narghile loiter around **Mis Sokak** and **Büyük Parmakkapı Sokak**.

Kaktüs

Imam Adnan Sokak 4, off Istiklal Caddesi (0212 249 5979). **Open** 8am-2am daily. **Licensed.** **Credit** MC, V. **Map** p249 O2 ㉚

Kaktüs's elegant dark-wood interior owes a great deal to the classic French café. Its patrons do their best to recreate the ambience of a Godard movie by chain-smoking and sipping blonde beers or black coffee. Stand-offish staff process the short-order menu that changes daily. Since opening in the early 1990s, Kaktüs has spawned countless imitators, but it remains the coolest hang-out with some of the highest prices. Cadde-i Kebir across the street is similar in style, but sells beer for about half the price. **Other locations** 16 Cihangir Caddesi, Cihangir (0212 243 5731).

Klub Karaoke

Zambak Sokak 15 (0212 293 7639, www.klub-karaoke.com). **Open** 8pm-3am Mon-Thur, Sun; 8pm-5am Fri, Sat. **Licensed.** **Credit** MC, V. **Map** p249 O2 ㉛

This karaoke club near Taksim Square consists of a small bar and two private rooms that are available for hire – the intimate, red-leather Tokyo Room and the larger, darker Fetish Room. Look out for the theme nights dedicated to ladies, men, Turkish tunes or disco hits. Things don't really get going until around 11pm, then everyone wants a turn on the mike.

Old City

Turnacı Başı Sokak 5/5, off Istiklal Caddesi (0212 244 28 96, www.oldcitycomedyclub.com). **Open** 8pm-midnight Mon-Thur; 8pm-4am Fri-Sat. **Licensed.** **Credit** MC, V. **Map** p249 O3 ㉜

Old City has been a late-night haunt of nocturnal Istanbullus for years. The place is a bit of a hit or miss affair. But on the right night, you're guaranteed shot-fuelled dancing or live cover bands until all hours. The best way to avoid the wrong night (and the occasional entrance fee) is to peek through the windows on Istiklal Caddesi: there's no mistaking if the joint is jumping. It's also a comedy club, but nearly always in Turkish.

Pia

Bekar Sokak 4A, off Istiklal Caddesi (0212 252 7100). **Open** 10am-2am daily. **Licensed.** **Credit** MC, V. **Map** p249 O2 ㉝

The uncluttered decor and gallery-style mezzanine create a sense of space where there isn't much at all. Ornate mirrors and a single George Grosz print set the tone. This is a hang-out for writers, film-makers and other creative types. It's also the kind of place where single women will feel comfortable – in fact, some of the city's most beautiful women have been seen to drop into Pia. Dishes inspired by the owners' travels are served all day. The daily specials are usually worth a gamble.

NIŞANTAŞI & TEŞVIKIYE

For a different take on Istanbul's bar life, head up to **Nişantaşı** or **Teşvikiye**, a pair of upper-class neighbourhoods north of Taksim with a lively bar scene.

Corridor

Milli Reasürans Çarşışı 47/48, Abdi İpekci Caddesi, Teşvikiye (0212 343 0241). **Metro** Osmanbey. **Open** 6pm-2am Mon-Sat. **Licensed.** **Credit** AmEx, MC, V.

A shopping mall may seem like a rather strange place for a bar, but Nişantaşı's Milli Reasürans Çarşışı is full of them. Corridor has a lively but laidback atmosphere, without the snob factor and dismissive doormen of so many Nişantaşı locations.

CONSUME

And the hipsters don't seem to mind taking their drinks out to the closed shopping centre.

Touchdown

Milli Reasürans Carşışı 61/11, Abdi Ipekci Caddesi, Teşvikiye (0212 231 3671, www.touchdown.com.tr). Metro Osmanbey. **Open** 11am-midnight Mon-Thur; 11am-2am Fri, Sat. **Licensed**. **Credit** MC, V.

Touchdown manages to successfully recreate the atmosphere of an American corner bar, despite the fact that it's in a shopping small. It's a popular spot for drinks after work; on busy nights, customers trickle down the stairway of the Reasürans Centre. Although a favourite with media and advertising executives, it's not flashy. In fact, it feels more like a student union bar.

THE BOSPHORUS VILLAGES

On the shores of the Bosphorus, picturesque, well-to-do **Ortaköy**, **Arnavutköy** and **Bebek** are made for indolent afternoons measured out in coffee cups and moonlit evenings fuelled by martinis. The most successful venues owe as much to their waterfront settings as their designer decor and fancy drinks.

Angelique

Muallim Naci Caddesi, Salhane Sokak 5, Ortaköy (0212 327 2844). **Open** 6pm-4am daily. **Licensed**. **Credit** MC, V.

Angelique, run by the prolific Doors Group, is an upmarket restaurant serving Asian and Mediterranean dishes before turning into a club and cocktail bar. In a restored three-storey mansion, it has superb views over the Bosphorus. The music policy is key, and it even has its own *Sounds of Angelique* CD volumes. Big name DJs regularly attend. Recently at the turntable was Argentinian DJ Hernan Cattaneo.

Aşşk Café

Muallim Naci Caddesi 64/B, Kuruçeşme (0212 265 4734). Bus 25E, 40T. **Open** 9am-2am Tue-Sun; noon-2am Mon. **Licensed**. **Credit** AmEx, MC, V.

Once you get past that name – the Turkish word for 'love' drawn out into a lisping 'aşşk' – this place has a lot to recommend it. To find it, follow the unmarked staircase down to the Bosphorus from the Macrocenter in Kuruçeşme. The setting is gorgeous: a clubhouse beside the Bosphorus with a lovely garden. The lavish breakfasts and organic salads are deservedly renowned, but rather expensive.

★ Lucca

Cevdetpaşa Caddesi 51/B, Bebek (0212 257 1255, www.luccastyle.com). Bus 22, 22R, 25E, 30D, 40, 42T. **Open** 9am-2am daily. **Licensed**. **Credit** AmEx, MC, V.

If you're caught in a traffic jam in Bebek, the likely cause is the string of SUVs double-parked outside this neighbourhood hotspot. By night, sleek society girls pick at plates of sashimi and check each other out from the pavement seating or through the floor-to-ceiling windows. At weekends, the party people like to kick off the night with exotic cocktails, and big-name DJs hit the decks (Giles Peterson has been here recently). By day, it's a pleasant café with Mediterranean mains (YTL20-YTL40). The modern decor works well, and different artists show their work every month.

Sedir

Mecidiye Köprüsü Sokak 16-18, Ortaköy (0212 327 9870). Bus DT1, DT2. **Open** 9.30am-midnight daily. **Not licensed**. **Credit** MC, V.

In a converted house next door to Ortaköy mosque, Sedir is a laid-back choice for all-day dining or a coffee break, although conversation is punctuated by the wail of the muezzin. The decor is deliberately designed to feel like home, with sofas, old books, and hand-painted patterns on the walls. The split-level conservatory, with its creeping ivy and stained-glass windows, is especially inviting.

ASIAN SHORE

Savvy residents of the Asian side turn their noses up at the prospect of crossing the Bosphorus for a night out. Kadıkoy's **Kadife Sokak** is packed with bars and cafés offering cheap beer and live music. It's also worth checking out the lively nightlife at bars such as **Moda Terrace** in Moda, near Kadıköy.

Isis

Kadife Sokak 26, Kadıköy (0216 349 7381). Ferry from Karaköy or Beşiktaş to Kadıköy. **Open** 11am-2am daily. **Licensed**. **Credit** MC, V. **Map** p251 W8 ㉔

This Egyptian-themed bar, with wall paintings and statues, is incongruously located in a converted three-storey townhouse. The top-floor wine bar holds regular tastings accompanied by live music. The large garden gets crammed on summer nights.

Karga

Kadife Sokak 16, Kadıköy (0216 449 1725, www.kargart.com). Ferry from Karaköy or Beşiktaş to Kadıköy. **Open** 11am-2am daily. **Licensed**. **Credit** AmEx, DC, MC, V. **Map** p251 W8 ㉟

This much-loved haunt in the heart of Kadıköy's bar strip is known for three things: alternative music, cheap beer and fine art. The music policy can only be described as eclectic, with themed nights ranging from Belgian pop to Bill Laswell. These usually take place in the ground-floor bar, which is like a pub, with lower lighting and louder music. Changing art exhibitions are held in the quieter space upstairs.

CONSUME

Hubbly Bubbly

Put this in your pipe and smoke it.

Waterpipe, hookah, or 'hubbly-bubbly'. Call it what you will, Turks have been smoking the narghile since the early 17th century, despite religious authorities periodically denouncing the practice and calling for it to be banned. The tyrannical Murat IV (1623-40) decreed that anyone caught having so much as a quick puff should be sentenced to death.

In the late 19th and early 20th century, narghile smoking was all the rage in high society, particularly among women. That fad passed and in republican Istanbul the narghile was relegated to a pastime of the peasantry. Why it should suddenly be making a comeback in the 21st century is anybody's guess. But in the last few years a slew of cafés devoted to the waterpipe have opened. A few are aimed squarely at tourists, but most custom comes from students.

Narghile tobacco is typically soaked in molasses or apple juice, giving it a slightly sweet flavour; but you can get it straight and strong by asking for *tömbeki*.

Narghile cafés serve tea and coffee, but no alcohol. Prices are around YTL5-YTL9 a pipe, which lasts a good hour or more. Contrary to popular misconception, hashish is not an option, nor, sadly, is the traditional Ottoman blend of opium, perfume and crushed pearls.

The best place to sample a narghile is on the nameless pedestrian strip by the American Pazarı, below the old cannon foundry at Tophane. Until recently there was just a row of small shops; now it's lined with nothing but narghile cafés. At any time of day or night, there might be 300 to 400 people here, an extraordinary mix of students, couples and families, all belching forth great clouds of grey smoke. Certain cafés at the north end of the strip have drawn fire in the press for providing cushion-strewn banquettes, which apparently encourage al fresco canoodling. But with or without the bodily contact, this is a fine place to wind down after a night out in Beyoğlu.

In Sultanahmet, meanwhile, the **Enjoyer Café** (*see p141*), one of the most touristy of the many narghile cafés on the pedestrianised street north of Divan Yolu, is a good bet if you avoid the fruity tobaccos. Over in Beyazit, in the idyllic

courtyard of an Ottoman seminary, **Erenler Çay Bahçesi's** (*see p142*) has low tables and benches, shaded with ivy-hung trellises. Despite signs advertising 'Magic Waterpipe Garden', few tourists visit; it's filled with students from nearby Istanbul University.

Perhaps the most popular place on this side of the Golden Horn is **Meşale** (*see p141*). This sunken café beside an arcade of tourist shops is very pleasant when the shops close and locals descend. There are nightly performances of Turkish classical music and dervish dancing shows on Friday, Saturday and Sunday between 8pm and 10pm.

CONSUME

Shops & Services

A rug, designer clothes or a pair of retro sunglasses.

Istanbul's image as a blend of ancient and modern may be a cliché, but that doesn't mean it isn't true, and the old-new fusion is as apparent in the city's shops as anywhere else. The oriental shopping experience, with a visit to the **Grand Bazaar** (*see p52*) or the **Egyptian Bazaar** (*see p58*), may be an integral part of an Istanbul itinerary, and the antique and vintage shops of **Çukurcuma** have plenty to entice shoppers too.

Shopping mall culture came to the city some years ago – and stayed. There are enough aspirational and sophisticated consumers to support local fashion designers and retailers, and enough with sufficient cash to spend on big international labels, too. Upmarket **Nişantaşı** and the newly redeveloped **Akaretler** district reflect this buying power.

CONSUME

General

DEPARTMENT STORES

Beymen
Akmerkez Mall 107, Nispetiye Caddesi, Etiler (0212 316 6900, www.beymen.com.tr). Metro Levent. Bus 59R, 59UL, 559C, U1, U2, UL57. **Open** 10am-10pm daily. **Credit** AmEx, MC, V.
Beymen started life as a men's clothing store, but is now synonymous with designer clothing and accessories for men and women, combining own-label products with select international brands. You'll also find cosmetics and home accessories.
Other locations Abdi Ipekçi Caddesi 23/1, Nişantaşı (0212 373 4800); Bağdat Caddesi 330/1, Erenköy, Asian Shore (0216 468 1500).

Boyner
Metro City Mall, Büyükdere Caddesi 171, Levent (0212 344 0566, www.boyner.com.tr). Metro Levent. **Open** 10am-10pm daily. **Credit** MC, V.
Part of the eponymous Boyner Group, which also owns Beymen, Boyner is a less label-conscious version of its sister store. It stocks a comprehensive selection of clothes, shoes, sportswear, cosmetics, fabrics, china, glass and home accessories.

Vakko
Kanyon Mall, Büyükdere Caddesi 138-140, Levent (0212 353 1080, www.vakko.com.tr). Metro Levent. **Open** 10am-10pm daily. **Credit** AmEx, DC, MC, V.

Vakko was once Turkey's authority on fashion and still has huge cachet locally. Aside from some eye-catching window displays, the store has lost much of its originality today. The exceptions are own-label scarves and ties (worth checking out in the duty free store at Atatürk Airport) and some lavish Ottoman-design furnishings and fabrics.
Other locations Akmerkez Mall 122, Nispetiye Caddesi, Etiler (0212 282 0695); Bağdat Caddesi 422, Suadiye, Asian Shore (0216 416 4204).

YKM
Halaskargazi Caddesi 368, Şişli (0212 248 4120, www.ykm.com.tr). Metro Şişli. **Open** 10am-10pm Mon-Sat; noon-7pm Sun. **Credit** MC, V.
Turkey's oldest department store started life as a humble shop behind the Spice Bazaar in 1950. Today, it's the closest thing Istanbul has to a real department store. Unlike its more exclusive rivals, it caters to a broad market, selling everything from unisex clothing to sports gear, toys, home accessories and electronics.
Other locations Cevahir Mall, Büyükdere Caddesi, Şişli (0212 382 0342).

MALLS

Mall mania has seized the city since the arrival of the first one in 1988. Since then, Istanbullus have eagerly embraced the whole lifestyle package from across the pond. **Kanyon** and the paparazzi-friendly **Istinye Park** are recent additions to Istanbul's mall roster. **Akaretler** isn't a mall, but this redeveloped area, once an estate of houses for workers at Dolmabahçe Palace, it's now a row of shops, including Marc Jacobs and other luxury brands. The centrepiece is the new W Hotel (*see p116*).

Akmerkez

Nispetiye Caddesi, Etiler (0212 282 0170, www.akmerkez.com.tr). Metro Levent. Bus 59R, 59UL, 559C, U1, U2, UL57. **Open** 10am-10pm daily.

An upmarket mall with 250 shops, a food court, cinema and one of the city's better Italian restaurants, Paper Moon (www.papermoon.com.tr). But its infuriating design means it's hard to find your way out. Akmerkez suffers from an inconvenient location a good 15 minutes from the metro.

Cevahir

Büyükdere Caddesi 22, Şişli (0212 380 0893/4, www.istanbulcevahir.com). Metro Şişli. **Open** 10am-10pm daily.

Where to Shop

Istanbul's best shopping neighbourhoods in brief.

SULTANAHMET

Sultanahmet is prime tourist territory, and is well supplied with tacky souvenir stores and pushy carpet sellers. Prices are marked up accordingly. That said, some of the handicraft places and rug stores, particularly off the main drag, can turn up some interesting stuff – just don't expect bargains. Things get spicier as you head west towards the **Grand Bazaar** area, which may have lost its lustre to locals now attuned to the mall, but remains the oriental shopping experience par excellence (*see p54* **Shopping the Bazaar**).

BEYOĞLU

By comparison, Beyoğlu offers an altogether more western shopping experience. The street that is the backbone of the area, **Istiklal Caddesi**, is fast becoming bland anywhere-in-the-world high-street territory. The current line-up includes Top Shop, the Body Shop, Mango, Nike and multiple Starbucks, with at least one massive mall under construction at the time of writing. But dive into the side streets, be enticed by the Paris-style passages, and things start to get more interesting. That's also the case as you head away from the mainstream Taksim end of the street, and head past Galatasaray to the more off-beat Tünel end.

ÇUKURCUMA

This is the principal art, antiques and collectibles district. In the labyrinth of steep, narrow streets are dozens of dealers. Antiques, mid-century modern furniture and quirky knick-knacks from the last century can all be found, along with paintings in various artists' ateliers. **Bostanbaşi Caddesi** and **Turnacı Başi Sokak** are the best streets to start, but nothing beats wandering.

NIŞANTAŞI

For committed shoppers in search of sophistication, head to Nişantaşı and neighbouring **Teşvikiye**, two districts about a mile north of Taksim Square. This is serious label territory. On **Abdi Ipekçi Caddesi** the likes of Armani, Louis Vuitton and Tiffany sit alongside Turkish jewellers.

THE ASIAN SHORE

The Asian Shore is great for food. In Kadıköy, at the top end of **Yasa Sokak**, are delis stocking a huge range of regional Turkish produce. **Güneşlibahçe Sokak** has more excellent food shops, including one devoted exclusively to honey, another to olive oil, and some fantastic fishmongers. **Dellalzade Sokak** is lined with antique shops.

Grand Bazaar.

Market Day

A bit of everything.

Once a week, in most Istanbul neighbour-hoods, a few streets are taken over by the *mahalle pazarı*, or local market. The awnings go up, wooden stalls jam the streets, and stallholders compete for custom at high volume.

Stalls are heaped with everything from jumbo olives and village cheese (*köy peyniri*) to cheap clothing, cooking pots and tools. Apples, melons and all manner of seasonal fruit and vegetables are stacked in colourful pyramids.

Bargain hunters can sometimes find well-known European and American clothing brands at knock-down prices. Turkey's factories produce garments for the likes of Gap and Calvin Klein, and manufacturers sometimes sell surplus stock to market traders. But be sure to check items for faults. (For more on picking up surplus fashion stock, see *p161* **Begoğlu's Fashion Arcades**.)

As a general rule, trading kicks off around 9am and winds down around 5pm (later during the summer), when prices are slashed for the small pickings that remain.

For some of the city's best-known markets, *see right*.

Salı Pazarı.

Europe's biggest mall, and the second largest in the world; its six storeys can seem confusing. Besides direct access from the metro, the mall's greatest asset is Koc Taş, one of the city's only DIY stores reachable by public transport.

Istinye Park

Istinye Bayuddesi 185, Levent (0212 345 5555, www.istinyepark.com). Bus 29, 40, 42. **Open** 10am-10pm daily.

The latest addition to Istanbul's malls is also the most exclusive. Itinye Park is home to Gucci, Louis Vuitton and the usual roll call of designer stores. It's mostly covered, but there's a more pleasant outdoor precinct area. Among the mall's various restaurants and cafés, it is Masa where shoppers go to be seen; paparazzi often hang about the place. Pizzas are the pick on the menu.

▶ *Istinye Park is fairly close to Müzedechanga (see p137), the restaurant in the Sakıp Sabancı Museum in Emirgan.*

★ Kanyon

Büyükdere Caddesi 185, Levent (0212 353 5300, www.kanyon.com.tr). Metro Levent. **Open** 10am-10pm daily.

Kanyon is a mall with a difference. Open to, and yet sheltered from, the elements, its canyon-inspired design shelters 170 boutique-style shops, a plethora of restaurants, including branches of fashionable Kitchenette (*see p127*) and House Café (*see p137*), not to mention the plushest cinema in town. When it comes to shopping, the accent is on prestige fashion and lifestyle labels, both local and foreign: the likes of Harvey Nichols, Georg Jenson, Vakko and Swarovski. There's also a new Apple reseller store.

Metrocity

Büyükdere Caddesi 171, Levent (0212 344 0660, www.metrocity.com.tr). Metro Levent. **Open** 10am-10pm daily.

Like Kanyon across the road, this four-storey mall is served by a direct link to the metro. What's different is that it pitches to a far more middle-of-the-road clientele. Among the 140 stores, you'll find Marks & Spencer vying for business with Benetton, Zara, Mavi Jeans and the like. There's also a food court offering standard mall fare.

MARKETS

For food markets, *see p164*.

Fatih Pazarı

Darüşşafaka Caddesi, Fatih. **Open** Wed. **Map** p291 G7.

This vast open-air market surrounds the Fatih Mosque and fills its rambling courtyard. Join the headscarved crowds ever Wednesday to tussle over leopard-print lingerie, surplus clothing and household items. It also has an excellent reputation for food: expect to find top village produce, including local cheeses, baskets of fresh rosehips and, in season, cornelian cherries.

Ortaköy Market
Ortaköy Quayside. **Open** Sat, Sun.
Istanbul's answer to London's Camden Market. Go for mounds of tacky jewellery and plentiful kitsch imported from India and Africa. You might also happen to find the odd interesting antique, reproduction print or choice piece of trinketry.
▶ *For a post shopping snack visit the House Cafe (see p137).*

Salı Pazarı
Corner of Uzunçayır Caddesi & Mandıra Caddesi, Kadıköy. **Open** Tue, Sun.
This is the best-known, biggest and most popular of the city's street markets, so be prepared to mix it up with middle-class matrons and beetle-browed Anatolian mamas in search of bargain bras and the freshest of figs. A new location means it's further out of town.

Ulus Pazarı
Kürkadı Sokak, Etiler. **Open** Thur.
It may be sited in a sophisticated neighbourhood but don't expect a genteel crowd. This is the place for knock-off designer labels and an upmarket range of household ware, fruit, veg and deli items. A free bus service runs between the market and the Akmerkez mall.

Specialist
BOOKS & MAGAZINES
English-language

★ Homer Kitapevi
Yeniçarşi Caddesi 12A, Galatasaray (0212 249 5902). **Open** 10am-7.30pm Mon-Sat. **Credit** AmEx, MC, V. **Map** p248 N3.
Set alongside the Galatasaray Lycée, this smart, air-conditioned book shop has what is widely considered to be the best collection of foreign non-fiction in Istanbul. It's particularly strong on art and academic subjects.

Pandora
Büyükparmakkapı Sokak 3, Beyoğlu (0212 243 3503, www.pandora.com.tr). **Open** 10am-8pm Mon-Wed; 10am-9pm Thur-Sat; 1-8pm Sun. **Credit** AmEx, MC, V. **Map** p249 O3.
A fine little bookshop squeezed into three tight floors. The top one is filled with English-language titles, including fiction, poetry, art, local interest and a decent history section. Flyers and posters downstairs advertise events around town.

Robinson Crusoe.

★ Robinson Crusoe
Istiklal Caddesi 195/A, Beyoğlu (0212 293 6968, www.rob389.com). **Open** 9am-9.30pm Mon-Sat; 10am-9.30pm Sun. **Credit** AmEx, DC, MC, V. **Map** p248 M4.
A good-looking but cramped space saved by its tall ceilings, the store has an especially well-chosen selection of English-language fiction, international music and art mags, plus an array of titles on Istanbul and Turkey.

General

Galeri Kayseri
Divan Yolu 58, Sultanahmet (0212 512 0456, www.galerikayseri.com). Tram Sultanahmet.
Open 9am-8.30pm daily. **Credit** AmEx, MC, V. **Map** p243 M10.
This shop is devoted exclusively to books about Istanbul and Turkey. Whatever the genre, you'll find it here: fiction, non-fiction, guidebooks and coffee-table volumes.

Selim Mumcu Sahaf
Yeniçarşı Caddesi 33/C, Galatasaray (0212 245 4496). **Open** 10am-8pm Mon-Sat. **Credit** AmEx, MC, V. **Map** p248 N3.
What the stock lacks in depth it more than makes up for in eclecticism. There are also hundreds of old movie posters, photos, postcards and other memorabilia for sale.

Specialist

Denizler Kitabevi
Istiklal Caddesi 199/A, Beyoğlu (0212 243 3174, www.denizlerkitabevi.com). **Open** 10am-8pm daily. **Credit** MC, V. **Map** p248 M4.

CONSUME

The 130-year-old premises once housed the Dutch Consulate. This shop specialises in books on a maritime theme (*deniz* means 'sea'), but is also strong on travel guides, especially on Turkey.

Used & antiquarian

There are about half a dozen shops packed with second-hand books, many in English, in the **Aslıhan Pasajı**, an inconspicuous passage just off the Balık Pazarı halfway down Istiklal Caddesi. Some shops also deal in vinyl, magazines and old film posters.

★ Booksellers Bazaar
Kapalı Çarşı, Beyazıt (0212 522 3173, www.karpalicarsi.org.tr). Tram Beyazıt or Çemberlitaş. **Open** 8.30am-7pm Mon-Sat. **Map** p288 L9.
West of Çadırcılar, in Sahaflar Çarşısı Sokak, is the Booksellers' Bazaar, a lane and courtyard where the written word has been traded since early Ottoman times. Because printed books were considered a corrupting European influence, only hand-lettered manuscripts were sold until 1729, the year the first book in Turkish was published. Today, much of the trade at this historic bazaar is in textbooks (the university is nearby), along with plentiful coffee table volumes and framed calligraphy. Booksellers now have to compete with itinerant merchants peddling everything from Byzantine coins to used mobile phones.

Librairie de Pera
Galipdede Caddesi 22, Tünel (0212 243 7447, www.librairiedepera.com). **Open** 9am-7pm daily. **Credit** AmEx, MC, V. **Map** p248 M5.
Situated just downhill from Tünel Square, this shop carries old and rare books in numerous languages, many concerned with travel and Turkey.

CHILDREN
Toys

★ Porof Zihni Sinir
Kuloğlu Mahallesi Ağahamam Caddesi, Cihangir (0212 252 9320, www.zihnisinir.com). **Open** 10am-7.30pm Mon-Sat. **Credit** MC, V. **Map** p249 O3.
This remarkable store is at its core a toy shop, but the inventiveness of Irfan Sayar's creations could have found it a place in the Galleries chapter. Irfan is a cartoonist, whose character, a teacher called Porof Zihni Sinir, features in many Turkish children's books. However, his sculptures, at once tactile, fantastical and imaginative, have one thing in common: fun. Alongside the large-scale pieces, there are plenty of unique souvenirs and knick-knacks that would fit in a suitcase.
▶ *To learn more about the Turkish cartoon culture, visit the Cartoon Museum (see p61).*

ELECTRONICS & PHOTOGRAPHY
General

The best place to buy electronics – both big-name and discount brands – is in the underground arcade in **Karaköy Square**, directly under the tram stop.
   Photographic shops can be found on almost every high street. Many will do portrait and passport-size (*vesikalık*) photos, as well as selling and developing film. There are dozens of photographic shops around **Ankara Caddesi** in Eminönü.

Stüdyo Mor Ipek
Selvi Han, Sıraselviler Caddesi 61, Taksim (0212 249 5877/251 9253, www.moripek.com). **Open** 8.30am-8pm Mon-Sat. **Credit** MC, V. **Map** p249 O3.
This basement shop caters to both professionals and amateurs. Staff are also able to take colour passport photographs.

Teknosa
Kanyon Mall, floor B2, 185 Büyükdere Caddesi, Levent (0212 353 0460, www.kanyon.com.tr). Metro Levent. **Open** 10am-10pm daily. **Credit** AmEx, MC, V.
A new electronics shop in Kanyon Mall that sells laptops, telephones, white goods, TVs and cameras.

Yalçınlar
Ankara Caddesi 159, Sirkeci (0212 514 3009, www.yalcinlar.com.tr). Tram Sirkeci. **Open** 8.30am-8pm Mon-Sat. **Credit** AmEx, MC, V. **Map** p243 M10.
One of 30 branches offering developing and printing services for professionals and amateurs.
Other location Cevahir Shopping Mall, Büyükdere Caddesi 22, Şişli (0212 380 0292).

Specialist

There are several camera shops along Hüdavendigar, where the tram passes, in Sultanahmet. Lenses, filters and parts for all the major brands can be bought here.

Bilgisayar Hastanesi
Inönü Caddesi 72/3, Gümüşsuyu, Taksim, (0212 252 1575, www.bilgisayarhastanesi.com). **Open** 9am-6pm Mon-Fri. **Credit** MC, V. **Map** p247 P2.
An authorised service provider for Compaq, Hewlett Packard and Epson. Staff will clean, maintain and repair computers and order spare parts. Bilgisayar Hastanesi also operates an emergency service, but you pay a 50 per cent premium for any work done outside office hours. Otherwise, expect a long wait. You can also buy second-hand laptops here.

Yargıcı.

Troy Apple Centre
Kanyon Mall, floor B2, 185 Büyükdere Caddesi, Levent (0212 353 0460, www.kanyon.com.tr). Metro Levent. **Open** 10am-10pm daily. **Credit** AmEx, MC, V.
All the usual Apple goods you'd expect from a certified reseller. Repairs and parts available.

FASHION
Designer

★ Berrin Akyüz
Akarsu Caddesi 20, Cihangir (0212 251 4125, www.berrinakyuz.com). **Open** 10am-8pm Mon-Fri; 10am-5pm Sat, Sun. **Credit** AmEx, MC, V. **Map** p249 O4.
Designer Berrin Akyüz works half the time in her atelier in Üsküdar, and the other half in this Cihangir shop that sells her skirts, tops, scarves, bags, children's wear and jewellery. She works with Polish designer Lucasz Budzisz, who specialises in corsets, and between them offer four collections every year.

Damat Tween
Akmerkez Mall 214, Nispetiye Caddesi, Etiler (0212 282 0112, www.damat.com.tr). Bus 59R, 59UL, 559C, U1, U2, UL57. **Open** 10am-10pm daily. **Credit** AmEx, MC, V.
A local boy made good, Damat has branches in a dozen countries in addition to his mini-empire in Turkey. His stock-in-trade is classic menswear, ranging from suits to knitwear. The Tween label features casual collections in bold styles that are distinctive both for design and quality.

★ Gönül Paksoy
Atiye Sokak 1/3, Teşvikiye (0212 261 9081). Metro Osmanbey. **Open** 1-7pm Mon; 10am-7pm Tue-Sat. **Credit** AmEx, MC, V.
Ms Paksoy claims her designs are unique, not just in Turkey but worldwide. She's probably right. Her collections reinterpret Ottoman designs, using original fabrics and the finest natural weaves hand-dyed in subtle shades. She also does a great line in Ottoman-style slippers, handbags and shoes.

Mavi Jeans
Istiklal Caddesi 195, Beyoğlu (0212 244 6255, www.mavi.com). **Open** 10am-10pm Mon-Sat; 11am-10pm Sun. **Credit** AmEx, DC, MC, V. **Map** p249 O3.
Since making it big in the US, Mavi's prices have rocketed, but compared with imported brands, prices are still reasonable. Designs aren't cutting-edge, but they are very wearable. T-shirts, sweatshirts and casual co-ordinates complete the look.
Other locations Akmerkez Mall 235-238, Nispetiye Caddesi, Etiler (0212 282 0423); Metrocity Mall 134-135, Büyükdere Caddesi 171, Levent.

★ Simay Bülbül
Camekan Sokak 5, Galata (0212 292 7899, www.sim-ay.com). **Open** 10am-7pm Mon-Fri; 11am-8pm Sat, Sun. **Credit** AmEx, MC, V. **Map** p248 N5.
At the bottom of a quiet cobbled street off Istiklal Caddesi, designer Simal Bülbül's eponymous store sells her delicate leather and fabric clothes. She elegantly integrates leather into dresses and blouses with the lightest of touches. There are also shoes and leather accessories.

Ümit Ünal
Ensiz Sokak 1B, Tünel (0212 245 7886, www.umitunal.com). **Open** 10am-7.30pm Mon-Fri; 10am-noon Sat. **No credit cards. Map** p248 M5.
Ümit Ünal is an Istanbul-based designer who is plugged into the international fashion scene. His avant-garde fashion shows are more like performances, and his multi-layered, complex creations are art installations as much as garments. Ünal's influences are diverse – Celtic banshees, Himalayan mountain tribes, gypsies. He travels the globe in search of unusual fabrics and accessories.

Yargıcı
Valikonğı Caddesi 30, Nişantaşı (0212 225 2952, www.yargici.com.tr). Metro Osmanbey. **Open** 9.30am-7.30pm Mon-Sat; 1-6pm Sun. **Credit** AmEx, DC, MC, V.
Middle-of-the-road fashion both sexes. You're talking dependable quality rather than cutting-edge design. Beware the sizing, which can be baffling. (You thought you were a 36? Well, here you're a 32.)
Other locations Akmerkez Mall 208, Nispetiye Caddesi, Etiler (0212 282 0501).

CONSUME

WORLD'S TOP BRANDS
WORLD'S TOP TRENDS

Discount

See right **Beyoğlu's Fashion Arcades**.

Leather

For the best selection of leather (*deri*) head to the **Grand Bazaar** *(see p52)*. Be careful though, because quality can often be poor: 'antelope skin', for example, is unlikely to be genuine. You'll have to work hard to get a fair price. If it all seems like too much hassle, there are stores that specialise in quality leather at fixed prices, but they aren't that much cheaper than stores at home.

Derimod
Akmerkez Mall 362, Nispetiye Caddesi, Etiler (0212 282 0668, www.derimod.com.tr). Bus 59R, 59UL, 559C, U1, U2, UL57. **Open** 10am-10pm daily. **Credit** AmEx, DC, MC, V.
Classic and contemporary designs in top quality leather for both men and women, as well as an extensive range of leather accessories.

Matraş
Akmerkez Mall, Nispetiye Caddesi, Etiler (0212 282 0215, www.matras.com). Bus 59R, 59UL, 559C, U1, U2, UL57. **Open** 10am-10pm daily. **Credit** AmEx, DC, MC, V.
Classic, high-quality designs from Turkey's leading leather accessories label. As well as handbags, wallets and belts, pieces also include briefcases, luggage and smaller items such as leather purses and cardholders.
Other locations Bağdat Caddesi 273, Erenköy, Kadıköy (0216 385 0622).

Used & vintage

Binbavul
Galipdede Caddesi 66, Kuledibi, Galata (0212 243 7218, binbavul@gmail.com). **Open** 11am-9pm Sun-Thur; 11am-11pm Fri, Sat. **Credit** AmEx, MC, V. **Map** 248 M5.
Binbavul is located in the basement of an old building along an alley off the touristy Galipdede Caddesi at the southern end of Istiklal Caddesi. The small street stall only hints at the cavernous space behind that is rammed with vintage clothes, military regalia, theatre props, luggage, ball dresses, vinyl, designer goods and any whimsical item the owner picks up.

★ Mozk
Kuloğlu Mahallesi, Ağahamam Caddesi 13, Cihangir (0212 252 3499, www.mozk.co.uk). **Open** 9am-9pm Mon-Sat. **Credit** AmEx, MC, V. **Map** p249 O3.
Run by two fashion designers, this vintage store exudes cool. Retro sunglasses, leatherwear, floral

Binbavul.

dresses, shirts, hats – just about any item of clothing, can be found in this little shop. Only items in excellent condition are sold. Some other vintage items, such as telephones are available.

Roll
Turnacıbağı Sokak 11, Galatasaray (0212 244 9656). **Open** 10am-10pm Mon-Sat; noon-10pm Sun. **Credit** MC, V. **Map** p248 N3.
Most vintage stock here is from Europe and dates from the 1960s and '70s – loud nylon shirts, suede and velvet jackets, and vintage Adidas tracksuit tops.

FASHION ACCESSORIES & SERVICES

Accessories

See also p166 **Seyitağaoğulları Carpet Kilim Hand Crafts**.

Antique Objet
Zennecilere Caddesi 48-50, Grand Bazaar (0212 526 7451/www.antiqueobjet.com). Tram Beyazıt. **Open** 9am-7pm Mon-Sat. **Credit** AmEx, MC, V. **Map** p79.
Crammed into an awkward space by the entrance to the market's İç Bedesten, this den of delights stocks own-label boots, Cinderella slippers and jackets in velvet Suzani cloth, sleek short coats of rich Ottoman fabric and a line of bags in Suzani and ikat. Workmanship is top notch.

Ipek
Istiklal Caddesi 230, Beyoğlu (0212 249 8207). **Open** 9am-8pm Mon-Sat. **Credit** MC, V. **Map** p248 M4.

CONSUME

If it's neckwear you're after, this is the place to head. Along with charmingly persuasive service, you'll find an exhaustive range of scarves, shawls and ties.

Cleaning & repairs

The bespoke tailoring business may be foundering, but there's still a living to be made from mending and alterations. Tailors (*terzi*) are found throughout the city.

There are still some laundries in Istanbul, though these are a dying breed now that most people have washing machines at home. Dry-cleaners are plentiful and reasonably priced.

Acar Terzihane

Yeni Yuva Sokak 30, Cihangir (0212 251 3745/0535 762 7320). **Open** 8am-8pm Mon-Sat. **No credit cards. Map** p249 O4.

A long-running outfit, competent at all kinds of stitching and mending, as well as more ambitious custom-made outfits for ladies and gents.

Can Laundry

Bakraç Sokak 32/A, off Sıraselviler Caddesi, Cihangir (0212 252 9360). **Open** 8.30am-7.30pm Mon-Fri; 8.30am-4pm Sat. **No credit cards. Map** p249 O4.
Neighbourhood laundry services come with a smile a smile at this Cihangir laundry. You can either pay per load or by individual item. Ironing is optional and is charged per item.

Celal Akagün Tuhafiye

Marpuççular Alacahamam Caddesi 53, Eminönü (0212 526 5828). Tram Eminönü. **Open** 8.30am-6pm Mon-Fri; 8.30am-4pm Sat. **Credit** MC, V. **Map** p243 M8.

Beyoğlu's Fashion Arcades

Hunt out budget clothes in Istiklal's hidden pasajs.

In the last few decades, Turkey has become one of the world's most prolific producers of clothing, with over 40,000 factories nationwide. Many leading American and European brands now manufacture their clothing in Turkey.

Savvy local shoppers can reap the benefits by visiting factory outlets, where seconds and overruns can be bought for a fraction of the retail price. In Istanbul, you don't even have to trek to the suburbs to find a factory outlet: you can find seconds at unofficial outlets right in the city centre, if you know where to look.

Off Beyoğlu's Istiklal Caddesi are a number of *pasajs* (covered arcades) tucked away in backstreets, bursting with cheap clothing, stacked in bins or hung on rails, at knock-down prices. A pair of jeans, say, might be YTL35 or YTL40. Be prepared to rummage, as clothes are often crammed indiscriminately on to racks and it's up to you to find the right size.

As part of the trade agreement between the fashion companies and factories, extras usually have their labels removed. Part of the fun is trying to figure out whether you've got your hands on the latest style from H&M or Miss Sixty. Some companies don't allow their factory cast-offs to be resold, although you may well find faithful rip-offs of well-known brands anyway.

Popular with the grungy and black-clad, the **Atlas Pasajı**, behind the Atlas cinema,

is more structured than most, and its stock is of a higher quality, with a better claim to street cred than the Beyoğlu *pasaj* norm. Atlas is also home to an interesting selection of jewellery, second-hand clothes, kitsch collectibles, records, posters and comics. Its vaguely gothic vibe is reminiscent of London's Camden Market.

Beyoğlu İş Merkezi, opposite the Odakule building (286 Istiklal Caddesi), is a vast *pasaj* that has three underground floors packed with real bargains. Most of the clothes are casual and sporty, with the emphasis on denim.

With a rather hard-to-find entrance across from the Dutch consulate at 393 Istiklal Caddesi, **Terkoz Çıkmazı Karaaslan İş Merkezi Pasaj** has piles and piles of clothing at rock-bottom prices, as well as some small boutiques with more discriminating selections.

Atlas Pasajı.

After 60 years in the business, Mr Akagün is the oldest haberdasher in town, and still works from his original store. His stock, 90 per cent of which is Turkish-made, includes a bewildering array of buttons, lace, embroidered trimmings and ribbons.

Çınar

Sıraselviler Caddesi 152/A, Cihangir (0212 251 4204/252 1938). **Open** 8am-7.30pm Mon-Sat. **Credit** MC, V. **Map** p249 O3.
A dry-cleaner and laundry running a pick-up and delivery service in the Taksim area (hotels included). A same-day service is available. Mending/alteration jobs are outsourced to a local tailor.

Hats

For felt hats visit **Cocoon** (*see p165*).

Hat Quarters

Shop 185, Kanyon Shopping Mall, Büyükdere Caddesi 185, Levent (0212 353 0926, www.kanyon.com.tr). Metro Levent. **Open** 10am-10pm daily. Credit MC, V.
All manner of designer hats, berets and various other accessories.

Jewellery

The **Grand Bazaar** (*see p52*) houses the largest selection of jewellery and gold under one roof, and where designs once stopped at the classic, a new tide of creativity has been creeping in over the last few years. Still, for definitively modern pieces, try **Teşvikye**, home to several small, creative showrooms.

Mor

Turnacıbaşı Sokak 10B, Galatasaray (0212 292 8817). **Open** 10am-7.30pm Mon-Sat. **Credit** MC, V. **Map** p248 N3.
A stylish, glass-fronted studio just down from the Galatasaray Hamam, selling inspired originals designed by an in-house team. Most pieces are fashioned from silver and bronze, often combining scraps of ethnic jewellery from eastern Turkey, Turkmenistan and Afghanistan.

Nelia

Valikona 35 Caddesi, Halil Bey Pasajı 40/19, Nişantaşı (0216 451 7438, www.nelia.com.tr). Metro Osmanbey. **Open** 10am-7.30pm Mon-Sat. **Credit** AmEx, DC, MC, V.
A newly opened space at the back of a Nişantaşı passage, Nelia produces funky, chunky jewellery with a tribal twist. In-house designer Banu Kosifoğlu works with a multitude of materials – from semi-precious stones and sterling silver to ribbon, silk tassels and snippets of ethnic cloth – crafting weird and wonderful combinations that work as unique pieces.

INSIDE TRACK
FIT FOR A SULTAN

Akaretler is a newly redeveloped area in Beşiktas. Its terraced buildings were once the homes of officers who worked at the nearby Dolmabahçe Palace, residence of Ottoman sultans. It now houses clothing stores, design brands and a W hotel. For details, see www.akaretler.com.tr.

★ Sanatanik

Kuloğlu Mallahesi, Faikpaşa Caddesi 1/1, Çukurcuma (532 372 8581). **Open** 10am-10pm daily. **No credit cards**. **Map** p249 O3.
Friendly Aziz makes his own jewellery from antique beads. The folk pieces are inspired by a mix of Turkish and Central Asian influences. Earrings, beautiful necklaces (some made from antique spoons) and wall decorations are part of the unique mix.

★ Urart

Abdi Ipekçi Caddesi 18/1, Nişantaşı (0212 246 7194, www.urart.com.tr). Metro Osmanbey. **Open** 9am-7pm Mon-Sat. **Credit** AmEx, DC, MC, V.
Sophisticated jewellery with an Anatolian slant. Designs are drawn from the countless civilisations that have peopled Anatolia from palaeolithic to Ottoman times, using a combination of silver, gold and semi-precious stones. Pricey, but beautiful.
Other locations Topkapı Museum, Swissôtel.

Lingerie & underwear

Zeki

Akkavak Sokak 47/9, Tunaman Çarşısı, Nişantaşı (0212 233 8279, www.zekitriko.com.tr). Metro Osmanbey. **Open** 9.30am-7.30pm Mon-Sat. **Credit** AmEx, MC, V.
Not only is Zeki the premier swimwear label at home, it's also one of Turkey's most successful exports. Prices are high, but so is the quality. Check out the own-label lingerie.
Other locations Akmerkez Mall 366, Nispetiye Caddesi, Etiler (0212 282 0591); Cevahir Mall, Büyükdere Caddesi 22, No.146, Şişli (0212 380 0807).

Luggage

Paşalar Çanta

Istiklal Caddesi 56/D, Beyoğlu (0212 293 9080). **Open** 10am-10pm Mon-Sat; 10am-8pm Sun. **Credit** AmEx, MC, V. **Map** p248 N3.
All types of luggage and accessories for the traveller can be found at this shop along Istikal. The prices are good, but you might need to look elsewhere if it is high-end luggage you are looking for. There are a couple of similar luggage stores on the same block.

FOOD & DRINK

Bakeries

★ Güllüoğlu

Mumhane Caddesi 171, Karaköy (0212 293 0910, www.karakoygulluoglu.com). Tram Karaköy. **Open** 7am-10pm Mon-Sat. **Credit** AmEx, MC, V.

Güllüoğlu is the king of baklava and *su böreği* (baked layers of cheese, fresh herbs and filo pastry).

Kitchenette

Marmara Hotel, Taksim Square, Taksim (0212 292 6862, www.kitchenette.com.tr). **Open** 8am-midnight daily. **Credit** AmEx, DC, MC, V **Map** p249 P2

The in-house bakery at this successful brasserie sells its superior bread to outside customers as well.

▶ *For a review of the restaurant, see p127.*

Konak Patisserie

Bereket Zade Mahallesi, Hacı Ali Sokak, Galata, Beyoğlu (0212 252 5346). **Open** 7am-7pm daily; 7am-midnight *terrace*. **Credit** AmEx, MC, V. **Map** p246 M6.

This French-influenced patisserie has been serving its colourful cakes since 1975. Alongside the cakes are sweet Turkish bite-sized pastries. There is a great view from the terrace.

★ Savoy Pastanesi

Sıraselviler Caddesi 181, Taksim (0212 249 1818, www.savoypastanesi.com). **Open** 7am-10.30pm daily. **Credit** AmEx, MC, V. **Map** p249 O3.

Mor.

One of Istanbul's best cake shops, and now something of an institution. There's a reasonably sized café up on the first floor, which gets especially busy at breakfast.

Drinks

La Cave

Sıraselviler Caddesi 109A, Cihangir (0212 243 2405, www.lacavesarap.com). **Open** 9am-9pm Mon-Sat; 9am-8pm Sun. **Credit** MC, V. **Map** p249 O4.

One of the city's first speciality wine shops and certainly the most serious. Owner Esat Ayhan keeps a comprehensive cellar filled with wines from all over Turkey, Europe and the New World. He also stocks imported spirits, bar accessories and a limited range of Havana cigars.

Mimolett

Sıraselviler Caddesi 55/A (0212 245 9858, www.mimolett.com.tr). **Open** 10am-2am Mon-Sat. **Credit** AmEx, DC, MC, V. **Map** p249 O3

There's a selection of more than 400 wines at the wine boutique attached to the Mimolett restaurant and bar. Aimed at a discerning, upmarket clientele , it excels in stocking wines from Turkey's boutique vineyards. Use of enomatic machines means there are lots of wines to try by the glass.

▶ *For a review of the restaurant, see p131.*

★ Sensus

Bereketzade Mahallesi, Büyükhendek Caddesi 5, Galata, Beyoğlu (0212 245 5657, www.sensus wine.com). **Open** 10am-10pm daily. **Credit** AmEx, MC, V. **Map** p246 M5.

There are more than 370 different types of wine in this underground cellar by Galata Tower. A tasting bar allows customers to try 50 wines by the glass (a five-glass flight is YTL20-YTL25; and for only YTL7.50 this can be accompanied by regional cheese).

▶ *For more on Turkish wines, see p146* **Grape Expectations**.

General

Carrefour Express

Sıraselviler Caddesi 74A, Cihangir (0212 293 5158/355 8080, www.carrefourexpress.com). **Open** 9am-10pm daily. **Credit** MC, V. **Map** p249 O3.

This central and well-stocked supermarket also offers a home delivery and online ordering service. **Other locations** Eski Büyükdere Caddesi 5/7, Şişli (0212 219 6439).

Macro

Abdi İpekçi Caddesi 24-26, Nişantaşı (0212 231 3999, www.tansas.com.tr). Metro Osmanbey. **Open** 8.30am-9pm daily. **Credit** AmEx, MC, V.

CONSUME

Saray.

Macro caters for the upper end of the market, with a wide selection of imported foods and prices to match. The deli, fresh fish and meat counters are especially good and there's a wide, fairly priced selection of local wines.
Other locations Akmerkez Mall 325, Nispetiye Caddesi, Etiler (0212 282 0310); Muallim Naci Caddesi 170, Kuruçeşme (0212 257 1381).

Markets

For the freshest, best-quality produce, visit the **Halk Pazarı**, situated opposite the jetty in Beşiktaş, and the more upmarket **Balık Pazarı** (fish market) next to Çiçek Pasajı, off Istiklal Caddesi. As well as fish, you'll find delicacies from quail's eggs to fresh clotted cream. For regional specialities, head for the stalls lining the west side of the **Egyptian Bazaar** or the many delicatessens in the backstreets of **Kadıköy** on the Asian shore. For general markets, *see p154*.

Specialist

★ Ali Muhiddin Hacı Bekir
Istiklal Caddesi 83/A, Beyoğlu (0212 244 2804, www.hacibekir.com.tr). **Open** 8am-10pm Mon-Sat; 9am-10pm Sun. **Credit** MC, V. **Map** p248 N3.
You can't come to Turkey without trying Turkish delight. This place, which has been in the confection business since 1777, is where to try it and buy it. You should also suck on some *akide*, colourful boiled sweets that come in every conceivable flavour.

Other tasty gifts include halva, baklava and marzipan (*badem ezmesi*), which all come in beautiful gift-wrapped boxes.
Other locations Hamidiye Caddesi 83, Sirkeci (0212 522 0666).

Ambar
Kallavi Sokak 6, off Istiklal Caddesi, Beyoğlu (0212 292 9272, www.nuhunambari.com). **Open** 8am-8pm Mon-Fri; 9.30am-8pm Sat. **Credit** AmEx, MC, V. **Map** p248 M3.
One of the few places in Istanbul that sells fresh tofu. Other worthwhile buys include wholegrain bread, organic grains and pulses, hulled pumpkin and sunflower seeds and a range of organic fruit and veg.

★ Antre Gourmet Shop
Akarsu Caddesi 52, Cihangir (0212 292 8972, www.antregourmet.com). **Open** 9am-9pm Mon-Sat; 9am-8pm Sun. **Credit** AmEx, MC, V. **Map** p249 O4.
Antre stocks around 40 regional cheeses, all bought from local producers and free from additives. There's also a fair selection of cold meats, Austrian wholegrain breads, teas, home-made mezedes and jams, olive oil, honeycomb (in season), Turkish wines and natural yoghurt.

Kurukahveci Mehmet Efendi
Tahmis Sokak 66, Eminönü (0212 511 4262, www.mehmetefendi.com). **Open** 8.30am-7pm Mon-Fri; 9am-6.30pm Sat. **No credit cards. Map** p242 L8.
Reputedly the first shop to sell bagged Turkish coffee, Mehmet Efendi has been doing a roaring trade since it opened in 1871. It's opposite the west entrance to the Egyptian Market – just follow your nose. Besides the traditional Turkish variety, there's filter and espresso coffee, whole roasted beans, cocoa and *sahlep*, a winter drink made from ground orchid root.

Namlı Pastırmacı
Hasırcılar Caddesi 14-16, Eminönü (0212 511 6393, www.namlipastirma.com.tr). *Tram Eminönü.* **Open** 8.30am-8pm Mon-Sat. **Credit** MC, V. **Map** p242 L8.
A hugely popular deli just along from the west end of the Egyptian Market. It specialises in *pastırma* (Turkish pastrami) but also has a tantalising selection of cold cuts, cheeses, halva, honeycomb, *pekmez* (fruit-based molasses), olives and pickles.

Saray
Istiklal Caddesi 173, Beyoğlu (0212 292 3434, www.saraymuhallebicisi.com). **Open** 6am-2am daily. **Credit** MC, V. **Map** p248 L8.
Delectable Turkish desserts, from milk puddings to *aşure*, popularly known as Noah's pudding. Since 1949, Saray has served as a sugar-fuelled pit stop during or after a night out in the bars and

cafés of Beyoğlu. There are smoking and non-smoking sections, and a takeaway service.
Other locations 105/1 Teşvikiye Caddesi, Teşvikiye (0212 236 1617).

Şütte
Dudu Odaları Sokak 21, Balık Pazarı, Galatasaray (0212 293 9292). **Open** 9am-8pm Mon-Sat. **Credit** AmEx, MC, V. **Map** p248 N3.
This long-established deli, owned by Macedonians, is one of the few places in Istanbul that stocks pork products other than bacon. It also carries pricey but wonderful imported cheeses, plus cheaper local cheeses, ready-made meze and condiments.

GIFTS AND SOUVENIRS
Handicrafts

Besides carpets, Turkey offers a wealth of lesser-known – and equally traditional – handicrafts. The ceramics trade dates back to the Selçuk Empire of the 11th century. Tiles, vases and plates with the traditional Ottoman tulip motif are now displayed in museums worldwide. The tradition lives on in Kütahya, western Anatolia, where artists hand-craft reproductions and more contemporary designs. Then there's *ebru*, a Central Asian variation of paper marbling, which took off during calligraphy's heyday. Today, the technique is also applied to fabrics. Other craft-work includes carved meerschaum pipes, prayer beads, backgammon sets, and silks. Most of these crafts can be found at the **Grand Bazaar** (*see p54* **Shopping the Bazaar**).

For carpets and rugs *see p169* and *p168* **The Rug Trade**.

Abdulla
Halıcılar Caddesi 53, Grand Bazaar (0212 522 3070, www.abdulla.com). Tram Beyazıt. **Open** 9am-7pm Mon-Sat. **Credit** MC, V. **Map** p54.
Abdulla is all about a contemporary take on traditional crafts. The bywords are 'natural' and 'handmade'; the main product line is hamam accessories, so you will find towels, *peştemals* and olive oil soaps in scents from cinnamon and tea to sesame. Other good buys include sheepskin throws and hand-spun silk and wool.

★ Cocoon
Küçükayasofya Caddesi 13 & 17, Eminönü (0212 638 6450, www.cocoontr.com). Tram Sultanahmet. **Open** 8.30am-7pm Mon-Sat. **Credit** AmEx, MC, V. **Map** p243 N11.
Cocoon is housed in two fabulous shops by the Blue Mosque, on Küçükayasofya. The first (no.13) has an incredible array of felt hats. Coupled with four floors of accessories, hamam wear, shirts, scarves and all manner of knick-knacks, it is the only souvenir shop

Cocoon.

you'll need. A couple of doors down is a more serious affair. Owner Şeref Özen has collected antique rugs, clothing and textiles from across Turkey and Central Asia for collectors and enthusiasts.
Other location Arasta Bazaar 93, Blue Mosque.

Deli Kızın Yeri
Halıcılar Caddesi 82, Grand Bazaar (0212 526 1251, www.delikiz.com). Tram Beyazıt. **Open** 8.30am-7pm Mon-Sat. **Credit** AmEx, MC, V. **Map** p54.
Linda Caldwell, a retired American and self-styled crazy lady (*deli kız*) turns traditional Turkish handicrafts, motifs and fabrics into something more offbeat. Her unique designs include hand-made clothes, tablecloths, placemats and dolls.

Derviş
Keseciler Caddesi 33-35, Grand Bazaar (0212 514 4525, www.dervis.com). Tram Beyazıt. **Open** 9am-7pm Mon-Sat. **Credit** MC, V. **Map** p54.
Derviş nestles behind the narrowest of shop fronts. Here, Anatolian traditions are reinvented. Bathroom accessories are big, including handmade soaps in a host of natural flavours, super-soft unbleached cotton towels, and *peştemals* in linen, cotton and silk. But there are also shimmering scarves of hand-spun silk, felt slippers, rugs and throws, and mohair and patchwork fur blankets; plus brimming shelves of original dowry items, trawled from the depths of Anatolia by owner Tayfun Utkan. Look out for the hand-stitched bolero jackets, ethnic coats and dresses in fabulous colours and fabrics, and exquisitely embroidered linens.

CONSUME

Istanbul Handicrafts Centre

Kabasakal Caddesi 5, Sultanahmet (0212 517 6784/8). Tram Sultanahmet. **Open** 9am-6.30pm daily. **Credit** AmEx, MC, V. **Map** p243 N10.

The Istanbul Handicrafts Centre is located in a restored *medrese* (religious school), opposite the Baths of Roxelana. It now houses a warren of workshops, each with its own specialisation. The most accomplished handicrafts are the illuminated manuscripts, miniatures and calligraphy. Other highlights include cloth-painting, dolls, ceramics, glassware and hand-bound books. The artists work on site, so you can watch them at their trade.

Seyitağaoğulları Carpet Kilim Hand Crafts

Avrupa Pasajı 15 (off Balık Pazarı), Meşrutiyet Caddesi 16, Beyoğlu (0212 249 2903). **Open** 9.30am-8.30pm daily. **Credit** MC, V. **Map** p248 N3.

Kilim accessories are everywhere these days, but what you'll find here – from belts and footwear to bags, purses and stationery – is a cut above the rest. The products are all handmade, the kilims are kosher and the leather trim really is leather.

Other locations Küçükayasofya Caddesi 35, Sultanahmet (0212 518 1295); Arasta Çarşısı, Sultanahmet (0212 516 9351).

HEALTH & BEAUTY

Hairdressers & barbers

Grooming is next to godliness for Turkish girls, which means that the beauty salon (*güzellik salonu*) is a second home and the city is brimming with them. For the face, it's tweezers and expertly teased thread; for the body it's waxing (*ağda* – Turkey is the home of the all-over wax), plus manicures (*manikür*), pedicures (*pedikür*), and all manner of hair treatments.

INSIDE TRACK
TAXES AND REFUNDS

VAT (KDV) on goods and services is a standard 18 per cent. Non-residents are eligible for refunds on purchases of goods (not services) over YTL118 from stores displaying the tax-free sticker, and reclaiming the money is not the tedious process it used to be. The retailer fills out a special receipt in quadruplicate and gives you three copies, which you then present to customs – along with your purchases – upon departure; this must be within three months of the purchase. You can then get a cash refund in the currency of your choice on the other side of passport control.

Dyeing (*boya*) is a favourite, and the blow-dry (*fön*) – involving at least two attendants and an army of brushes – essential.

Cihangir Erkek Kuaförü

Akarsu Yokuşu Caddesi 49/1, Cihangir (0212 251 1660). **Open** 8am-8.30pm Mon-Sat; 10am-5pm Sun. **No credit cards. Map** p249 O4.

All the usual barber services, delivered with a smile and some English. The Cihangir neighbourhood is popular with expats, so the staff are used to dealing with foreigners.

Hüseyin Günday

Sıraselviler Caddesi 80, Cihangir (0212 251 0005/252 0947). **Open** 8am-8pm Mon-Sat. **Credit** MC, V. **Map** p249 O3.

A typical neighbourhood *kuaför* offering the full range of beauty services. Bright young things attend to your every whim. Prices are very reasonable.

MOS

Bronz Sokak 65/7, off Abdi Ipekçi Caddesi, Maçka, Teşvikiye (0212 240 1970/246 3222). Metro Osmanbey. **Open** 9am-7pm Mon-Sat. **Credit** MC, V.

MOS equates with class on the Istanbul hairdressing scene. Despite being production-line stuff, it's a great favourite with the well-heeled of both sexes, who book in for all manner of treatments. But beauty doesn't come cheap: prices are high by Turkish standards.

Other locations Akmerkez Mall 122, Nispetiye Caddesi, Etiler (0212 282 0554).

Herbal remedies

Bünsa

Dudu Odaları Sokak 26, Balık Pazarı, Galatasaray (0212 243 6265). **Open** 9am-8pm Mon-Sat. **Credit** MC, V. **Map** p248 N3.

Herbal remedies and healing tonics, from medicinal teas to ginseng, karakovan honey and rare varieties of *pekmez* (fruit molasses). Tell them your ailment, and they'll prescribe a potion. The most popular panacea is a concoction of honey, royal jelly, nettle and ginseng, guaranteed to beat fatigue.

Kalmaz Baharat

Mısır Çarşısı 41/1, Eminönü (0212 522 6604). Tram Eminönü. **Open** 8am-7pm Mon-Sat. **No credit cards. Map** p243 L8.

One of the oldest stores in the Egyptian Bazaar, this atmospheric place – just east of the main intersection – still has its original drawers and tea caddies. Specialities include spices, medicinal herbs, healing teas and aromatic oils.

Toiletries & cosmetics

Toiletries and a limited range of cosmetics are available in most supermarkets. Some

Eski Fener. See p168.

pharmacies also stock imported brands like Vichy and RoC. For upmarket labels, go to a specialist *parfümeri*, but note that prices are pushed up by stiff import taxes. Better to stock up in duty free before your trip.

Erkul Cosmetics
Istiklal Caddesi 311, Beyoğlu (0212 251 7662).
Open 10.30am-10pm Mon-Sat; noon-10pm Sun.
Credit AmEx, MC, V. **Map** p248 N3.
A one-stop cosmetics store where you can find every grooming product imaginable. In addition to its own range, Erkul stocks reasonably priced perfumes and cosmetics from around the world.

Opticians

Emgen Optik
Istiklal Caddesi 45, Beyoğlu (0212 292 3577).
Open 9am-7.30pm Mon-Sat. **Credit** AmEx, MC, V. **Map** p249 O2.
Emgen Optik does a roaring trade in fashion-conscious frames and shades. Around since 1925, this local institution carries a huge selection of big brands like Ray-Ban, Police, Gucci and Armani. It also deals in prescription lenses and repairs.

Pharmacies

Pharmacies (*eczane*) are plentiful. Pharmacists are licensed to measure blood pressure, give injections, clean and bandage minor injuries and suggest medication for minor ailments – many prescription medicines are available over the counter in Turkey. However, few pharmacists speak English. Opening hours are typically from 9am-7pm Mon-Sat. Every neighbourhood also has a duty pharmacy (*nöbetçi*) that is open all night and on Sundays.

Filibeli Eczane
Istiklal Caddesi 27A, Beyoğlu (0212 245 6440).
Open 9am-7.30pm. **Credit** MC, V. **Map** p248 L2.

There are dozens of pharmacies on Istiklal Caddesi, as there are throughout the city. Some of the staff at this branch near Taksim Square speak some English and they're very helpful.

Spas & salons

For the best spas and salons, *see p116* **Hotel Hamams**.

HOUSE & HOME
Antiques

One of the best places for browsing is **Çukurcuma**, a quiet Beyoğlu backwater behind the Galatasaray Lycée. Its roller-coaster streets harbour a plethora of small shops with a wealth of antiquaria from rural Anatolia – anything from oil lamps and painted trunks to carved doors. There's also a fair amount of sophisticated glass and porcelain ware, Ottoman screens and chandeliers, as well as shops specialising in single items such as tin toys. Items over a century old must be cleared by the Museums Directorate before being taken overseas. Dealers should know the procedure.

★ Artrium
Tünel Gecidi İş Hanı, A Blok 3, 5, & 7, Tünel (0212 251 4302). **Open** 9am-7pm Mon-Sat.
Credit AmEx, MC, V. **Map** p248 M4.
A shop attracting a more sophisticated breed of collector, with three spacious display rooms and a prime location in the passage just across from KV Café. It has a fine selection of miniatures, maps, prints and calligraphy, along with Kütahya ceramics and the odd film and advertising poster.

Can Shop
Avrupa Pasajı 7, Meşrutiyet Caddesi 16, Galatasaray (0212 249 3280). **Open** 10am-7pm Mon-Sat. **No credit cards. Map** p248 N3.

Tins, pins, coins and toys, from clanky cars to planes and tanks. There's a lot of Turkish stuff, dating mostly from Ottoman and early Republic times.

Eski Fener
Aga Hamam Sokak 77, Çukurcuma (0212 251 6278). **Open** 11am-7pm Mon-Sat. **No credit cards. Map** p249 O3.

A select assortment of furniture, doors, oil lamps and copperware, mostly picked up in rural Anatolia. There are things like low-legged dough-rolling tables, wooden butter churns and storm lamps. All items have been painstakingly restored. *Photo p167.*

Leyla Seyhanli
Altıpatlar Sokak 6, Çukurcuma (0212 293 7410). **Open** 10am-7pm Mon-Sat. **Credit** AmEx, MC, V. **Map** p249 O3.

A massive selection of antique clothes, hats, embroidered linens, wall hangings and tapestries. Prices are quite high, but it's all top quality stuff.

Popcorn
Turnacıbaşı Caddesi, Faikpaşa Sokak 2, Çukurcuma (0212 249 5859, www.popcorn istanbul.com). **Open** 10am-7pm Mon-Sat. **No credit cards**.

The Rug Trade

Follow our guide to getting the best deal, and having fun while you do it.

Buying a carpet in Istanbul has unfortunate associations with hassle, hustle and hoodwinking. It doesn't have to be that way. With a bit of homework and common sense, you can enjoy the buying process and go home with a beautiful carpet at the right price.

To be a confident and successful bargainer and buyer, first you need to determine how much you are prepared to spend. If you're interested in hand-made carpets or kilims made of natural fibres, expect to spend YTL450 and above. Unless you're an expert, don't bother paying a premium for vintage; modern carpets are just as high quality and are usually made with natural dyes (*kök boya*). Under no circumstances should you tell the dealer your budget. Instead, ask the prices, get a feel for what's on offer, and be prepared to shop around. Look at carpets that are double your price range, then offer what you have.

Carpet dealers have all the time in the world. It is their job to answer your questions, explain details of origin and design, and unroll hundreds of kilims, all the while keeping you fortified with miniature glasses of strong tea.

Ultimately, the final price depends a great deal on your rapport with the dealer and your determination to buy a carpet. It all comes down to one thing: how much do you want it? If you have the slightest hesitation concerning patterns or colours, keep looking.

Nearly all shops, including those listed in this chapter (*see right*), have English-speaking staff, can be trusted to handle overseas shipping, and allow exchanges if you are unhappy with your purchase. And if you find the Grand Bazaar too bewildering, try browsing at the more peaceful **Arasta Bazaar** on Küçük Ayasofya Caddesi in Sultanahmet (map p243 N11) – also home to a branch of Cocoon (*see p165*).

CONSUME

This eclectic shop specialises in rare books, furniture and knick-knacks from the 1950s.

★ The Works: Objects of Desire

Faikpaşa Sokak 6/1, Çukurcuma (0212 252 2527, www.fleaworks.com). Open 11am-6.30pm Mon-Sat. No credit cards.

A remarkable shop that goes the extra mile in collecting the kitsch, the old and the downright bizarre. Owner Karaca Borar follows his own whims, and those of the collectors and film crews that buy and rent the goods. The shop, dubbed 'for the slightly deranged collector seeking identifiable memories', is stuffed with coats, hats, mannequins, old porn, unworn designer clothes, snow globes, and pretty much anything else. Prices are good, and as the sign says, 'no bargaining under YTL10, it's embarassing'.

Carpets

For tips on buying carpets, *see left* **The Rug Trade**.

Ahmet Hazım

Takkeciler Caddesi 61-63, Grand Bazaar (0212 52 9886, www.ahmethazim.com). Tram Beyazıt. Open 8.30am-7pm Mon-Sat. Credit MC, V. Map p54.

One of the oldest rug merchants in the bazaar, specialising in kilims and carpets from Turkey, Iran and the Caucasus and Suzanis from Uzbekistan. What you get is quality service and none of the hard sell.

Ethnicon

Kapalıçarşı Takkeciler Sokak 58-60, Grand Bazaar (0212 345 5620, www.ethnicon.com). Tram Beyazıt. Open 8.30am-7pm Mon-Sat. Credit MC, V. Map p54.

Ethnicon (short for 'ethnic contemporary') creates kilims with a modern twist. They are made without child labour and using environmentally friendly processes, so colours tend to be muted. Browsing in Ethnicon is a very different – and more peaceful – experience compared to the rest of the bazaar. Prices are fixed.

Kalender Carpets

Tekkeciler Caddesi 24-26, Grand Bazaar (0212 527 5518). Tram Beyazıt. Open 8.30am-7pm Mon-Sat. Credit AmEx, MC, V. Map p54.

Kalender stocks a great collection of full-size, deep pile Anatolian carpets, which start from as little as YTL1,500. A good place to start your mission in 'carpet row', in the heart of the bazaar.

Sisko Osman

Zincirli Han 15, Grand Bazaar (0212 528 3548, www.siskoosman.com). Tram Beyazıt. Open 8.30am-6.30pm Mon-Sat. Credit AmEx, MC, V. Map p54.

Sisko 'Fat Man' Osman is acknowledged around the Grand Bazaar as the leading authority on carpets and kilims. His well-stocked shop fills most of the historic Zincirli Han, and his international clientele has included many well-known people over the years. So while you can be sure of quality, don't expect a bargain.

Yörük

Kürkçüler Çarşısı 16, Grand Bazaar (0212 527 3211). Çar Beyazıt. Open 8.30am-7pm Mon-Sat. Credit AmEx, DC, MC, V. Map p54.

The shop may be tiny, but it has some of the finest treasures to be found in the bazaar. There are lots of kilims here, although the real emphasis is on old ethnic rugs of all sizes, mostly from the Caucasus. Guide yourself towards Gürsel, one of the dashing young partners, and you're promised entertainment, little pressure to buy and, quite probably, the rug of your dreams.

General

Turkey has a strong textile industry, so towels, linens, curtains and fabrics are excellent buys. Quality towels and linens are found in Sultanhamam, around the back of the **Egyptian Bazaar** (*see p58*) – look out for the Taç label.

Özgül Çeyiz

Mısır Çarşısı 83, Sultanhamam, Eminönü (0212 522 7068, www.begonville.com.tr). Tram Eminönü. Open 8am-7.30pm Mon-Sat. Credit MC, V. Map p243 L8.

The east end of the Egyptian Bazaar was once crammed with stores in the trousseau (*çeyiz*) business. In days of yore, young ladies were wheeled along by their female relatives to make wholesale purchases that would improve their prospects. Özgül is one of the few survivors from those days. It's a minimal store packed with fancy embroidered sheets, quilts, towels and robes. Trousseau-hunting or not, there's some great stuff at very reasonable prices – like the fluffy Begonville towels.

Paşabahçe

İstiklal Caddesi 314, Beyoğlu (0212 244 0544, www.pasabahce.com.tr). Open 10am-8pm Mon-Thur; 10am-8.30pm Fri, Sat; 11am-7pm Sun. Credit AmEx, MC, V. Map p248 M4.

This stylish shop on three floors, a favourite with Istanbul's upwardly mobile, is Turkey's answer to Habitat. Head to the basement for kitchenware, basic china and glass, the ground floor for vases and ornaments, and the first floor for special collections. The latter includes some impressive hand-blown glass, using traditional motifs – a conscious revival of time-honoured techniques.

Other locations Teşvikiye Caddesi 117, Teşvikiye (0212 233 5005).

CONSUME

MUSIC & ENTERTAINMENT

CDs, records & DVDs

Ada Müzike
Orhan Adli Apaydin Sokak 20, off Istiklal Caddesi, Tünel (0212 251 3878). **Open** 9am-10pm Mon-Thur, Sun; 9am-11pm Fri, Sat. **Credit** AmEx, V, MC. **Map** p248 M4.
Owned by local record company Ada, this was Istanbul's first shop to specialise in Turkish rock and protest music. There's a small café and Biletix ticket booth attached. There's also a decent range of foreign CDs, newspapers and magazines.

★ De Form Müzik
Turnacıbaşı Caddesi 45, Çukurcuma (0212 245 3337). **Open** noon-8pm Mon-Sat; 1-7pm Sun. **Credit** AmEx, MC, V. **Map** p248 N5.
Vinyl fans look no further. De Form, run by two friends, is an old-school music shop, with a turntable to test your potential purchases. Most of the records are Turkish editions of international artists, but there is a small selection of Turkish folk too. There is also dance music and, shhh, some CDs.

★ Lale Plak
Galipdede 1, Tünel (0212 293 7739). **Open** 9am-7.30pm Mon-Sat; 11.30am-7pm Sun. **Credit** MC, V. **Map** p248 M5.
The city's top jazz, ethnic and classical music retailer is a favourite hangout of visiting jazz musicians. There is also a comprehensive selection of traditional Turkish music. Staff are knowledgeable and helpful.

De Form Müzik.

Mimplak
Aslıhan Sahaflar Çarşısı 49, Beyoğlu (0212 252 6877). **Open** noon-8pm daily. **Credit** MC, V. **Map** p248 M3.
In a passageway crammed with second-hand book and record shops, this tiny shop is the best of the lot. Look for bargain deals on old disco and soundtrack albums, plus rare Turkish releases.

Musical instruments

Look no further than **Galipdede Caddesi**, which extends towards Galata Tower on the southern end of Istikal Caddesi. There are dozens of music shops along this street and many more in the close vicinity. Each has a specialism, whether it be stringed instruments, wind instruments, percussion or electronic goods. It is also the place to pick up traditional Turkish instruments, such as the *saz* long neck lute, *baglama* or *tar*.

SPORTS & FITNESS

There are sports shops all around the city. Along Beyoğlu's main thoroughfare are Nike, Adidas and other general sports stores. All the shopping malls will also have stores where you can pick up a pair of running shoes and sporting equipment. **Kanyon** (*see p154*), for example, has Adidas and Intersport (www.intersport.com.tr).

TICKETS

Sporting events and musical events are listed in the local press. Tickets for many of them are available from online ticketing agencies **Biletix**, which is an arm of Ticketmaster, and **Ticket Turk** (www.ticketturk.com). Both have a good website in English.

Biletix
www.biletix.com/0216 556 9800. **Open** *Call centre* 8.30am-11pm Mon-Fri; 10am-9pm Sat, Sun. **Credit** DC, MC, V.
Tickets can be booked on the phone or the website (in English and Turkish), or at one of the many desks in selected outlets of Vakkorama, Ada (*see p170*), supermarket Migros, and at music retailer Raksotek (Istiklal Caddesi 162, Beyoğlu). There's a booking charge of YTL3 per transaction if you buy online or on the phone (irrespective of the number of tickets purchased), while an extra YTL2 will buy delivery to your home address.

TRAVELLERS' NEEDS

For luggage, *see p162*. For shipping, *see p221*. For mobile phone rental, *see p226*. For a computer repair shop, *see p156*.

CONSUME

Arts & Entertainment

Reina. *See p201.*

Calendar

See the city's festive spirit.

Back in the golden days of the Ottoman Empire, extravagant celebrations were held on every possible occasion, with the sultan providing most of the excuses. But when the republic was founded in 1923, Ottoman imperial traditions and overt religious celebrations were replaced by a dour bunch of annual excuses for flag-waving, such as Republic Day (29 October) and Victory Day (30 August).

In recent years, though, the full-blown festive spirit has returned to the city. Nowadays, winter apart, every month sees a festival some kind, with the city's youthful population giving events a dynamism that more than makes up for any lack of experience. Many of these events are superbly managed by the Istanbul Foundation for Arts and Cultures (Istanbul Kültür ve Sanat Vakfı; www.iksv.org), which consistently attracts a roster of international big names.

Tickets for events can often be bought through **Biletix** (*see p170*).

(*see p170*)

SPRING

★ International Istanbul Film Festival

Various venues (0212 334 0700, www.iksv.org). **Date** April. **Tickets** venues, Biletix. **Admission** YTL2.50-YTL15.

An annual highlight, eagerly anticipated for the glamour factor of visiting movie stars. Be warned: this is the city's most popular cultural jamboree, and tickets sell out in advance. For more information on this and other film festivals, *see p180*.

Orthodox Easter

Patrikhane (Orthodox Patriarchate Building), Sadrazam Ali Paşa Caddesi 35, Fener (0212 531 9674). **Date** Apr/May. **Admission** free. **Map** p245 G4.

The city's last remaining Greek residents – as well as hundreds of pilgrims from Greece – flock to Easter Sunday mass in the venerable Patriarchate in Fener on the Golden Horn. In a church illuminated by hundreds of candles, the aura of ancient ritual is powerful enough to move even the most ardent of atheists.

★ International Istanbul Theatre Festival

Various venues (0212 334 0700/334 0777, www.iksv.org). **Date** May (even years). **Tickets** venues, AKM, Biletix. **Admission** varies.

One of the few opportunities to see international theatre in Istanbul. In the past, big draws have included the likes of Robert Wilson, Pina Bausch, the Berliner Ensemble, the Piccolo Teatro di Milano and Britain's Royal Shakespeare Company. The programme also features a selection of the year's best Turkish plays. Most performances are held at city theatres including the Atatürk Cultural Centre, the Kenter Theatre and the Aksanat Cultural Centre (for venues, *see p202*). A few events take place at more unusual venues, such as Rumeli Hisarı on the Bosphorus.

★ International Istanbul Puppet Festival

Akkarga Sokak 22, Elmadağ (0212 232 0224). **Date** 2nd week of May. **Tickets** venues, Biletix. **Admission** varies. **Credit** MC, V.

Puppet, marionette and shadow theatre was big in Ottoman times, but is rarely performed today. This festival is an opportunity to witness this almost forgotten art, with around a dozen shows by Turkish and international companies at the Kenter Theatre (*see p202*) and various other venues. Most plays are silent and suitable for children and adults.

Conquest Week Celebrations

Various venues (0212 449 4000, www.ibb.gov.tr). **Date** late May. **Admission** free.

A lively celebration of the Turkish conquest of Constantinople (29 May 1453), featuring exhibitions

of traditional Turkish arts and parades by the 'Ottoman' Mehter band, plus concerts, conferences, lectures, screenings, fireworks and some rabble-rousing by nationalist and Islamist parties.
▶ *The Panorama 1453 History Museum (see p62) details the siege of Istanbul.*

SUMMER

International Istanbul Music Festival

Various venues (0212 334 0700/334 0736, www.iksv.org). **Date** June-July. **Tickets** AKM, Biletix. **Admission** YTL10-YTL200.
Inaugurated in 1973 on the occasion of the 50th anniversary of the republic, the IMF is the most prestigious event on the city's cultural calendar. It comprises about 30 performances of orchestra and chamber music, dance and ballet. Big hitters at past festivals have included Kiri Te Kanawa, Philip Glass, the Michael Nyman Ensemble, Cecilia Bartoli and the Kronos Quartet. It's worth attending just to get a rare peek inside Haghia Irene church (*see p46*), normally closed to the public.

★ International Istanbul Jazz Festival

Various venues (0212 334 0700/334 0708, www.iksv.org). **Date** July. **Tickets** venues, Biletix. **Admission** varies.
This two-week festival pushes the boundaries of what defines modern jazz. Keith Jarrett, Wynton Marsalis and Dizzy Gillespie have all performed in the 4,000-seat Harbiye open-air theatre, as have less likely musicians like Grace Jones, Nick Cave, Lou Reed and Martha Wainwright. Consistently the best programme of any Turkish music festival.

INSIDE TRACK
TICKETS & INFORMATION

For information about festivals and events, try the English-language *Time Out Istanbul*, or www.istanbul.com, which lists events on a day by day basis. Istanbul Foundation for Arts and Cultures (Istanbul Kültür ve Sanat Vakfı, www.iksv.org) will also have details of major events. Tickets for festivals are often available through Biletix (www.biletix.com) or Ticket Turk (www.ticketturk.com).

Traditional Istanbul Açıkhava (Open-Air) Concerts

Harbiye Cemil Topuzlu, Açıkhava Tiyatrosu (0212 257 6200, www.mostproduction.com). **Date** mid July/early Aug. **Tickets** Açıkhava Tiyatrosu (box office 0212 232 1652), Biletix. **Admission** varies.
This season of open-air concerts in Harbiye is worth checking out. The line-up mixes mainstream names from Turkish pop, rock and folk with a variety of alternative genres. It's a good opportunity to see the more innovative end of the local music scene. Past performers have included the Mercan Dede Fusion Project, alongside Balkan stars such as Goran Bregovic.

Rock 'n' Coke

Hezarfen Airfield (0212 334 0100, www.pozitifist.com, www.rockncoke.com). **Date** early Sept, odd years only. **Tickets** Biletix. **Admission** YTL65 (one day), YTL125 (camping, two days).

International Istanbul Jazz Festival.

ARTS & ENTERTAINMENT

Since it began in 2003, Rock 'n' Coke has become Istanbul's biggest (late) summer opportunity to stand in a beer queue with 50,000 of your closest friends. In 2009, groups appearing included the Prodigy, Nine Inch Nails and Linkin Park. Smashing Pumpkins and Franz Ferdinand have also appeared. Turkey's largest open-air festival is now held every two years, the next will be in 2011.

AUTUMN

International Istanbul Biennial
Various venues (0212 334 0700, 334 0763, www.iksv.org). **Tickets** venues. **Admission** YTL7-YTL15; Festival Pass YTL25. **Credit** MC, V.
Alternating with the Istanbul Theatre Festival (*see p172*), every other year more than 50 artists from around 50 countries exhibit around a theme set by a guest curator. Expect to find paintings, installations, screenings, walkabouts, films, panel discussions, lectures and daily guided tours (in English). The next Biennal will be held in 2011 and will be curated by Adriano Pedrosa and Jens Hoffmann.

Akbank Jazz Festival
Various venues (0212 334 0100, www.pozitif-ist.com). **Date** Oct. **Tickets** venues, Biletix. **Admission** YTL5-YTL40.
Unlike July's international jamboree (*see p173*), this festival is less about big names and more about jazz. Some ten bands perform every day over a two-week period, with jam sessions at venues including Babylon (*see p191*) and Nardis (*see p194*). Joe Lavano, Marilyn Mazur and Cecil Taylor have all participated in recent years. In addition to great music, there are film screenings and workshops.

Phonem/Electronic Music Plateau
Various venues (0212 334 0700, www.iksv.org). **Date** late Oct-early Nov. **Tickets** venues, Biletix. **Admission** varies.

An international platform for exploring electronic music, with discussions, technology exhibitions and performances. Expect a string of parties featuring local and international DJs, plus concerts, video art, film and video screenings, and workshops.

Istanbul Arts Fair
Tüyap Centre, E5 Hwy (Karayolu), Gürpınar Jcn, Kavşağı, Beylikdüzü (0212 886 6843, www.tuyap.com.tr). **Date** Oct/Nov. **Admission** YTL5; free students. **No credit cards**.
Relocated from its city centre home to the less accessible Tüyap Centre near the airport, this vast, week-long sales fair has retained its massive appeal. Some 50 Istanbul galleries plus a handful of international art dealers come to offload paintings, sculpture and ceramics on to an increasingly receptive local market. Don't let the remote location put you off: free shuttle services depart from AKM on Taksim Square, Atatürk airport, the Bakırköy ferry stop and the Esenler bus terminal.

Anniversary of Atatürk's Death
Date 10 Nov.
Every 10 November at 9.05am, the death of Mustafa Kemal Atatürk is commemorated with a minute's silence. Sirens howl mournfully and the Bosphorus ferries sound their foghorns, while buses, cars, and people everywhere come to a sudden standstill. The experience is both moving and eerie – a testament to the great leader's lasting grip on the Turkish public's imagination.

Istanbul Book Fair
Tüyap Centre, E5 Hwy (Karayolu), Gürpınar Jcn Kavşağı, Beylikdüzü (0212 886 6843, www.tuyap.com.tr). **Date** Nov. **Tickets** at the door. **Admission** YTL5; students free. **No credit cards**.
Over 200 of Turkey's publishing houses, as well as several publishers from abroad, gather for ten days to trade their wares. Leading writers, academics and intellectuals participate in non-stop conferences and round-table discussions. Attendees get discounts on new publications. Free shuttle services run from AKM on Taksim Square, Atatürk airport, the Bakırköy ferry stop and Esenler bus terminal.

WINTER

Efes Pilsen Blues Festival
Lütfü Kırdar Convention Centre, Harbiye (0212 334 0100, www.pozitif-ist.com). **Date** Nov/Dec. **Tickets** Biletix. **Admission** varies. **No credit cards**.
This hugely popular festival, running since 1990, is a showcase for new talent, with three bands performing every night. This doesn't stop the occasional star (such as Bobby Rush or Long John Hunter) from showing up.

Children

Turkish delights for mites.

The allure of the bazaars, large carpeted mosques with lots of space to run around, and boat trips on the Bosphorus will keep the kids happy and entertained for quite a while. But after a week, say, it may be time to turn to more conventional types of entertainment. Istanbul doesn't have a big, centrally located park or zoo, but there are several neighbourhood playgrounds to run around in.

Childhood is a different experience here. Kids are the centre of attention, as everywhere, but rather than parents accompanying children into a children's world, kids tend to accompany their parents into the adult world; they enjoy being part of almost all aspects of adult life, from smoky restaurants to gossip sessions with the neighbours.

MUSEUMS

The museum with the most direct appeal to kids is probably the **Toy Museum** (*see p88*). As well as old Anatolian toys and *karagoz* puppets, there is a Wild West section highlighting the lives of native Americans, and puppets of American presidents from George Washington to Nixon. At weekends there are puppet shows, magic shows and plenty of other activities. The puppet theatre starts at 1.30pm.

The **Archaeology Museum** (*see p48*) has a small area set aside for children, with displays at youngsters' eye level. The **Military Museum** (*see p74*) has tanks and soldiers' uniforms. The **Ural Ataman Classical Car museum** (Nuripşa Caddesi, 41, Tarabya, 0212 299 4539) displays cars, trucks, motorbikes and war vehicles dating back more than 100 years.

Best of the lot is the **Rahmi M Koç Museum** (*see p75*), which has a heaps

of interactive displays and working models, and a submarine to clamber around.

Sakıp Sabancı Museum (*see p84*) and **Istanbul Modern** (*see p77*) both arrange free programmes to make the visual arts fun for kids. At the time of writing they take place in summer only.

PARKS & PLAYGROUNDS

There are two nice playgrounds in Cihangir (Güneşli Caddesi) and Bebek (Cevdetpaşa Caddesi). They tend to get overcrowded on sunny weekends.

There are also some lovely parks further from the centre. Just north of the city centre, in Beşiktaş, **Yıldız Park** is beautiful and leafy. The small fairground **Maçka Luna Park** is in a park north of Taksim. A little further north of Bebek is the large **Emirgan Park**, located just beside the Bosphorus, with an ornamental lake, playground and some of the nicest landscaping to be found in Istanbul. The coast road is heavy with traffic at the weekends; go early and leave early to beat it.

Park Orman is a lovely woodland area in Maslak, north of the city, with sports facilities including a swimming pool, picnic areas, a playground and fast-food outlets. It also hosts organised parties and activities for children.

OUTSIDE THE CENTRE

Kilyos and **Demirciköy** (*see p216*), villages on the Black Sea coast north of Kemerburgaz

---

ARTS & ENTERTAINMENT

on the European side, have beaches that are popular in summer, with food, umbrellas and loungers available. The Black Sea has some strong currents, so be sure not to let children swim outside the designated areas. But wave-surfing and the beach itself are fun enough for the kids. Just make sure you leave home early so you can have a decent time at the beach and leave before the early evening rush; the journey can be as long as two hours each way, instead of the usual 30 minutes at peak times.

Polonezköy, the old Polish village on the way to Şile on the Asian side, is also a 30-minute drive (traffic permitting). For many Istanbullus, a visit here is a rare opportunity to see large patches of grass you're actually allowed to walk on. It's a great place for children to run around, kick a ball and ride horses. There are several restaurants. **Leonardo's** (Köyiçi 32, 216 432 3082, www.leonardo.com.tr) in the centre is among the best. Brunch, served 11am-5pm daily, costs YTL45 per person (with a 50 per cent discount for children between three and seven). A swimming pool (and a small pool for kids) and a large playground are major assets.

ACTIVITIES

For babies under two, the free mother-and-baby group at the British International School (Fulyalı Sokak 24, Levent, 0212 270 7801) is pretty good; the International Women of Istanbul (IWI, www.iwi-tr.org) organises similar free groups.

Bab Bowling Café

Yeşilçam Sokak, 24, Beyoğlu (0212 251 1595, www.babbowling.com.tr). **Open** 10am-midnight daily. **Games** YTL6 daytime, YTL7 evening Mon-Fri; YTL9 Sat, Sun. **Credit** MC, V. **Map** p246 N3.

This bowling café is one of the most popular among young people in Istanbul. There are also pool tables, and a café serving fast food and snacks.

★ Bosphorus Zoo

Tuzla Caddesi 15, Bayramoğlu, Izmit (0262 653 8315, www.hayvanat-bahcesi.com). **Open** *May-Oct* 8.30am-8pm daily. *Nov-Apr* 8.30am-5pm daily. **Admission** YTL15; free under-6s. **Credit** MC, V.

Located way out in Darıca, 45km (30 miles) from the city centre, but worth the trip for its wide range of exotic birds and animals, gardens and playground.

Dance Akademik

Tepecik Yolu, Cevher Sokak 6, Etiler (0212 352 7046, www.dansakademik.com). *Metro Levent.* **Credit** MC, V (not for beginners' classes).

Ballet and jazz classes start at YTL180 for a course.

Emirgan Park. *See p175.*

Enka Sports Centre

Sadi Gülçelik Spor Sitesi, Istinye (0212 276 5084). *Bus 40, 40T/Metro 4 Levent then dolmuş.* **Open** 7am-10pm daily. **Credit** MC, V.

Facilities for swimming, tennis, basketball, football, volleyball and athletics, with nine-week courses for children in swimming and tennis (YTL295).

Galleria Ice Skating

Galleria Shopping Mall, Sahilyolu, Ataköy (0212 560 8550). *Bus 71T, 72T, E-50.* **Open** 10am-10pm daily. **Admission** YTL12 children, YTL15 adults, 40mins Mon-Fri; YTL17 30mins for all Sat, Sun. **Credit** MC, V.

Galleria, the first shopping mall in Istanbul, still offers the most entertaining shopping experience for families with kids, thanks to its skating rink. Private lessons are also available for YTL30 a session.

In the Kitchen with the Kids

Çocuğumla Mutfatktayız

Tepecik Yolu 28/2, Etiler (0212 358 1825, www.mutfaktayiz.com). *Metro Levent.* **Open** 9am-6pm Mon-Fri; weekend hrs vary according to course times. **Credit** AmEx, MC, V.

Organises cooking courses for parents and their children. Cooking activities for kids take place once a month on Saturday or Sunday. Call ahead for the date and reservation. One course is YTL89 (plus VAT) for the parent and the child.

ARTS & ENTERTAINMENT

★ Miniaturk

Imrahor Caddesi, Sütlüce (0212 222 2882,
www.miniaturk.com.tr). Bus 47E, 54H. **Open**
Nov-Apr 9am-7pm daily. *May-Oct* 9am-7pm
Mon-Fri; 9am-9pm Sat, Sun. **Admission**
YTL10; free under-9s. **Credit** MC, V.

An absolutely magical attraction, which recreates
105 of Turkey's most famous sights in miniature.
The models range from a palm-sized Leander's
Tower to a Sultanahmet Mosque the size of a small
car and an Atatürk airport complete with taxiing
jumbos; the level of detail is incredible. Card-
operated speakers deliver commentary in English
and Turkish. There is also a train going around the
sights, a playground and a maze for the kids.

Play 'n' Learn

Havyar Sokak, 46, Cihangir, Beyoğlu (0212 244
9151, www.playnlearn-tr.com). **Open** 8.30am-
6pm Mon-Sat. **Admission** YTL2.5/hr. **Credit**
MC, V. **Map** p247 O4.

Activities for children up to six. There are workshops on arts and crafts, drama, experiments and
games. Arrangements are flexible: you can join in
with your child, or drop him off for a few hours.

Play Barn

Kirazlıbağ Sokak 4, Yeniköy (0212 215 3049,
www.theplaybarn.com.tr). **Open** 9am-7pm daily.
Admission YTL25/hr. **Credit** MC, V.

This indoor playground has three different rooms –
all supervised – and a great outdoor playground, featuring mazes and tube slides. There's also a half- or
full-day crèche for three days a week for children
between one-and-a-half and four (YTL475 per month
half-day, YTL575 full day), a twice-weekly mother
and baby group (YTL25 for three hours), plus a couple of child-friendly cafés.

RESTAURANTS

Although most Istanbul restaurants welcome
children, and it's usual to bring children to
restaurants, few offer special amenities such
as high chairs or children's menus. If asked,
though, many will serve children's portions
and cook special requests. The restaurants
we list in this section go out of their way to
cater for children.

INSIDE TRACK GETTING ABOUT

Children can be taken almost everywhere
in Istanbul, though it's not always
physically easy to do so: pushing a pram
is a battle involving encounters with steep
hills, high kerbs and narrow passes –
which is why most Turks carry their
children in their arms.

Mezzaluna

Abdi İpekçi Caddesi 38/1, Nişantaşı (0212 231
3142, www.mezzaluna.com.tr). Metro Osmanbey.
Open noon-11.30pm daily. **Main courses**
YTL15-YTL30. **Credit** AmEx, DC, MC, V.

This famous Italian chain restaurant is always
crammed with children. It's noisy, but kids love it.
Highchairs are available.

Secret Garden

Kalender Üstü, Atadan Sokak, Yeniköy (0212
299 0077, www.secretgardenistanbul.com).
Open 10am-1am daily. **Main courses** YTL10-
YTL15. **Credit** MC, V.

In summer, tables are laid out in this big hilly garden overlooking the Bosphorus, which also has a
play area with swings, slides and a big lawn. The
restaurant serves decent food: pancakes and
sausages, barbecued meatballs and lamb chops.

TGI Fridays

Nispetiye Caddesi 19, Etiler (0212 257 7078,
www.fridays.com.tr). Metro Levent. **Open**
11.30am-midnight daily. **Kids courses** YTL10-
YTL15. **Credit** AmEx, MC, V.

Burgers, hot dogs and fancy ice-cream desserts.
There is a dedicated kids' menu.

SHOPPING

Kids' clothing and toy stores can be found
at all the large malls (*see p152*). There are
pharmacies (*eczane*) in most neighbourhoods.
Almost all supermarkets sell a good selection
of Milupa baby food and Turkish brands like
Ülker. Nappies and wipes can be found at most
grocery stores. For supermarkets, *see p163*.

Gelar

Nispetiye Caddesi, Petrol Sitesi 1, Blok 4, Levent
(0212 351 9515). Metro Levent. **Open** 9am-6pm
Mon-Fri. **Credit** MC, V.

Imported educational tools, wooden toys and playground equipment of excellent quality. Prices are
high but the range is unique in Turkey.

Toys 'R' Us

Migros Building Ground Floor, Büyükdere
Caddesi, Maslak (0212 217 9616). Metro 4
Levent then dolmuş. **Open** 10am-10pm daily.
Credit AmEx, DC, MC, V.

The largest selection of toys in the city. It also has
kids' clothing, shoes, baby food and nappies.

BABYSITTING

Deluxe hotels provide babysitting services.
Smaller hotels will usually make every effort
to find someone. Beyond that, Anglo Nannies
London (0212 287 6898, www.anglonannies.com),
provides live-in nannies from England.

ARTS & ENTERTAINMENT

Film

Rich pickings for cinephiles – and cinematographers.

Istanbul's movie-goers are well served with more than 200 screens, an annual world-class film festival and several smaller cinematic events. The dominance of Hollywood blockbusters still prevails, but an increasingly diverse programme is on offer, with a handful of theatres now specialising in independent and art-house films, many of them Turkish-made. Big names in the Turkish film world today include Cannes winner Nuri Bilge Ceylan, creator of the acclaimed *Uzak* (*Distant*) and the brutally realistic Zeki Demirkubuz, who also wowed the Cannes crowd with *Kader* (*Destiny*). Young directors are also being increasingly recognised, notably Yüksel Aksu.

ARTS & ENTERTAINMENT

CINEMAS

All films, except animation and the biggest blockbusters, are shown in the original language with Turkish subtitles, but don't expect English subtitles for Turkish films. Contrary to expectations, the once over-zealous censors have retreated into virtual oblivion under the current Islamist government.

Tickets cost an average of YTL9-YTL14. Most cinemas have a 'People's Day' once or twice a week, when all seats are reduced. The first screening of the day is often cheaper, and students and OAPs generally qualify for a discount at all times with proof of identity.

Phone and online reservations are accepted at some cinemas, and a growing number take credit cards. Seating is assigned. In the older cinemas, ushers often expect a tip; the going rate is around YTL1. Be prepared for an intermission during all screenings. To find out what's on where, check the *Turkish Daily News*.

Sultanahmet

Şafak Movieplex

Darüşşafaka Sitesi Pasajı, Yeniçeriler Caddesi, Çemberlitaş (0212 516 2660, www.ozen film.com.tr). Tram Çemberlitaş. **Tickets** YTL9; YTL7 Mon. **Credit** MC, V. **Map** p242 L10.
Sultanahmet's only cinema couldn't be better positioned, right by a tram stop. All screens have Dolby Digital sound and offer a range of current US, European and local releases.

Beyoğlu

AFM Fitaş

Fitaş Pasajı, Istiklal Caddesi 24-26 (0212 251 2020, www.afm.com.tr). **Tickets** YTL11-14. **Credit** MC, V. **Map** p249 O2.
Just below Taksim Square, this US-style multiplex has 11 screens, showing a mix of Hollywood hits, indie and Turkish film. The IF Festival (*see p171*) takes place here early in the year.

Atlas

Atlas Pasajı, Istiklal Caddesi 209 (0212 252 8576). **Tickets** YTL10; YTL7 Mon, Wed. **No credit cards. Map** p248 N3.
This once imposing cinema has been carved into three smaller screens. The largest still boasts the city's most steeply raked auditorium. *Photo p180.*

Emek

Yeşilçam Sokak 5, off Istiklal Caddesi (0212 293 8439). **Tickets** YTL10; YTL7 Wed. **No credit cards. Map** p248 N3.
During the golden age of Turkish cinema, Yeşilçam Sokak was Turkey's answer to Hollywood. No more. But the Emek still stands as a relic of former glories, built in the 1920s with an impressively ornate 875-seat hall. Forgive the newer lino flooring and sagging upholstery and catch a film here if you can.

Sinepop

Yeşilçam Sokak 22, off Istiklal Caddesi (0212 251 1176, www.ozenfilm.com.tr). **Tickets** YTL10; YTL8 Mon, Thur. **Credit** MC, V. **Map** p248 N3.

And... Action

Turkish cinema comes of age.

The Turkish film industry didn't really get going until the 1950s: from the 50s to the 70s, around 250 films were made a year. By the 1990s, the average number was down to ten. But now this number is creeping slowly up again, with around 60 Turkish films being released annually over the last couple of years.

Commercial success usually calls for a star-studded cast borrowed from TV soaps, pop bands and the catwalk, with a celebrity director to boot. Slapstick comedy is perenially popular, but there are more intelligent films, too. Ömer Faruk Sorak's *G.O.R.A.*, a sci-fi parody written by comedian Cem Yılmaz, in which a carpet seller is abducted by aliens, is crammed with cultural references, with subtle swipes at Turkey's deference to the US and Europe. Another recent hit was actor-director Yılmaz Erdoşan's latest comedy *Organize Işler* (*Magic Carpet Ride*), a spoof on Istanbul's organised crime racket.

But box office bounty is not confined to comedy. A case in point is Çağan Irmak's drama *Babam ve Oğlum* (*My Father and Son*), a rural tale of father and son relationships, set against the backdrop of Turkey's troubled political past. And action thrillers are entering the fray, among them the crudely nationalistic *Kurtlar Vadisi – Irak* (*Valley of the Wolves: Iraq*), a spin-off of a popular TV series that raised hackles across the Atlantic early in 2006 and earned record box office takings at home. Built around a real-life event in 2003, when US troops arrested and hooded a group of Turkish officers in northern Iraq, the film sets the scene for hero Polat Alemdar to avenge the incident.

For all its domestic success, Turkish cinema rarely gets released or recognised

abroad. This is less true of lower-budget art-house productions, which have sparked growing interest in Turkish cinema abroad through the festival circuit. The best known director is probably Nuri Bilge Ceylan, creator of the acclaimed *Uzak* (*Distant*), whose latest feature *Iklimler* (*Climates*) also won an award at the Cannes Film Festival. While Ceylan's cinema is a simple but subtle reflection on the human condition, director Zeki Demirkubuz has made waves with his ruthless realism. In 2002, two of Demirkubuz's films were simultaneously selected for Cannes. His latest feature *Kader* (*Destiny*), a grim love triangle and prequel to *Masumiyet* (*Innocence*), merits similar attention.

New directors are also commanding international recognition. Özer Kızıltan's debut feature *Takva* (*Takva – A Man's Fear of God*), an ironic look at the inner workings of an Islamic sect, won the Swarovski Cultural Innovation Award at the Toronto Film Festival. Yüksel Aksu's debut *Dondurmam Gaymak* (*Ice Cream, I Scream*) took the comic and colourful tale of a small trader struggling hopelessly against globalisation to the Oscars as Turkey's official entry for best foreign language film.

ARTS & ENTERTAINMENT

It's hard to imagine that this modern theatre was used as a club by the Germans during World War I. Two screens show varied local and international fare.

Taksim-Beyoğlu
Halep Pasajı, Istiklal Caddesi 140 (0212 251 3240, www.beyoglusinemasi.com.tr). **Tickets** YTL10; YTL7 Wed. **No credit cards. Map** p248 N3.
The Beyoğlu has an authentic art-house feel with a programme to match. From July to September, there's a daily programme of critics' picks from the past year, but this soon slides into anything from

the past decade. Across from the foyer/café is the small-screen Pera, with the same management.

★ Yeşilçam
Imam Adnan Sokak 10, off Istiklal Caddesi (0212 293 6800, www.yesilcamsinemasi.com). **Tickets** YTL6; YTL5 Wed. **No credit cards. Map** p249 O2.
At this small, basement art-house cinema, the programming leans towards local and European independent film. The charming foyer is full of old projection machines and fading film posters.

Atlas. See p178.

Levent

★ Kanyon Mars
Kanyon Mall, Büyükdere Caddesi 185 (0212 353 0853). Metro Levent. **Tickets** YTL12.50; YTL8 Thur. **Credit** MC, V.
The ultimate cinema experience. Step into the cutting-edge complex and you're in a world of plush design and smooth service, from the ticket booths to the conveniences. Worth every penny.

★ Levent Kültür Merkezi Sinema
Çalıkuşu Sokak 2 (0212 325 7371). Metro Levent. **Tickets** YTL5. **No credit cards**.
Run by TÜRSAK (the Turkish Foundation of Cinema and Audiovisual Culture), this art-house venue shows almost exclusively indie fare, as well as hosting various festivals. There's a pleasant café with seats outside in summer.

Karaköy

★ Istanbul Modern
Liman İşletmeleri Sahası, Antrepo 4, off Meclis-i Mebusan Caddesi (0212 334 7300, www.istanbul modern.org). Tram Karaköy. **Tickets** YTL10. **No credit cards**.
A state-of-the-art theatre within the new museum (*see p77*), which runs a monthly programme dedicated to home-grown and international art-house movies, including retrospectives, documentaries, animation and shorts.

FESTIVALS

★ IF AFM Independent Film Festival
AFM Fitaş, Fitaş Pasajı, Istiklal Caddesi 24-6 (0212 251 2020, www.ifistanbul.com). **Date** Feb.
This hugely popular event is run by the cinema chain AFM. The programming is distinctly right-on, with strands dedicated to digital, political, and gay/lesbian cinema, plus hardcore sex and violence. Try to book tickets in advance, either online or at the AFM Fitaş cinema (*see p178*), where all screenings are held.

Istanbul International Short Film Festival
Various venues (0212 252 5700, www.istanbul filmfestival.com). **Date** late March.
A long-running event masterminded by short film aficionado Hilmi Etikan, this week-long festival is based at various cultural centres in Beyoğlu and the Istanbul Modern. The programme includes short fiction, experimental fare and animation from all over the world. All films have English subtitles and all screenings are free.

★ International Istanbul Film Festival
Various venues (0212 334 0723, www.iksv.org). **Date** Apr. **Tickets** Biletix (www.biletix.com), participating cinemas.
A highlight of the Turkish cultural calendar, this glamorous festival brings a real buzz to Beyoğlu. Some 200 films from around the world, plus all the latest Turkish productions, are crammed into a two-week programme. Alongside national and international competitions, themes include tributes, documentaries, animation, adaptation and world cinema. Festival season is also a chance to stargaze, with an impressive contingent of heavyweight directors and actors in attendance most years. Buy tickets in advance to guarantee seats and qualify for a discount.

International 1001 Documentary Film Festival
Various venues (0212 245 8959, www.bsb.org.tr). **Date** late Sept.
Refreshingly, this one-week festival run by the Association of Documentary Film Makers (BSB) does not focus on any particular theme. As well as unusual factual films, there are panel discussions, master classes and Q&A sessions. Admission is free.

International Meeting of Cinema and History Film Festival
Various venues (0212 244 5251, www.tursak.org.tr). **Date** mid Dec.
One of a string of festivals run by TÜRSAK (the foundation for cinema and audiovisual culture), this is a showcase for over 50 features and documentaries from around the world with a political or human rights dimension. Most screenings are held around Beyoğlu and at the TÜRSAK cinema in Levent. Admission fees are nominal.

ARTS & ENTERTAINMENT

Galleries

Istanbul's contemporary arts scene comes of age.

After the success of **Istanbul Modern**, the
Turkish contemporary art movement continues
to gather pace with new galleries such as
Santralistanbul and **Arter**. Today, Istanbul
galleries are multidisciplinary spaces that host
photography, multimedia installations, sculpture
and, increasingly, video. International recognition
was further bolstered by the city's status as the
European Capital of Culture in 2010.

Some of the city's best galleries, many owned by
banks, are along Beyoğlu's main thoroughfare of
Istiklal Caddesi and are easily accessible. It is here
that you will find some of the more cutting-edge art that has previously struggled
to find a place in more conservative spaces.

GALLERIES

For many years, the **International Istanbul
Biennial** (*see p173*) was the only specialist
art event that invited international artists to
exhibit in Istanbul, and also gave selected local
artists the opportunity to present their work in
professionally curated, large-scale exhibitions.
With the Biennial taking place only every
two years, the city lacked a more permanent
support structure for ongoing artistic
production and presentation.

Over the last few years, the situation has
shifted to the opposite extreme. Although there
is almost no state funding for contemporary
culture in Turkey, wealthy patrons and banks,
which have a history of providing charitable
financial support to the arts, have taken it
upon themselves to create their own 'branded',
non-commercial galleries, cultural centres and
museums. It is now so fashionable to own an
art institution that Istanbul – or rather the
relatively small area around Beyoğlu, Karaköy

INSIDE TRACK HOTEL GALLERIES

Some of the city's hotels host art
exhibitions, notably the **Çıağan Palace
Hotel Kempinski** (*see p115*), which
has its own gallery. Many of these
exhibitions are actually put on by
government departments.

and the Golden Horn – is bursting with new
developments and prospective projects.

In 2004, **Istanbul Modern** (*see p77*) opened
in an old customs warehouse on the Bosphorus.
Alongside a fairly standard collection of
modern Turkish art, the museum showcases
some interesting recent acquisitions and
photography, and stages several temporary
exhibitions each year.

Hot on the heels of Istanbul Modern
came the **Pera Museum** (*see p72*), with an
historical collection displayed alongside work
by young contemporary artists. The **Sakip
Sabanci Museum** (*see p84*), meanwhile,
has raised its profile over the last few years
by hosting big-name touring exhibitions by
artists including Picasso and Rodin. And a
lot of excitement surrounded the opening of
the opening of **Santralistanbul** (*see p67*),
a gallery and cultural centre at at Bilgi
University. Recent shows have featured work
from photographer Martin Parr and political
painter Yüksel Arslan.

On the face of it, these projects and
developments suggest a sudden wave of artistic
movement and production; but critics maintain
that Istanbul continues to lack the artist-led
initiatives and independent spaces that would
fuel their expansion.

★ Akbank Kültür Sanat Merkezi

*Istiklal Caddesi 8, Beyoğlu (0212 252 3500,
www.akbanksanat.com).* **Open** 10.30am-7.30pm
Tue-Sat. **Map** p249 O2.

Casa Dell'Arte.

Of the many galleries affiliated to a bank, this one has perhaps the most interesting programme. Close to Taksim Square, the first-floor space is accessible via the main entrance on the side of the building. The exhibition programme fluctuates between externally curated shows of international artists and exhibitions by Turkish art students.

★ Arter
Istiklal Caddesi 211, Beyoğlu (0212 243 3767, www.arter.org.tr). Open 11am-7pm Tue-Thur; noon-8pm Fri-Sun. Map p249 M4.
An initiative of the Vehbi Koç Foundation, this new 'Space for Art' showcases a multidisciplinary collection of some of Turkey's most interesting artists from the last 50 years. Videos, paintings, photography and installation pieces are shown over five floors. The programme will also include work from international partner foundations.

BAS
Meşrutiyet Caddesi 166, Beyoğlu (0555 503 3847, www.b-a-s.info). Open 2-6pm Tue-Sat. Map p248 M4.
Launched by artist Banu Cennetoğlu to display and produce art books and publications, BAS has already published several books by Turkish artists, which can be purchased here. The rest of the collection is a useful reference resource.

★ Casa Dell'Arte
Mısır Apartment 163/3, Istiklal Caddesi, Beyoğlu (0212 251 4288, www.casadellartegallery.com). Open 10am-7.30pm Tue-Fri; noon-7pm Sat.
In the Mısır Apartments building on Istiklal, Casa Dell'Arte – with its side gallery, CDA Projects – is one of the finest in Istanbul. It's a commercial gallery, with exceptionally high standards. CDA Projects, on the second floor, focuses on up-and-

coming Turkish and international artists, while the main gallery displays interesting work from more well-known artists.
▶ *Galerist is the same building, as is the 360 restaurant (see p125).*

Galeri Apel
Hayriye Caddesi 5A, Galatasaray, Beyoğlu (0212 292 7236, www.galleryapel.com). Open 11.30am-6.30pm Tue-Sat. **No credit cards.** Map p248 N3.
Apel hosts exhibitions in a variety of media that verge on craft and design. Expect weird and wonderful works from Turkey's avant garde, as well as surreal paintings by international artists. As you might expect for an underground space, it's a little hard to find: up a few steps at the corner of the street right behind the Galatasaray Lycée.

Galeri Nev
Maçka Caddesi 33, Maçka (0212 231 6763, www.galerinev.com). Bus 30A, 30M. Open 11am-6.30pm Tue-Sat.
Founded in 1984 by architects Ali Artun and Haldun Dostoğlu, Galeri Nev has a sister gallery in Ankara. Essentially a commercial space, it represents Turkish artists such as Inci Eviner, as well as exhibiting work by artists from abroad.

Galerist
Mısır Apartment 163/4, Istiklal Caddesi, Beyoğlu (0212 244 8230, www.galerist.com.tr). Open 10am-6pm Mon-Fri; noon-6pm Sat. **Credit** AmEx, MC, V. Map p248 N3.
Galerist has the strongest international reputation of any contemporary art gallery in Istanbul, with a roster of illustrious local artists. The gallery stages about eight temporary exhibitions a year; Julian Opie showed here in 2010.

★ Galeri X-Ist
Açıkhava Appartment 15, Eytam Caddesi,
Nişantaşı (0212 291 7784, www.artxist.com).
Metro Osmanbey. **Open** noon-7.30pm Mon;
11am-7.30pm Tue-Sat. **No credit cards**.
Galeri X-Ist is committed to working with young
Turkish artists, giving them the opportunity to
show and develop their work from an early stage in
their career. Photography and painting are high on
the agenda. Cutting-edge work by artists such as
Ahmet Polat, who won the New York International
Center of Photography's Infinity award in 2006, are
definitely worth checking out.

★ Garanti Galeri (GG)
Istiklal Caddesi 115A, Beyoğlu (0212 293 6371).
Open 11am-8pm Tue-Sat. **Map** p248 N3.
The only gallery in Istanbul dedicated exclusively
to architecture and design, GG is corporate in feel
and intellectual in concept. In the past, it has shown
work by internationally renowned architects such
as Zaha Hadid, but also works with local talents.

Kargart
Kadife Sokak 16, Kadıköy (0216 330 3151,
www.kargart.org). Ferry from Karaköy or
Eminönü. **Open** 12.30-8pm Tue-Sat.
No credit cards. **Map** p251 W8.
Located above a popular student hang-out in
Kadıköy, Kargart is easily the most experimental
and interesting gallery on the Asian side. The exhibitions often feature works by young artists from
the area, which attract a loyal local following. This
is a good place to grab a beer and find out what's
happening beyond Beyoğlu.

Karşı Sanat
Gazeteci Erol Dernek Sokak 11/4, Hanif Han,
Beyoğlu (0212 245 7153, www.karsi.com). **Open**
11am-7pm Mon-Sat. **Credit** MC, V. **Map** p248 N3.
A well-hidden location adds to the exclusive air of this
gallery. The unusual space – a U-shaped corridor –
hosts group and solo exhibitions, which focus mainly
on young local and international artists. To find it, go
up to the third floor of the Elhamra Han and ring the
bell by the door on the left of the landing.

Milk Gallery & Design Store
Ṭahkulu Mah. Balkon Çıkmazı, Galata, Beyoğlu
(0212 251 57 97, www.whatismilk.com). **Open**
noon-7pm Wed-Sun. **Map** p246 M6.

INSIDE TRACK PERA MUSEUM

The **Pera Museum** (*see p72*) displays a
historical art collection alongside work by
young contemporary artists and temporary
exhibitions. Recent high-profile exhibition
subjects have included Marc Chagall.

Milk is a small gallery that shows work influenced
by graffiti, street art, illustration and comics, by both
local and international artists. There is also a display room for common design objects, such as Lomo
cameras, Ndeur shoes and artwork.

Pist
Dolap Dere Sokak 8/A/B/C, Şişli (no phone,
www.pist.org.tr, http://pist-org.blogspot.com).
Metro Şişli. **Open** check website for details.
An independent gallery located in the unlikely, off-
centre district of Pangaltı. In a large, street level
space, Pist offers a lively interdisciplinary programme that includes solo installations displayed in
the window, performances and collaborations with
international artists' collectives. There are also pop-
up exhibitions. Check the blog for details.

Platform Garanti Contemporary Art Centre
Istiklal Caddesi 115, Beyoğlu (0212 293 2361,
www.platform.garanti.com.tr). **Open** *Gallery*
10am-8pm Tue-Sat. *Library & archive* 10am-6pm
Mon-Fri. **Map** p248 M4.
Right on Istiklal Caddesi, Platform Garanti is home
to an exhibition space, archive centre, and an international artist-in-residence programme. The gallery
has quite a high profile: Tracey Emin held her first
solo show in Turkey here back in 2004. The emphasis is on video art, performance and installations. If
you're interested in researching the local art scene,
check out the extensive archives on the first floor.

Proje4L Elgiz Museum
Meydan Sokak, Beybi Giz, Plaza B Block, Maslak
(0212 290 2525, www.proje4l.org). Metro
Levent. **Open** 10am-5pm Wed-Fri; 10am-4pm Sat;
by appointment Tue.
Originally created as a museum for temporary exhibitions, Proje4L is now devoted to the private collection of art aficionado Can Elgiz, which combines
contemporary Turkish art with international pieces.
In 2009, the gallery moved to its new premises in
Maslak. The Artvarium gallery hosts exhibitions by
Turkish artists that change every month. There is a
small café.

Yapı Kredi Kültür Merkezi Kazım Taşkent Galerisi
Istiklal Caddesi 285, Galatasaray, Beyoğlu
(0212 252 4700, www.ykykultur.com.tr).
Open 10am-7pm Mon-Fri; 10am-6pm Sat;
1-6pm Sun. **Map** p248 M4.
This spacious 'culture and art bank' is on the first
floor of the Yapı Kredi Bank (just south of the
Galatasaray Lycée). It specialises in retrospectives of
important Turkish artists such as sculptor Ilhan
Koman, and also hosts an eclectic mix of international artists. Work shown ranges from figurative
and abstract painting to exhibitions on Anatolian
culture. Yapı Kredi is also an important art publisher.

ARTS & ENTERTAINMENT

Gay & Lesbian

Forget your preconceptions.

In Istanbul, where nothing is ever quite what it seems, sexuality is no exception. And when it comes to homosexuality, it's that much more complicated. No, those moustachioed men in tight jeans and bomber jackets, sauntering down the street hand in hand, are not the local Greenwich Village clones. They're just a couple of traditional guys in a country where public displays of male affection have been assumed to mean just that – and only that. And no, that doesn't mean you and your boyfriend can walk down the street hand in hand. Urban Turks are savvy enough to know when male affection means more, and you'd draw the same reactions in the streets of Istanbul as in a small city in the American South, or in 1950s London.

That doesn't mean there is no gay culture in the city: there is, but it's a little different, with its own idiosyncracies.

THE GAY SCENE

While Turkey's strictly secular nature means the gay community is not subjected to the ranting of religious figures, the traditional family structure is still firmly in place, and there is enormous pressure to marry. A high premium is placed on knuckle-dragging masculinity, which is one reason why so many bisexual and gay men present themselves in public as straight. Even for those few gay men with the financial means and firmness of character to strike out on their own, the downside of strong neighbourly ties is that liberated anonymity, even in large cities, is very difficult to achieve.

The whole concept of a gay rights movement complete with full social acceptance is a foreign import. The same is true of gay sex. Oscar Wilde's 'love that dare not speak its name' had been expressed in loving detail in Ottoman court literature centuries earlier. It didn't need a name. It was just love, and nothing at all to be afraid of.

Ironically, it is in comparison to European norms that Turkey is now found wanting. And the legal codification of gay rights is among the criteria Turkey must fulfil in order to join the EU. As is the case in terms of geography and culture, Turkey lies somewhere between Europe and the Middle East, but Istanbul still has the most vibrant gay nightlife scene to be found between Prague and Cape Town.

Bars and clubs abound, Turkish baths are as steamy as ever, cyber hook-ups are an increasingly favoured sexual and social outlet for the closeted majority, and secluded public parks are wildly cruisy. While home-grown transsexual diva Bülent Ersoy has been revered for nearly two decades, and fellow singer Zeki Muren's gold lamé boots and thigh-baring tunics did his career no harm, until very recently even the campest celebrities have not been subjected to the 'outing' campaigns of the West, or pressured to 'admit' to their sexual orientations.

When it comes to gay culture, Turkey is neither permissive nor repressive, and the long, slow march to full acceptance will be won the same way it will (eventually) be won in the West: a family member, a friend, a colleague, a neighbour at a time. In the meantime, momentum continues in the form of a gay presence at the annual 1 May parade, and positive publicity in the form of the Istanbul Gay and Lesbian Film Festival (www.iksv.org), not to mention the unstoppable determination of a small but swelling group of queers, dykes and trannies determined to meet, party, have sex and settle down, whether society likes it or not.

VENUES

If you come to Istanbul expecting to find a gay nightlife scene comparable to that of major cities in the US and Europe, you will be disappointed – although incredible strides have been made, from just one bar in the 1980s to over a dozen by the turn of the 21st century. In the last few years, however, the scene has grown decidedly less diverse.

While there have never been 'niche bars' catering exclusively to a mature crowd, leather queens or other subsets, there used to be a wider selection of more upmarket 'Western-style' venues. Of the three Western-style clubs that remain open, **Privé** has gone downmarket, and **Bar Bahçe** and **Love Point** have become the victims of their own success, unless well-heeled suburban PR ladies and their banker boyfriends are elements you'd like in your social mix.

That said, if you're in search of a truly Turkish experience, you're still in luck. There are at least half a dozen clubs and bars within walking distance of each other in Beyoğlu, tucked into side streets on both sides of Istiklal Caddesi. Expect a mix of scratchy techno dance tunes and Turkish pop, an average age barely over 20, minimal decor at best, a ventilation system unable to cope with the summer heat and clouds of cigarette smoke, and drinks costing YTL15. What you won't see much of are lesbians, although venues catering for them have risen – from none to one.

On the other hand, even if all of that's not your thing, on the right night, in the right mood, after the right number of overpriced cocktails, you just might find yourself somewhere, appreciating the sheer energy and lack of pretension, and a realisation will strike you that you have indeed strayed far from home.

Most places fill up only on Wednesday nights and weekends, if then. Don't bother turning up before midnight unless you're particularly enamoured of your own company, and be prepared to pay a nominal admission, usually in exchange for a drink ticket.

Western

Not places in which chaps with chaps and cowboy hats hang out; by Western we mean the sort of bar where monied, liberated and largely moustache-free Turks tend to congregate. While still distinctly local in flavour, they're the kind of places where straights and women – lesbian or otherwise – will feel comfortable.

★ Bigudi Pub
Istiklal Caddesi, Balo Sokak 20/4&5, Beyoğlu (0555 835 1822, www.bigudiproject.com). **Open** 2pm-2am daily. *Club* 10pm-5am Wed-Fri. **Admission** free. **Credit** MC, V. **Map** p248 N3.

Lipstick chic is the order of the evening at Istanbul's first lesbian bar. The terrace club is all girls; the café/pub, one floor below, is open to everyone LGBT, and friends.

► *Lesbians will also enjoy the Rocinante Café Bar (Öğut Sokak 6/2, Sakızağacı Caddesi, Beyoğlu, 0212 244 8219), where Turkish pop and arabesque is played on Friday and Saturday nights.*

★ Love
Cumhuriyet Caddesi 349/1, Harbiye (0212 296 3357). **Open** 11.30pm-4am Tue-Thur; 11.30pm-5am Fri, Sat. **Admission** free Tue-Thur; YTL20 Fri, Sat. **Credit** MC, V. **Map** p247 P1.
Istanbul's only gay venue worthy of the title 'club', Love Point has a full-size dancefloor, a no riff-raff door policy, professional sound system and groovy DJs. It draws a mixed crowd, most of whom are too focused on dancing and preening to notice anyone else but themselves.

Other Side
Zambak Sokak 2/5, Beyoğlu (0212 235 7914). **Open** 8pm-3am daily. **Admission** free. **Credit** MC, V. **Map** p247 O1.
What used to be Istanbul's first gay restaurant is now a club, complete with house music, go-go boys and a tiny dancefloor. It's on the fourth floor of an apartment building, and decor is mismatched and glitzy. The main bar is in the former living room and the back room is the place to discreetly make bedroom eyes at your new friend.

Privé
Tarlabaşı Bulvarı 28A, Taksim, Beyoğlu (0212 235 7999). **Open** 11pm-5am daily. **Admission** free Mon-Thur, Sun; YTL25 Fri, Sat. **Credit** MC, V. **Map** p247 O2.
An after-hours club that used to mix the slightly sordid with the upmarket, Privé was the place where minor celebrities and socialites could slum in safety. In the las t few years, though, the more unsavoury elements seem more in evidence. Be thankful for the hulking bodyguards at the door. The DJs shift a surprisingly progressive set.

Xlarge
Caddesi Kallavi Sokak 12, Beyoğlu (0506 788 7372, www.xlargeclub.com). **Open** 11pm-5am Wed-Sat. **Admission** varies. **No credit cards.** **Map** p248 M3.

INSIDE TRACK LEGALLY FOND

Homosexuality is not illegal in Turkey. It was decriminalised by the Ottomans in 1858, after a short-lived ban that had come about mainly as a result of European influences.

True to its name, this is a mega club. It features a ballroom-sized chandelier, the biggest bar of the venues in this chapter and two giant beds flanking the mezzanine bar. It's pretty busy, largely thanks to the recent DJ Mus-T programmes for avid dance music lovers. The Las Vegas style drag revue brings Lady Gaga and Madonna to the stage. A straight and pansexual crowd often roars in appreciation of the spectacle.

▶ *With Xlarge filling up with a straight crowd these days, the owner has opened Xlarge Chicos, an intimate and dimly lit room (Hüseyin Ağa Malhallesi Küçük, Bayram Sokak 1, Beyoğlu, 0212 245 6898).*

A la Turca

Be warned: some of these venues are minefields for anyone not sufficiently attuned to the local social dynamics. That tall, dark number cruising you from his dim corner could well be more of a homophobe than the most rednecked straight. Our list includes only the safer venues, but even so, brace yourself for the unexpected.

★ Alternative

Şehit Muhtar Mahallesi, Taksim Caddesi, Kargin Apt, Taksim. **Open** 10pm-5am daily. **Admission** free. **Credit** MC, V. **Map** p247 O1.
Up a narrow, creaking staircase is this fantasy land inspired by a New Orleans bordello – all dim lighting, red velvet, purple lights, tassels and beads. In a separate area, away from the crowded bar, is a sitting room with faded armchairs. Alternatively, take

the spiral staircase to the even more secluded second floor, where there's occasional live music.

Chianti Café-Pub

Balo Sokak 31/2, Istiklal Caddesi, Beyoğlu. **Open** 10pm-12.30am Wed-Sun. **Admission** free. **Credit** MC, V. **Map** p248 N3.
A recent addition to the ever-changing nocturnal landscape of Balohood (otherwise known as Balo Sokak), Chianti caters mainly to locals who fancy themselves as singers and enjoy the communal singing of Turkish pop. There's dancing between tables late into the evening. As much local flavour as you can find anywhere.

Deja Vu

Sadri Alışık Sokak 26/1, Beyoğlu (0535 614 8164). **Open** 10pm-4am daily. **Admission** varies. **No credit cards**. **Map** p249 O3.
One of the few clubs with room to wander and a crowd midweek, Déjà vu is inconspicuously tucked into a side-street across from a 24-hour men's health club (and, handily for uniform queens, just around the corner from the local police station). Most of the ground floor is taken up by a dancefloor filled with 18-year-olds who look as though they've pilfered their mother's purses for the admission money. Head downstairs for the dungeon-like 'chat room' and relief from the thumping Eurotrash music.

Mon Key

Eski Yeşilcam Sokak 9/1, Beyoğlu (0536 983 6476). **Open** 10pm-4am daily. **Admission** free. **No credit cards**.

Sugar Café.

Across from a backstreet lined with tranny brothels, Mon Key is unusually roomy and well-designed for a club of its kind – a pity the management didn't spend more on speakers. A second floor affords a haven from the distorted thumping and a bird's-eye view of the dancers below. A sofa for two is helpfully positioned just outside the men's toilets on the third floor.

★ Tek Yön

Sıraselviler Caddesi 63/1, Taksim, Beyoğlu (0535 233 0654, www.tekyonclub.com). **Open** 10pm-4am daily. **Admission** free. **No credit cards.** **Map** p248 M3.

Still one of the most happening places in town, able to retain a few bears even as its new sound system, video screen and club tunes have begun packing in the clubbers, middle classes and foreigners. For a Turkish night on the tiles in an unthreatening environment, this is your best bet.

Transgender

There are an estimated 3,000 transsexuals in Istanbul, nearly all of whom survive through prostitution. Tranny admirers are drawn primarily from the ranks of the straight, and the bars and clubs they frequent are pick-up scenes dominated by moustachioed men in badly cut suits. You're bound to catch a glimpse of scantily clad 'girls' flocking towards **Sahra** (Sadri Alışık Sokak 42/A, off Istiklal Caddesi, 012 244 3306), the only tranny club where a gay presence is tolerated, if not necessarily appreciated.

RESTAURANTS & CAFES

Durak Bar

Muratpaşa Sokak 9, Yusufpaşa, Aksaray (0212 244 1275). Tram Aksaray. **Open** 8pm-2am daily. **No credit cards.**

Turkish bears and other earthy types who won't do with the bright lights and thumping electronica of Beyoğlu gather here in the comparatively more exotic neighbourhood of Aksaray. The beer is cheap and folk music raunchily doled out by live performers. It gets busy around midnight at weekends.

Sugar Café

Sakasalim Çıkmazı, off Istiklal Caddesi, Beyoğlu (0212 244 1275). **No credit cards.** **Map** p248 N3.

Istanbul's first gay café offers smart decor, strong espresso and homemade Turkish sweets. The cafe's handy location and evening crowds make it a good starting point for a night of carousing.

HAMAMS & SAUNAS

None of Istanbul's hamams and saunas is officially gay, but the ones listed below cater almost exclusively to men unabashedly seeking

a bit more than a good exfoliation. Their sheer numbers, and the decline in the popularity of public bathing among the population at large, have resulted in the small local hamams listed below becoming gay by default, simply because they've been swamped by an almost exclusively queer clientele. No matter how zealous the management's efforts to stamp out any monkey business, boys will be boys: clingy cloths are hitched up or allowed to slip down, groins are repeatedly lathered and rinsed. One notoriously busy hamam in the Sultanahmet district responded by adopting a women-only policy; others have helplessly thrown in the towel and sexual activity is tolerated as long it is not seen. Pointing out that a couple in the next room were moments ago having sex won't necessarily save you from a rapid ejection if you're spotted doing the same.

Çeşme Hamam

Yeni Çeşme Sokak 9, off Perşembe Pazarı Caddesi, Karaköy (0212 252 3441). **Open** 8am-7pm daily. **Admission** YTL20. **No credit cards.** **Map** p246 L6.

A makeover several years ago did little to improve the forbidding appearance of this hard-to-find hamam, hidden among the backstreet hardware stores. The staff are apathetic enough to take a relaxed approach to the sight of great tubby things flirting (and more) in the underground bathing area.

Yeşildirek Hamam

Tersane Caddesi 74, Azapkapı (0212 297 7223). **Open** 6am-9.30pm daily. **Admission** YTL20; YTL27 with massage. **No credit cards.** **Map** p246 L5.

A neighbourhood hamam across from the Azapkapı Mosque at the base of the Atatürk Bridge. As good an introduction to the bathing scene as you'll get anywhere, with the added bonus of being relatively clean. The large, jam-packed sauna reeks of sweat and testosterone, if that's your thing.

ARTS & ENTERTAINMENT

Hamams

Scrub up on history.

Paying a burly, near-naked stranger to scrape, knead and pummel your flesh, while you're laid flat out on a steamy slab of marble, is one of Istanbul's hedonistic highlights. Although the process can appear daunting, all the hamams listed are used to visitors looking slightly bemused. English might not always be common, but the international language of gesture will get the job done. For an introduction, many hotels have a version of a hamam, but it's worth making the effort to go to a real one. As British novelist Maggie O'Farrell put it: 'If heaven exists, I hope it's a hamam.'

HAMAM HISTORY

Hamams were always intended to purify. Part of Islamic tradition is that followers should adhere to a strict set of rules for ablutions, washing hands, arms, face and feet with running water before praying. This was not necessarily carried out in a hamam, but the link between the mosque and hamam was always close, and the precincts of all major mosques incorporated a public bathhouse.

In the earliest times, the hamam was for men only, but the privilege was later extended to women. No mixing, of course: either the hamam would have two sections, one for each sex, or it would admit men and women at separate times of day. This is still the case. In male-dominated Ottoman times, women particularly valued their visits as a rare freedom: far more than just somewhere to get clean, the hamam was a rare opportunity to be away from the home unchaperoned. Hamams were the favoured places for arranging marriages, somewhere a mother could get a good eyeful of any prospective daughter-in-law. When the wedding came along, the equivalent of an Ottoman stag or hen night was spent getting steamed, lathered, hennaed and depilated. For a husband to deny his wife access to the hamam was grounds for divorce.

Newborn babies would be taken out of the family home for the first time 40 days after birth for a visit to a hamam, an event that also marked the end of housebound confinement for the mother. And after a lifetime of hamam-going came to its inevitable end, a person's body would be carried in one last time to be washed, before being laid out at the mosque. Thankfully, this tradition has passed away; these days, there's no chance that you might have to share your steam room with a corpse.

Hamam-going itself has been on the verge of extinction since the advent of affordable internal plumbing. Whereas 80 years ago there were more than 2,500 bathhouses in Istanbul, now there are only about a hundred. Many of these struggle to survive. The few that flourish do so largely by courting the tourist dollar – hence some exorbitant admission prices.

BARE ESSENTIALS

For the uninitiated, entering a hamam for the first time can be a daunting experience. Lengthy menus offer such treats as massage, depilation and pedicures (also soap and shampoo, although you may prefer to bring your own – and don't forget a hairbrush or comb). Outside tourist-frequented hamams such as Çemberlitaş, Cağaloğlu and Galatasaray, this will all be in Turkish. It all boils down to whether you just want to look after yourself, or whether you want to pay extra for the services of a masseur (who'll also give you a good soaping and scrub).

INSDE TRACK FAMILY WASH

Familes and couples who don't mind a touristy experience should go to the **Süleymaniye Hamam** near its namesake mosque. Attendents speak some English. Children are welcome.

Once you've paid, you enter the *camekan*, a kind of reception area. Some of these are splendid affairs with several storeys of wooden cubicles, like boxes at an opera house, and a gurgling central fountain. This is where you get changed. You will be given a colourful checked cloth, known as a *peştemal*, to be tied around the waist for modesty. Keep this on at all times – it's bad form to flash. Women are less concerned and often ditch the *peştemal* in the steam room, though many keep on their knickers. Both sexes also get *takunya*, wooden clogs that can be lethal on wet marble floors. Plastic slippers are often substituted nowadays.

A door from the *camekan* leads through to the *soğukluk*, which is for cooling off and has showers and toilets; another gives into the hararet, or steam room. These can be plain or ornate, but are nearly always covered in marble and feature a great dome inset with star-shaped coloured glass admitting a soft, diffuse light. Billowing clouds of steam fog the air.

There are no pools, as still water was traditionally considered to be unclean. Instead, the *hararet* is dominated by a great marble slab known as the *göbektaşı* or 'navel stone'. Here, customers lie and sizzle like eggs on a skillet.

THE HAMAMS

For anyone who is interested in the unique architecture of hamams but doesn't fancy the heat, a few hamams have been converted to other uses. Built in the mid 16th century by Sinan, and named in honour of Süleyman the Magnificent's wife, the **Baths of Roxelana** on Sultanahmet Square now serve as an exhibition centre and carpet store.

Be warned that many hamams are run-down to the point of being downright filthy. We recommend sticking to the places reviewed below. For gay-friendly hamams, *see p187*. For hamam-style spas in hotels, *see p116*.

Büyük Hamam

Potinciler Sokak 22, Kasımpaşa, Beyoğlu (men 0212 238 9800/women 0212 256 9835). **Open** *Men* 5.30am-10.30pm daily. *Women* 9am-7pm daily. **Admission** *Men* YTL14; YTL18.50 with massage. *Women* YTL12.50; YTL16.50 with massage. **No credit cards. Map** p246 L3.
This no-frills hamam is favoured by locals. The name means 'the big bathhouse' – and it is Istanbul's largest. The *hararet* has 60 wash stations, compared to the usual dozen or so. The beautiful details are courtesy of the Ottoman architect Sinan. An open-air swimming pool has been added to the men's section. The Büyük is a ten-minute walk from central Beyoğlu. Cross six-lane Tarlabaşı Bulvarı beside the Pera Palas Hotel and head west along Tepebaşı Caddesi, looking out for the minaret of Kasımpaşa Mosque.

Cağaloğlu Hamamı

Prof Kazım İsmail Gürkan Caddesi 34, Cağaloğlu, Sultanahmet (0212 522 2424, www.cagalogluhamami.com.tr). Tram Gülhane or Sultanahmet. **Open** *Men* 8am-10pm daily. *Women* 8am-8pm daily. **Admission** YTL38; YTL57 with massage. **No credit cards. Map** p243 M9.

Gedikpaşa Hamamı. *See p190.*

ARTS & ENTERTAINMENT

More or less unchanged since it was built in 1741, Cağaloğlu – pronounced 'jaah-lo-loo' – is Istanbul's most famous hamam. It is often used as a backdrop for soap ads and pop videos. The two-storey *camekan* has a baroque fountain, while the grand *hararet* seems inspired by the domed chamber of an imperial mosque. Illustrious bathers include Franz Liszt, Florence Nightingale and Tony Curtis.

★ Çemberlitaş Hamamı

Vezirhan Caddesi 8, Çemberlitaş (0212 522 7974, www.cemberlitashamami.com.tr). Tram Çemberlitaş. **Open** 6am-midnight daily. **Admission** YTL35; YTL55 with massage. **Credit** AmEx, MC, V. **Map** p243 M10.

Possibly the cleanest and most atmospheric hamam in town. Built in 1584 by Sinan, it was commissioned by Nurbanu, wife of Sultan Selim the Sot, as a charitable foundation for the poor. The hamam has been in continual use ever since. There are sections for both sexes, but part of the ladies' wing was torn down in the 19th century. Women now change in a corridor rather than a proper *camekan*, although the main *hararet* is lovely. Close to the Grand Bazaar, the hamam is frequented by foreigners; as a result, the masseurs are perfunctory and more interested in hassling for tips. But there's usually someone at reception who speaks English, and if you're a hamam virgin, this is a good place to begin.

Galatasaray Hamamı

Turnacıbaşı Sokak 24, Galatasaray, Beyoğlu (men 0212 252 4242/women 0212 249 4342). **Open** *Men* 7am-10pm daily. *Women* 8.30am-8pm daily. **Admission** YTL50; YTL75 with massage. **Credit** MC, V. **Map** p248 N3.

Built in 1481, for almost 500 years this hamam was for men only. A small women's section was finally added in 1963. Little else has been altered. The camekan is particularly fine, and there's some beautiful tilework at the entrance to the men's steam room. Unlike other hamams, the Galatasaray has marble slabs in the *soğukluk* where you can have a massage in semi-privacy. Because it's used largely by locals, the steam room is hot, hot, hot – towels have to be laid on the *göbektaşı* before anyone can lie on it. Staff are shameless about hustling for tips, but at least they give a good massage. To find the place, take the side-street off Istiklal Caddesi immediately north of the Galatasaray Lycée.

Gedikpaşa Hamamı

Hamam Caddesi 65-7, off Gedikpaşa Caddesi, Beyazıt (0212 517 8956). Tram Beyazıt. **Open** *Men* 6am-11.30pm daily. *Women* 9am-10.30pm daily. **Admission** YTL30; YTL50 with massage. **No credit cards. Map** p242 L10.

One of Istanbul's oldest hamams, Gedikpaşa was built in 1457 by one of Mehmet the Conqueror's viziers, next door to the mosque that also bears his name. Although not in the same architectural league

Galatasaray Hamamı.

as the Çemberlitaş or Cağaloğlu, the interior remains largely intact. Both men's and women's sections are a little run-down but clean. The men's area includes a small pool and sauna. *Photo p189.*

★ Sülemaniye Hamam

Mimar Sinan Caddesi 20, Süleymaniye, Eminönü (0212 519 5569, www.suleymaniyehamami.com). Tram Eminönü. **Open** 10am-midnight daily. **Admission** YTL70 with scrub and soap massage. **No credit cards. Map** p242 K8.

This hamam was built by the venerable Mimar Sinan in 1557. It was once part of a structure that included a mosque, hospital, school and an asylum. It's tourist friendly – in fact few locals visit – and so it's a comfortable option for an introduction. Couple and families can go in together. All the soapers are male. It's best to make reservations.

★ Üsküdar Çinili Hamam

Çavuşkapı Sokak, opposite Üsküdar ferry terminal (men 0216 553 1593, women 0216 334 9710 , http://site.mynet.com/cinilihamam). **Open** 8am-10pm daily. **Admission** YTL12; massage YTL5, scrub YTL 5. **No credit cards. Map** p250 W2.

The best option on the Asian shore for a newcomer, this hamam was built in 1648 by Kösem Sultan, with a section for each gender. You'll have an authentic experience here – this hamam has remained immune from modernity.

Music

The soundtrack of the city.

Turkey is a nation in love with music. Not always the best music, mind you, but you'll hear music of some kind everywhere you go. Pop, rock and arabesque, which dominate the city's high streets and airwaves, are a lot easier to sample live these days, thanks to venues like **Balans** and **Babylon**. For traditional *fasıl* music, simply head to the restaurants on Nevizade Sokak to hear wandering minstrels – its common for groups of eaters to interrupt the meze and start dancing. Even people strolling along Istiklal will find time to dance in front of buskers.

TICKETS AND INFORMATION

To find current information on live music events, visit the venues or pick up flyers in cafés and bookshops around Istiklal Caddesi. The monthly *Time Out Istanbul* (in English) has listings and previews, as does the fortnightly *Zip* (distributed free in bars and cafés around Beyoğlu, but only in Turkish). For online listings try: www.pozitif-ist.com, www.echoesproduction.com, www.biletix.com and www.ticketturk.com.

Biletix sells tickets online and at ticket booths around town, including downstairs at the Ada bookshop at 330 Istiklal Caddesi.

ROCK & WORLD MUSIC

Most of Istanbul's music venues are located on the side-streets off Istiklal Caddesi – and they tend to be cramped and smoky. At many venues, the bouncers are in charge of the door policy, which means that men may have trouble entering if not accompanied by women, although foreigners usually get the nod. Many places include a drink in the price of admission. In addition to venues listed below, **Park Orman** in Maslak (Büyükdere Caddesi, 0212 328 2000) hosts some big names.

Beyoğlu

★ Babylon

Şehbender Sokak 3, Asmalımescit (0212 292 7368, www.babylon-ist.com). **Open** 9.30pm-2am Tue-Thur; 10pm-3am Fri, Sat. Closed mid July-mid Sept. **Admission** varies. **Credit** AmEx, DC, MC, V. **Map** p248 M4.

Far and away Istanbul's finest live music venue, this modestly sized brick vault with a mezzanine is located in the backstreets near Tünel. There's a lot of jazz, but Babylon is also the place for world music, electronica and anything avant-garde. The management, which also runs the Doublemoon record label and the city's best music festivals, consistently attracts the best local and international names. Pick up the well-distributed monthly brochure for details.
▶ *Also on the premises is the Babylon Lounge, which serves food and decent cocktails.*

★ Balans

Balo Sokak 22, off Istiklal Caddesi (0212 251 7020, www.jollyjokerbalans.com). **Open** 9pm-3am Mon-Thur; 10pm-4am Fri, Sat. **Admission** YTL10-YTL30. **Credit** AmEx, DC, MC, V. **Map** p248 N3.

The home of 'pop-rock' in Istanbul, Balans started out with huge ambitions and attracted huge international

---

INSIDE TRACK
CROSSING THE BRIDGE

For a great introduction to the music scene in Istanbul, pick up a copy of *Crossing the Bridge*. The highly regarded 2005 film is directed Fatih Akın and presented by Alexander Hacke, a bass player for German experimental band Einstürzende Neubauten. The two explore the many musical styles, crossing ethnic, social and age groups, that converge on the Bosphorus.

---

bands to its well-appointed stage. It's still a smart venue that occasionally pulls in global guests, but today you're more likely to find local stars.

Indigo

Akarsu Sokak 1-5, off Istiklal Caddesi (0212 244 8567, www.livingindigo.com). **Open** 10pm-4am Mon-Thur, Sun; 11pm-5am Fri, Sat. **Admission** YTL25. **Credit** AmEx, MC, V. **Map** p248 N3.

Better known as a nightclub, Indigo is also at the cutting edge for electronic live acts. As one of very few venues with an interest in new music, it has built up a loyal audience of electro-rockers, so it's best to arrive early or buy tickets in advance.

Mojo

Büyükparmakkapı Sokak 26, off Istiklal Caddesi (0212 243 2927, 243 2991, www.mojomusic.org). **Open** 10pm-4am daily. **Admission** YTL10 Mon-Thur, Sun; YTL20 Fri; YTL25 Sat. **Credit** MC, V. **Map** p249 O3.

A basement decorated with giant posters of rock 'n' roll legends, Mojo is the type of bar where long hair and leather jackets never go out of fashion. Istanbul has dozens of similar joints, including many more on this very street. Cover bands have struck chords here every night of the week for almost a decade. Gigs usually begin around midnight.

★ Peyote

Kameriye Sokak 4, off Nevizade Sokak (0212 251 4398, www.peyote.com.tr). **Open** midnight-4am daily. **Admission** varies. **Credit** MC, V. **Map** p248 N3.

Spread over several floors, this joint is a favourite of the city's alternative crowd. There's a small performance space on the second floor, where various local bands play original material. With capacity limited to 100, it's the place to discover some of Istanbul's finest new talent. The beer is cheap, too. ▶ *Peyote is in the heart of the Nevizade area – perfect for drinks and dinner beforehand (see pp131-32).*

Riddim

Sıraselviler Caddesi 69/1, Taksim (0212 251 2723, www.riddim.com.tr). **Open** 9pm-4am daily. **Admission** free Mon-Thur, Sun; YTL15 Fri; YTL20 Sat. **Credit** MC, V. **Map** p248 N3.

Formerly the long-running Kemancı rock bar, this venue is an odd mixture of musical genres, with one floor devoted to rock, and another to hip hop and R&B. Locals seem to love it.

Roxy

Arslan Yatağı Sokak 3, off Sıraselviler Caddesi, Taksim (0212 2491283, 245 6539, www.roxy.com.tr). **Open** 9pm-3am Wed, Thur; 10pm-5am Fri, Sat. Closed July-Sept. **Admission** YTL30. **Credit** MC, V. **Map** p249 O3.

Roxy used to be a major live venue, but its weekend club nights became so successful that live music has been relegated to the odd midweeker or an addendum to city-wide festivals. These live events are eclectic, with artists ranging from Luke Haines to Chumbawumba via Japanese 'acid mothers' Afrirampo.

Doing the Oryantal

Swivel those hips.

The pelvis plays a prominent role in Turkish life. Belly-dancing shows are a staple of the package-holiday circuit, gyrations are a required movement for Turkish pop stars, while hip-swaying *dansöz* are celebrities.

Funny, then, that belly-dancing isn't a Turkish tradition. Sure, there were dancing girls in the harems, but the belly-dancing familiar to most – long-haired female *dansöz* in gauzy, sequined garments, undulating rhythmically – is actually an Egyptian import, which only caught on here during the 20th century. Turks acknowledge the dance's Arab heritage in their name for it: *oryantal*.

The Turks have embraced hip-swivelling with gusto. Ordinary Turks can perform similar moves to the professionals, but they don't call it *oryantal*: when civilians gyrate it's referred to as *gobek atmak*, which literally means 'to fling one's belly'.

Belly-flinging wasn't always so acceptable. Once upon a time, the *dansöz* was considered a fallen woman, whose spangles and lamé were confined to entertaining men in seedy nightclubs.

That changed in the late 1970s, when a *dansöz* appeared on Turkish television for the first time. Nesrin Topkapı's five-minute spot transfixed the country, and she became an overnight celebrity. In the 1990s, it was the turn of Sibel Can to make the leap from seedy belly-dancing clubs to the charts. And in the 2003 Eurovision Song Contest, winner Sertap Erener brought belly-dancing into millions of living rooms across the world.

But traces of the demi-monde vibe remain. These famous names aside, the world of professional dancing is still pretty much wedded to its image of greasy banknotes stuffed into skimpy costumes.

International Jazz Festival.

Studio Live

*Atıf Yılmaz Caddesi 17/A (0212 244 7712,
www.studiolive.com.tr).* **Open** 10pm-4am Fri,
Sat. **Admission** varies. **Credit** MC, V.
Map p248 N2.

Along with Balans, Studio Live caters for both international acts and local cover bands, with the occasional DJ party thrown into the mix.

The Asian Shore

Buddha

*Kadife Sokak 14/1, Kadıköy (0216 345 8798,
www.kadikoybuddha.com). Ferry from Karaköy
or Eminönü to Kadıköy.* **Open** 9pm-2am Mon-
Thur, Sun; 9pm-4am Fri, Sat. **Admission** free
Mon-Thur, Sun; YTL10 Fri, Sat. **Credit** MC, V.
Map p251 W8.

This popular student hangout on two floors is sup-
plemented with a pleasant garden in summer. It gets
busy early, with crowds turning up for passable
Britpop and rock cover bands. The beer is cheap, the
atmosphere convivial and relaxed.

Shaft

*Osmancık Sokak 13, off Serasker Caddesi,
Kadıköy (0216 349 9956, www.shaftclub.com.tr).
Ferry from Karaköy or Eminönü to Kadıköy.*
Open 2pm-4am daily. **Admission** free Mon-
Thur, Sun; YTL10 Fri, Sat. **Credit** MC, V.
Map p251 W7.

The most established live venue on the Asian side,
Shaft has a varied programme of rock, blues and jazz
concerts, featuring original artists, cover bands and

an open stage on Monday nights. There's not very
much to lure anyone over from Beyoğlu, but this is
one of the few late-night options on this side of the
water. Be warned: the last *dolmuş* back to Taksim
leaves the bus station at about 2am.

JAZZ

In Istanbul, jazz has a revered status, with a
hardcore of devotees and musicians who keep
the scene varied and vibrant. Jazz is the focus of
the prestigious **International Jazz Festival**
(*see p173*), the **Akbank Jazz Festival** (*see
p174*), and a wonderful jazz bar called **Nardis**.
Both festivals draw a glittering array of global
stars (partly because of a very broad definition
of jazz); thanks to Nardis, the line-ups feature
strong local players, too.

In the past, many of Istanbul's great jazz
musicians found recognition abroad before they
made it big back home: Maffy Falay (discovered
by Dizzy Gillespie), percussionist Okay Temiz
and guitarist Önder Focan all emigrated to
Scandinavia; percussionist Burhan Öçal moved to
Switzerland; drummer Selahattin Can Kozlu went
to Africa; and tenor saxophonist Ilhan Erşahin
moved to New York, where he has a bar, a record
label and high-profile friends like Norah Jones.

Today, many Turkish musical talents are
returning to their roots, encouraged by the
fresh group of musicians making a name for
themselves in Istanbul. Names to watch
are pianists Kerem Görsev and Aydın Esen,
who has worked with Pat Metheny, and

Eylül.

trumpeter Imer Demirer. Of the old school, Öçal now records for the Doublemoon label, Erşahin makes regular visits, while percussionist Temiz now runs a 'rhythm school' in Galata (www.okaytemiz.com).

★ Jazz Café
Hasnün Galip Sokak 20, off Büyükparmakkapi Sokak, Beyoğlu (0212 245 0516, www.jazzcafe istanbul.com). **Open** 6pm-4am Mon-Sat. Closed July-mid Sept. **Credit** MC, V. **Map** p251 O3.
A dimly lit and cosy little venue allied to the 24-hour Jazz Café FM. Downstairs is a standard bar; upstairs is where the musicians perform to respectful silence. The main draw is veteran guitarist Bülent Ortaçgil, whose Wednesday night sessions have been going strong for ten years. His highly talented backing band includes fretless guitar maestro Erkan Oğur.

KV
Tünel Geçidi 10, off Tünel Square, Beyoğlu (0212 251 4338). **Open** 8am-2am daily. **Admission** free. **Credit** MC, V. **Map** p248 M4.
This laid-back café, (pronounced 'Kahve') situated in a gorgeous, old-fashioned arcade off Tünel Square, hosts low-key jazz every evening in winter, including regular appearances by former Mingus sideman and Istanbul resident Ricky Ford.

★ Nardis Jazz Club
Galata Kulesi Sokak 14, Galata (0212 244 6327, www.nardisjazz.com). **Open** 8.30pm-2am Mon-Sat. **Admission** YTL30. **Credit** MC, V. **Map** p246 M5.
Nardis is a dedicated jazz venue, just a few steps downhill from the Galata Tower, for patrons who

know their jazz. Small and sparsely decorated – bare floorboards and brick walls – Nardis benefits from an intimate atmosphere. The place is run by guitarist and regular performer Önder Focan and his wife, who also edit *Jazz* magazine. Food is served, if you want it. Reservations are essential for tables near the stage. The music usually kicks off at around 9.30pm or 10pm.

TURKISH MUSIC

Turkish music – blasting from taxis, echoing out of kebab joints, wafting through markets – is one of the more startling sensory surprises for the visitor to Istanbul. The market may be inundated with mainstream pop and rock, but locals haven't lost their taste for indigenous sounds. Turkey has a local music scene as diverse as world music centres like Brazil, Cuba or West Africa.

Some of the music you'll hear is what's known as 'arabesque'. Much maligned by serious musical commentators – often with good reason – arabesque is a melancholic fusion of Turkish folk with borrowed 'oriental' frills.

In the days before electrified arabesque conquered Istanbul with its incessant dum-shikka-shikka, traditional Turkish music was one of the most influential in the world. The Ottomans understood a thing or two about melting pots. Instruments and musical styles from Central Asia and Persia were mixed with elements of Byzantine music, which encouraged many new sounds to flourish. Echoes of Ottoman music are still audible today in genres ranging from Jewish *klezmer* to Greek *bouzouki* to Romanian *lautar*. Today,

Turkey's musical roots are still expanding and spreading in different directions.

SONGS OF OLD STAMBOUL

To get a sense of how this music flows through the city, spend an evening in a *meyhane*, one of the boozy backstreet restaurants. As you nibble on meze, a quartet of musicians (usually Roma) warms up the crowd with nostalgic songs from 'old Stamboul'. By the time the main courses arrive – several hours and shots of rakı later – the rhythm has stepped up and the diners are dancing around, or on the tables.

One striking feature of this music is the wide variety of rhythms. If you can't keep time clapping, that could be because it's in 9/8, 10/16, or some other bizarre signature. Also, Turkish scales often employ notes between the notes, sometimes referred to as quarter-tones.

Although crossovers abound, traditional Turkish music can be divided into four basic styles: folk, which generally has a regional or rural flavour; *fasıl*, the boisterous music found most often in *meyhanes*; Turkish classical (or Ottoman) music, the refined soundtrack of the court; and Sufi music, the ethereal sounds that inspire the dervishes to whirl.

Folk music

Halk müziği (folk music) is an important part of the local music scene. Usually what gets labelled as folk are the slightly modernised, *bağlama*-heavy songs played in bars. The *bağlama*, a long-necked lute also called a *saz*, was adopted by Atatürk's reformers as a national folk symbol because of its rural Anatolian connotations.

It's also the instrument favoured by the Alevi and Bektaşi, sects of Islam that stress inter-sectarian tolerance and equality between men and women, and are frowned upon by the orthodox majority. Their folk poets, known as *aşıks*, have been wandering the Anatolian plains since the tenth century or earlier.

Istanbul is also home to many immigrants from the Black Sea coast, whose characteristic instrument is the *kemençe*. The wonderfully chaotic music that comes out of this pear-shaped fiddle accompanies improvised musical 'duels' between the singers and players.

INSIDE TRACK
RAISING THE BAR

Some of the best live music can be heard in the bars of Beyoğlu. **Badehane** (*see p144*), in particular, has live music, notably from legendary gypsy jazz clarinet player Selim Sesler.

Bağlama bars, identified by signs announcing *halk müziği*, are especially prevalent in **Hasnün Galip Sokak** off Istiklal Caddesi and in **Kadıköy** on the Asian shore. With low seating, folk art and cosy kilims, these cosy venues exude Anatolian nostalgia. It's not unusual to see family groups late at night, and men and women mingling more freely than is the norm in Turkey. Most venues offer two live sets a day, providing non-stop music from mid-afternoon until after midnight. Booze is served, tables are shared, and in addition to singing along, there's bound to be dancing. There is usually no admission charge, but patrons are, of course, expected to drink.

For a more sober experience, and probably more polished performances, head for the **Atatürk Cultural Centre (AKM)** (*see p202*), which hosts recitals by state ensembles such as the Modern Folk Music and Turkish Music Groups. Closed at the time of writing, it is scheduled to reopen in early 2011.

★ Eylül
Erol Dernek Sokak 16, off Istiklal Caddesi, Beyoğlu (0212 245 2415). **Open** noon-2am daily. **Credit** MC, V. **Map** p249.

Eylül means September, but this bar engenders a kind of balmy, best-years-of-our-lives vibe all year round. A long-established venue with reliably good musicians and an all-singing, all-dancing crowd of regulars, it's a great place in which to while away the afternoons. The music kicks off at around 3pm, so you don't have to eat. Evenings get much busier and tables are at more of a premium.

★ Munzur
Hasnün Galip Sokak 21A, Beyoğlu (0212 245 4669). **Open** 6pm-4am daily. **Credit** MC, V. **Map** p249 O3.

From the outside, Munzur doesn't look that special. The inside is pretty nondescript too, but when the live music starts this little bar suddenly becomes extraordinary. The outstanding quality of the musicians, who have a wicked way with a *bağlama*, is inspirational. Highly recommended.

Fasıl

Defining *fasıl* is one for the musicologists. At times it sounds like gypsy music, but it's also quite classical; or maybe it's just folk. In fact, it's all three – and more.

The word *fasıl* comes from Ottoman classical music. It refers to a suite involving different types of vocal and instrumental works strung together on the basis of their *makam* (mode and melodic shape). Today, *fasıl* bears very little resemblance to this style, except for the tendency of musicians to organise their compositions in a *makam*.

Andon.

Unlike folk, which is basically bar music, *fasıl* is most commonly encountered in *meyhanes*. The musicians tend to appear later in the evening, by which time most of the diners are already warmed up by a few drinks. The vast majority of *fasıl* musicians touring the restaurants are Roma, skilled at working their audience into a state of *keyif* – or ecstasy. Not that anyone needs much encouragement to lose their inhibitions: most Turks don't have any. Every song is belted out by everyone in the room and tables are often pushed aside to create an impromptu dance floor. Nostalgia is an essential element of *fasıl*, and most *meyhanes* are decorated with photos and prints that evoke the good old days of Beyoğlu.

Most *fasıl* venues offer set menus with drinks and music included, although it is customary to tip the musicians a few lira per person at the end of each set. Bring an appetite and try to go with a group of Turkish friends, and don't forget a *fasıl* night is a participatory event.

A word of warning: if it's a slow night and the *meyhane* isn't filling up, the musicians may not play or the management may send them home early. This is more likely to occur early in the week and during the summer.

Andon

Sıraselviler Caddesi 89, Taksim (0212 251 0222, www.andon.com.tr). **Open** 7pm-5am daily.
Credit MC, V. **Map** p249 O3.
A four-storey multi-purpose venue close to Taksim. As well as being a *meyhane*, it's equipped with a

wine bar, terrace restaurant and disco bar, not to mention Bosphorus views, accomplished musicians and smart service. The dimly lit interior creates a flattering backdrop for the dressed-up diners. A good place to start exploring *fasıl* if you're not ready to jump in at the deep end.

Despina

Açıkyol Sokak 9, Kurtuluş (0212 232 6720). Bus 70KE, 70KY. **Open** noon-midnight daily.
Credit MC, V.
Located in the far-from-glamorous district of Kurtuluş, an area that was once home to a sizeable Greek community, Despina doesn't look promising at first. Its fluorescent lights and plastic flowers are a far cry from the snug *meyhanes* of Beyoğlu. However, some fine musicians frequent the place, drawing an appreciative and demonstrative audience, who submit requests for their favourite *oyun havaları* (dance songs). On the right night, this can be the best party in town. The easiest way to find it is by taxi.

Ehli Keyif

Kallavi Sokak 20, off Istiklal Caddesi, Beyoğlu (0212 251 1010). **Open** noon-2am Mon-Sat.
Credit MC, V. **Map** p248 M3.
Tucked away on its own little street off Istiklal, this classic little *meyhane* has decent food and, most weekend nights, an exhilarating atmosphere. It has one of the best reputations for *fasıl*, which makes reservations essential. Dancing in the street is not uncommon. Highly recommended.

Shout Out to Istanbul

Turkey's hybrid hip hop scene.

Turkish hip hop has only recently hit the streets of Istanbul, but its roots can be traced back to late 1980s inner-city Berlin. The style, then as today, mixes the arabesque sounds of Turkish pop with the young, urban voice of the Turkish diaspora and those living in the *gecekondu*, or unplanned shanty areas, of Istanbul.

Islamic Force, originally from Berlin and with a name chosen to both reflect and combat negative stereotypes of Muslims, are credited with being the first to blend Turkish music with hip hop rhythms. But the first Turkish hip hop to make it to vinyl was 'Bir Yabancn Hayat' ('The Life of the Stranger') by King Size Terror, a Nuremberg band. It told of the disenchantment and difficulties of life in Germany for the first and second generation immigrants who form the largest non-EU minority group in the country, numbering 1.7 million.

But it was the group Cartel that really brought Turkish hip hop to the fore. Based in Berlin, three groups of rappers came together for one eponymously named album, which has sold around half a million copies. They rapped mainly in Turkish, with just the odd smattering of German, and included traditional Anatolian instruments with the beats and bass of US hip hop. The album's artwork featured a red background with the letter C (representing the crescent on the Turkish flag), and on the sleeve was written, in English, 'What are they sayin?!'. Despite *Cartel* being banned in Turkey when it was released, it found its way into the underground scene, paving the way for the group Karakan – part of the Cartel line-up – to win Best European Act at the 1995 MTV awards. Around this time, Turkish hip hop became known as oriental hip hop.

At the beginning of the 21st century, artists such as Kool Sava, who released his album *Die John Bello Story 3* in March 2010, Bass Sultan Hengzt and Eko

Fresh found success in Germany, a resurgence that was documented by Neco Celik, a Turkish-German director in his film *Alltag*, filmed around Berlin's heavily Turkish Kreuzberg area.

In 2001, Turkish hip hop found its most successful proponent: Ceza, meaning 'the punishment'. Ceza (Bilgin Özçalkan) was born in Üsküdar on the Asian shore of Istanbul in 1976. Working with Turkish rappers Dr Fuchs, Sagopa Kaimer, Sahtiyan and Fuat, Ceza has done more than others to promote the mix of arabesque and hip hop. He is based in Turkey, but with connections with Germany, one of his biggest markets.

An international breakthrough came when he was featured freestyling in the documentary *Crossing the Bridge* (*see p191* **Inside Track**) and his song 'Holocaust' was featured on the movie's soundtrack. The film's producers described his staccato style as sounding 'as if he swallowed an Ak-47, like a preacher on speed'. His latest album, *10 Köy*, was released in 2010.

The most successful female oriental hip hop artist is Aziza A (*pictured*), a Turkish German. One of the early stars of the genre, she is now also an actor and presenter. Born in Kreuzberg, she is known for her support of Turkish women in Germany. As her style has matured, elements of funk, soul, jazz and R&B have crept into her work, to great effect. Yet she remains true to her roots. In 'Powerful Sister', she raps: Now I'm going to take a liberty, man!/Aziza A does what she takes to be right/Even if banned from her family's sight/For not being sweet, not Turkish Delight/I don't give a damn/I speak out when and wherever I can.'

Süheyla
Balık Pazarı, Galatasaray, Beyoğlu (0212 251 8347). **Open** 7pm-2am daily. **No credit cards**. **Map** p248 N3.

Another prime *fasıl* venue, in the Nevizade Sokak area, with two large rooms and above-average musicians. The set menu includes unlimited *rakı* for YTL60 per head. The place gets packed at weekends.

Turkish classical

Real Turkish classical music is rarely performed in public these days. In the new Turkish Republic of the 1920s, Ottoman music was considered elitist and backward, so the state did its best to bury it. There has been a slow revival over the last couple of decades; percussionist **Burhan Öçal** is the latest to pay his respects, with his classically inspired *Yeni Rüya* album. To hear other faithful renditions, look in music shops for Turkish classical music on the Kalan label.

Also known as Ottoman, Osmanlı or Court-Enderun music, Turkish classical music is based on the principle of *makam*. Like Indian *ragas*, the *makams* are modal. The melodies are subtle, the rhythms gentle and sometimes quite slow, although towards the end of a programme you'll often hear lively numbers as the pace picks up.

No single venue in Istanbul devotes itself exclusively to performances of Turkish classical music, although it does feature in the annual **International Istanbul Music Festival** (*see p173*).

Atatürk Cultural Centre
Atatürk Kültür Merkezi/AKM, Taksim Square (0212 251 5600/251 1023). **No credit cards**. **Map** p247 P2.
The most likely place to find Turkish classical music. When the centre is open, the Türk Müziği chorus performs in the lower auditorium most Sundays from autumn to late spring. Closed for refurbishment until early 2011.

Cemal Reşit Rey Konser Salonu
Cemal Reşit Rey Konser Salonu Darülbedai Caddesi 1, Harbiye (0212 232 9830). **Open** Box office 10am-8pm daily. **Admission** YTL8-21 **Credit** MC, V.
This large, comfortable auditorium with excellent acoustics is not far north of Taksim Square. Run by the Istanbul Municipality, the venue hosts occasional concerts of Turkish classical music.

Sufi music

They may be promoted as one of the enduring symbols of Turkey abroad, but the Whirling Dervishes, better known locally as the Mevlevi order of Sufis, are quite rare in Istanbul – not least because the sect is still technically outlawed in Turkey. You can catch a *sema* (performance) in designated tourist spots, but this is promoted as a colourful historical oddity, rather than an ecstatic connection with God through music, dance and *zikr* (a form of rhythmic breathing).

The **Galata Mevlevihanesi** in Tünel (*see p72*), a centre for whirling dervishes sanitised as a Museum for Classical Literature (Divan Edebiyat Müzesi), stages two performances a month exclusively for tourists.

Genuine dervish ceremonies are not always accessible to the outsider. One place to catch one is in Fatih, where the Cerrahi brotherhood operates the Museum for the Study and Preservation of Tasavvuf Music (Nurettin Tekkesi Sokak, Karagümrük), actually a fully functioning mosque. Visitors are not necessarily welcome, as the place is obliged to keep a low profile, but if you go with a respectful attitude and an open mind, you may be able to witness a ceremony on Monday nights starting from 10pm. On Thursday evenings, the brotherhood holds *zikr* ceremonies – a rousing chorus of Sufis locked together in concentric dancing circles around a solo singer and a drummer. More an act of worship than a concert, it's an unforgettable experience.

Another opportunity to hear Sufi music in Istanbul is during the **Mystic Music Festival** held at Cemal Resit Rey Concert Hall every November. Check www.biletix.com for details.

FESTIVALS

The number of music festivals is multiplying every year. Events range from one night of performances in a touring show to a month of citywide activities. The Istanbul Culture and Art Foundation (www.iksv.org) organises an ambitious two-week **Jazz Festival** every July. Another key player on the festival scene is Pozitif (www.pozitif-ist.com), the organisation behind October's **Akbank Jazz Festival** (www.akbanksanat.com), the **Efes Pilsen Blues Festival** (www.efesblues.com), which tours Turkey and much of Russia, the **One Love Festival** (www.en.istanbul2010.org), two days of eclectic bands in a park north of the city, and the **Rock 'n' Coke Festival** (www.rockncoke.com), a three day event that hosts international and local acts at an airstrip, complete with a Glastonbury-style camp site.

Local stars of pop and arabesque perform series of concerts each summer at the open air theatres in Rumeli Hisarı and Harbiye. Look out for details on www.biletix.com.

The summer festivals held at beach clubs on the Black Sea coast usually include some kind of shuttle service from Taksim Square, but standards of organisation vary widely.

Nightlife

Istanbul embraces club culture.

The club scene came late to Istanbul, but Istanbullus are making up for it now. On every night of the week, the bars and pavements of Beyoğlu fill up with partygoers enjoying an evening drink before hitting a club. This city knows how to party – and the superstar DJs know this, visiting Istanbul regularly.

In summer, the nightlife moves outside to the superclubs strung along the Bosphorus. **Reina** and **Sortie** are classic destinations to drink cocktails as the sun sets, and dance until the sun comes up.

THE LOCAL SCENE

Given that Turks are obsessive followers of fads, club promoters tend to stick to tried and tested formulas. So although smaller clubs cater to most musical tastes, from rock and jazz to Latin or electronica, the majority of big clubs play house and techno. But what could be a lack of variety is offset by the frequency and variety of guest DJs who come to the city – the likes of Tiesto, Kruder & Dorfmeister, John Digweed and Paul Oakenfold. Istanbul also has plenty of talented DJs of its own: look out for Yunus Güvenen, Barış Türker and Murat Uncuoğlu.

Although new venues crop up every month, it's safest to stick with big names like **Crystal** (electronic, after hours), **Roxy** (rock, pop, theme parties), **NuPera** (electronic, dance, disco), or **Babylon** (excellent live acts and DJ nights).

Istanbul's lively party scene has its idiosyncracies. Turks like to dress up, so make an effort not to look too casual. You won't find any rowdy, alcohol-induced behaviour at clubs or on the streets. But although disturbances are rare, belligerent bouncers can be a hassle. Drinks are generally expensive, due to heavy taxes on alcohol. Be warned that police sometimes raid clubs and crack down hard on anyone caught in possession of drugs.

The party doesn't really get started until after midnight, with clubs peaking between 1am and 4am. Fridays and Saturdays are the busiest nights, although there are sometimes special events on Wednesdays. Bars are busy on Thursdays, but it's usually dead in the clubs. From July to September, the party shifts to the shores of the Bosphorus

(*see p201* **Bosphorus Bling**). When it comes to getting around, taxis are cheap, reliable, and generally safe.

Finding up-to-date nightlife listings is a challenge. Check out *Time Out Istanbul* and its online edition www.timeoutistanbul.com.

FESTIVALS & EVENTS

Despite drawbacks like heavy-handed security and expensive taxi rides home, one-off raves and annual festivals in far-flung locales are a growth industry. Many events are held at the **Venue**, (better known as Maslak Venue, www.re-fresh. com.tr), with its huge indoor and outdoor arenas, on the outskirts of Maslak business district. Just beyond Maslak is **Park Orman**, a huge bar/restaurant complex with a pool. **Yeni Melek** is a giant space that hosts parties and concerts in the heart of Beyoğlu. During summer, the action moves to **Solar Beach** or **Burç Beach** in Kilyos on the Black Sea coast (*see p216*).

Big events are advertised around town, and clubs distribute flyers at bars, cafés and bookshops in Beyoğlu. You can buy tickets online at Biletix (www.biletix.com) or Ticket Turk (www.ticketturk.com). Websites that list upcoming events include www.pozitif-ist.com, www.hippro.com and www.kodmuzik.com.

CLUBS

★ **11:11**
Tepebaşı Mahallesi, Meşrutiyet Caddesi 69, Beyoğlu (0212 244 8834, www.1111.com.tr).
Open 6pm-4am Wed-Sat. **Admission** varies.
Credit MC, V. **Map** p248 M4.

Looking somiething like a James Bond baddie's lair, also possibly resembling the inside of an ice cube, 11:11 (named after its opening date of 11.11.2009) is a busy venue that's popular with a more mature crowd. There are several different areas, each playing a different genre of music. A lounge bar also serves Asian and fusion food alongside good cocktails.

★ Anjelique
Salhane Sokak 5, off Muallim Naci Caddesi, Ortaköy (0212 327 2844). Bus DT1, DT2. **Open** 6pm-4am Mon-Sat. **Admission** varies. **Credit** MC, V.
The most tasteful of the Bosphorus bunch of clubs. Anjelique's assets include stunning views over the water, above- average food at the refined Da Mario restaurant, and delicious apple martinis. There are resident and excellent guest DJs, but Western and Turkish sing-along pap predominates. *See right* **Bosphorus Bling**.

★ Babylon
Şehbender Sokak 3, Tünel, Beyoğlu (0212 292 7368, www.babylon.com.tr). **Open** 9.30pm-4am Tue-Sat. **Admission** varies. **Credit** AmEx, DC, MC, V. **Map** p248 M4.
More of a live music venue (*see p191*) than a club, the intimate Babylon hosts some of the best parties in town. Run by the prolific Pozitif group, it's one of the few places in Istanbul that offers more than techno. Nights range from funk to Oldies But Goldies parties, where cheesy ballads and dirty dancing are *de rigueur*.

Blackk
Muallim Naci Caddesi 71, Ortaköy (0212 236 7256, www.blackk.net). Bus DT1, DT2. **Open** 8pm-late Tue-Sat. **Admission** varies. **Credit** AmEx, MC, V.
Blackk is giving its upmarket neighbours a run for their money. Dinner will set you back about YTL90-YTL120. Try a frozen watermelon cocktail on the upper terrace, decked out with antiques and ceramics. The music policy tends towards vocal house. Occasional live jazz.

INSDE TRACK PLUSONE

Beer for YTL3 and no guest list are just two reasons to keep an eye out for the next PlusOne DJ collective event – the antithesis of the flashy superclubs. PlusOne members describe themselves as 'open source excitement', and anything can happen at their parties. See www.plusoneistanbul.com for the collective's Facebook page to find out about the next one.

Çubuklu Hayal Kahvesi
Çubuklu Ağaçlık Mesire Yeri, Burunbahçe (0216 413 6880). Ferry from Beşiktaş to Üsküdar, then bus 15. Or ferry from Karaköy or Eminönü to Kadıkoy, then bus 15BK, 15F. **Open** 7pm-4am daily. **Admission** varies. **Credit** MC, V.
Right on the waterfront in a leafy Asian suburb. Free boats whisk you across the Bosphorus to the club's private jetty (departing from Istinye Motor Iskelesi every 30 minutes from 7pm until closing time).

★ Dirty
Erol Dernek Sokak 11/1, Hanif Han Apt, Beyoğlu (536 399 6151). **Open** 10pm-2am Wed-Sat. **Admission** YTL5. **No credit cards**. **Map** p248 N3.
The underground venue of Dirty is known for its pop-art decor and constant stream of electronic DJs. Some frequent guest DJs include Mabbas, Style-Ist, Disc Jokey Ari, 7-Erhan.

Dogzstar
Tosboğa Sokkak 22, Galatasaray, Beyoğlu (0212 244 1081). **Open** 10.30am-10.30pm Mon-Thur, Sun; 2pm-4am Fri, Sat. **Admission** free. **Credit** MC, V. **Map** p248 N3.
It may be small, but Dogzstar proves that size doesn't matter: this diminutive club in Beyoğlu has garnered quite a reputation: the laid-back, let-loose, neo-punk vibe here packs a punch. It can get a little cramped, but it's a good place to boogie, thanks to resident DJ Ari.

Indigo
Akarsu Sokak 1-5, Beyoğlu (0212 244 8567). **Open** 10pm-4am Tue-Thur, Sun; 11pm-5am Fri, Sat. **Admission** YTL20-30. **Credit** MC, V. **Map** p248 N3.
Attracting a mix of local and foreign bands and DJs, Indigo is the definitive venue for fans of electronic music. Smack in the centre of Beyoğlu, it is also jammed every weekend. So be warned: if you don't like people pushing you around, rubbing up against you and treading on your toes, it might be best to steer clear. In the summer, Indigo moves to its other venue, Blanco.

Nu Club
Meşrutiyet Caddesi 67, Beyoğlu (0212 245 6070). **Open** *Oct-May* 11pm-4am Fri, Sat. Closed June-Sept. **Admission** free. **Credit** AmEx, MC, V. **Map** p248 M3.
The Nu Pera complex is known for great modern Turkish cuisine (Lokanta) and amazing views (Nu Teras). Come winter, the action moves downstairs to this intimate basement club, where everyone knows everyone, and anyone who doesn't soon will. Top-notch local DJs like Yunus Güvenen and Barış Türker are complemented with a guest DJ from Paris once a month. Unpretentious and great fun.

Bosphorus Bling

When Istanbul gets hot, the hot people move outside.

If you like your nightlife flashy, you'll love the clubs along the Bosphorus between Ortaköy and Kuruçeşme. So-called superclubs like **Reina** and **Sortie** (for both, *see below*) are a gaudy swirl of swaggering playboys, C-list celebs and anorexic gold-diggers sipping exorbitant cocktails as they sway to trashy Turkish and European pop. Patrons roll up in sports cars, or even speedboats. They might be soap stars eager to flash their cash; or nouveau-riche upstarts trying to scramble up the social ladder.

These clubs – particularly Reina – are notoriously elitist. A beer can cost YTL17, a cocktail YTL35, and a meal around YTL150 per person. You have to pay around YTL45 just to get in – if, that is, you're lucky enough to make it past the bouncers.

Other popular clubs include **Çubuklu Hayal Kahvesi** (*see left*) on the Asian shore and **Blackk** (*see left*), which moves to the Sortie complex in summer.

All these venues are at the peak of their popularity in summer, when the fine moonlit views offer cool respite for those stuck in the city. Some close in winter, others keep their indoor dancefloors open and close the outdoor spaces. Some, like chic **Anjelique** (*see left*), are more relaxed than the others.

Reina.

ARTS & ENTERTAINMENT

Peyote
Kameriye Sokak 4, off Nevizade Sokak, Beyoğlu (0212 251 4398, www.peyote.com.tr). **Open** midnight-4am daily. **Admission** varies. **Credit** MC, V. **Map** p248 N3.
Spread over several floors, this joint is a favourite with the city's alternative crowd. Each floor has a different vibe. It's well known for live music, and the open roof terrace is also a popular place for drinks, to be enjoyed before descending to the ground floor for the trance and electronica music from the resident DJ. Peyote also has a small performance space on the second floor, where various local bands play original material.

Reina
Muallim Naci Caddesi 44, Ortaköy (0212 259 5919, www.reina.com.tr). Bus DT1, DT2. **Open** 7pm-4am daily. **Admission** varies. **Credit** AmEx, MC, V.
The city's most famous nightclub, Reina is paparazzi heaven. It's a stunning waterfront venue with the expected amazing views, and resembles a swanky food court with a big dancefloor in the middle. It

attracts rich brats, playboys, celebs and wannabes. The music is pure Euro Med trash, and loud.

Roxy
Arslan Yatağı Sokak 7, off Sıraselviler Caddesi, Beyoğlu (0212 249 1283, 245 6539, www.roxy. com.tr). **Open** 10pm-5am Fri, Sat. **Admission** YTL35. **Credit** MC, V. **Map** p249 O3.
Not exactly cutting edge, this established venue is a showcase for mainstream rock and pop bands. The place is usually packed with sociable, easy-going regulars, swigging bottled Sex On The Beach. Look out for the regular theme parties.

Sortie
Muallim Naci Sokak 141-142, Kuruçeşme (0212 327 8585). Bus 25T, 40. **Open** Summer only 6pm-5am daily. **Admission** varies. **Credit** MC, V.
Sortie has successfully replicated the Bosphorus bling formula. Like many of the area's neighbouring clubs, it's a nightspot that is well known for the collection of pricey restaurants that surround the central bar area. Though big and brash in the summer, Sortie is closed in winter.

Performing Arts

A small scene, but some great venues.

Despite the best efforts of the reformist Turkish state in the early years of the republic, Western performing arts generally appeal only to a minority of Turks, drawn almost entirely from the westernised upper classes. The rest of the population prefer homegrown folk and traditional art. However, a trend for international events, especially the **Istanbul Theatre Festival** and the **International Puppet Festival** (for both, *see p172*), the success of local talent at home and abroad, and regular visits by some exceptional foreign theatre companies, dance troupes, and musicians from around the world seem to be making a difference. It's an emerging market, reflected in new venues such as **Garajistanbul**.

CLASSICAL MUSIC, OPERA & BALLET

Turkey doesn't have a long tradition of western-style classical music. The Ottomans had their own courtly music (*see p198*), but it was banned by Atatürk, who considered it regressive and elitist. He promoted western-style music instead, which in the early years of the republic was put to the service of Turkish nationalism.

Today, Istanbul is home to a respectable – if small – classical music, opera and ballet scene. Although the choice is pretty limited, Istanbul has some decent symphonic and chamber music orchestras, and also hosts the major annual **International Istanbul Music Festival** (*see p173*). And there is one area in which Istanbul can compete with any major city in the world, and that's the unique venues where concerts and events are held; these include ancient underground cisterns, Byzantine churches and Ottoman palaces.

The standard modern venues are also very good, if few; chief among them is the **Atatürk Cultural Centre (AKM)**, where the Istanbul Symphony Orchestra and the Istanbul State Opera and Ballet perform, along with foreign companies. Other leading local companies are the Akbank Chamber Orchestra, Borusan Istanbul Philharmonic Orchestra, and the Cemal Reşit Rey Symphony Orchestra.

Tickets for concerts, opera and theatre (as well as sports events) can be bought online from Biletex (www.biletix.com).

VENUES

★ Akbank Culture and Arts Centre
Akbank Kültür ve Sanat Merkezi (Akbank Sanat)
İstiklal Caddesi 8, Beyoğlu (0212 252 3500, www.akbanksanat.com). **Performances** 8pm Mon-Sat. **Credit** DC, MC, V. **Map** p249 O2.
This arts centre boasts its own chamber music orchestra and a cosy, 135-seat, multi-purpose concert hall. The six-storey building hosts all sorts of cultural activities, from theatre to exhibitions to workshops.

Atatürk Cultural Centre (AKM)
Atatürk Kültür Merkezi
Taksim Square (box office 0212 251 5600, opera & ballet enquiries 243 2011/251 1023, www.idobale.com). **Box office** 10am-6pm daily. **Performances** usually 3.30pm, 8pm Mon-Sat. **Credit** MC, V. **Map** p247 P2.
Istanbul's premier performing arts venue. Behind the brutalist 1960s design, the interior is surprisingly grand and vibrant. It has two main concert halls, with a capacity of 1,300 and 520. Ticket prices are kept low through state subsidies. The venue is currently under renovation, scheduled to reopen in 2011.

Bosphorus University Albert Long Hall Cultural Centre
Boğaziçi Üniversitesi Albert Long Hall Kültür Merkezi
Boğaziçi Üniversitesi, Bebek (0212 359 5400). **Bus** 22, 22R, 25E, 30D, 40, 42T. **Performances** vary. **No credit cards.**

The Albert Long Hall building is an iconic symbol of Bosphorus University. The 479-seat hall is an important venue for classical music concerts by leading local and foreign musicians, orchestras and companies. The Bosphorus University campus is in Rumeli Hisarı, near the Fatih Sultan Mehmet Bridge.

Cemal Reşit Rey Concert Hall
Cemal Reşit Rey Konser Salonu
Darülbedai Caddesi 1, Harbiye (0212 232 9830, www.crrks.org). Bus 43, 46Ç, 46ÇYm, 46H, 46KY. **Box office** 10am-8pm daily. **Performances** 8pm daily. Closed June-Sept. **Credit** MC, V.
This venue, the 860-seat home of the municipal CRR Symphony Orchestra, has a diverse programme, including Turkish religious and traditional music. It's a key venue for several festivals, including October's International Mystic Music Festival, December's International CRR Piano Festival, January's International Istanbul Baroque Days, April's International Dance Festival and the International Youth Festival in May. Tickets are available from www.biletix.com.

★ Enka Ibrahim Betil Auditorium
Enka Ibrahim Betil Oditoryumu
Sadi Gülçelik Spor Sitesi, Istinye (0212 276 2214, www.enkasanat.org). Metro Şişli. **Performances** 8pm Mon-Sat; 11.15am Sun. **Credit** MC, V.
A 600-seat modern auditorium with perfect acoustics. It hosts a variety of events, including drama, concerts, folk dancing and ballet, and regularly plays host to the local metropolitan and state music and dance companies.
▶ *There is also an open-air venue, Enka Eşref Denizhan Açık Hava Tiyatrosu (Sadi Gülçelik*

Spor Sitesi, Istinye, 0212 276 2214), which is used for events during June and July.

★ Garajistanbul
Tomtom Mahallesi, Yeni Çarşi Caddesi, Kaymakam Reşat Bey Sokak 11, Galata, (0212 212 4499, www.garajistanbul.org). **Performances** varies. **Credit** MC, V.
A forward-thinking performing arts centre, not afraid to lend its stage to any discipline, from cutting-edge theatre to the International Puppet Festival. The programme covers theatre, dance, music, literature and arts shows, both home-grown and from abroad. The non-profit organisation that runs the centre produces its own shows, tours and a magazine. The centre is also open to touring companies.
▶ *There is a bar and café on the premises.*

Iş Art and Culture Centre
Iş Sanat Kültür Merkezi
Iş Towers (Iş Kuleleri), Kule 1 17, Levent (0212 316 1083, www.issanat.com.tr). Metro Levent. **Box office** 9am-6pm daily. **Performances** 8pm Mon-Sat; 3pm Sun. Closed June-Oct. **Credit** MC, V.

ARTS & ENTERTAINMENT

Garajistanbul.

INSIDE TRACK
CHILDREN'S THEATRE

The **Atatürk Cultural Centre**, when it reopens at the end of 2010, will stage opera and ballet for kids on Saturdays at 11am (admission YTL4). For more information, go to www.idobale.com.

An 800-seat concert hall with a prestigious programme and an unconventional location: the basement of the highest skyscraper in Levent. Classical music concerts are performed by Turkish and foreign symphony and chamber orchestras. Other draws include jazz and world music. The centre also hosts exhibitions and plays, and has a shopping centre.

Lütfi Kırdar Convention & Exhibition Centre
Lütfi Kırdar Kongre ve Sergi Sarayı
Darülbedayi Caddesi 60, Harbiye (0212 373 1100, www.icec.org/en). Bus 43, 46Ç, 46ÇY, 46H, 46KY.
The convention centre houses one of the city's biggest auditoriums, seating up to 3,500 people. Although it's not a dedicated music venue, it's actually one of Istanbul's top venues for classical music, along with the AKM.

THEATRE

Theatre in Istanbul is far more vital and varied than the classical music, opera or ballet scenes. More than 30 stages are scattered across the city, even in the remotest districts.

The best chance for seeing good theatre in English is during the **International Istanbul Theatre Festival** (*see p172*) and the **Location Theatre Festival** (Mekan Tiyatro Festivali). Both feature performances from dozens of foreign companies, in their original languages.

In most cases, though, performances will be in Turkish. Also be aware that many theatres are closed from June to September.

Kenter Theatre
Kenter Tiyatrosu
Halaskargazi Caddesi 9/B, Harbiye (0212 246 3589, www.kentersinematiyatro.com). Bus 43, 46Ç, 46ÇY, 46H, 46KY. **Box office** 11am-6pm daily. **Performances** 8pm Wed-Sat; 3pm Sun. **Credit** MC, V.
A private 450-seat theatre, founded in 1968 by Yıldız Kenter, one of Turkish theatre's leading actresses. Here, the City Players (Kent Oyuncuları) perform two or three plays a year, usually classics by the likes of Shakespeare and Chekhov. Performances usually star Yıldız Kenter and tend towards the old-fashioned and earnest.

Maya Sahnesi
Halep İş Hanı, 140/20 Istiklal Caddesi, Beyoğlu (0212 252 7452, www.mayasanat.com). **Box office** 9am-7pm daily. **Performances** 8.30pm Wed, Sat, Sun. **No credit cards.** Map p248 N3.
This 100-seat venue has attracted a loyal following of young theatre buffs since it opened in 2001. It hosts several young theatre companies. There is also a cosy café complete with a piano, library and snack bar. Music performances, film screenings and workshops take place here, too. Closed for most of 2010.

★ Muhsin Ertuğrul Stage
Muhsin Ertuğrul Sahnesi
3 Gümüş Caddesi, Harbiye (0212 455 3919, www.ibst.gov.tr). Bus 43, 46Ç, 46ÇY, 46H, 46KY. **Box office** 10am-6pm Sun. **Performances** 8.30pm Tue-Sat; 3pm Sun. Closed May-Sept. **Credit** MC, V.
Founded in 1914 as a conservatory, this venue had significant influence on the development of Turkish theatre. Of the plays performed here, half are by Turkish writers and include musicals and children's plays. Low ticket prices ensure packed houses.

Pera Theatre
Tiyatro Pera
Billurcu Çıkmazı 10, Sıraselviler Caddesi, Taksim (0212 245 4460, www.tiyatropera.com). **Performances** 8pm Fri, Sat; 6.30pm Sun. **Credit** AmEx, MC, V.
The Pera Theatre is an ambitious project realised by Turkish actor/director/writer Nesrin Kazankaya. It's a theatre company and a drama school rolled into one. Good news for foreigners: the company performs works in both English and Turkish.

Ses-1885 Ortaoyuncular Theatre
Ses-1885 Ortaoyuncular Tiyatrosu
Istiklal Caddesi 140/90, Beyoğlu (0212 251 1865, www.ortaoyuncular.com). **Box office** 11am-8pm daily. **Performances** 8pm Thur-Sat; 6pm Sun. Closed June-Sept. **No credit cards.** Map p248 N3.
Istanbul's oldest functioning theatre and one of its most beautiful. The wooden hall, with 554 seats on two floors, plus boxes and a balcony, is dripping in nostalgia. It usually hosts performances by the Ortaoyuncular Company.

Small Stage
Küçük Sahne
Istiklal Caddesi 209, Taksim (0212 244 5256, www.istdt.gov.tr). **Box office** 10am-8pm daily. **Performances** 8pm Tue-Sun. **Credit** MC, V. Map p249 O3.
This intimate hall, owned by the Turkish Ministry of Cultural Affairs, is a new home to the Istanbul State Theatre. Around four different plays are put on every month, each for one-week runs. Productions tend to be bit po-faced.

ARTS & ENTERTAINMENT

Sport & Fitness

Football, more football, and the occasional bout of oil wrestling

Ask most Istanbullus about sport and they'll tell you about football. Turks are dedicated to the game, and Istanbul teams can rely on fervent support from armies of fans, whose fearsome reputation may have softened in recent years. In other sports, Turks have only made their mark at world-class level in weightlifting and Greco-Roman wrestling, but in recent years, Turkish basketball teams have also begun making a name in the international arena.

Failed bids to host the Olympic Games in 2000, 2004, 2008 and 2012 haven't quite soured the city on the project. The government continues to invest in sport – building the spectacular 80,000-seat Olympic Stadium at Ikitelli and investing billions of lira on other sports projects – and the public passion remains.

SPECTATOR SPORTS

All sporting events and fixtures are listed in the local press and at the online ticketing agency **Biletix** (www.biletix.com) or **Ticket Turk** (www.ticketturk.com).

Football

Istanbul is home to Turkey's three biggest clubs: **Galatasaray**, **Beşiktaş** and **Fenerbahçe**. The Black Sea side **Trabzonspor** supposedly completes the 'big four,' but has struggled to keep up in recent years. The domestic league runs from August to May. For a really intense atmosphere, try to catch one of the Istanbul derbies.

To satisfy the TV companies, matches are staggered over the whole weekend, from Friday evening to Sunday evening. Tickets usually go on sale two or three days before a match, although for all but the biggest games it is surprisingly easy to pick them up at the stadium on the day. For matches involving the big teams, tickets can also be bought in advance via booking agency Biletix (www.biletix.com).

★ **Beşiktaş**
İnönü Stadium, Dolmabahçe Caddesi, Beşiktaş (0212 236 7202/227 8780, www.bjk.com.tr). **Tickets** League games YTL25-YTL200. **Tickets** from Biletix. **Credit** MC, V. **Map** p247 R1/2.

National league champions and Turkish Cup winners in 2009, the Beşiktaş 'Black Eagles' are resurgent. The club's İnönü Stadium is the city's most conveniently located, just uphill from Dolmabahçe Palace. Some stands offer great views over the Bosphorus.

★ **Fenerbahçe**
Şükrü Saraçoğlu Stadium, Kadıköy (0216 261 1907, www.fenerbahce.org). Ferry from Eminönü or Karaköy to Kadıköy, then 10B bus. **Tickets** League games YTL30-YTL225. **No credit cards**. **Map** p251 Y8.

Despite winning a record number of Turkish league championships, Fener's European record is weak. Atatürk's favourite team, Fenerbahçe has historic links with the Turkish army, despite its decidedly unmilitary nickname – 'the Canaries'. The home stadium is in the wealthy suburb of Fenerbahçe, on the Asian side.

Galatasaray

Ali Sami Yen Stadium, Mecidiyeköy (0212 261 1500, www.galatasaray.org). **Tickets** League games YTL13-YTL160. **No credit cards.**
Easily Turkey's most famous club, Galatasaray boasts a string of European successes, crowned by victory over Arsenal in the UEFA Cup final in 2000. Known to fans as 'Cim Bom' for reasons no-one can explain, Galatasaray see themselves as the aristocracy of Turkish football. Shuttles transfer fans from Taksim Square and Eminönü and Topkapı bus stations. The fans have a fierce reputation, though problems with hooliganism are improving since their late 1990s nadir.

▶ *For the Galatasary football club museum, see p74*

Basketball

While international soccer success has tended to eclipse Turkey's long-running love affair with basketball, the game still has a large fan base, and a handful of Turkish-born players have moved on to the NBA. Hopes run high at the time of writing for the chances of Turkey's '12 Dev Adam' ('12 Giant Men), as the national team is fondly known, during the 2010 World Championships, which Turkey is hosting (28 August to 12 September).

The basketball season lasts roughly from October to June. Tickets for all but the biggest games are readily available on the day, or can be bought in advance. Information on games and fixtures is available on the Turkish Basketball Federation website (www.tbf.org.tr).

Beşiktaş ColaTurka

BJK Akatlar Spor ve Kültür Kompleksi
Gazeteciler Sitesi Mayadrom Arkası, Beşiktaş (0212 283 66 01, www.biletix.com.tr). Bus 105. **Tickets** YTL6-YTL8. **No credit cards.**
Lagging behind their footballing colleagues, Beşiktaş haven't won the basketball championship since 1975.

★ Efes Pilsen

Abdi Ipekçi Spor Salonu
Onuncu Y5l Caddesi, Zeytinburnu (0212 414 7700, www.efesbasket.org). Bus 93C, 93M, 93T. **Tickets** YTL5-YTL17. **No credit cards.**
Founded in 1976, Efes Pilsen have won the Turkish title 13 times. In 1996, they scored their biggest success when they bagged the European Korac Cup.

Fenerbahçe-Ülker

Fenerbahçe Spor Kulübüğ Tesisleri
Dereağzı Tesisleri, Basketbol Şubesi, Kızıltoprak (0216 347 8438). Ferry from Eminönü or Karaköy to Kadıköy, and then 10B bus. **Tickets** YTL7.50-YTL15, from Biletex.
Fenerbahçe won the national championship in 2007, 2008 and 2010. In 2006, they merged with Ülkerspor and pilfered the stronger squad's roster in a bid to unseat perennial champions Efes Pilsen. This address is the training ground; games are played elsewhere, including the Abdi Ipekçi Spor Salonu (*see above*).

Galatasaray CafeCrown

Galatasaray Spor Kulübü
Metin Oktay Tesisleri, Basketbol Şubesi, Florya (0212 574 2901, www.galatasaray.org). Bus E-52. **Tickets** YTL5-YTL15. **No credit cards.**
While both the men's and women's teams once topped their respective Istanbul leagues, neither is the team it once was. Games take place at Ahmet Cömert Spor Salonu in Ataköy (Ataköy 4. Kısım Sonu, Olimpiyatevi Yanı).

ACTIVE SPORTS

With sparse facilities and little leisure time, few Turks actively participate in any sports other than the odd football match played on one of the city's many five-a-side pitches. The Kadıköy and Bakırköy municipalities have established cycle paths along coastal roads, which are usually filled with joggers. Exercise in Istanbul is otherwise a habit confined to the well-heeled.

Adventure sports

Ministry of Tourism efforts to pitch Turkey as an ideal destination for adventure enthusiasts have at least got more locals interested.

Fans of **Beşiktaş**. See p205.

ARTS & ENTERTAINMENT

Grease is the Word

Take a jar of olive oil, pour it all over yourself, then wrestle.

Two heavily set men, with moustaches, are covered in oil and grappling on the floor. One hand slips down the other's leather trousers – it's the only place to get a good grip – and a man is thrown on his back. Yes, you are reading the sport chapter: this is Turkey's national sport of oil wrestling. The Kırkpınar oil-wrestling tournament, held every year in Edirne, near the Bulgarian and Greek border, is the world's longest-established sporting event. With the first tournament taking place 1346, it preceded football's FA Cup by more than half a millennium.

Grappling while covered in oil has been an essential part of the Central Asian Turkic culture for more than 3,000 years. The word *pehlivan*, meaning wrestler, was first used around the turn of the first millennium. As the Turks spread across Western Asia and into Anatolia, they brought the sport of *yagli gures* with them. The original function of the oil is disputed. Some believe it was used to repel mosquitoes, while others maintain that it was just used to make it more difficult to grapple – which it undoubtedly does.

The sport really rose to prominence during the Ottoman conquest of Rumeli, the area that would become the southern Balkan regions of the Ottoman Empire, during the reign of Orhan I (1326-1361). Wrestling became popular in military camps during the campaigns, to fend off boredom. Legend has it that one bout lasted for two days, leading to the death of both fighters from exhaustion. The prize, as decreed by Orhan's brother, Süleyman Pasha, was some trousers made from buffalo hide – known as *kispet*, and still worn today. The two soldiers were buried under a fig tree and several years later, upon returning to the site, springs had developed; the area became known as Kırkpınar (Forty Springs), and a tournament has been held here most years since 1362 (only an estimated 70 years have been missed).

During the Ottoman era, wrestlers studied the art in schools called *tekke*. Much like Japanese sumo wrestling, spiritual development was considered at least as important as the physical aspect of the sport. Today, the rituals remain. The leather *kispet* is worn by all the *pehlivans* and, of course, gallons of olive oil are used to grease themselves up beforehand. Unlike Olympic wrestling (a sport in which Turkey excels, with 28 golds to date), a fight is won when someone manages to carry their opponent or, to put it another way, 'when one umbilicus is exposed to heaven'.

The Kırkpınar tournament is usually held at the end of June in Erdine. See www.kirkpinar.org for details.

Adrenalin

Büyük Beşiktaş Çarşısı 19, off Ortabahçe Caddesi, Beşiktaş (0212 260 6002, www. adrenalin.com.tr). Bus 22E, 28, 28T, 30A, 30M. **Open** 10am-8pm Mon-Sat. **Credit** MC, V.
Adrenalin offers training in outdoor adventure sports, prefaced by classroom sessions on surviving the experience. Activities run the gamut from weekends camping in the Istanbul suburbs to mountain-climbing courses. Trainers all speak English.

Adre-X Extreme Organisation

Necatibey Caddesi, Gayret Han 53/A, Beyoğlu (0212 293 1530, www.adre-x.com). Bus 129T. **Open** 9am-8pm Mon-Fri; noon-6pm Sun. **Credit** V, MC.
This organisation provides outdoors training and adventure-sport weekends. Activities include low- and high-rope systems, navigation and bungee jumping. English is spoken.
Other locations Bağdat Caddesi 200-3, Selamiçeşme (0216 368 7864).

DSM Doğa

Kayışdağı Caddesi 17, second floor, Özplaza, İçerenköy (0216 469 4858, www.dsm.com.tr). Ferry from Eminönü or Karaköy to Kadıköy, then bus 10B. **Open** 9am-6pm Mon-Sat. **Credit** MC, V
An adventure sports centre that organises group activities including rafting, mountain climbing, caving, camping, trekking and paragliding, all under the leadership and guidance of expert trainers. English is spoken.

Gezici YAK

Selçuk Apt, Recep Paşa Caddesi 14/10, off Cumhuriyet Caddesi, Taksim (0212 238 5107, www.geziciyak.com). **Open** 9am-7.30pm Mon-Sat. 11am-4pm Sun. **Credit** MC, V. **Map** p247 P1.
Organises day treks in the local area and river and rafting trips further afield. The company also organises scuba diving trips and training, for which a doctor's certificate is required. English is spoken.

ARTS & ENTERTAINMENT

Çırağan Palace
Hotel Kempinski.

Swimming

The city's few Olympic-size pools are located in university campuses or members-only sports complexes, but you can get a day pass or membership at several hotels. Call in advance, as terms and conditions change frequently.

★ Çırağan Palace Hotel Kempinski

Çırağan Caddesi 32, Beşiktaş (0212 258 3377, www.kempinski.com). Bus DT1, DT2. **Open** 7am-11pm daily. **Rates** Day pass YTL100 Mon-Fri; YTL160 Sat, Sun. 40% discount under-12s; free under-6s. **Credit** AmEx, DC, MC, V.
Right on the banks of the Bosphorus, this 33m-long (108ft) outdoor pool has the most spectacular setting in Istanbul. The indoor pool is a third of the size.

Hilton Istanbul

Cumhuriyet Caddesi, Harbiye (0212 315 6000, www.hilton.com). **Open** *Outdoor pool* 7am-6pm daily. *Indoor pool* 7am-10pm daily. **Rates** YTL60 Mon-Fri; YTL95 Sat, Sun. Half price under-12s; free under-6s. **Credit** AmEx, MC, V. **Map** p247 P1.

INSIDE TRACK WEIGHING GOLD

The failure of Turkey's bids to host the Olympic Games hurt, but as a competing nation they have excelled in two sports: wrestling and weightlifting. Halil Mutlu is Turkey's most famous Olympian, winning three consecutive golds (1996, 2000, 2004) in the 56kg category. He also won five World Championships and broke more than 20 world records. Mutlu's hero and countryman, Naim Süleimanov, also won three Olympic Golds. Most of Turkey's Olympic golds (28) have been won for wrestling.

The outdoor pool is approximately half Olympic size, while the indoor pool is 18m (60ft) long. The price includes use of all the health club facilities. After 3pm, the price of a day pass drops to YTL30 on weekdays and YTL60 on weekends.

Beaches

Although Istanbul is surrounded by water and the municipality has sponsored numerous high-profile clean-up campaigns, swimming within city limits is still a dodgy proposition. The upper Bosphorus, near Sarıyer, is cleaner but subject to treacherous currents.

★ Solar Beach & Party

Eski Turban Yolu 4, Kilyos (0212 201 2139, www.kilyossolarbeach.com).
In addition to jet skiing, bungee jumping and trampolining, Solar Beach hosts rave parties most summer weekends come nightfall. In past years, shuttle buses have picked up revellers from Taksim Square.

FITNESS

Weightlifting and bodybuilding are beloved of Turkish men of all ages and income brackets. Cheaper gyms tend to be dominated by men, but women should find this one hassle-free, because it's expensive enough to keep out the oglers. Most big hotels also have fitness centres.

★ Marmara Gym

The Marmara Hotel, Taksim Square (0212 251 4696, www.themarmarahotels.com). **Open** 7am-9.45pm daily. **Rates** *Day pass* YTL40 gym only, YTL60 all facilities. *Monthly membership* YTL360 gym only, YTL480 all facilities. **Credit** AmEx, MC, V. **Map** p249 P2.
Hi-tech equipment, English-speaking trainers and panoramic views over Taksim Square, which provide a welcome distraction from the treadmill.

Escapes & Excursions

Buyukada. *See p215.*

Escapes & Excursions

Take a cruise along the Bosphorus.

For centuries, the narrow waterway that separates Europe and Asia and snakes through the city's heart was Istanbul's *raison d'etre*. The Bosphorus was essentially the city's main drag, and consequently Istanbul has always presented its best face to its shore. The twisting shoreline is punctuated by imperial palaces, diplomatic hideaways and gorgeous old Ottoman *yalıs* (waterfront mansions), all ageing gracefully. A cruise up the **Bosphorus** is as crucial to any Istanbul experience as a visit to Haghia Sophia or haggling in the Grand Bazaar. At its north end, the Bosphorus widens to meet the **Black Sea**, much of its shoreline sadly scarred by overdevelopment.

To the north-east of the city, the miles of greenery of the **Belgrad Forest** make for an idyllic retreat.

THE BOSPHORUS CRUISE

The standard Bosphorus cruise takes six hours and costs all of YTL25. Ferries depart daily all year round from Eminönü's Boğaz Hattı dock, 100 metres east of the Galata Bridge. Buy your tickets at the window labelled Eminönü-Kavaklar Boğaziçi Özel Gezi Seferleri (Eminönü-Kavaklar Bosphorus Special Tourist Excursions). Cruises depart at 10.30am and 1.30pm, with an extra service at noon from June to September. In summer and at weekends, board the boat at least 30 minutes before departure to get a seat.

From Eminönü, the first stop is Beşiktaş near Dolmabahçe Palace. The ferry then tacks back and forth between the European and Asian shores, stopping at several Bosphorous villages along the way: notably Kanlıca, Yeniköy, Sarıyer, Rumeli Kavağı and Anadolu Kavağı. You can get off wherever you like, but you will have to make your own way onwards or back into town. Most first-timers stay on board until Anadolu Kavağı, where there's enough time for lunch at one of the fish restaurants before reboarding the ferry, which then makes a beeline back to Beşiktaş and Eminönü, with no other stops en route.

From June to September, a Moonlight Trip (YTL20) leaves Eminönü at 7.15pm or Ortaköy at 7.40pm. The ferry arrives at Anadolu Kavagi at 8.50pm, and departs at 10pm, returning to Beşiktaş at 11.05pm and Eminonu at 11.30pm. For further information call 0212 444 44 36 or check www.ido.com.tr and click on Special Bosphorus Trip in the timetable section.

Numerous private operators run shorter boat trips too. These typically only go as far as Rumeli Hisarı, where passengers have an hour for lunch before the boat returns to Eminönü. There are no stops en route. Boats depart from Eminönü roughly every half hour between 10.30am and 6pm (4pm October to April). Touts who roam the wharfs sell tickets for YTL10-YTL15, but it's worth bargaining.

KANLICA

The first major sights – and, indeed, the last if you opt for the shorter cruise – are the twin fortresses of **Rumeli Hisarı** (*see p84*) and **Anadolu Hisarı**, looming on opposite shores of the Bosphorus.

Just before the second great suspension bridge, the 1,096-metre Fatih Mehmet Bridge, a battered, barn-like structure hangs over the water on the Asian side. This is the historic **Amcazade Hüseyin Paşa Yalısı**, Istanbul's oldest waterfront mansion. Built in 1699, its scandalous state of disrepair is nothing new: when French writer and long-time local resident Pierre Loti visited in 1910, he pleaded, 'Of all the *yalıs* on the Bosphorus, you must save the Amcazade Yalı'.

First stop on the standard Bosphorus cruise is **Kanlıca** on the Asian Shore, a lovely village dotted with picturesque mansions and backed by the lush Mihribad Forest Preserve. But Kanlıca's main claim to fame is bacterial: since the 17th century, it has been celebrated for its rich yoghurt; the milk coming from sheep grazing on the hills around nearby Beykoz. A pleasant diversion is a walk up a leafy path to **Khedive's Villa** (Hıdiv Kasrı), a former summer residence of the 19th-century rulers of Egypt. The villa itself is a stately structure built in 1907. It has manicured lawns, a children's play area and an outdoor café, making it ideal for a tranquil morning. The restaurant serves Ottoman and Turkish cuisine – without alcohol. Weekend brunch buffet will set you back YTL23-YTL32. During weekdays it's open from 9am to 11pm for breakfast, lunch or dinner. Dishes are between YTL8 to YTL19.

Kanlıca is linked by regular ferries to Arnavutköy and Bebek on the European shore. On departing Kanlıca, the ferry noses back towards Europe. Shortly after Istinye Bay is the stunning **Ahmet Atıf Paşa Yalı**, a white neo-baroque fantasy of turrets and Ottoman roofs, created by Italian architect Alexandre Villaury for the original proprietor of the Pera Palas hotel (*see p103*).

Further north is **Beykoz**, a larger and livelier town. This working settlement offers a sense of real Turkish life among the wealth of other coastal towns. There are more amenities and shopping options than Kanlıca. Of interest is the house of Ahmed Midhat Efendi (1844-1912), the respected journalist, author and publisher of Tercüman-i Hakikat, the longest running Turkish newspaper. The polymath published more than 250 works that covered subjects such as philosophy, the Turkish identity and papers decrying the Ottoman rule.

YENİKÖY

The ferry then pulls in at **Yeniköy**. As the Ottoman Empire deteriorated in the early 19th century, increasingly desperate rulers used lavish gifts of land as a way of securing the support of foreign embassies in Istanbul. Yeniköy was considered choice real estate, and the waterfront is lined with the greatest concentration of restored Bosphorus mansions, several of which remain the summer residences of the city's consulates.

Just south of the landing is the boxy, white shuttered Sait Halim Paşa, also known as the Pink Lion Mansion because of the two stone lions on the quay. Sait Halim was grand vizier under Sultan Abdül Hamit in the dying days of the empire. The hapless Halim ended up taking much of the rap for the empire's disastrous decision to fight on Germany's side in World War I. Adding fatal injury to insult, he was shot dead by an Armenian extremist soon after the war. North of the landing is another Bosphorus landmark, the **Twin Yalı**, a symmetrical semi-detached, whose art nouveau scrollings mark it out as a work by Raimondo D'Aronco.

As the ferry departs Yeniköy it passes a string of rambling European summer embassies, including a vast pink edifice, partially screened by trees, belonging to Austria. About a mile north, spires and gables mark out the fantastic **Huber Mansion**, another D'Aronco design. The Hubers made a vast fortune flogging Mauser rifles to the Ottoman government in the dying days of the empire. The Hubers were renowned for their lavish parties, earning them regular appearances in the late-19th-century versions of *Hello!* magazine. The Huber Mansion is now the official Istanbul residence of the Turkish president. The forested slopes surrounding both these mansions give an idea of how most of the Bosphorus shoreline looked not so long ago.

Several more summer embassies follow in quick succession. With its distinctive bell tower, Germany's looks rather like a Black Forest town hall. Though dilapidated, the Italian Embassy remains supremely elegant. And the British ambassador's summer retreat is a small cottage set in luxuriant gardens.

SARIYER

The shoreline recedes to accommodate Büyükdere Bay, where the Bosphorus is at its widest (3.5 kilometres, or just under two miles). As the ferry approaches land, you will see a curious, flat-fronted building distinguished by bold yellow-and-white cross-hatching; this houses the **Sadberk Hanım Museum**, stuffed with Ottoman costumes, archaeological and ethnographic artefacts, and old tiles.

The ferry's next port of call is Sarıyer, beside the turreted **Naval Officers' Club**. Built in 1911, it bears the seal of Sultan Mehmet V Reşat. It is now a restaurant and social club for naval officers and their families.

Sarıyer, the largest village on the Upper Bosphorus, is one of Greater Istanbul's most conservative suburbs. As recently as 1995, a local woman was stoned to death here on suspicion of being a prostitute. For the morally unblemished, it is a lovely place to wander (if you disembark here, you can catch bus 25E back to Kabataş). There's a fine old fish market just north of the ferry landing, plus several good seafood restaurants.

On Sular Caddesi *dolmuş* depart for the next waterside village, Rumeli Kavağı. En route they pass the **burial place of Telli Baba**, a mystic Muslim saint. Would-be brides come to pray at his tomb and take away a charmed piece of golden wire, apparently guaranteed to secure them a husband. Newlyweds traditionally return on their wedding day to reattach the wire to the saint's tomb and pay homage to Telli Baba's matchmaking skills. On Saturday and Sunday afternoons, there are usually major traffic jams as convoys of husband-seekers pile up along the narrow road beside the Bosphorus.

RUMELI & ANADOLU KAVAĞI

Rumeli Kavağı is a sleepy little place – no more than a string of houses and restaurants clustered around the ferry landing and the coastal road. From here, the road runs north up the Bosphorus, passing dozens of restaurants set into the cliffs and a few small, sandy private beaches, which usually charge entrance fees of around YTL3-YTL6.

Just before the coastal road ends abruptly at the gates of an army base is Altınkum, the best of the area's beaches, accessible via a narrow footpath between the trees. There is a restaurant serving meze and cold beer. The water is marked off by a line of buoys – stick within this line if you're swimming, as the Bosphorus is swept by strong currents further from the shore.

From Sarıyer, a couple of metres left of IDO harbour, boats depart between 8am and 1pm for Büyük Liman and Menekşe beaches, returning to Sarıyer between 5pm and 7pm. The round trip costs YTL6, including the entrance fee for the beaches. Menekşe beach is conservative: one day a week, it's ladies only.

The last stop for the ferry cruise is **Anadolu Kavağı** on the Asian Shore, which is almost opposite Rumeli Kavağı. Passengers have time to explore the village and eat in one of the many fish restaurants, which cater exclusively to passing tourist trade.

Alternatively, clamber up to Yoros Castle, which looms on the headland north of the village, offering commanding views of the Black Sea. Originally, the site of a temple to Zeus, where ancient Greek sailors would make a sacrifice to ensure safe passage through the straits, the present fortress was built by the Byzantines, occupied by the Genoese in the mid 14th century, until it was seized by the Turks, who fortified the battlements. The castle lay abandoned until it was opened to the public in the 1980s. Descending from the castle, take the steep path across the heath, which leads to a teahouse with half a dozen rickety tables and amazing views.

Khedive's Villa
Hıdiv Kasrı
Çubuklu Yolu 32, Kanlıca (0216 413 9253, www.beltur.com.tr). **Open** 9am-10pm daily. **Admission** free.

Sadberk Hanım Museum
Sadberk Hanım Müzesi
Piyasa Caddesi 27-29, Büyükdere (0212 242 3813, www.sadberkhanimmuzesi.org.tr). **Open** 10am-5pm Mon, Tue, Thu-Sun. **Admission** YTL5. **No credit cards**.

BELGRAD FOREST

Stretching over the hills and valleys north-east of the city, Belgrad Forest is popular with summer picnickers, cyclists and joggers. All leafy glades and oak, pine, plane and beech trees, the place has a distinctly Balkan feel. It is actually named after the Serbian residents entrusted by Süleyman the Magnificent with guarding the forest reservoirs that served as the city's water supply under the Byzantines and Ottomans. Even today, you'll come across the remains of the reservoirs and aqueducts. The Serbs were booted out in the 1890s by the paranoid sultan Abdülhamit II, who suspected they were poisoning the water.

In centuries past, the wealthy European residents of Istanbul would retreat to Belgrad Village in summer to escape the heat and bouts of pestilence. In 1771, Lady Mary Wortley Montagu described the village as an Arcadian idyll, whose inhabitants would meet every night 'to sing and dance, the beauty and dress of the women exactly resembling the ancient nymphs'. All that's left of Belgrad village are a few bumps in the forest floor, hidden near one of the main picnic areas by Büyük Bend reservoir, one of the oldest parts of the Byzantine water system.

Following Mahmut II's purge of the Janissary corps in 1826, those who escaped the massacre fled into the forest, where they took up traditional woodland pursuits such as shooting the sultan's deer and ambushing local traders. The sultan's radical response was to set the whole forest on fire.

Also worth visiting is the *Long Aqueduct*, on the road to Kısırmandıra, another work by Mimar Sinan, built for Süleyman the Magnificent in 1563. The stream it crosses is the Kağıthane Suyu, which eventually flows into the Golden Horn.

Getting there

From Kabataş take the 25E bus (or the 40 from Taksim) to Büyükdere. Take a *dolmuş* for Bahçeköy, on the east side of the forest, a one-mile (1.5 kilometre) walk to Büyük Bend.

Bosphorus cruise.

Exploring the Princes' Islands

Dissidents, minorities and horse-drawn carriages – island life, Istanbul style.

Set in the Marmara Sea off Istanbul's Asian Shore, the Princes' Islands have come a long way since they were used as a place of exile and imprisonment. In the 19th century, they were 'discovered' as a luxury location for the summer houses and pleasure palaces of Istanbul's mainly non-Muslim elite. Today, they are some of the last places to offer a glimpse of the old ethnic mix of Istanbul. Greeks, Armenians and Jews still rub shoulders with Turks in the local squares in a way that's no longer the case in the city itself.

Almost all the houses are built of wood, fretted and carved into lacy designs and set in well-tended gardens. The streets are completely car-free and echo with the clip-clop of horse-drawn carriages. The overall effect is of a 19th-century time capsule.

There are nine islands in total, of which four can be visited. Furthest from European Istanbul (20 kilometres, or 12 miles) is **Büyükada**, the largest and most popular island. It has traditionally been home to a large Jewish population. **Kınalıada** is predominantly Armenian, **Burgazada** is Greek and **Heybeliada** is mostly Turkish.

KINALIADA

Kınalıada, the smallest of the islands and the closest to Istanbul, is the least green. Its name (from *kınalı*, Turkish for 'dyed with henna') comes from the reddish tinge of the shoreline cliffs, although the absence of greenery today is down to the fact that the island is almost completely scabbed over by modern housing.

Sights in the town include a fine modernist mosque, the **Kınalıada Camii**, erected in 1964, and an Armenian church, the **Surp Krikor Lusavoria**, on Narciciyi Sokak, a ten-minute walk inland from the ferry landing. En route, pass by the grilled sheep's head vendors on **Akasya Caddesi**, which is also the place to hire bicycles.

Where to stay & eat

There is no accommodation on Kınalıada. The Greek taverna, **Çınaraltı Plaka** (6 Çınaraltı Köşk Sokak, 0216 381 5407) in Çınaraltı Meydanı, or square, has been going for 125 years. In summer, live Greek and Armenian music is thrown in.

BURGAZADA

Burgazada is best known for its connections with Turkish short-story writer Sait Faik (1906-54), who lived on the island from 1939 until his death. He was a specialist in brief vignettes of the lives of his neighbours. Gay, or at least bisexual, Faik probably enjoyed the freedom from the censorious mores of the city that island life could offer. His former home is now the modest and free **Sait Faik Museum** (15 Burgaz Çayırı Sokak, 0216 381 2132), which includes a musty collection of his works and his death mask. The local landmark is the Greek Orthodox **Church of St John the Baptist**.

Where to stay & eat

The **Mehtap 45 Butik Otel** (45 Mehtap Caddesi, 0216 381 2660, doubles $85-$120) is set on top of a peaceful hill, but still close to town. The area around the ferry landing is laden with fish restaurants, of which the Greek-owned **Barba Meyhane** (6B Yalı Caddesi, 0216 381 2404, meal with drinks YTL35-YTL45) has live Greek music on Fridays and Saturdays.

HEYBELIADA

The name means 'saddlebag island' – a good description of how Heybeliada looks, with a low landmass between twin summits. It's a summer favourite with picnickers, although much of the island is occupied by the military.

The best way of getting around is in a horse-drawn carriage, picked up on Ayyıldız Caddesi, parallel to the seafront. An island tour takes 45 minutes and costs YTL15; a trip to the monastery YTL15 (you can't get in, but the views are good).

Where to stay & eat

The **Merit Halki Palace** (94 Refah Şehitleri Caddesi, 0216 351 0025, www.halkipalace hotel.com, doubles YTL100-YTL125) is set in a 19th-century Ottoman mansion. In summer its swimming pool is open to non-residents (YTL30 weekdays, YTL45 weekends). The waterfront is brimming with restaurants. For value for money, hit **Gökşins Ambrosia** (30B Ayyıldız Caddesi, 0216 351 1388), for fish and meze.

BUYUKADA

The largest Prince's island is suitably named: *büyük* means 'big', while *ada* is the word for 'island'. From 1929 to 1933, Büyükada was the home of Leon Trotsky, who bashed out his *History of the Russian Revolution* in exile at the **Izzet Paşa Köskü**, a restored wooden mansion at 55 Çankaya Caddesi. The island was probably the safest place for him, given that at the time Istanbul was also home to some 34,000 White Russians, living in exile after a crushing defeat by Trotsky's Red Army.

The island is now a hugely popular but exclusive summer resort – a kind of Turkish take on the Hamptons. For the casual visitor, it's a gorgeous place for a long walk along leafy lanes scented heavily with blossom. The main settlement and ferry landing are on the northern tip of the island. East is a corral of horse-drawn carriages. Drivers offer big (YTL40) or small (YTL35) tours of the island, both of which end up at the foot of the hill, where you can climb up a cobbled path to **St George's Monastery** – or hire a donkey for YTL4. As you climb the steep slope up to the monastery, note the hundreds of pieces of cloth tied to the branches of the trees: each represents a prayer, tied by the faithful of all religions, mostly women desperate for a child.

At the top are fine views and an excellent restaurant. The monastery's chapel is usually open to visitors, with icons depicting the old dragon-slayer, plus an assortment of saintly relics. Up from the harbour on Çankaya Caddesi stands the Ottoman-era Büyükada Kültürevi Cultural Centre, with a garden restaurant.

Where to stay & eat

The **Hotel Princess** (1 Iskele Caddesi, 0216 382 1628/2930, www.buyukada princess.com, doubles $90-$110) is right by the clock tower square. A little further west on the same street is the **Splendid Palas** (23 Nisan Caddesi 53, 0216 382 6950, www.splendidhotel.net, doubles from $90, closed Nov-Apr). To sample authentic island life, try the **Kıyı Restaurant** (2 Çiçekliyalı Sokak, 0216 382 5606), a run-down meyhane that plays Greek music and is famous for its meze. A meal costs around YTL25-YTL30.

GETTING THERE

Regular ferries to the islands depart from Eminönü's Adalar Iskele, which is the dock nearest Sirkeci railway station. They stop at each of the islands in turn, taking an hour and a half to reach Büyükada (50 minutes to Kınalıada). The fare is YTL2. Departure times from Eminönü change with the season, but in summer there are at least a dozen sailings a day from 9.20am onwards. For schedules and information, call 0212 444 4436 or visit www.ido.com.tr. There is also a less frequent and more expensive fast catamaran service from Eminönü, but the time saved is not significant – and anyhow, the slow sail is a pleasure in itself.

Black Sea coast.

THE BLACK SEA COAST

North of the twin landmarks of Rumeli
Kavağı and Anadolu Kavağı, the mouth of
the Bosphorus widens to meet the **Black Sea**
(Karadeniz). Much of the coast is an off-limits
military zone, but there are small enclaves of
civilian life. On the European side, there's the
fishing port of **Rumeli Feneri** and **Kilyos**,
one of Istanbul's most popular beach resorts,
mirrored on the Asian side by the resort of **Şile**.

RUMELI FENERI

Rumeli Feneri means 'European Lighthouse'.
Perched atop sheer cliffs overlooking the
entrance to the Bosphorus, the lighthouse was
built by the British during the Crimean War.
But the namesake village is most famous for
the ancient Symplegades or 'clashing rocks'
– two large humps at the end of the L-shaped
harbour. In ancient mythology, these rocks
were regarded as living creatures that would
dash out to crash into passing boats. One such
vessel was Jason's *Argo*, which managed to
make it through the straits to the Black Sea,
thanks to a neat trick with a pigeon and a
helping hand from the goddess Athena.

These days, Rumeli Feneri is a working
fishing village – a laid-back Sunday lunch venue
for the few Istanbullus who have discovered it.
On the Black Sea side of town is an Ottoman fort,
once the area's main customs clearing house.
Also of archaeological interest is the stone altar
on top of the Symplegade closest to shore, which

was used to make sacrifices to the sea god,
Poseidon, and to light fires to warn passing
ships. You can scale the rocks as long as you've
got walking shoes and a head for heights.

One of the most exclusive spots on Istanbul's
Black Sea coast, the **Golden Beach Club** at
Rumeli Feneri, boasts an attractive beach and
endless facilities including a restaurant, beach
bar, beach volleyball, cycling tracks, climbing
wall, mini golf, paintball, and sea-trampoline. If
you make a reservation one day in advance, you
can be picked up from Sarıyer.

Golden Beach Club
*Marmaracık Bay, Rumeli Feneri (0212 325 5583,
www.goldenbeachclub.net).* **Admission** YTL15
Mon-Fri; YTL25 Sat, Sun, incl lounger & umbrella.

KILYOS AND DEMIRCIKOY

Kilyos's long sandy beaches – **Nonstop Beach**
(0212 201 2305, www.nonstopbeach.com,
admission YTL10, YTL15 with lounger &
umbrella) and **Solar Beach** (0212 201 2139,
admission YTL15, inlcuding lounger &
umbrella) – have been badly scarred by overdevelopment. Tragically, this formula is being
repeated all along the Black Sea coast.

Both these beaches become party venues
during the summer nights, when raves,
concerts, and other special events draw crowd.
Solar beach is the more upmarket of the two,
with lifeguards and a food court.

People's Beach (admission YTL5) is the
most downmarket of Kilyos's options. The cost
of admission includes use of the shower and a
locker, but you have to bring your own lounger
and umbrella. **Dalia Beach** (0212 204 0368,
www.clubdalia.com, admission YTL20, YL25
weekends, including lounger & umbrella) at
Demirciköy, two kilometres from Kilyos, is
much quieter and has a small fish restaurant.
Access is by taxi (YTL3-YTL5); or you can
take the 151 bus from Sarıyer.

Getting there

Kilyos is ten miles (15 km) north of Sarıyer,
where regular *dolmuş* depart from Sular
Caddesi (the *dolmuş* rank is just before you
arrive at Sarıyer bus terminal, opposite the old
municipality building). The journey takes half
an hour and costs YTL1.50. The last *dolmuş*
back to Sarıyer from Kilyos leaves at about
8pm. Rumeli Feneri can be reached by bus or
taxi (around YTL15) from Sarıyer.

Buses 150 (Rumeli Feneri), 151 (Kilyos/
Demirciköy) and 152 (Kısırkaya) depart from
Sarıyer every 15 minutes during summer
weekends and every 20 minutes on weekdays.
In winter, buses depart every 45 minutes, with
the last bus returning at around 10pm.

Directory

Getting Around

ARRIVING & LEAVING

By air

Istanbul's international **Atatürk Airport** is around 25km (15 miles) west of the city centre in Yeşilköy. The compact international terminal (Dış Hatlar) has several shops, restaurants, bars, a massage parlour, post office, 24-hour banking, exchange bureaux, car hire, a tourist office and hotel reservation desk. From landing to clearing customs usually takes 20 minutes. Security checks can delay check-in, so arrive at least 90 minutes before your flight.

A second international airport, **Sabiha Gökçen**, in Kurtköy on the Asian side was intended to handle three million travellers a year, and is finally beginning to reach its potential. Easyjet and many charter flights arrive there. It is 35km (22 miles) from the city centre, but improved transport means it's not the hassle it once was.

Atatürk International Airport
Atatürk Hava Limanı Yolu
24-hr English flight info 0212 465
3000, www.ataturkairport.com.
Sabiha Gökçen Airport
Kurtköy
0212 585 500 3000, English flight
info at www.sgairport.com.

There are three options for getting from the airport to the city centre: bus, light rail/underground or taxi. The choice depends on where you're staying and how much time you've got.

The easiest option is with Havaş (0212 444 0487, www.havas.net). Havaş operates the reliable **express airport bus service** from both airports, which leaves for four different destinations from a signposted stop outside the arrivals hall. The only one of use to visitors is the Taksim service – fine if you're staying in Beyoğlu or Taksim – which starts at 4am then half-hourly until 11.30pm (4am-midnight to Sabiha Gökçen), stopping en route at the Bakırköy Sea Bus Terminal, Aksaray and Tepebaşı (just short of Taksim). The fare is YTL10 (YTL13 from Sabiha Gökçen), collected by a conductor on board the bus.

The **underground**, or 'light metro', takes you to Aksaray in

half an hour and costs just YTL1.50; from here, you can get a bus to Taksim or a tram to Sultanahmet. Services run 6.15am-midnight Mon-Sat, 6.30am-midnight Sun.

Taxis can be taken from the rank outside the arrivals hall. Fares are metered. Journeys to the centre of Sultanahmet should be around YTL18-YTL20 (half as much again at night). The ride takes about 20 minutes but can stretch to 45 minutes if the traffic's bad. To Taksim, it costs around YTL23 and takes anywhere between 20-50 minutes. Taxis from Sabiha Gökçen will be around half as much again.

By rail

The days of the Orient Express are long gone. Rail travel from Europe to Istanbul is now the preserve of backpackers and the lower-income end of Turkey's Balkan diaspora.

The only direct route to Istanbul from Greece is from Thessaloniki, with a daily 7.25am departure taking around 15 hours to cover the 850km (510 miles). The other direct service from Europe is the daily Bosphorus Express, departing Bucharest at 2.05pm and pulling into Istanbul at 8.27am the following morning.

Trains from Europe arrive at Sirkeci Station (*gar*), beside the Golden Horn in Eminönü. From here, it's a short walk or tram ride up the hill to **Sultanahmet**. A taxi to Taksim costs YTL5-YTL6.

Trains from destinations to the south and east terminate at **Haydarpaşa Station** on the Asian shore. International arrivals include the Trans-Asya, which departs from Tehran every Thursday at 8.15pm and limps into Istanbul some 69 hours later.

Sirkeci and Haydarpaşa stations are connected by ferries, though there is also a tunnel link on the drawing board. Information lines serve Sirkeci (0212 527 0051) and Haydarpaşa (0216 348 8020 ext 336) between 7am-midnight daily, but are in Turkish only. Timetables for international and national services are posted on the state railway (TCDD) website (www.tcdd. gov.tr); the English-language version of the site is refreshingly good.

Sirkeci Station
Istasyon Caddesi, Eminönü
(0212 520 6575 ext 417, for
reservations 6am-6pm daily).
Haydarpaşa Station
Haydarpaşa Istasyon Caddesi,
Kadıköy (0216 336 0475, for
reservations 6am-6pm daily).

By road

Turkish coach companies (such as Ulusoy and Varan) run regular services from many European cities. Be prepared for lengthy waits at border crossings – particularly with Bulgaria, where it can take up to three hours to clear customs.

Travellers arriving by coach disembark at the international and inter-city bus terminal (*otogar*) in Esenler, about ten kilometres (six miles) from the city centre. There are courtesy minibuses to Taksim and Sultanahmet. The underground 'light metro' connects the terminal to Aksaray, where you can trudge to the Taksim bus stop across the road, or take a tram to Sultanahmet.

Esenler bus terminal
Uluslararası Istanbul Otogarı
Büyük Istanbul Otogarı,
Bayrampaşa (0212 658 0505,
www.otogaristanbul.com).
Open 24hrs daily.
Ulusoy
İnönü Caddesi 59, Gümüşsuyu
(0212 244 6375/International
journeys 0212 658 3006,
www.ulusoy.com.tr). **Open** 24hrs
daily. **Credit** AmEx, MC, V.
Twice-weekly buses to and from
Greece (Thessaloniki, 12hrs, YTL88;
Athens, 21hrs), Germany (Münich,
48hrs; Frankfurt, 55hrs) and Italy
(Ancona via Munich). Bookings can
be made through the website.
Varan
İnönü Caddesi 29/A, Gümüşsuyu
(0212 444 8999, www.varan.
com.tr). **Open** 24hrs daily.
Credit MC, V.
Weekly buses to and from Austria
(Vienna, 33hrs, Salzburg, 37hrs,
Linz, 39hrs, YTL240-255); Germany
(Berlin, YTL295).

PUBLIC TRANSPORT

Public transport is cheap and improving all the time, thanks to a municipal campaign to defeat the city's chronic traffic problem. The result is reinforcement to the entire transport infrastructure: extensions to metro and tram lines, new bypasses and underpasses, new sea bus routes and funiculars are all under way or completed, and a trans-Bosphorus tunnel (Marmaray) is now under construction. But for the time being, Istanbul endures gridlock along major arteries.

Happily, the two areas where visitors are likely to spend most time – Beyoğlu and Sultanahmet – are easily explored on foot. However, buses are useful for heading up the Bosphorus coast to Ortaköy, Arnavutköy, Bebek and beyond, while trips to the districts of Üsküdar and Kadıköy on the Asian shore are best undertaken by ferry or sea bus. The easiest way to get to shopping and business districts in Nişantaşı, Teşvikye, Etiler and Levent is via the new metro line that runs north from Taksim.

The informative website of the IETT (www.iett.gov.tr), the local transport authority, has an excellent English version that includes maps and timetables.

Fares & tickets

Akbil, the 'smart card', is an electronic travel pass that can be used on all public transport except *dolmuş* and minibuses. You get a ten per cent discount on fares. Akbils are available for a small refundable deposit (YTL6) from booths at all main bus, sea bus and metro stations. To use it, firmly press the circular metal stud into the socket on the orange machine located next to the driver on buses, or to the left of turnstiles at all metro, light rail, tram and ferry stations. Recharge at Akbil machines located at bus, metro and tram stations, ferry terminals or Akbil booths.

Particularly useful for visitors is the *mavi* (blue) travel pass valid for a day, a week, 15 days or a month.

Metro, trams & Tünel

The new metro and tram systems provide a comfortable and efficient alternative to clogged roads and crowded buses. However, coverage currently remains scant. At present, the metro runs from Şişhane north to Maslak, stopping at Taksim, Osmanbey, Şişli, Gayrettepe, Levent and 4. Levent. Extensions

will take the line south of Şişhane to the sea bus jetty at Yenikapı.

Another option is the 'light metro', which connects Aksaray (west of the Grand Bazaar) to the Esenler bus terminal and on to the airport.

The city's only modern tram runs from Zeytinburnu via Aksaray, Sultanahmet, Eminönü by the Galata Bridge and six more stops including Karaköy and Kabataş; the ferry and sea bus terminal.

This is a useful service for visitors, linking the Grand Bazaar, Haghia Sophia, Sultanahmet, Topkapı, the Egyptian Bazaar and the Golden Horn. You can also use the tram to visit the city walls. Buy tokens in advance from kiosks at tram stops or from nearby shops – the attendant will point you in the right direction) and feed them into the automatic barriers outside the platform. A single trip on the tram costs YTL1.50 irrespective of your destination. The service runs from around 6am-midnight.

A funicular connects Kabataş to Taksim Square, (connecting at the metro).

A 125-year-old funicular, known as the *tünel*, ascends from Karaköy to Tünel Square at the southern end of Istiklal Caddesi. It's a very short run, but saves a tiring climb up (or down) the sheer slope. The service runs 7am-10pm Mon-Sat and 7.30am-10pm Sun and rests around YTL1. At Tünel, it connects with a century-old tram that shuttles up mile-and-a-half-long Istiklal Caddesi to Taksim Square and back. Akbil can be used for either, but not regular bus tickets. You need to buy a token for the funicular at the entrance, and a ticket for the tram from Tünel Square funicular station or from a vendor in Taksim Square. Tickets for either the tram or funicular cost YTL1.

Buses

Most city buses (*belediye otobüsü*) are operated by the municipality, but there are also private versions (*halk otobüsü*). Municipal buses are red and white or green; all have IETT written on the front. Private ones are pale blue and green, and usually more modern.

Buy tickets (*bilet*) for municipal buses before boarding (they won't take money on the bus). On private buses, pay a conductor seated in the doorway (they will begrudgingly accept coins, but no large bills). Both IETT and private buses accept Akbil (*see above*) and charge the same fare (YTL1.50). Tickets

for municipal buses are sold from booths at main stops and stations, or newsstands, nearby stalls and itinerant street vendors for a 30 per cent premium.

Newer buses have electronic signboards with route information. Bus stops also have route maps. Still, the sheer number of routes and the interminable traffic and roadworks can make bus travel tricky – consider buses with the same number but different proceeding letter as different routes. Bus services run from 6am to 11pm. Kabataş and Taksim are the two main bus terminals north of the Golden Horn. These are useful bus routes:

Taksim – Topkapı 83
Taksim – Bahçeşehir 76E, 76D
Taksim – Sultanahmet T4
Taksim – Ortaköy DT1, DT2
Taksim – Edirnekapı 87
Taksim – Kadıköy 110
Taksim – Aksaray (metro) 83MT
Taksim – Sarıyer 25T, 40
Taksim – Otogar 83O
Otogar – Eminönü 91O
Otogar – Beşiktaş 28O
Kabataş – Beşiktaş 22E
Kabataş – Reşitpaşa 22RE, 58A
Kabataş – Sarıyer 25T
Topkapı – Beşiktaş 28T
Topkapı – Sarıyer 341T
Topkapı – Kadıköy 127
Sarıyer – Kilyos 151
Sarıyer – Beşiktaş 40B
Aksaray – Airport light metro
Edirnekapı – Beşiktaş 28

Dolmuş & minibuses

A *dolmuş* (which means 'full') is basically a shared taxi that sets off once every seat is taken. *Dolmuş* run fixed routes (starting points and final destinations are displayed in the front window) but with no set stops. Passengers flag the driver down to get on (if there's room) and holler out to be let off (*Inecek var!*). For local journeys, there's one fixed fare (usually YTL1.50). Ask a fellow passenger how much it is or just watch what everyone else is paying. *Dolmuş* run later than buses, often as late as 2am.

Minibuses are more crowded than *dolmuş*, and less frequent. Minibus fares are lower, but chances are you'll make your journey standing while being blasted by tinny Turkish pop. Pay and get on/off as you would a *dolmuş*. The main routes are from Beşiktaş to the upper Bosphorus districts.

DIRECTORY

Water transport

Boats and ships of all sizes shuttle between the European and Asian shores, operating to summer (mid June-mid Sept) and winter timetables. Timetables are available from ferry terminals; times are also posted online. The main services run between Eminönü, Karaköy, Kabataş and Beşiktaş on the European side, and Üsküdar and Kadıköy on the Asian shore. Departures are every 15 minutes or so.

There are also regular services running up the Golden Horn to Eyüp from Üsküdar via Eminönü. Less frequent commuter services criss-cross the Bosphorus, starting from Eminönü and calling at Haydarpaşa, Ortaköy, Arnavutköy, Bebek, Kandilli and beyond.

Ferries also depart from Eminönü and Kabataş to the Princes' Islands. The popular Bosphorus tour departs from Eminönü three times daily – *see p210*.

The modern catamarans (called *deniz otobüsleri* or 'sea buses') are faster but more expensive and generally restricted to commuter hours. You can pick up timetables from the ferry terminals or check online (*see below*).

Turkish Maritime Organisation
Türkiye Denizcilik İşletmeleri Şehir Hatları İşletmesi AŞ
Rıhtım Caddesi 4, Karaköy (0212 251 5000, www.tdi.com.tr).

Istanbul Fast Ferry
Istanbul Deniz Otobüsleri AŞ
Kennedy Caddesi, Sahil Yolu, Hızlı Feribot İskelesi, Yenikapı (0212 444 4436, www.ido.com.tr).

TAXIS

You won't have a problem finding a taxi, day or night. Licensed taxis are bright yellow, with a roof-mounted *taksi* sign. They're all metered, and relatively cheap by European standards. If the meter isn't running, get out.

During the day, the meter displays the word *gündüz* (day rate); the clock should start with YTL2.50. From midnight to 6am the *gece* (night) rate kicks in, adding 50 per cent to the fare. The day rate is YTL1.40 per kilometre. A trip between Sultanahmet and Taksim Square costs YTL6-YTL7. There's no room for haggling and no need to tip. Cabbies are not necessarily streetwise. It's not unusual for your driver to ask you, other drivers or passers-by the way. If you cross the Bosphorus bridges, the toll (YTL4) will be added to the fare.

DRIVING

Driving is not recommended. Heavy congestion doesn't stop speeding, although the limit is 50kmh (30mph), rising to 120kmh (75mph) on motorways. Seat belts are the law, but observance of regulations is laughable.

If you take your own car to Turkey, prepare to be entangled in red tape. Drivers must provide registration documents and a valid international driving licence at point of entry. Cars, minibuses, caravans, and motorbikes can be taken into Turkey for up to six months without a *carnet de passage* or *triptyque*. Your vehicle is registered in your passport and you're issued a certificate that should be carried at all times along with your driving licence and passport. If you stay in Turkey for more than six months, you must leave and re-enter the country, or apply to the Turkish Touring & Automobile Association for a *triptyque*. You won't be allowed to visit another country without taking your vehicle, unless you cancel the registration at the local customs office. Drivers from Europe also need a Green Card, which is available from your insurance company.

A rarely enforced law requires all cars to be equipped with a fire extinguisher, first-aid kit and two triangles.

Turkish Touring & Automobile Association
Türkiye Turing ve Otomobil Kurumu
1 Sanayi Sitesi Yanı, Seyrantepe, 4.Levent (0212 282 8140, www.turing.org.tr).
Turkey's equivalent of the AA.

Breakdown services

Gökşenler
Atatürk Oto Sarayı Sitesi 2, Kısım. Gökşenler Plaza 213, Maslak (0212 276 3640). **Open** 8.30am-6.30pm Mon-Fri; 8.30am-3.30pm Sun. **Credit** MC, V.
24-hour emergency service.

Istanbul Traffic Foundation
0212 289 9800.
24-hour towing services.

Car hire

Rental rates generally include VAT, insurance with third-party liability, and unlimited mileage, but are still relatively high. The rates below include VAT and insurance.

Avis
Abdülhakhamit Caddesi 72/A, off Cumhuriyet Caddesi, Taksim (0212 444 2847, www.avis.com.tr). **Open** 9am-7pm daily. **Rates** YTL105-YTL195 per day. **Credit** AmEx, DC, MC, V.
Other locations Atatürk Airport (0212 465 3455/56).

Budget
Cumhuriyet Caddesi 19, Taksim (0212 444 4722, www.budget. com.tr). **Open** 8.30am-7pm daily. **Rates** YTL60-YTL105/day. **Credit** AmEx, MC, V.
Other locations Atatürk Airport (0212 465 5807).

Europcar
Topçu Caddesi 1/A, off Cumhuriyet Caddesi, Taksim (0212 254 7710, www.europcar.com.tr). **Open** 8.30am-7pm daily. **Rates** YTL95-YTL240/day. **Credit** AmEx, DC, MC, V.
Other locations Atatürk Airport (0212 465 3695).

Parking

Street parking is difficult and not always legal, in which case you're liable to get towed. Use the plentiful car parks; you may have to leave the keys so that cars can be shuffled.

CYCLING

Terrrible traffic, steep hills, slippery cobbles, and countless potholes make Istanbul very challenging for cyclists. However, the wide road alongside the Bosphorus north of Ortaköy is great for biking, with lovely views and a sea breeze. A hired bike is ideal for getting around the Princes' Islands where cars are banned.

WALKING

The tourist hubs of Sultanahmet, the Bazaar Quarter and Beyoğlu are all perfect for exploring on foot (and Beyoğlu's main drag, Istiklal Caddesi, is pedestrianised). There are very few main roads, while the narrow, sloping backstreets are better suited to pedestrians than cars. Pay attention when crossing roads, as drivers often jump lights.

GUIDED TOURS

All hotels will be able to organise guided tours. Istanbul Walk (www.istanbulwalks.net) is a highly regarded, independent tour organiser.

Resources A-Z

ADDRESSES

When writing an address, the house number comes after the street name, with a slash separating the flat number. If it's on a side street (*sokak*), the custom is to include the nearest main street or avenue (*caddesi*). This main street is usually written first. So the address of Mehmet Aksoy, who lives in Flat 7 at 14 Matrar Sokak, off Sıraseviler Street, in the district of Cihangir, will be written like this:

Mehmet Aksoy
Sıraseviler Caddesi
Matar Sokak 14/7
Cirhangir
Istanbul

ATTITUDE & ETIQUETTE

Istanbullus are generally polite, open and interested in foreigners. It's a laid-back city, so don't be surprised if a meeting starts late or food takes a while to turn up. The relaxed vibe extends even to high-end restaurants. Diners will generally look smart, but jackets and ties aren't necessary.

BUSINESS SERVICES

Although Istanbul is alive with opportunity, the city is also fraught with difficulties for business. Of the many foreign companies that have successfully entered the Turkish market, few have done so alone. Foreign concerns have either bought controlling interests in local businesses, or work with Turkish partners. Corruption and interminable bureaucracy make it essential to have an efficient local representative, preferably with plenty of *torpil* ('influence').

Turkish employees work long hours and take few holidays, but seem to have inherited their administrative methods from the Byzantines. Things are slowly changing, but official paperwork still takes forever to complete, while the vocabulary of the average civil servant more often than not seems to consist entirely of negatives. Most foreign companies farm out tasks such as getting work permits and residence permits to local lawyers or accountants. Dealings with private-sector business are less fraught, and the AKP government has been trying to ease red tape to encourage more foreign investment.

Conventions & conferences

Istanbul Convention Bureau
Halaskargazi Caddesi 143/5, Şişli (0212 373 0000, www.icvb.org). Help with arranging a conference.
Istanbul Convention & Exhibition Centre
Lutfi Kirdar Uluslararasi Kongre ve Sergi Sarayi (0212 373 1100, www.icec.org). Large convention centre near Taksim.

Courier & shippers

DHL
Yalçın Koreş Caddesi 20, Güneşli (0212 478 1225, www.dhl.com.tr). **Open** 9am-6pm Mon-Sat. International service only. Customer services 24 hours daily.
UPS
Mevlana Caddesi 85, Zeytinburnu (0212 413 2222, www.ups.com.tr). **Open** 8.30am-7.45pm Mon-Fri; 8.30am-5pm Sat. International and national deliveries.

Federal Express
Fabrikalar Caddesi Tasoca 35 Yolu 19 Mahmutbey (0212 444 0606, www.fedex.com.tr). **Open** 8am-11pm Mon-Fri; 8am-8pm Sat. International service only.

Office services

Deloitte & Touche
Dereboyu Sokak 24, Sun Plaza, floors 23-24, Maslak (0212 366 6000, www.deloitte.com).
PricewaterhouseCoopers
Ninth floor, B Blok, BJK Plaza, Süleyman Seba Caddesi 48, Akaretler, Beşiktaş (0212 326 6060, www.pwc.com/tr).
IBS
Agahamami Caddesi, Aga Han 17/6, Cihangir (0212 252 2460, www.ibsresearch.com). **Open** 9am-6pm Mon-Fri.
English-owned and run. It produces the comprehensive, indispensable guide *Doing Business in Turkey*.
Wordsmith
Refik Saydam Caddesi, Akarca Sokak 39, kat 5, Beyoğlu (0212 237 1979, www.wordsmith.com.tr).
Open 9am-6pm Mon-Fri. Advertising, promotional films and translation.

Useful organisations

Foreign Economic Relations Board
Dış Ekonomik İlişkiler Kurulu *Ekonomik İlişkiler Kurulu TOBB Plaza Talatpaťa Cad. No:3 Kat:5 Gültepe Levent (0212 339 50 00).* **Open** 9am-6pm Mon-Fri. **Map** p248 N3.
Organises joint business councils between Turkey and 56 countries worldwide. Also has a small library and resource centre.

TUGEV Istanbul Convention & Visitors Bureau

Istanbul Kongre ve Ziyaretçi Bürosu

Bürosu Halaskargazi Caddesi 143/5, Şişli (0212 243 0000, istanbul@icvb.org). **Open** 9am-5.30pm Mon-Fri.
Provides information and services related to conventions and meetings in Istanbul.

CUSTOMS

Foreign visitors can import up to one 100cc (or two 75cc) bottle(s) of alcohol (including wine), 200 cigarettes, 50 cigarillos and ten cigars. You may be asked to register electronic equipment to ensure it leaves Turkey with you. You may need proof of purchase for antiques and a carpet. If an item is more than 100 years old there is some red tape which the dealer should help with. For more details, visit www.gumruk.gov.tr or call 0212 465 5244/45.

DISABLED ACCESS

Hilly Istanbul is tough on anyone with a mobility problem. Roads and pavements are narrow, bumpy, and often cobbled, kerbs are high, and stairs ubiquitous. However, public transport is more accessible than before: the new metro has elevators, the light railway and trams are accessible; and some 450 'low-riding' Mercedes buses have been provided to facilitate disabled access. Apart from a handful of top hotels, few buildings make any provisions for the disabled, although Mayor Kadir Topbaş has put this issue high on his agenda.

DRUGS

Turkey is a major transit point for heroin smugglers. The use of marijuana, cocaine and ecstasy is also on the rise. Enforcement is uneven, but heavy-handed; police conduct random sweeps of bars and nightclubs. You may be body-searched and checked for needle tracks. Sentencing for drug offences is mild by American standards, but harsh compared to Europe. Carry ID at all times, especially if you're out on the town.

ELECTRICITY

Electricity in Turkey runs on 220 volts. Plugs have two round pins. Adaptors for UK appliances can be found in hardware shops and on

street stalls, but it's still best to bring one from home. Transformers are required for US 110-volt appliances. There are frequent, brief power cuts (more often in winter), so it's not a bad idea to bring a torch.

EMBASSIES & CONSULATES

All foreign embassies are located in Ankara, but many countries also have a consulate in Istanbul.

Australian Consulate
Askerocağı Caddesi 15, Süzer Plaza 16nd Floor, Şişli (0212 243 1333-36, www.dfat.gov.au). **Open** 8.30am-12.30pm, 1.30-5pm Mon-Fri.

Canadian Consulate
Istiklal Caddesi 189/5, Beyoğlu (0212 251 9838). **Open** 9.30am-12.30pm, 1.30-5.30pm Mon-Thur; 9.30am-12.30pm Fri. **Map** p248 M4.

Republic of Ireland Honorary Consulate
Merter İş Merkezi 417, General Ali Rıza Gürcan Caddesi, Merter (0212 482 1862, www.irlconsulist.com). **Open** 9am-5pm Mon-Fri.

New Zealand Honorary Consulate
İnönü Caddesi 48/3, Gümüşsuyu, Taksim (0212 244 0272). **Open** 9am-7pm Mon-Fri. **Map** p247 P2.

UK Consulate
Meşrutiyet Caddesi 34, Tepebaşı, Beyoğlu (0212 334 6400, www.fco.gov.uk). **Open** 8.30am-4.45pm Mon-Fri. **Map** p248 M3.

US Consulate
Kaplıcalar Mevkii Sokak 2, Istinye Mahallesi, Istinye (0212 335 9000, 340 4444 visas, http://istanbul. usconsulate.gov). **Open** 8am-4.30pm Mon-Fri.

EMERGENCIES

For police, *see p225.* For hospitals and health, *see right.*
Police 155
Fire 110
Ambulance 112

GAY & LESBIAN

For more information on the gay and lesbian scene, *see pp184-87.*

LAMBDA Istanbul (0212 233 4966, www.lambdaistanbul.org).
This umbrella group has links to international organisations, including the International Gay and Lesbian Association. LAMBDA is involved in a wide range of legal, social, cultural, health and political issues of concern to the gay community.

HEALTH

Turkey's health services suffer from an overstretched, underfunded public sector. There is no GP system, state hospitals are jammed, and underpaid doctors often have to take on private patients. In contrast, private hospitals have state-of-the-art equipment, look like five-star hotels, and milk their patients royally. If you need medical aid, the simplest solution (especially if you have insurance) is to go straight to a private hospital, where you'll get immediate attention and are pretty sure to find English speakers. Many private hopsitals also run dental clinics.

No vaccinations are required for Istanbul, although cases of rabies were reported as recently as 1999. It's best to avoid tap water; cheap bottled water is readily available.

Accident & emergency

American Hospital

Amerikan Hastanesi
Güzelbahçe Sokak 20, Nişantaşı (0212 444 3777, www.amerikanhastanesi.com.tr). **Credit** AmEx, MC, V.
Well equipped and well staffed, the American Hospital also has a dental clinic.

European Florence Nightingale Hospital
Abide-i Hürriyet Caddesi 164, Şişli (0212 212 8811 or 444 0436, www.florence com.tr). **Credit** AmEx, MC, V.
Modern and well equipped, specialises in treating children.

German Hospital
Sıraselviler Caddesi 119, Cihangir, Taksim (0212 293 2150, www.almanhastanesi.com.tr). **Credit** AmEx, MC, V. **Map** p249 O3.
Part of the Universal Hospitals Group, it incorporates an eye hospital and dental clinic.

International Hospital
Istanbul Caddesi 82, Yeşilköy (0212 444 0663, www.international hospital.com.tr). **Credit** AmEx, DC, MC, V.
Five minutes from the airport, it has cutting-edge technology, eye and dental clinics.

Taksim State Emergency Hospital

Taksim Ilkyardım Hastanesi
Sıraselviler Caddesi 112, Cihangir, Taksim (0212 252 4300). **No credit cards. Map** p249 O3.
A state-run hospital that recently got a much-needed overhaul. It only deals with emergencies.

Contraception & abortion

Contraception can be found at any pharmacy (*see below*).

Kürtaj
Halaskargazi Caddesi Doğançay apt 216 (532 354 0553, www.doktornevra.com).

Dentists

ADENT Dental Clinic
Çamlık Girişi 6, Etiler (0212 263 1649, www.dentinn.com.tr).
An English-speaking practice.

Opticians

See p167 **Shops & services**

PHARMACIES

Pharmacies (*eczane*) are plentiful. Pharmacists are licensed to measure blood pressure, give injections, clean and bandage minor injuries, and suggest medication for minor ailments – many prescription medicines are available over the counter in Turkey. However, few pharmacists speak English. Opening hours are typically from 9am-7pm Mon-Sat. Every neighbourhood also has a duty pharmacy (*nöbetçi*) that is open all night and on Sundays. *See p167.*

STDs, HIV, AIDS

Yeniden
Halaskargazi Caddesi, Kücükbaçe Sokak, Yuvam Apart 351/1 (0212 219 0303, www.yeniden.org.tr).
Yeniden works mainly with young people regarding AIDS, STDs, HIV and on addiction issues.

ID

It is illegal not to carry ID at all times. It's unlikely that tourists are asked by authorities to show ID, and almost never to buy alcohol.

INSURANCE

Turkey is not covered by EU mutual health insurance schemes, so visitors are advised to take out private insurance policy. Anyone with a full residence permit is entitled to national health care.

INTERNET

Particularly around Sultanahmet, most hotels offer internet access and many travel agents have a couple of online computers. Wireless access is available in most upscale cafés and restaurants, including Gloria Jeans and Starbucks.

The majority of phone sockets take the US-style RJ11 plug, although a few older hotels use a Turkish model for which there don't seem to be any adaptors.

The following are reputable internet providers with English-speaking technical staff and back-up services.

Superonline
0212 473 7475, www.superonline.com
Turknet
0212 444 0077, www.turk.net
Netone
0212 355 1700, www.netone.net.tr

There are also many internet cafés in Sultanahmet, especially on and round Divan Yolu.

Robin Hood Internet Café
Yeniçarşı Caddesi 8/4, Galatasaray (0212 244 8959). **Open** 9.30am-11pm daily. Rates YTL2/hr.
No credit cards.
This pristine, fourth-floor café has 30 computers. Provides printing, fax and scanning services, plus English-speaking technical support. No smoking.

LANGUAGE

For more on language, *see p229,* **Vocabulary**. For **language classes,** *see p225.*

LEFT LUGGAGE

There are left luggage facilities at both **Sabiha Gökçen Airport** and **Atatürk Airport**. It costs between YTL8-YTL15 depending on the size. They are open 24 hours. There's also left luggage storage at Istanbul's Esenler Bus Terminal but not at the train stations.

LEGAL HELP

For criminal legal help, contact the consulates, *see p222.*
Ertan & Oran
Adnan Saygun Caddesi, Belediye Sitesi D1 Blok, Daire 82, Ulus (0212 225 0952, ayhanoran@superonline.com). **Open** 9am-6pm Mon-Fri.
A consultancy and law firm that specialises in commercial, corporate, international trade and maritime law.

LIBRARIES

While there are excellent Spanish and French libraries in Beyoğlu, there isn't a single English-language library open to the public since the closure of the British Council library after the 2003 bombing. Your best bet for English-language resources is to visit Bilgi or Boğaziçi university.
**Istanbul Library/
Çelik Gülersoy Foundation**
Ayasofya Pansiyonları, Soğukçeşme Sokak, Sultanahmet (0212 512 5730). **Open** 9am-noon, 1-4.30pm Mon-Fri. **Map** p243 N10.
Antique and modern books on Istanbul in several languages, stored in an Ottoman house beside Topkapı Palace. Used mainly by academics and specialists.

LOST PROPERTY

To report a crime or lost property, go to the Tourist Police station (0212 527 4503) opposite Yerebatan Sarnıcı in Sultanahmet. Most officers speak English or German. If your passport is lost or stolen, you generally have to fill out a police report before the consulate will deal with you.

MEDIA

Magazines

Most magazines are ephemeral unless backed by one of the big media groups. Established leaders are *Tempo* and *Aktüel*, which mix news, fashion and gossip. There's a slew of licensed international titles, including the monthly *Time Out Istanbul* with both English and Turkish editions.

Our competitor *Istanbul: The Guide* also includes hotel, restaurant and club reviews, but only appears every other month.

Newspapers

National newspapers fall into two broad categories, secular and pro-Islamist. The secular press is monopolised by two empires – the Doğan and Sabah groups; between them, they account for around 60 per cent of the market.

The most highbrow papers are *Cumhuriyet* (*Republic*), a foundering left-of-centre paper, and *Radikal*, a Doğan title. Competition comes from three big hitters: *Hürriyet*, *Sabah* and *Milliyet*, indistinguishable popular dailies that occupy the centre. Journalistic standards are undermined by low pay. The real news comes from the columnists – usually at least one per issue.

The main pro-Islamist daily is *Zaman*, distinguished by good

DIRECTORY

coverage of international literature and film, and the first Turkish newspaper to go online. By far the worst Islamist paper is the hate-mongering *Akit*, with its habit of insinuating that successful business leaders are closet Jews or Christians.

Weekly satirical comics sell well. Popular titles include *Gır Gır*, *Penguen* and *LeMan*. No subject is taboo, and the humour, while crude, is usually on the mark.

For such a cosmopolitan city, Istanbul is low on foreign-language publications. The only daily English newspaper is the semi-literate *Turkish Daily News*, which has reasonable coverage of domestic politics, but suffers from indigestible features and soapbox columnists. The monthly *Turkish Business World* does what is says on the cover, but reads suspiciously like advertorial. The new *Pera Weekly* (*Beyoğlu Gazetesi*), sold by street vendors, at bookstores and newsstands, has several pages of English summary of local news.

Foreign newspapers and magazines are easy to find, but rarely arrive before late afternoon. The best places to look are the news stands in Sultanahmet and around Taksim Square, or the bookshops on Istiklal Caddesi.

Radio

The airwaves over Istanbul are so crammed with broadcasts that it's practically impossible to pick up any station without overlapping interference. Stations generally offer either Turkish or foreign music, but rarely both. One exception is Açık Radyo (94.9), which intercuts topical talk shows (often in English) with world music. Stations offering dance and pop music include Kiss FM (90.3), Radio Oxygen (95.9), Metro FM (97.2), Capital Radio (99.5), Power FM (100) and Number One FM (102.5). Radyo Blue (94.5) specialises in Latin and jazz, and Energy FM (102) in jazz. Radyo Eksen is the best channel for alternative music. For Turkish music, try Kral FM (92.0), Best FM (98.4) and Lokum FM (89.0). For Western classical music tune into ITU Radyosu (103.8). You can pick up the BBC news in English on NTV Radyo (102.8) at 6pm daily, and at 7am and 10.30pm Monday to Friday.

Television

Turkey now has 30 national channels, and countless more regional stations. Perhaps unsurprisingly, production values are low. The exceptions are CNN Turk and NTV, which feature excellent news, documentary and sports programmes. Cable TV is available in many areas, offering improved reception of terrestrial channels, plus BBC Entertainment, CNN, Discovery, Eurosport and MTV. Digital TV is represented by Digitürk, which carries programmes from Europe and the US, plus all the biggest Turkish TV and radio stations.

MONEY

Local currency is the Turkish lira, or YTL. High inflation (which hovered around 70-80 per cent for years) was down to a modest 6.5 per cent in 2009, but is estimated to rise again to 10 per cent. After taming inflation with IMF help, Turkey lopped six zeros off its currency in 2005 and the New Turkish Lira (YTL) was born. YTL banknotes come in denominations of 5, 10, 20, 50, and 100. New notes and coins have come in, so beware of being fobbed off with the old ones – if they are a noticably different style than the uniform new ones, query it

Travellers' cheques can be cashed at banks or post offices, but are usually not accepted at exchange bureaux. You always need to have your passport with you to cash cheques. Banks charge different commissions, and some charge none at all; but the post office usually offers the best deal.

Banks & ATMs

Cashpoints are common. Most machines will accept cards linked into the Cirrus or Plus networks, and supply Turkish lira or cash advances on major credit cards, provided you know your PIN number.

Most banks provide telephone and internet banking, which can be less frustrating than shabby counter service. Non-residents can open a savings account at a Turkish bank in any currency: just go to any branch with your passport. You'll be asked to sign a routine account agreement. Be sure to choose a branch that is near your place of residence or work, because you'll only be able to draw cash from this branch without incurring charges. Cash can be deposited at any branch. With a current account, you can also apply for an ATM card. Getting a credit card isn't so easy: you need a residence permit, employment,

proof of income, and a Turkish guarantor, as well as patience.

Most banks will accept transfers even if you don't have an account. The drawback is that the money doesn't always arrive instantly, and the bank will block the money for up to 20 days. There is a way around this: you can withdraw the money in Turkish lira at the bank's discretionary rates, or by paying a hefty commission. The quicker and more reliable alternative is to use Western Union Money Transfer. This service is now offered by all branches of Denizbank, Dışbank, Oyak Bank, Finansbank and Ziraat Bankası. If you're expecting to receive money, just turn up at any branch of these banks with your passport and transfer details (time and amount of transfer, plus 'money transfer control number'). You should be able to draw the money instantly in dollars, euros or YTL.

Akbank
www.akbank.com.
Citibank
www.citibank.com.tr.
Garanti Bank
www.garantibank.com.tr.
HSBC
www.hsbc.com.tr.
Yapı Kredi Bank
www.yapikredi.com.tr.

Bureaux de change

Many shops and restaurants accept payment in US dollars, sterling or euros, but there are dozens of exchange bureaux (*döviz bürosu*) in the main tourist districts. These are easier to deal with than banks, where transactions can take forever and exchange rates are generally lower. Bureaux de change have long opening hours, generally from from 9am to 7.30pm Monday to Saturday. Some exchange offices also open on Sundays, but they tend to offer considerably worse exchange rates.

Çetin Döviz
Istiklal Caddesi 39, Beyoğlu (0212 252 6428). **Open** 9am-8pm daily. **Map** p249 O2.
Çözüm Döviz
Istiklal Caddesi 53, Beyoğlu (0212 244 6271). **Open** 9am-7.30pm Mon-Sat; 11am-6pm Sun. **Map** p249 O2.
Klas Döviz
Sıraselviler Caddesi 51, Taksim (0212 249 3550). **Open** 8.30am-10pm daily. **Map** p249 O2.

Lost/stolen credit cards

American Express
0212 444 2525,
www.americanexpress.com.tr.

Represented in Turkey by Akbank, AmEx is far less widely accepted than Mastercard or Visa because of high commission charges.

Mastercard
00 800 13 887 0903.

Visa
00 800 13 535 0900.

OPENING HOURS

Opening hours are extremely variable in Istanbul, but here are some general guidelines:
Banks 9am-12.30pm, 1.30-5pm Mon-Fri.
Bars 11am or noon-2am daily.
Businesses 9am-6pm Mon-Fri.
Municipal offices 8am-12.30pm, 1.30-5.30pm Mon-Fri.
Museums 8.30am-5.30pm Tue-Sun.
Petrol stations 24 hrs daily.
Post offices see below.
Shops 10am-8pm Mon-Sat. In main shopping areas shops stay open until 10pm and also open on Sunday. Grocery stores (bakkals) and supermarkets are open 9am-10pm daily. Most neighbourhoods will have a 24hr grocery store.

POLICE

See p222 **Emergencies**.
Crime is low in Istanbul. The main thing to beware of is bag-snatching and pickpocketing, especially in tourist areas like Sultanahmet, or crowded places such as Eminönü and Beyoğlu.

Single women can get hassled, but this is generally confined to verbal comments. That said, women should not wander around the quieter streets of Beyoğlu or Taksim late at night unaccompanied. Steer clear of the seed Tarlabaşı district.

The police have a reputation for incompetence, excessive use of force, and an appetite for back-handers – which they have generally deserved. Determination to change this image has resulted in a major PR drive: the new police website (www.iem.gov.tr) has an exhaustive catalogue of services in ten languages.

Tourist police
Yerebatan Caddesi 6, Sultanahmet (0212 527 4503). Tram Sultanahmet. **Open** 24 hrs daily.
Map p243 N10.
The place to report thefts, losses or scams. Most officers speak English.

POST

Post offices are recognisable by their yellow and black PTT signs.
Stamps can only be bought at post offices. Postcards cost YTL0.70 to

Europe, YTL0.80 to the US and Australia. Airmail letters up to 50g cost YTL1.50 to Europe, YTL1.75 to the US and Australia.

For parcels, airmail rates start at YTL39 to the UK, YTL38 to the US, and YTL45 to Australia for the first kg, with an extra YTL8, YTL17 and YTL24 respectively for every additional kg. Rates for surface mail are YTL34 to the UK, YTL24 to the US and YTL29 to Australia.

The contents of all parcels will be inspected at the post office, so it's best not to seal them and bring tape with you.

Beyoğlu
Yeniçarşı Caddesi 4A, Galatasaray (0212 444 1788, www.ptt.gov.tr). **Open** 8.30am-5pm Mon-Fri; 8.30am-7pm Sun. **Map** p248 N3.

Sirkeci
Büyük Postane, Büyük Postane Caddesi (0212 444 1788, www.ptt.gov.tr). **Open** 8.30am-9pm daily. **Map** p243 N9.

Taksim
Cumhuriyet Caddesi 2 (0212 444 1788, www.ptt.gov.tr). **Open** 8.30am-12.30pm, 1.30-5.30pm Mon-Sat. **Map** p249 P2.

Post restante

Poste restante mail should be sent to the central post office at Sirkeci, addressed as follows:

Recipient's name
Poste Restante
Büyük Postane
Büyük Postane Caddesi
Sirkeci
Istanbul

To collect mail, you need to bring your passport, and to pay a small fee for each letter that you receive.

RELIGION

Istanbul has a strong Jewish tradition and is still the home of the Greek and Armenian Orthodox Patriarchates.

Christian

Christ Church (Anglican)
Serdari Ekrem Sokak 52, Tünel, Beyoğlu (0212 251 5616). **Services** 9am, 6pm Mon-Sat; 9am,10am Sun. **Map** p248 N5.
Union Church of Istanbul (Protestant)
Postaclar Sokak, Beyoğlu (0212 244 5212, www.union churchofistanbul.org). **Services** 9.30am, 11am, 1.30pm Sun. **Map** p248 N4.

St Anthony's (Catholic)
Istiklal Caddesi 325, Beyoğlu (0212 244 0935). **Open** 8am-7.30pm Mon-Sat, 9am-12.30pm and 3-7.30pm Sun. **Services** English 8am Mon-Sat, 10am Sun. **Map** p248 N3.
Haghia Triada (Greek Orthodox)
Meşelik Sokak 11/1, Taksim (0212 244 1358). **Services** Short 8.30am, 5pm daily (4pm in winter). Full-length 9am Sun. **Map** p249 O2.
Üç Horon (Gregorian Armenian)
Balık Pazarı, Sahne Sokak 14/1, Beyoğlu (0212 244 1382). **Open** 9am-5pm daily. **Services** 9.30am-1pm Tue; 9am-1pm Sun. **Map** p248 N3.

Jewish

Security at Istanbul's synagogues has been tighter than ever since two suicide bombings on synagogues in November 2003. To visit, you must first obtain permission. Call the office of the Chief Rabbinate for further information. Prayers are usually held daily at 7.30am, with Shabbat services at 8am. Friday evening services take place at sunset.

Chief Rabbinate
Yeminiçi Sokak 23, Tünel (0212 293 8794/5). **Open** 9am-5pm Mon-Thur; 9am-1pm Fri.

SMOKING

Smoking bans are slowly creeping in: first it was public transport, now it's public offices, banks, shops and even private offices. Offenders are supposedly liable to fines of up to YTL500. In practice, this is rarely enforced and only a few restaurants and cafés offer non-smoking sections.

STUDY

The most significant public universities are **Istanbul University**, Beyazıt (0212 440 0000, www.istanbul.edu.tr/english) and **Galatasaray University** (Çırağan Caddesi 36, 0212 227 4480, www.gsu.edu.tr/en).

Language courses

Turkish is taught at various private schools and colleges; many also offer individual tuition. You can also find private tutors in the classified ads in the *Turkish Daily News*.
Bilgi University
Kurtuluşderesi Caddesi 47, Dolapdere (0212 444 0428, www.bilgi-egitim.com). **Open** 10am-6pm daily.

English First (Turkish Department)
Aydn Sokak 12, off Korukent Yolu, Levent (0212 282 9064, www. turkish lesson.com). **Open** 9am-10pm Mon-Fri; 9am-5pm Sat, Sun.

Taksim Dilmer Language Teaching Centre
Tarık Zafer Tunaya Sokak 18, off Inönü Caddesi, Taksim (0212 292 9696, www.dilmer.com). **Open** 9am-8pm Mon-Fri; 9am-5pm Sat, Sun. **Map** p247 Q2.

TELEPHONES

Dialling & codes

Istanbul's districts have different area codes: 0212 for Europe; 0216 for Asia. You must use the code whenever you call the opposite shore, but when dialling from abroad omit the zero. The country code for Turkey is 90. Call 118 for directory inquiries, 115 for the international operator.

Mobile phones

There are three GSM networks: Turkcell, Telsim and Avea. If you bring your UK mobile, you'll have no problem using your phone as long as you've set up a roaming facility. However, because the Turkish system operates on 900 MHz, US mobile phones won't work.

A cheaper option is to invest in a local SIM card, or *hazır kart*, available through all the GSM operators. Find an authorised dealer (Turkcell is the most popular), present a photocopy of your passport, and pay the subscription fee (around YTL30-YTL40) which includes 100 units, or roughly 25 minutes of talk-time within Turkey. Top-up cards are sold all over the place (look for the *hazır kart* sign in units of 100 (YTL12.50), 250 (YTL28), 500 (YTL53), or 1000 (YTL98).

Getting a contract mobile phone is tricky and expensive, thanks to a 40 per cent tax. You'll need a residence permit plus a Turkish guarantor prepared to stump up $900.

Operator services

Call 115 for the international operator. Directory assistance is 118, but ony in Turkish.

Public phones

Public phones now operate with pre-paid cards (*telefon kartı*). There are two types: a floppy version, or a rigid 'smart card'. Some newer phones also take credit cards. Phone cards can be bought at post offices or, at a small premium, from street vendors and kiosks. They come in units of 30 (YTL2.15), 60 (YTL4.30), 100 (YTL7.20) and 120 (YTL8.60). Metered calls (*kontörlü*) can be placed at post offices or private phone and fax offices (*telefon ofisi*), but they charge over the odds.

Public phone rates are about YTL1.50 a minute to the UK and US, YTL2.25 to Australia. Reduced rates for international calls operate from 10pm to 9am Monday to Saturday, and all day Sunday and holidays. For local and national calls, cheap time is 8pm to 8am midweek and all weekend.

TIME

Turkey is two hours ahead of Greenwich Mean Time (GMT) and seven hours ahead of New York. There is no Turkish equivalent of am and pm, so the 24-hour clock is used. Daylight-saving runs from the last Sunday in March to the last Sunday in October. This creates a three-hour time difference between Turkey and the UK in October only.

TIPPING

Although not obligatory, the rule of thumb is to leave about ten per cent of the bill at cafés and restaurants. Service is occasionally included, in which case it'll say *servis dahil* at the bottom of the bill. If in doubt ask: '*Servis dahil mi?*' Tipping hotel staff, porters and hairdressers is discretionary, but YTL1-YTL2 is the norm. Hamam attendants expect more like 25 per cent. It's not necessary to tip taxi drivers.

TOILETS

Public toilets are plentiful. They'll be signposted 'WC' (when asking, use the term *tuvalet*); the gents' is Bay; the ladies' is Bayan. Public facilities usually consist of a hole in the floor. Toilet paper in these places is a rarity, so carry a pack of tissues (*selpak*). City plumbing cannot cope with toilet paper, so use the bin provided. Hotels, bars and restaurants all have Western-style (*alafranga*) toilets.

TOURIST INFORMATION

The Ministry of Culture and Tourism has tourist information kiosks, where staff speak English, all over town.

Atatürk Airport
International Arrivals (0212 465 5555). **Open** 24 hrs daily.

Beyazıt
Beyazıt Square (0212 522 4902). **Open** 9am-6pm daily. **Map** p242 K10.

Hilton Hotel
Cumhuriyet Caddesi, Şişli (0212 233 0592). **Open** 9am-5pm daily. **Map** p247 P1.

Karaköy Seaport
Kemankeş Caddesi, Karaköy (0212 249 5776). **Open** 9am-5pm Mon-Sat. **Map** p246 N6.

Sirkeci Station
Istasyon Caddesi, Sirkeci (0212 511 5888). **Open** 9am-5pm daily. **Map** p243 N8.

Sultanahmet Square
Divan Yolu 3 (0212 518 1802). **Open** 9am-5pm daily. **Map** p243 N10.

International Turkish tourist offices

Australia
Room 17, Level 3, 428 St George Street, Sydney NSW 2000 (02 9223 3055, 9223 3204).

Canada
Constitution Square, Suite 801, 360 Albert Street, Ottawa, Ontario K1R 7X7 (613 230 8654, 230 3683).

UK
29-30 St James Street SW1A 1HB (020 7839 7778, 7839 7802, www.gototurkey.co.uk).

USA
821 UN Plaza, New York, NY 10017 (212 687 2194, 599 7568, www.tourismturkey.org).

VISAS & IMMIGRATION

Visas are required by most nationalities; they can be bought at the airport upon arrival. At press time, rates were as follows: UK $20; USA $20; Canada $60; Australia $20; Ireland $20. New Zealanders don't need a visa. Fees must be paid in Euros or dollars. UK passport holders can pay £10 in sterling; Turkish lira, credit cards or travellers' cheques are not accepted. Visas are valid for three months. Overstaying your visa, even by a single day, will earn you a fine of around YTL150 ($100) when you finally leave the country. *See p227* for information on work visas.

If you have a work permit, you're automatically entitled to residence as long as your permit is valid. Otherwise, residence applications should be filed with the Turkish Consulate General in your country of residence. The laborious application procedure for British passport holders is detailed online at www.turkconsulate-london.com.

Upon arrival in Istanbul, you must register with the Foreigners' Branch of the Police Department (Emniyet Müdürlüğü Yabancılar Şubesi) on Vatan Caddesi (Aksaray) within one month of the visa/work permit being issued. Residence permits are valid for one or two years; you can also apply for a five-year permit. Expect to pay upwards of YTL225.

WEIGHTS & MEASURES

The metric system (kilogrammes and metres) is used across Istanbul.

WHEN TO GO

Between December and March Istanbul is cold, grey and blustery. Temperatures average 5C (42F), but humidity and windchill make it feel much colder. Sleet and snow showers are not uncommon; the city is usually buried under several feet of snow at least once every winter.

Summers can be oppressive; temperatures average 25-30C (78-88F) from June to August, occasionally rising beyond 35C (104F). The heat and humidity can be draining during the day, but when things cool down at sunset city dwellers descend to the Bosphorus to enjoy languid evenings at waterfront cafés.

The best weather is in spring and autumn, when days are temperate and evenings mild. Occasionally, *poyraz*, a chill Balkan wind, and *lodos*, hot, humid gusts from the south, can result in a 'four seasons in a single day' effect. Both spring and autumn are busy festival seasons.

Public & religious holidays

Turkey's five secular public holidays last one day each. Banks,

offices and post offices are closed, but many shops stay open and public transport runs as usual.

Religious holidays are different. They last three or four days; if these happen to be midweek, the government often extends the holiday to cover the whole working week. The city shuts down as Istanbullus flock to the country. Coaches and flights are jammed, so book ahead if your travel plans coincide.

Observance of Ramazan, the Islamic month of fasting, is widespread. Many Turks abstain from food, drink and cigarettes between sunrise and sunset. This has little impact on visitors, as most bars and restaurants remain open, but it's bad form to flaunt your non-participation by smoking or eating in the street, especially in religious districts, such as Fatih and Üsküdar. Here, Ramazan nights are the busiest of the year. At sundown, eateries are packed with large groups breaking their fast together. Sultanahmet Square turns into an extravaganza of food and music at twilight. The end of Ramazan is marked by the three-day Şeker Bayramı, or 'Sugar Holiday', when sweets are traditionally given to friends and family.

The main event in the Islamic calendar is Kurban Bayramı (the Feast of the Sacrifice), which marks Abraham's near-sacrifice of Isaac. Traditionally, families buy a *kurban*, which could be a sheep, bull, goat or camel, which they sacrifice on the first or second day of the feast. The meat is shared with relatives, neighbours and the poor. There are now stricter regulations on slaughtering sites and methods, which has reduced the bloodbath effect, but the faint-hearted are advised to keep away from mosques.

Islamic religious holidays are based on a lunar calendar, approximately 11 days shorter than the Gregorian (Western) calendar.

Consequently, Islamic holidays shift forward by ten or 12 days each year.
New Year's Day (*Yılbaşı Günü*)
1 Jan.
The Feast of the Sacrifice (*Kurban Bayramı*) 16-19 Nov 2010; 6-9 Nov 2011.
National Sovereignty & Children's Day (*Ulusal Egemenlik ve Çocuk Bayramı*) 23 Apr.
Youth & Sports Day (*Gençlik ve Spor Bayramı*) 19 May.
Victory Day (*Zafer Bayramı*) 30 Aug.
Republic Day (*Cumhuriyet Bayramı*) 29 Oct.
Ramazan Holiday (*Ramazan Bayramı*) 30 Aug-2 Sept 2011; 20 July-18 Aug 2012.

WOMEN

Few special rules apply for women in Istanbul. With some provisos, you needn't dress any differently than at home, certainly not in the more European areas such as Beyoğlu. Probably best to leave the micro minis and short shorts at home, though. To avoid being stared at, wear trousers or skirts that come to the knee. And in more conservative areas, and particularly in mosques and churches, keep your shoulders covered.

In touristy areas you may get hit on. It's usually harmless, but all the same it can be annoying. It's also generally easy to shrug off. Avoid eye contact; don't beam wide smiles. Don't respond to invitations, come-ons or obnoxious comments. If a man is persistent and in your face, try saying '*Ayıp*', literally 'shame on you'. Chances are someone will intervene on your behalf. It seldom extends beyond that, but should you need help, the word is '*İmdat*'.

WORK

Work permits can only be obtained through a sponsoring employer. In principle, your job should only be doable by a foreigner. Getting the permit is a long, bureaucratic process. First, the employer submits an application for authorisation to the Treasury in Ankara. This can take a couple of months. You then submit your own application to the Turkish Consulate General in your country of residence (which shouldn't be Turkey) and wait about six weeks for it to be processed. When it's ready, you must collect it from the consulate in person with your passport. Back in Turkey, you still need a residence permit (*see p226* **Visas & immigration**.

DIRECTORY

AVERAGE TEMPERATURES

Month	Minimum °C	Maximum °C
January	3	8
February	2	9
March	3	11
April	7	16
May	12	21
June	16	25
July	18	28
August	19	28
September	16	24
October	13	20
November	9	15
December	5	11

Vocabulary

Making the effort to use a few phrases will be greatly appreciated. For information on language courses *see p225*.

PRONUNCIATION

All words are written phonetically and except ğ there are no silent letters; so post office, *postane*, is pronounced 'post-a-neh'. Syllables are articulated with equal stress. The key is to master the pronunciation of the few letters and vowels that differ from English:

c – like the 'j' in jam; so cami (mosque) is 'jami'
ç – like the 'ch' in chip, so çiçek (flower) is 'chi-check'
ğ – silent, but lengthens preceding vowel
ı – an 'uh', like the 'a' in cinema
ö – like the 'ir' in girdle
ş – like the 'sh' in shop, so şiş (as in kebab) is pronounced 'shish'
ü – as in the French 'tu'

ACCOMMODATION

air-conditioning klima
bathroom banyo
bed yatak
bed & breakfast pansiyon
breakfast kahvaltı
double bed çift kişilik yatak
hotel otel
no vacancies yer yok
room oda
shower duş
soap sabun
towel havlu
vacancy yer var

DAYS OF THE WEEK

Monday pazartesi
Tuesday salı
Wednesday çarşamba
Thursday perşembe
Friday cuma
Saturday cumartesi
Sunday pazar

EMERGENCIES

accident kaza
ambulance ambülans
doctor doktor
fire yangın
help! imdat!
hospital hastane
medication ilaç

pharmacy eczane
police polis
sick hasta

ESSENTIALS

a lot/very/too çok
and ve
bad/badly kötü
big büyük
but ama/fakat
good/well iyi
I don't speak Turkish Türkçe bilmiyorum
I don't understand anlayamadım
leave me alone (quite forceful) beni rahat bırak
Mr/Mrs bey/hanım (with first name)
no hayır
OK tamam
or veya
please lütfen
small küçük
sorry pardon
thank you teşekkürler/mersi/sağol
yes evet
this/that bu/şu

GETTING AROUND

airport havalimanı
bus otobüs
bus/coach station otogar
car park otopark
entrance giriş
exit çıkış
left sol
map harita
no parking park yapılmaz
petrol benzin
platform peron
right sağ
road yol
station gar
street sokak
train tren

GREETINGS

good morning günaydın
good afternoon/goodbye iyi günler
good evening/goodbye iyi akşamlar
good night/goodbye iyi geceler
goodbye güle güle (to the person leaving)
hello merhaba

QUESTIONS

do you have change? bozuk paranız var mı?

do you speak English? ingilizce biliyor musunuz?
how? nasıl?
what? ne?
when? ne zaman?
where? nerede?
where to? nereye?
which (one)? hangi(si)?
who? kim?
why? niye/niçin/neden?

SHOPPING

bank banka
cheap ucuz
credit card kredi kartı
expensive pahalı
how many? kaç tane?
how much (price)? kaç para?
I would like....istiyorum...
is there/are there any? var mı?
post office postane/PTT
price fiyat
stamp pul
till receipt fiş

SIGHTSEEING

castle kale
church kilise
closed kapalı
free bedava/ücretsiz
open açık
mosque cami
museum müze
palace saray
reduced price indirimli
ticket bilet

TIME

at what time? saat kaçta gün
hour saat
minute dakika
today bugün
tomorrow yarın
week hafta
what time is it? saat kaç?
when? ne zaman?
yesterday dün

NUMBERS

0 sıfır; 1 bir; 2 iki; 3 üç; 4 dört; 5 beş; 6 altı; 7 yedi; 8 sekiz; 9 dokuz; 10 on; 11 onbir; 12 oniki; 20 yirmi; 21 yirmibir; 22 yirmiiki; 30 otuz; 40 kırk; 50 elli; 60 altmış; 70 yetmiş; 80 seksen; 90 doksan; 100 yüz; 1,000 bin; 1,000,000 milyon; 1,000,000,000 milyar.

Further Reference

BOOKS

Istanbul has a lively literary scene. Authors whose work has been translated include Turkey's national poet, **Nazım Hikmet**, and award-winning fiction writers **Orhan Pamuk** (*see p70* **The City's Narrator**) and **Yaşar Kemal**. Most of the titles listed here are available in Istanbul.

Fiction

Ali, Tariq *The Stone Woman* (2000)
Historical novel by former Trotskyist activist in which an Ottoman noble family observes the decay of the empire.
Christie, Agatha *Murder on the Orient Express* (1934)
The fabled train is stuck in a snowdrift on the Turkish border when one of the passengers is bumped off.
de Souza, Daniel *Under A Crescent Moon* (1989)
True-life tale of a guy banged up in Istanbul for drug smuggling.
Greene, Graham *Stamboul Train* (1932)
Lesser yarn about a bunch of characters crossing central Europe on the Orient Express. Greene's advance wouldn't stretch beyond Cologne, so all the eastern detail was cribbed from Baedeker.
Kemal, Yashar *Memed, My Hawk* (1961)
The book that established Kemal as one of Turkey's greatest contemporary writers as a gritty insight into Turkish rural life.
Nadel, Barbara *Harem* (2002)
Taking on prostitution and mafia violence, this crime novel from the Inspector Ikmen series has won few friends in the Istanbul tourist board.
Pamuk, Orhan *Snow* (2005)
A sensation in his native Istanbul, Pamuk scooped the Nobel Prize for Literature in 2006. This poetic novel is set in the town of Kars.
Unsworth, Barry *The Rage of the Vulture* (1982)
Booker Prize-winner Unsworth once taught English in Istanbul. His detailed imagery enriches this tale of political intrigue, as the 'vultures of Europe' circle the dying Ottoman empire.

Non-fiction

Beck, Christa & Fausting, Christiane *Istanbul: An Architectural Guide* (1997)
Gazetteer of nearly 100 of the city's most significant buildings.
Hellier, Chris & Venturi, Franscesco *Splendors of Istanbul: Houses and Palaces Along the Bosphorus* (1993)
Glossy photos of the interiors of lavish waterside mansions.
Hull, Alastair & Luczyc-Wyhowska, Jose *Kilims: The Complete Guide* (2000)
Lavish but practical large-format paperback.
Hutchings, Roger & Rugman, Jonathan *Atatürk's Children: Turkey and the Kurds* (2001)
One of the best books on an explosive national issue – the conflict in the country's south-east.
Kinzer, Stephen *Crescent and Star* (2002)
Opinionated and engaging account of contemporary Turkey by the former *New York Times* correspondent for Istanbul.
Mango, Andrew *Atatürk* (2002)
Latest in a long line of Atatürk bios, with a strong narrative drive.
Mansel, Philip *Constantinople: City of the World's Desire* (1996)
Grand discourse on the rise and fall of the imperial capital.
Norwich, John Julius *A Short History of Byzantium* (1998)
An authoritative tour of the Byzantine Empire's 1,123-year history, which captures every tawdry and riveting detail.
Orga, Irfan *Portrait of a Turkish Family* (1989)
A haunting autobiography that follows a wealthy Istanbul family's demise following World War I, offering insight into Turkey's uneasy transition from crumbling empire to republic.
Pope, Hugh & Nicole *Turkey Unveiled* (2000)
Balanced assessment of the contemporary political and cultural landscape by two long-term Istanbul journalists.
Procopius *The Secret History* (1982)
The first-century Byzantine historian wrote the official biography of Justinian; in these salacious diaries, he gives his own, uncensored account of the tyrannical emperor.

Travel

Freely, John & Sumner-Boyd, Hilary *Strolling Through Istanbul* (2003)
An enlightening companion for city wandering, with an emphasis on history and architecture from the Byzantine to the Ottoman age. Itineraries are provided.
Kelly, Laurence (ed) *Istanbul: A Traveller's Companion* (1987)
Historical writings and travellers' tales covering places, people, courtly life, and social diversions.
Montagu, Mary Wortley *Turkish Embassy Letters* (1763)
London socialite Lady Montagu was a diplomatic wife in Istanbul from 1716-18 and an amusing correspondent, equally at home with court politics and harem gossip.

FILM

Journey Into Fear (Norman Foster, 1942)
World War II spy thriller co-written, produced by and starring Orson Welles as intelligence officer Colonel Hakkı.
Istanbul (Joseph Pevney, 1957)
Suspected diamond smuggler (Errol Flynn) returns to Istanbul to find his old flame, whom he thought was dead, is still alive.
From Russia with Love (Terence Young, 1962)
'He seems fit enough. Have him report to me in Istanbul in 24 hours.' 007 casually dispatches Eastern Bloc assailants in various tourist spots and gets to shag two wrestling gypsies.
America, America (Elia Kazan, 1963)
Autobiographical film (Kazan was born in Istanbul) picturing the working-class neighbourhoods of Istanbul through the eyes of the director's uncle, as he journeys from Anatolia to the New World.
Topkapı (Jules Dassin, 1964)
Caper movie in which a small-time con-man (Peter Ustinov) gets mixed up in a big-time jewellery heist. Good fun, and Istanbul looks stunning.
Murder on the Orient Express (Sidney Lumet, 1974)
Albert Finney, Lauren Bacall, Ingrid Bergman, Sean Connery and John Gielgud ham it up something rotten.

Midnight Express (Alan Parker, 1978)
Still misshaping views of Turkey and the Turks thirty years on. A great movie? Perhaps, but an inexcusably racist one.
Pascali's Island (James Dearden, 1988)
Based on a novel by Barry Unsworth. Pascali (Ben Kingsley) is a spy for the Ottoman sultanate. Although entirely shot in Greece, it successfully captures the period.
Hamam (Ferzan Ozpetek, 1996)
Italian man visits Istanbul, repairs bathhouse, falls for local boy. A gorgeously photographed, lushly scored ethno-homo romp.
In This World (Michael Winterbottom, 2002)
Award-winning account of two Afghans smuggled across countless borders between Pakistan and Britain, featuring dingy sweat-shop scenes in Istanbul.

MUSIC

Rock and pop releases on local labels are not widely available outside Turkey, but traditional Turkish music can be tracked down in the world music sections of specialist stores. Two fine labels are Kalan Music (www.kalan.com) and Traditional Crossroads (www.rootsworld.com). Golden Horn (www.goldenhorn.com), based in California, has a decent catalogue of traditional Turkish music and jazz.

For more on Turkish music *see pp191-98*; for places to buy CDs and tapes *see p170*.

Fasıl

There are surprisingly few *fasıl* recordings on the market. Generally, the older the recording, the better. Look out for albums by Müzeyyen Senar and Zeki Müren, reissues by Hamiyet Yüceses and Safiye Ayla, or newcomer Muazzez Erso's interpretations of standards and soundtracks.

Zeki Müren *1955-63 Recordings* (Kalan)
Double CD of gorgeous melodies complemented by Müren's gender-bending alto voice.

Folk music

Bosphorus *Balkan Dusleri* (Ada Müzik)
Turkish classical musicians revive the Istanbul Greek repertoire.
Ali Ekber Çiçek *Klasikleri* (Mega Müzik)

One of the most respected exponents of the *saz*.
Mehmet Erenler *Mehmet Erenler ve Bozlakları* (Folk Müzik Center)
Anything by *saz* maestro Erenler is worth picking up.
Neşet Ertaş (Kalan)
An eight-CD collection of work by Ertaş, a cult figure on the Turkish folk scene, now resident in Germany.
Muhabbet *Volumes 1-7* (Kalan)
Fantastic *aşık* – Alevi mystical songs – performed by top names such as Arif Sağ, Yavuz Top and Musa Eroğlu.

Ottoman, classical & court music

Erol Deran *Solo Kanun* (Mega)
This is what Turkish classical music should be: subtle and virtuosic.
Emirgan Assemble *Klasik Osmanlı Müziği* (Kalan)
A sampler of Ottoman instrumental works, featuring *kemençe, ud, kanun, ney* and percussion.
Kani Karaca *Kani Karaca* (Kalan)
Something of a national treasure, Karaca is a hafız, someone who can recite the Koran from memory, with voice bound to raise goosebumps.
Various *Gazeller 1&2* (Kalan)
Amazing archival recordings of traditional vocal improvisations, rescued from ancient 78rpm vinyl.
Various *Lalezar* (Istanbul Büyük Belediye)
Four-CD set of Ottoman music, including compositions by sultans and imperial dance music.

Rock & pop

Sezen Aksu *Serçe* (EMI)
The glitzy queen of pop churns out an album every two years, but this, her 1978 debut, is still her best.
Ceza *Med Cezir* (Hammer Müzik)
Ceza's intense lyrical flurries kick-started the Turkish hip-hop scene.
Cem Karaca *Best of* (Yavuz ve Burç Plakçilik)
Around since the 1960s, this old crooner is still a regular performer around town.
Erkin Koray *Şaşkın* (Kalite Ticaret)
Great intro to Turkish psychedelia by one of its leading lights.
Barış Mançolo *Mançoloği* (Stereo)
Anatolian rocker turned TV celeb whose early death immortalised him as a legend of Turkish rock.
Erkan Oğur *Fuad* (Kalan)
Erkan brings jazz and blues to Turkish instruments and melodies – or vice versa.
Tarkan *Dudu* (Istanbul Plak)
The sultry prince of pop is the sound of Istanbul for a huge

percentage of its population.
Various *East2West* (Doublemoon)
An eclectic, jazz-soaked sampler from the Doublemoon label.

Roma (Gypsy)

Ciguli *Ciguli* (Dost)
Accordion-led recording that made Ahmet Ciguli a star.
Roman Oyun Havaları *Volumes 1 & 2* (EMI-Kent)
Istanbul's top Roma session musicians thump out much-loved dance tunes.
Mustafa Kandıralı *Caz Roman* (World Network)
The 'Benny Goodman of Turkey', with cameos from other famous fasıl musicians.
Selim Sesler & Grup Trakya *The Road to Keşan* (Traditional Crossroads)
Songs and dances from Keşan, a Roma town on the Turkish-Greek border. Excellent sleeve notes.

Sufi religious

Asitane *Simurg* (Istanbul Ajans)
A young ensemble featuring *tanbur, kemençe, ney* and *bendir*.
Mercan Dede *Secret Tribe Nar* (Doublemoon)
Mercan Dede (aka DJ Arkın Allen) splices traditional mystic instruments with electronica.
Doğan Ergin *Sufi Music of Turkey Vol 2* (Mega)
Ephemeral and meditative improvisations.
Music of the Whirling Dervishes *Sufi Music of Turkey* (Mega)
Music to twirl by.
Various Mevlana *Dede Efendi* (Kalan)
1963 recording featuring some of the finest performers of the genre, including Kani Karaca.

WEBSITES

Great Buildings Online
www.greatbuildings.com
Take a virtual tour of Haghia Sophia or explore Sinan's masterpieces.
Istanbul City Guide
www.istanbulcityguide.com
English-language listings updated daily, plus features and news.
The Turkish Daily News
www.turkishdailynews.com
The World Factbook – Turkey
www.cia.gov
The CIA's factual take on Turkey.
Foreign & Commonwealth Office – Turkey
www.fco.gov.uk
The UK government's advice.

Content Index

INDEX

Venue Index

INDEX

Advertisers' Index

Please refer to relevant sections for addresses and/or telephone numbers.

INDEX

The travel apps city lovers have been waiting for...

Apps and maps work offline with no roaming charges

Search for 'Time Out Guides' in the app store

timeout.com/iphonecityguides

Maps

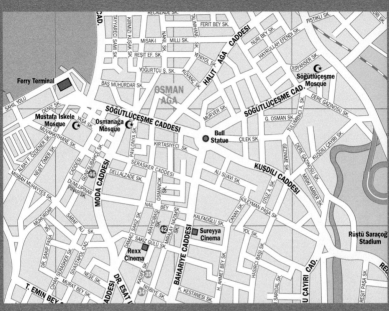

Major sight or landmark	■
Hospital or college	■
Railway station	■
Parks	■
River	■
Motorway	═
Main road	─
Main road tunnel	– –
Pedestrian road	▬
Steps	▬
City Wall	─
Tram	─●─
Airport	✈
Church	✚
Mosque	☾
Metro station	Ⓜ
Area name	FATIH

Istanbul Overview

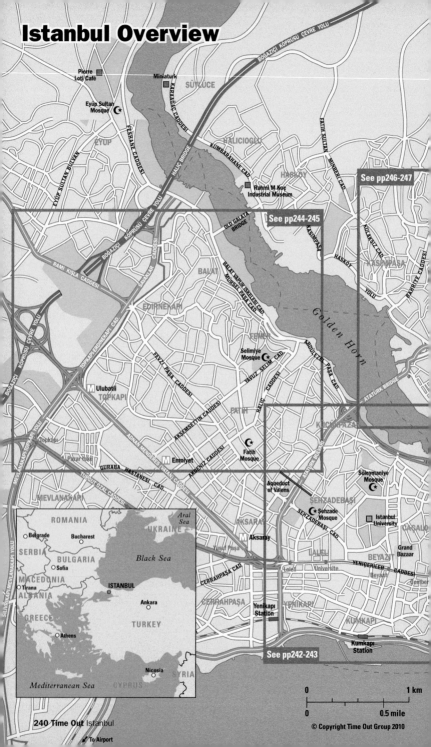

Pierre Loti Café ■

Miniaturk ■

SÜTLÜCE

Eyüp Sultan Mosque ☪★

KARAĞAÇ CADDESİ

FESRALE CADDESİ

EYÜP

EYÜP SULTAN BULVARI

HALİÇİOĞLU

KUMBARAHANE CAD.

HALİÇ BRIDGE

FATİH SULTAN

MÜNBELİ CAD.

HASKÖY

Rahmi M. Koç Industrial Museum ■

See pp246-247

KÜLAHLI CAD.

KASIMPAŞA

BOĞAZİÇİ KÖPRÜSÜ ÇEVRE YOLU

RAMİ KIŞLA CADDESİ

OLD GALATA BRIDGE

KASIMPAŞA YOLU

BAHRİYE CADDESİ

See pp244-245

HASKÖY

SAKAKLAR

TOPKAPI ERDİNEKAPI CAD.

BALAT

BALAT VAPUR İSKELESİ CAD.

MÜRSEL PAŞA CAD.

BOĞAZİÇİ KÖPRÜSÜ ÇEVRE YOLU

EDİRNEKAPI

Golden Horn

FENER

Selimiye Mosque ☪★

SELİM CAD.

YAVUZ SELİM CADDESİ

ABDÜLEZEL PAŞA CAD.

ATATÜRK BRIDGE

FEVZİ PAŞA CADDESİ

Ⓜ **Ulubatlı**

TOPKAPI

FATİH

HALİÇ CADDESİ

KÜÇÜKPAŞA

AKŞEMSETTİN CADDESİ

Topkapı

ADNAN MENDERES VATAN CADDESİ

Pazar Tekke

KARAGENÇ CADDESİ

Ⓜ **Emniyet**

Fatih Mosque ☪★

GURABA HASTANESİ CAD.

MACUNCU EDİRNE CAD.

MEVLANAKAPI TOPKAPI YOLU

SÜLEYMANİYE CADDESİ MÜTERCİM ASIM CAD.

Süleymaniye Mosque ☪★

MEVLANAKAPI

TURGUT ÖZAL CADDESİ

Aqueduct of Valens

ŞEHZADEBAŞI

Şehzade Mosque ☪★

ŞEHZADEBAŞI CAD.

Istanbul University ■

ÇAĞALO

AKSARAY

LALELİ

Grand Bazaar ■

BEYAZIT

Ⓜ **Aksaray**

Yusuf Paşa

Laleli

Universite

YENİÇERİLER CADDESİ

Beyazıt

Çember

CERRAHPAŞA CAD.

CERRAHPAŞA

Yenikapı Station

YENİKAPI

Kumkapı Station

KUMKAPI

See pp242-243

Inset map

ROMANIA

○ Belgrade

○ Bucharest

UKRAINE

Aral Sea

SERBIA

BULGARIA

○ Sofia

Black Sea

MACEDONIA

○ Tirana

ISTANBUL

ALBANIA

GREECE

○ Ankara

TURKEY

○ Athens

○ Nicosia

SYRIA

CYPRUS

Mediterranean Sea

0 ___ **1 km**

0 ___ **0.5 mile**

© Copyright Time Out Group 2010

★ To Airport

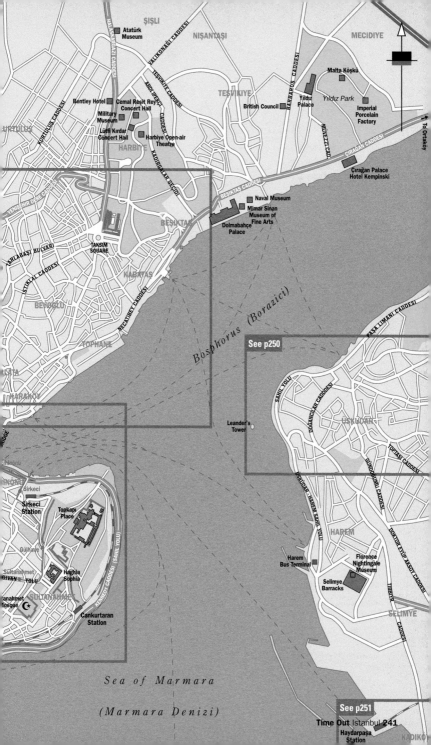

ŞİŞLİ

Atatürk
Museum

VALİKONAĞI CADDESİ

NİŞANTAŞI

MECİDİYE

TEŞVİKİYE CADDESİ

BARBAROS CADDESİ

Malta Köşkü

ABDİ İPEKÇİ CADDESİ

Bentley Hotel

Cemal Reşit Rey
Concert Hall

Military
Museum

Lütfi Kırdar
Concert Hall

Harbiye Open-air
Theatre

HARBİYE

KADIRGALAR GEÇIDI

TEŞVİKİYE

British Council

Yıldız
Palace

Yıldız Park

Imperial
Porcelain
Factory

MÜEZZİCAD.

ÇIRAĞAN CADDESİ

To Ortaköy

 URTULUŞ

KURTULUŞ CADDESİ

HALIL RIFAT PAŞA CADDESİ

BEŞİKTAŞ CADDESİ

BEŞİKTAŞ

Çırağan Palace
Hotel Kempinski

YENİŞEHİR DERE CADDESİ

ARI ARABAŞI BULVARI

İSTİKLAL CADDESİ

TAKSİM
SQUARE

KABATAŞ

MECATBEY CADDESİ

Naval Museum

Mimar Sinan
Museum of
Fine Arts

Dolmabahçe
Palace

BEYOĞLU

Bosphorus (Borazici)

TOPHANE

See p250

İSTA

KARAKÖY

Leander's
Tower

PAŞA LİMANI CADDESİ

SAHİL YOLU

DOĞANCILAR CADDESİ

ÜSKÜDAR

TOPTAŞI CADDESİ

BRIDGE

İNÖNÜ

Sirkeci

Sirkeci
Station

Topkapı
Place

Gülhane

Sultanahmet

DIVAN

YOLU

KENNEDY CADDESİ (SAHİL YOLU)

Haghia
Sophia

anahmet
osque

SULTANAHMET

Cankurtaran
Station

ÜSKÜDAR - HAREM SAHİL YOLU

GÜNDOĞUMU CADDESİ

DOKTOR EYÜP AKSOY CADDESİ

HAREM

Harem
Bus Terminal

Florence
Nightingale
Museum

Selimiye
Barracks

SELİMİYE

TIBBIYE CADDESİ

Sea of Marmara

(Marmara Denizi)

See p251

Haydarpaşa
Station

KADIKÖ

South of the Golden Horn

- Hotels pp40-59
- Restaurants pp113-130
- Bars & Cafés pp131-142

© Copyright Time Out Group 2010

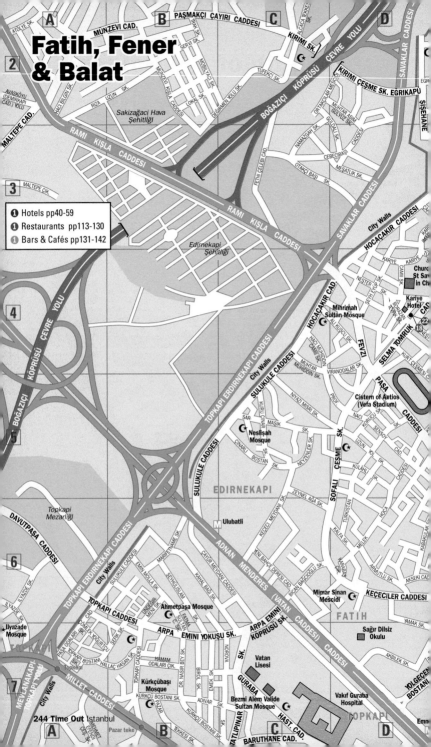

Fatih, Fener & Balat

❶ Hotels pp40-59
❶ Restaurants pp113-130
❶ Bars & Cafés pp131-142

Beyoğlu

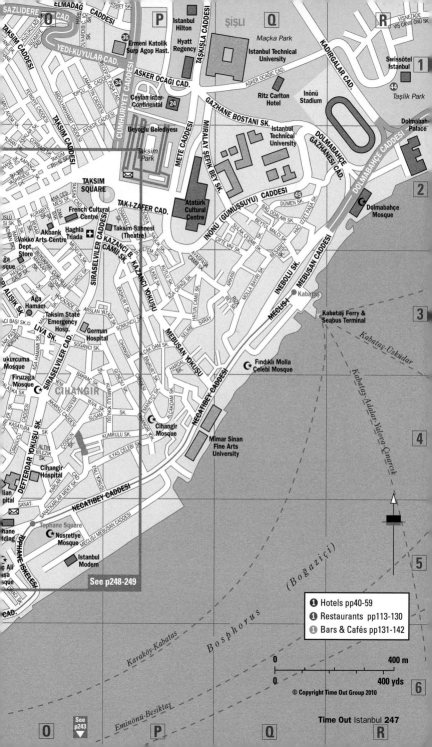

SAZLIDERE

ELMADAĞ CADDESI

NISBET SK.

O

P

Istanbul Hilton

TAŞKIŞLA CADDESI

ŞİŞLİ

Q

VISNEZCE VIŞ CAMI ONU SK.

R

Maçka Park

KADIRGALAR CAD.

Swissôtel Istanbul

1

TAKSIM CADDESI

YEDİ-KUYULAR-CAD.

Ermeni Katolik Surp Agop Hast.

Hyatt Regency

Istanbul Technical University

Taşlik Park

ASKER OCAĞI CAD.

36

Ceylan Inter-Continental

24

GAZHANE BOSTANI SK.

Ritz Carlton Hotel

Inönü Stadium

Dolmabahçe Palace

E

34

Beyoğlu Belediyesi

CUMHURIYET CADDESI

TAKSIM CADDESI

METE CADDESI

MIRALAY ŞEFIK BEY SK.

Istanbul Technical University

DOLMABAHÇE GAZHANESI CAD.

DOLMABAHÇE CADDESI

Dolmabahçe Mosque

2

Taksim Park

TAKSIM SQUARE

INÖNÜ (GÜMÜŞSUYU) CADDESI

DÜMEN SK.

45

TAK-I-ZAFER CAD.

French Cultural Centre

Atatürk Cultural Centre

MEBUSAN CADDESI

INEBOLU SK.

MECLIS-I

Kabataş

Akbank

Haghia Triada

Taksim Sahnesi (Theatre)

KAZANCI B. CAMII SK.

KAZANCI YOKUŞU

Kabataş Ferry & Seabus Terminal

3

Vakko Arts Centre Dept. Store

Ağa Hamam

MEBUSAN YOKUŞU

Kabataş-Üsküdar

Taksim State Emergency Hosp.

German Hospital

Fındıklı Molla Çelebi Mosque

Kabataş-Adalar-Yalova-Çınarck

LİVA SK.

ALİ SK.

ukurcuma Mosque

SIRASELVILER CAD.

CİHANGİR

4

Firuzağa Mosque

Cihangir Mosque

Mimar Sinan Fine Arts University

DEFTERDAR YOKUŞU SK.

Cihangir Hospital

NECATIBEY CADDESI

lian pital

NECATIBEY CADDESI

Tophane Square

Nusretiye Mosque

5

hane lding

ç Ali şa que

Istanbul Modern

See p248-249

(Boğaziçi)

❶ Hotels pp40-59

❶ Restaurants pp113-130

❶ Bars & Cafés pp131-142

Bosphorus

Karaköy-Kabataş

0   400 m

0   400 yds

© Copyright Time Out Group 2010

O

See p243 ▼

P

Eminönü-Beşiktaş

Q

R

6

Time Out Istanbul **247**

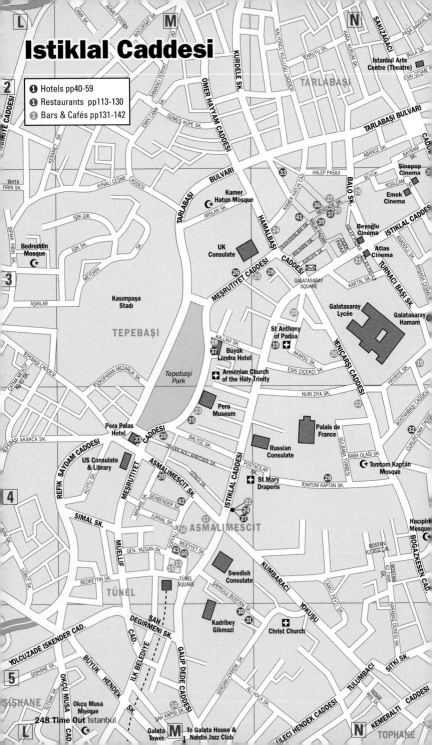

Üsküdar

Key:
1 Hotels pp40-59
1 Restaurants pp113-130
1 Bars & Cafés pp131-142

© Copyright Time Out Group 2010

To Beşiktaş
To Kabataş
To Eminönü

Leander's Tower

Bülbül Deresi Mezarlık

Çinili Mosque
Atik Valide Mosque
Karakadı Alaattin Mosque
Kara Davut Paşa Mosque
Şeyh Mosque
Mihrimah Sultan Mosque
Ağa Mosque
Mimar Sinan
Yeni Valide Mosque
Şehit Süleyman Paşa Mosque
Ahmediye Mosque
Doğancılar Mosque
Nasuhi Mosque
Kaptan Paşa Mosque
Rumi Mehmet Paşa Mosque
Şemsi Paşa Mosque
Ayazma Mosque
İmrahor Mosque

Atlas Çarşısı
Müsahipzade Celal Theatre

Hakimiyet-i Milliye Meydanı

HAREM USKUDAR YOLU
ÜSKÜDAR CAD.
DOĞANCILAR CAD.
HAKIMIYET - I MILLIYE CAD.
UNCULAR CAD.
SELAMI ALI EFENDI
SELMANIPAK CAD.
BULBULDERE
BAĞLARBAŞI CADDESI
EFENDI CAD.
KATIBIM AZIZ BEY SK.
SELAMI ALI CAD.
HATMI
ÇAVUŞDERE CAD.
TOPTAŞI CAD.
UK SELIM PAŞA CAD.
GÜNDOĞUMU CADDESI
TAVUKCU BAKKAL SK.
HALK DERHANESI SK.
TUNUS
PAŞA LIMANI

250 Time Out Istanbul

Kadıköy

KADIKÖY

HASANPAŞA
ZÜHTÜPAŞA

FAHRETTİN KERİM GOKAY (KAYIŞDAĞI) CADDESİ
Söğütlüçeşme Station
BAĞDAT CADDESİ

ULU SULUK SK.
SINAN BEY SK.
M. İBRAHİM P.
A. SADIK SK.
A. RUHİ SK.
A. MEMDUH SK.
A. RASİM SK.
ESAT SK.
NEBİZADE SK.

SÖĞÜTLÜÇEŞME CAD.
SARAY ARDI CADDESİ

Rüştü Saraçoğlu Stadium
RECEP PEKER CADDESİ
REŞİT PAŞA SK.

KIZILTOPRAK HATBOYU SK.
HASAN KAMİL SPOREL SK.
ÖMER EFENDİ SK.
CUMHURİYET SK.

SOKULLU SK.
İSMAİL HAKKI BEY SK.
FAİK SK.
NİĞDE BEY SK.
ÖMER CEMAL B. SK.
HASİBE B. SK.
FISTIKLI SK.
DİNÇSİPER SK.
Söğütlüçeşme Mosque

İNKIŞAF CAD.
AYRILIK ÇEŞMESİ SK.
DERE GAZİNOSU SK.
DERE GAZİNOSU SK.
GEZİNME SK.
G. OSMAN SK.

SÖĞÜTLÜÇEŞME CAD. CADDESİ
KUŞDİLİ CADDESİ

MISKİ AMBER SK.
KÜÇÜK ÇARE SK.

K. KAHVESİ SK.
KARAKOLHANE CAD.
ASLI BAYIR SK.
ERBİLDAR SK.
YEL DEĞİRMENİ
MACİT
AKİT BEY SK.

HALİT AĞA CADDESİ
TALİMHANE
FERİT BEY SK.
REYNOL SK.
NİBBİ BEY SK.
MÜFTER SK.
CİLEK SK.

Bull Statue

OTUZ A. SK.
SÜLEYMAN PAŞA SK.
AYNAN PAŞA SK.
ALİ SUAVİ SK.
MİRALAY NAZIM SK.
MİHRAB SK.
RIHTIM SK.

HAYDARPAŞA ÇAYIR CAD.
PROF. DR. VEHBİ SARIDAL SK.
HASIRCI BAŞI SK.
YOĞURTÇU ÇAYIRI CAD.

H. AHMET BEY SK.
K. KESTANESİ SK.
Süreyya Cinema
BAHARİYE CADDESİ
SAKIZLI SK.
LER SK.
SEMİ SK.
ANTER SK.

RASİMPAŞA RIHTIM CAD.
NEMLİZADE SK.
ORTAÇ SK.
UZUN HAFIZ SK.
İZZETTİN SK.

OSMAN AĞA

MİSAK-I SK.
NAKİL SK.
YOĞURTÇU SK.
REŞİT EF. SK.
RECAZADE SK.
KOYANCİ SK.
KIRTASİYECİ SK.

KARGA SK.
ALİ SAMİ SK.
SANO GÜLLÜ SK.
Rexx Cinema
AYRİOĞLU SK.
MADER SK.
MİSAFİR SK.

DR. ESAT İŞIK CADDESİ

HAYDARPAŞA RIHTIM CAD.
Dolmuş for Üsküdar
Bus Station

Ferry Terminal

BAŞ MUHURDAR SK.
SÖĞÜTLÜÇEŞME CADDESİ

KIRMIZI KUŞAK SK.
TAYYARECİ SAMİ SK.
PAVLONYA SK.
Osmanağa Mosque
SERASKER CADDESİ
BELLALIZADE SK.
OSMANCIK SK.
MODA CADDESİ

CAFERAĞA CADDESİ
Mustafa İskele Mosque
GÜNEŞLİBAHÇE SK.
DUMLUPINAR SK.
DUMLUPINAR SK.
SERASKER CADDESİ
ALİ SK.
MODA CADDESİ

MODA

GÜLŞEN SK.
SİNYASİYOL SK.
BEDRİ BEY SK.

Haydarpaşa Station

SAHİL YOLU

NİĞET ÖMER SK.
HACİ İZETBEGOVİÇ SK.
KAMİT EFENDİ SK.
MUHARREM SK.
SARAF
MİSBAH MUHAYYEŞ SK.
CİHAN SERASKER SK.
MUHURDAR CAD.
MUHTAR BEY SK.
T. EMİN BEY CAD.
DR. SAKIP PAŞA
RIZA BEY SK.

400 m
400 yds

To Karaköy & Eminönü

0

SEE MORE. BE MORE.

This is NEW YORK CITY™

Book Now. Get More.

*** travelocity**

Book your trip to NYC today with Travelocity on **nycgo.com**. Get the most out of your stay with special offers on hotels, dining, shopping, museums, arts, entertainment and more.

NYC
nycgo.com

Street Index

STREET INDEX

Istanbul transport

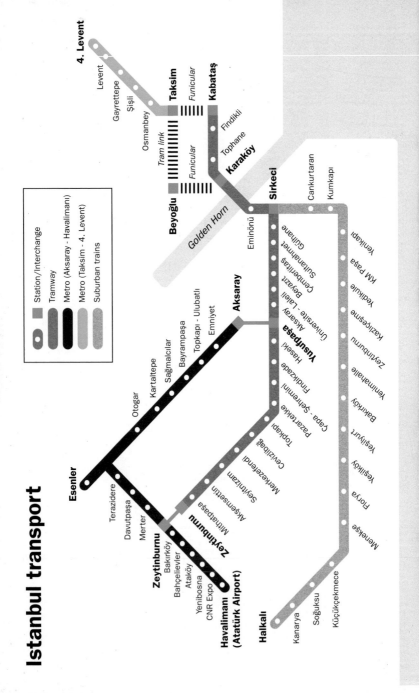

Legend:
- ○ Station/Interchange
- Tramway
- Metro (Aksaray - Havalimanı)
- Metro (Taksim - 4. Levent)
- Suburban trains

Metro (Taksim - 4. Levent):
4. Levent · Levent · Gayrettepe · Şişli · Osmanbey · Taksim

Funicular / Tram link:
Taksim · Kabataş · Beyoğlu

Tram:
Kabataş · Fındıklı · Tophane · Karaköy · Sirkeci · Eminönü · Gülhane · Sultanahmet · Çemberlitaş · Beyazıt · Üniversite - Laleli · Aksaray · Yusufpaşa · Haseki · Fındıkzade · Çapa - Şehremini · Pazartekke · Topkapı · Cevizilbağ · Merkezefendi · Seyitnizam · Akşemsettin · Mithatpaşa · Zeytinburnu

Metro (Aksaray - Havalimanı):
Esenler · Terazidere · Davutpaşa · Merter · Zeytinburnu · Bakırköy · Bahçelievler · Ataköy · Yenibosna · CNR Expo · Havalimanı (Atatürk Airport)

Aksaray line:
Aksaray · Emniyet · Topkapı - Ulubatlı · Bayrampaşa · Sağmalcılar · Kartaltepe · Otogar · Esenler

Suburban trains (Sirkeci line):
Sirkeci · Cankurtaran · Kumkapı · Yenikapı · KM paşa · Yedikule · Kazlıçeşme · Zeytinburnu · Yenimahalle · Bakırköy · Yeşilyurt · Yeşilköy · Florya · Menekşe · Küçükçekmece · Soğuksu · Kanarya · Halkalı

Golden Horn